# Mastering AspectJ

## Aspect-Oriented
## Programming in Java

Joseph D. Gradecki

Nicholas Lesiecki

Wiley Publishing, Inc.

Publisher: Robert Ipsen
Editor: Robert M. Elliott
Managing Editor: Vincent Kunkemueller
Book Producer: Ryan Publishing Group, Inc.

Copyeditors: Elizabeth Welch and Tiffany Taylor
Proofreader: Linda Seifert
Compositor: Gina Rexrode

Designations used by companies to distinguish their products are often claimed as trademarks. In all instances where Wiley Publishing, Inc., is aware of a claim, the product names appear in initial capital or ALL CAPITAL LETTERS. Readers, however, should contact the appropriate companies for more complete information regarding trademarks and registration.

This book is printed on acid-free paper. ∞

Wiley also publishes its books in a variety of electronic formats. Some content that appears in print may not be available in electronic books.

*Library of Congress Cataloging-in-Publication Data:*

Gradecki, Joe, 1967-
  Mastering Aspectj : aspect-oriented programming in Java / Joseph Gradecki, Nicholas Lesiecki.
    p. cm.
  ISBN 0-471-43104-4 (PAPER/WEBSITE : alk. paper)
  1. Object-oriented programming (Computer science) I. Lesiecki, Nicholas. II. Title.
  QA76.64 .G715 2003
  005.1'17—dc21

                        2002153175

10  9 8 7 6 5 4 3 2 1

# CONTENTS

## Dedication

This book is dedicated to Christ, my wife, and our sons.
—Joseph D. Gradecki


For S.H.
—Nicholas Lesiecki

## Acknowledgments

I'd like to thank Tim Ryan, Tiffany Taylor, Liz Welch, Nick Lesiecki, and the many reviewers who spent considerable time looking over the manuscript.

—Joseph D. Gradecki


First, I'd like to thank my wife Suzanne, who put up with not having a husband for months while I wrote this book. A sentence in the front of a technical manual will hardly make up for your good-natured sacrifice. Second, I'd like to thank our reviewers: Arno Schmidmeier and Andrew Barton. These dedicated souls put up with a hectic schedule and gave us invaluable advice and technical feedback on the manuscript. The book improved greatly as a result of your input. (Any errors remain our responsibility.) Third, I'd like to thank the AspectJ team (past and present) for delivering this book's *raison d'être* and for patiently answering my questions (and taking my suggestions!). In particular, I thank Jim Hugunin, Erik Hilsdale, Ron Bodkin, Gregor Kiczales, and especially Wes Isberg for their help and support. On a related note, thank you to Jan Hannemann and Vincent Massol whose contributions to the AspectJ community I drew on while writing my material. Finally, thank you to my cat, Juno, for sitting on my lap while I wrote.

To the Amherst College English Department: *this* is craft.

—Nicholas Lesiecki

**Joseph D. Gradecki** is a software engineer at Comprehensive Software Solutions, where he works on their SABIL product, a enterprise-level securities processing system. He has built numerous dynamic, enterprise applications using Java, AspectJ, servlets, JSPs, Resin, MySQL, BroadVision, XML, and more. He is the author of *Mastering JXTA* and the coauthor of *MySQL and Java Developer's Guide* (with Mark Matthews and Jim Cole). Mr. Gradecki holds Bachelor's and Master's degrees in Computer Science and is currently pursuing a Ph.D. in Computer Science.

**Nicholas Lesiecki** enjoys coding "in the zone"—the zone where code flows through your hands like water, your team shares a mind, and the results satisfy you and the client. The desire to achieve this zone has driven him to embrace techniques such as Extreme Programming and tools such as AspectJ. He is the best-selling coauthor of *Java Tools for Extreme Programming* (with Rick Hightower). He also contributed to the Cactus unit-testing framework. Most recently, he authored articles about AspectJ and testing for IBM's developerWorks. Mr. Lesiecki serves eBlox, Inc. as principle software engineer in Tucson, Arizona.

# Introduction

Most applications, particularly enterprise-level applications, are not one module of code that exists in a single file. Applications are collections of modules that work together to provide some desired functionality defined by a set of requirements. Theoretically, developers can create modules that contain discrete functions; so a security module and a login module might be combined with an HTTP module to create a Web server application.

Due to the nature of object-oriented tools and languages, however, this ideal of modular programming is seldom realized. Instead, developers are often forced to create modules that have mixed goals; a single function such as logging in a user might actually be distributed among several modules in an application. This is the case with the Apache Web server, for example; 37 of its 43 modules contain code that handles user login. This practice leads to tangled code that is more prone to errors and is difficult to debug, refactor, document, and support.

The goal of aspect-oriented programming (AOP) is to solve these types of development problems. AOP emphasizes the creation of *aspects*, which are modules that centralize distributed functionality. To put AOP theory into practice, the Palo Alto Research Center (PARC) created AspectJ. AspectJ is an open-source language that functions as an extension to Java. AspectJ is 100-percent compatible with Java: AspectJ's aspects work side by side with Java classes to deliver a comprehensive application. Benefits of using AspectJ with Java include:

- Less tangled code
- Shorter code
- Easier application maintenance and evolution

- Applications that are easier to debug, refactor, and modify
- Code that is more reusable—developers can create libraries of aspects in much the same way they already create libraries of objects in OOP

## What's in This Book

This book is designed to be a comprehensive introduction to the AOP paradigm, a complete handbook to the AspectJ language, and a guide for using both AOP and AspectJ in your next or current project. Some of the concepts you will read about are:

- **Join point**—A predictable point in the execution of an application
- **Pointcut**—A structure designed to identify and select join points within an AspectJ program
- **Advice**—Code to be executed when a join point is reached in the application code
- **Inter-type declarations**—A powerful mechanism to add attributes and methods to previously established classes
- **Aspect**—A structure analogous to a Java class that encapsulates join points, pointcuts, advice, and inter-type declarations

All the aspect concepts are discussed with code snippets and full explanations. With the AspectJ concepts in hand, we present a large number of examples that show how you can use AOP to solve real problems.

All the code in this book can be found on the book's Web site: www.wiley.com/compbooks/gradecki. The site contains a compressed file with code for each of the book's chapters. The examples in the book were built using version 1.4 of the Java SDK (you must have the Java SDK installed). In addition to Java, you need the AspectJ compiler and runtime components; these can be found at www.eclipse.org/aspectj.

## Who Should Read This Book

You should read this book if you currently design and develop software applications. All software contains requirements that crosscut the primary focus of the application and complicate its design and coding. Because AspectJ is built on top of Java, we assume you have a good understanding of that language.

# Book Organization

The book is organized in three parts. Part I is a comprehensive overview of AOP and the development of a language to support AOP. Part II discusses the primary concepts of AspectJ. These concepts are explained using short code samples. Part III takes the concepts from Parts I and II and applies them in practical ways to the development of software projects. The chapters are described next.

## PART I: Aspect-Oriented Programming Primer

### Chapter 1: Introduction to AOP

This chapter provides a comprehensive overview of what AOP is, where it came from, and how it's been used. The chapter begins with a complete discussion of object-oriented programming and some of the problems it cannot currently solve during software development. The discussion continues with a look at AOP and how it can be applied to the problem of separation of concerns.

### Chapter 2: Implementing AOP

Chapter 2 demonstrates how to translate AOP concepts from theory into concrete compiler support. The primary focus is on code weaving, which involves adding aspect code to join points at compilation time.

## Part II: Introduction to AspectJ

### Chapter 3: Obtaining and Installing AspectJ

Chapter 3 begins looking at the practical side of AOP by discussing how to obtain AspectJ and install it on your system. A simple example is presented, which will help you determine whether the system is installed correctly. Because AspectJ is built on and works in conjunction with Java, both Windows and Linux installations are covered.

### Chapter 4: Implementing AspectJ

Learning any new language or paradigm is much easier with an example. The Hello World application is discussed in this chapter. It covers most major concepts and compiling mechanisms and provides you with a view of what's ahead in the rest of the book.

## Chapter 5: Join Points

The most important concept in AspectJ is the join point. A join point is a well-defined point within an application that can be used as a trigger with AspectJ code. This chapter begins with a look at the Dynamic Join Point model used within AspectJ. AspectJ provides a variety of different types of join points for handling such constructs as methods, constructors, and the setting/getting of attributes. The signature is the defining part of a join point; it can be specified with text or using patterns and wildcards. The chapter uses a number of code snippets to illustrate a wide variety of join points.

## Chapter 6: Pointcuts

The pointcut is a language construct that selects a set of join points. Chapter 6 uses the knowledge you gained from writing a join point to demonstrate how to form pointcuts that implement requirements that crosscut the primary application. Within each user-defined pointcut are a number of different designators specifying when a join point should be matched. The chapter also discusses the use of reflection, which allows AspectJ code to see into the context of a join point.

## Chapter 7: Advice

Once you have picked out interesting points in your program with a pointcut (say, all calls to methods whose names begin with *set*), AspectJ allows you to define advice—code that runs after, before, or instead of that join point. For instance, you could log the executions of all set methods or inspect their parameters for legality. This chapter demonstrates how to define advice and covers the different types and uses of advice.

## Chapter 8: Inter-type Declarations

In addition to providing join points and advice, AspectJ also expands Java's type system by allowing inter-type declarations. Inter-type declarations let you add methods or attributes to a class (or even an interface) from outside that type. The ability to add concrete implementations onto interfaces allows for a type of multiple inheritance. Inter-type declarations also allow aspects to alter inheritance hierarchies—adding new interfaces or supertypes to any type in the system. This chapter covers the mechanics and uses of AspectJ's inter-type declarations and shows how they dramatically broaden the power of the previously presented constructs. The chapter also covers two less dramatic (but still important) capabilities: exception softening and custom compilation errors.

### Chapter 9: Aspects

AspectJ code is a combination of join points, pointcuts, advice, and inter-type declarations. It would be counter-productive to throw this new code into the same application you are trying to save from the mess of code tangling. An aspect is language construct provided by the AspectJ language for encapsulating the combination of constructs needed for AOP. This chapter provides a comprehensive view of aspects and how to build them in a number of different examples and situations.

## Part III: Using AspectJ

### Chapter 10: Development Uses of AspectJ

This chapter begins by showing some uses for AspectJ. The chapter covers topics including adopting AspectJ, testing uses, common concerns, production aspects, and performance tuning.

### Chapter 11: Using Aspect J Tools

Part of the overall power of AspectJ is its ancillary extensions to common Integrated Development Environments (IDEs). The current system includes extensions for JBuilder, Forte, Eclipse, and Emacs, and this chapter details the use of these extensions. AspectJ also provides a structure browser that gives a comprehensive view of the application and aspect code. This chapter also discusses debugging AspectJ code and use of Ant for building and compiling applications.

### Chapter 12: Error Handling and Common Problems

This chapter examines common compilation and runtime errors that occur when using AspectJ. It details both the origins of the errors and also suggest solutions.

### Chapter 13: Aspect-Oriented Examples: Patterns and Reuse

This chapter uses two medium sized examples to demonstrate how aspects can add a coherent layer of functionality to an application. Combining pointcuts, advice, and inter-type declarations, the examples show how you can add persistence and automatic cache invalidation to domain objects without modifying them. The second example leverages a reusable aspect version of the Observer pattern. The chapter concludes by considering implications of the examples for component reuse.

### *Chapter 14: Using AspectJ in the Real World*

This chapter brings together all the concepts learned throughout the book and applies them to two real-world scenarios. The first scenario involves using AspectJ and AOP in the addition of a new application feature. Topics covered include designing with aspects in mind, handling documentation, and coding the aspects. The second scenario involves refactoring an open-source project to use aspects for both timing and logging functionality.

### *Appendix A: AspectJ API*

This appendix provides a complete Application Programming Interface (API) for the AspectJ language. The API covers AspectJ 1.1.

### *Appendix B: Useful Sites*

This appendix provides a list of important Web sites covering AOP and AspectJ.

### *Appendix C: Other AOP Language Bindings*

Java isn't the only language to benefit from the use of AOP concepts. A large number of projects in the open-source community provide AOP support for C, C++, Ruby, and other languages. This appendix provides summaries of the additional language projects and where you can find more information.

# CHAPTER 1

# Introduction to AOP

Software development has come a long way since the days of toggle switches. Once the usefulness of software development was realized, its advancement became tied to finding techniques to more efficiently model real-world problems. Years ago, the common methodology for solving a problem was to break it into smaller and smaller modules of functionality, which in turn consisted of a dozen or more lines of code. This methodology worked, but it suffered from a system state being controlled through a large number of global variables that could be modified by any line of code in the application. The advent of object-oriented methodologies pulled the state of the system into individual objects, where it could be made private and controlled through access methods and logic.

This leads to the current situation: Developers are still having difficulty fully expressing a problem into a completely modular and encapsulated model. Although breaking a problem into objects makes sense, some pieces of functionality must be made available across objects. Aspect-oriented programming (AOP) is one of the most promising solutions to the problem of creating clean, well-encapsulated objects without extraneous functionality. In this chapter, we will explore what object-oriented programming (OOP) did right for computer science, problems that arise from objects, and how AOP can fill in the blanks.

## Where OOP Has Brought Us

Object-oriented analysis, design, and programming (OOADP) is no longer the new kid on the block; it has been proven successful in both small and large projects. As a technology, it has gone through its childhood and is moving into a mature adult stage. Research by educational establishments as well as audits by companies have shown that using OOP instead of functional-decomposition techniques has dramatically enhanced the state of software. The benefits of using object-oriented technologies in all phases of the software development process are varied:

- Reusability of components
- Modularity
- Less complex implementation
- Reduced cost of maintenance

Each of these benefits (and others you can think of) will have varied importance to developers. One of them, modularity, is a universal advancement over structured programming that leads to cleaner and better understood software.

## What OOADP Did for Computer Science

The object-oriented methodology—including analysis, design, and programming—brought to computer science the ability to model or design software more along the lines of how you envision a system in the real-world. The primary tool used for this modeling is the object. An *object* is a representation of some primary component of the problem domain. The object has attributes representing the state of the object and behaviors that act on the object to change its state. For example, if you were tasked with designing a system to handle selling DVD products, an OO design might include objects like a product, a DVD, and a Boxset, as well as many others.

The objects must be filled out with attributes and behaviors specific to their roles. A product might have a context defined as follows:

- Attributes
  - Price
  - Title
  - Suppliers
- Behaviors
  - Assign price
  - Assign title
  - Get suppliers

Of course, a production system would include many more attributes and behaviors, but those added to the product object here will suit our purpose. In defining the product, we create or acknowledge a relationship between the product and a supplier object. After further decomposition of the problem, DVD objects are created as well as Boxset objects, as shown in Figure 1.1.

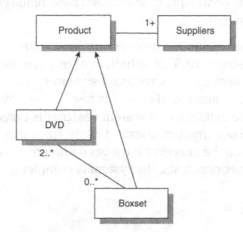

**Figure 1.1**  Example class model.

One of the goals in object design is encapsulating all the data and methods necessary for manipulating that data fully within the object. There shouldn't be any outside functions that can directly change the product object, nor should the product object make changes to any other object. Instead, a supplier object might send a message to a product object asking it to change its state by adding the supplier object to a list of suppliers in the product object. When a message is sent from one object to another, the receiving object is fully in control of its state. All the attributes of the object are encapsulated in a single entity, which can only be changed through an exposed interface. The exposed interface consists of the methods of the object having a public access type. The object could have internal private methods, but those methods aren't exposed to other objects. The encapsulation of the object is achieved by exposing an interface to other objects in the system. The interface defines the methods that can be used to change the object's state. The functionality behind the exposed interface is kept private.

Designing an object-oriented system in this manner aids in the functioning of the system, debugging if problems arise, and the extension of the system. All the objects in the system know their roles and perform them without worrying about malicious changes being made to their state. From a simplistic view, the system is just a group of objects that execute and send messages to each other, requesting information and changes in the other objects.

As the state of object-oriented technology has evolved, the vocabulary has, as well. As you know, an object is an instantiation of a class. The class is an abstract data-type used to model the objects in a system. A *class* is built based on a requirement extracted through an analysis phase (assuming there is an analysis phase). The class might be built on the fly during coding of a solution, with the requirement written in the comments of the class. These requirements and classes can be linked by a concern.

A *concern* is some functionality or requirement necessary in a system, which has been implemented in a code structure. This definition allows a concern to not be limited to object-oriented systems—a structured system can also have concerns. In a typical system, a large number of concerns need to be addressed in order for the system to accomplish its goals. A system designer is faced with building a system that uses the concerns but doesn't violate the rules of the methodologies being used. When all the concerns have been implemented with system code as well as related functional tests, the system is complete.

## Problems Resulting from OOP

If you read books and articles about object orientation, they commonly say that OOP allows for the encapsulation of data and methods specific to the goal of a specific object. In other words, an object should be a self-contained unit with no understanding of its environment, and its environment should be aware of nothing about the object other than what the object reveals. A class is the cookie cutter for objects in a system, and it implements a concern for the system. The goal of the class is to fully encapsulate the code needed for the concern. Unfortunately, this isn't always possible. Consider the following two concerns:

**Concern 1:** The system shall keep a price relating to the wholesale value of all products.

**Concern 2:** Any changes to the price shall be recorded for historical purposes.

The first concern dictates that all products in the system must have a wholesale price. In the object-oriented world, a Product class can be created as an abstract class to handle common functionality of all products in the system:

```
public abstract class Product {
   private real price;

   Product() {
      price = 0.0;
   }

   public void putPrice(real p) {
      price = p;
```

```
  }

  public int getPrice() {
    return price;
  }
}
```

The Product class as defined here satisfies the requirement in concern 1. The principles of OO have been maintained, because the class encapsulates the code necessary to keep track of the price of a product. The same functionality could easily be created in a structured environment using a global array.

Now let's consider concern 2, which requires that all operations involved in changing the price be logged. In itself, this concern does not conflict with the first concern and is easy to implement. The following class defines a logging mechanism:

```
public class Logger {
    private OutputStream ostream;
  Logger() {
    //open log file
  }
  void writeLog(String value) {
    //write value to log file
  }
}
```

A logger object is instantiated from the Logger class by the application's constructor or other initialization function, or individual logger objects are created within those objects needing to log information. Again, the fundamental object-oriented concepts remain in the Logger class.

To use the logger, you add the writeLog() method to code where the product price might be changed. Because you only have one other class, Product, its methods should be considered for logging inclusion. As a result of the class analysis, a new Product class emerges:

```
public abstract class Product {
  private real price;
  Logger loggerObject;

  Product() {
    price = 0.0;
    loggerObject = new Logger();
  }

  public void putPrice(real p) {
    loggerObject.writeLog("Changed Price from" + price + " to " +
p);
    price = p;
```

```
    }

  public int getPrice() {
    return price;
  }
}
```

The change made to the Product class is the inclusion of the logging method calls in the setPrice() method. When the price is changed using this method, a call is made to the logger object, and the old/new prices are recorded. All objects instantiated from the Product class have a local logger object to handle all logging functionality.

Let's look at the idea of encapsulation and modularity within object-oriented methodologies. By adding code to the Product class to handle a second concern in the system, it would appear that we've broken the idea of encapsulation. The class no longer handles only its concern, but also must fulfill the requirements of another concern. The class has been crosscut by concerns in the system.

Crosscutting represents the situation when a requirement for the system is met by placing code into objects through the system—but the code doesn't directly relate to the functionality defined for those objects. (Crosscutting is discussed in more detail in the next section.) A class like Product, which is defined to represent a specific entity within the application domain, should not be required to host code used to fulfill other system requirements.

Consider what would happen to the Product class if you added timing information, authentication, and long-term data persistence. Are all these concerns supposed to be designed into the Product object? Structured and object-oriented languages leave you no other choice when addressing crosscutting concerns. The additional concerns are forced to be part of another concern, thus breaking many of the rules of our favorite methodology.

This mixing of concerns leads to a condition called code scattering or tangling. With code scattering, the code necessary to fulfill one concern is spread over the classes needed to fulfill another concern. Code tangling involves using a single method or class to implement multiple concerns. Both of these problems break the fundamentals of OO and cause headaches for designers (for more information, see the following section). Consider the following Product class, where the two concerns mentioned earlier have been added in pseudocode form. This additional functionality is necessary, but it shouldn't be part of the Product class:

```
public abstract class Product {
  private real price;
  Logger loggerObject;
```

```
Product() {
  price = 0.0;
  loggerObject = new Logger();
}

public void putPrice(real p) {
 //start timing
 //Check user authentication
 loggerObject.writeLog("Changed Price from" + price + " to "
+ p);
  price = p;
 // log if problem with authentication
 //end timing
 //log timing
 }

public int getPrice() {
  //check user authentication
  return price;
 }

public void persistIt() {
  //start timing
  //save this object
  //end timing
  //log timing
 }
}
```

Once the Product class has been created, a DVD concrete class is formulated. The class inherits all the functionality found in the Product class and adds a few more attributes. The DVD class includes an attribute and associated methods for the number of copies currently available. This is important information that should be included in all logging activities:

```
public class DVD extends Product {

    private String title;
    private int count;
    private String location;

    public DVD(String inTitle) {
      super();
      title = inTitle;
    }

    private void setCount(int inCount) {
      //start timing
      //check user authentication
      count = inCount;
```

```
      //end timing
      //log timing
    }

    private int getCount() {
      return count;
    }

    private void setLocation(String inLocation, int two) {
      //start timing
      //check user authentication
      location = inLocation;
      //end timing
      //log timing
    }

    private String getLocation() {
      return location;
    }

    public void setStats(String inLocation, int inCount) {
      //start timing
      //check user authentication
      setLocation(inLocation, 0);
      setCount(inCount);
      //end timing
      //log timing
    }
}
```

Do you notice any problems with the code? The logging hasn't been included in the methods that change the count information. Unfortunately, the developer missed this concern when creating the new class.

## Results of Tangled Code

A developer doesn't have to be in the industry long to find out the effects of tangled and scattered code. Some of the effects are as follows:

- Classes that are difficult to change
- Code that can't be reused
- Code that's impossible to trace

Engineers and managers who need to refactor code commonly encounter one example of dealing with tangled code. If the code is written in clear components using well-defined objects, a relatively obvious cost-benefit ratio can be created. If the time and money can be justified, the components of the system can be refactored. However, in most cases, the code for the components is intertwined, and factoring becomes too cost prohibitive under traditional means. However, AOP allows the refactoring to be performed on a different level and in a manner that helps to eliminate some of the tangled code.

In one of the original AspectJ Tutorial presentations (http://aspectj.org/documentation/papersAndSlides/OOPSLA2002-demo.ppt), you could analyze the Jakarta Tomcat project to determine where code that performed logging was located in the source code. The result of the project showed that the logging code wasn't in just one place in the code, and not even in a couple of small places—it's spread throughout the source code.

As the Tomcat analysis project showed, code tangling is a major problem. Just think about the nightmare if the code for logging needed to change. The tangled code clearly accomplishes some defined functionality, like logging. The code is tangled because it needs to be spread throughout the application. When a requirement results in tangled code, we say that it *crosscuts* the system. The crosscutting isn't always a primary requirement of the system, just as logging isn't required for the application software to function properly; but sometimes it is required in the case of user authentication.

## How AOP Solves OOP Problems

Aspect-oriented programming is a paradigm created to solve the problems discussed so far without the difficulties and complexities encountered with subject-oriented programming (SOP) and multidimensional separation of concerns (MDSOC). AOP isn't necessarily a new idea; its roots lie in the separation of concerns movement, but it has moved into the forefront through work by Gregor Kiczales and his colleagues at Xerox's PARC (www.parc.com/groups/csl/projects/aspectj/).

AOP doesn't require the user to learn a host of new techniques, but instead relies on the features of its host language to solve crosscutting of concerns. Depending on the implementation of AOP, you need to learn only a handful of new keywords. At the same time, AOP supports reuse and modularity of code, to eliminate code tangling and scattering. With the advent of Java and the AspectJ support language, AOP is on the verge of becoming the next big thing in computer science since the adoption of OOP.

### What Is AOP?

Aspect-oriented programming is a paradigm that supports two fundamental goals:

- Allow for the separation of concerns as appropriate for a host language.
- Provide a mechanism for the description of concerns that crosscut other components.

AOP isn't meant to replace OOP or other object-based methodologies. Instead, it supports the separation of components, typically using classes, and provides a way to separate aspects from the components. In our example, AOP is designed to support the separation of the example concerns and to allow both a *Logger* and a *Product* class; it also handles the crosscutting that occurs when logging is required in the components supporting another concern.

## Development Process with AOP

To get an idea of how AOP helps with crosscutting, let's revisit the example concerns:

**Concern 1:** The system shall keep a price relating to the wholesale value of all products.

**Concern 2:** Any changes to the price shall be recorded for historical purposes

The two classes built to implement these concerns separated their functionality, as would seem appropriate. However, when concern 2 is fully implemented, it becomes clear that calls from the Product class will need to be made to the Logger class. Suddenly the Product class isn't completely modular, because it needs to incorporate within its own code calls to functionality that isn't part of a product.

AOP provides several tools that can help with this problem. The first is the language used to code the requirements or concerns into units of code (either objects or functions). The AOP literature commonly calls this the component language. The secondary or support requirements (aspects) are coded as well, using an aspect language. Nothing in the paradigm states that either language needs to be object-oriented in nature, nor do the two languages need to be the same. The result of the component and aspect languages is a program that handles the execution of the components and the aspects. At some point, the respective programs must be integrated. This integration is called weaving, and it can occur at compile, link, run-, or load time.

Using this information, let's look at how AOP handles the issue of putting logging code directly into the Product class. AOP is designed to respect the idea that some requirements can be modularly coded and others will crosscut the previously modular classes. In our example, concern 1 can be implemented in the Product class without violating the modularity of the class. Concern 2 cannot be implemented in a modular fashion within the Product class because it needs to be implemented in different spots throughout the Product class and other classes in the software system.

If we step back from the implementation details behind both concerns, we find that concern 2 doesn't necessarily need to be coded directly in the Product class (and the DVD class, the Boxset class, and so on). Instead, it would be ideal if the logging code could be called when the system calls any log-worthy methods.

For this to occur, an aspect must be created specifying that when the system encounters a call to the method setPrice(), it should first execute code defined in the aspect language. Here's an example of what the aspect might look like in a (fictional) object-oriented aspect language:

```
define aspect Logging{
  Logger loggingObject = new Logger();
  when calling set*(taking one parameter) {
    loggingObject.writeLog("Called set method");
  }
}
```

This aspect is compiled along with the component *Product* class using a compiler provided by the AOP system. The compiler weaves the aspect code into the component code to create a functioning system. Figure 1.2 shows graphically how the weave looks.

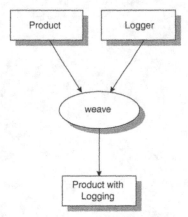

**Figure 1.2**  A graphical illustration of a weave.

The weave occurs based on the information provided in line 3, where the aspect is defined to act when a call is made to any method having a name starting with set and taking a single parameter. Once the system begins to execute, a call is made to the setPrice() method of the DVD object. Just before control is given to the setPrice() method of a target object, the code in line 4 executes and produces the statement "Called set method" in the system log. As a result of using

AOP, any call matching the aspect criteria produces an entry in the log—you don't have to scatter code throughout the entire program to support the concern.

## What's Next

In Chapter 2, we will look at some of the details behind implementing a language extension to support the functionality required in AOP. The primary consideration in any AOP tools is the weaver. We'll discuss the current state of AOP weavers as well as future implementations.

# Implementing AOP

Aspect-oriented programming (AOP) in accomplished by implementing a series of primary concerns in a given language. These crosscutting concerns are added to the system through an aspect-oriented language. The support code developed using the aspect-oriented language is used to implement any crosscutting concerns based on common AOP terms and must be weaved into the primary application. In most implementations, the support code is written in the same language as the primary application; that is the case for AspectJ. Figure 2.1 shows the generalized AOP process.

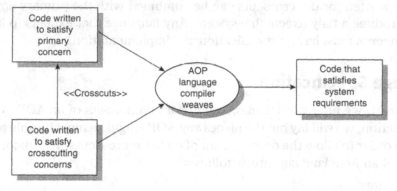

**Figure 2.1**   AOP process.

In this chapter, we will look at the language features of AOP and provide an overview of AspectJ. The topics covered are as follows:

- AOP language anatomy
- Concern implementation
- Weavers
- Compilers
- AspectJ

# AOP Language Anatomy

The primary goal of an AOP language is the separation of concerns. An application is written in a language that best satisfies the needs of the application and the developers. This language could be Java, C++, C#, Visual Basic, or even Cobol; in all these languages, a compiler converts the written language syntax into a format the machine can execute. In the case of Java or .NET, the language syntax is converted to byte code, which in turn is executed by a runtime environment.

During the development of the application, all the requirements are satisfied to produce the final system. As you saw in Chapter 1, "Introduction to AOP," the requirements include those necessary to meet the true needs of the application as well as conveniences such as logging and timing. Unfortunately, in most cases, this type of development (whether object-oriented or not) produces tangled code. When you use AOP, the development process isn't the same: The primary concerns are implemented using a language deemed appropriate for the application, and the crosscutting concerns are implemented in an aspect-oriented language.

It doesn't matter what language type is used for the implementation as long as the code written for the crosscuts can be combined with the primary application to produce a fully executable system. Any language that expects to implement concerns must have a specification and implementation.

## AOP Language Specification

In Chapter 1, we briefly touched on the major components of an AOP system. In this section, we will lay out the pieces any AOP language must be able to represent in order to allow the development of code for crosscuts. The major components of an AOP language are as follows:

- Join points
- A type of language to match join points
- Advice
- An encapsulating component, such as a class

## Join Points

A *join point* is a well-defined location within the primary code where a concern will crosscut the application. Join points can be method calls, constructor invocations, exception handlers, or other points in the execution of a program.

Suppose the specification document for a new system created by an AOP-aware team includes a concern stating that all SQL executions to the database should be logged. To facilitate the development of the primary system, a transaction component class is created to handle all database communication from business-level components. Within the transaction component, a method called updateTables() handles all database updates. To fully implement the crosscut concern, you need to add code to the method to register a timestamp when the method is first called. You must also include code at the end of the method to register a timestamp and add a success flag to the log. Thus, the join point to the implementation is the name of the method along with (possibly) the class name. For example, the following statement describes a join point:

```
public String DBTrans.updateTables(String);
```

The exact syntax will vary from language to language, but the goal of the join point is to match well-defined execution points.

## Pointcuts

Given that the join point is a well-defined execution point in an application, you need a construct that tells the aspect-oriented language when it should match the join point. For example, you may want the aspect language to match the join point only when it is used in a call from one object to another or possibly a call from within the same object. To handle this situation, you can define a designator named call() that takes a join point as a parameter:

```
call(public String DBTrans.updateTables(String))
```

The designator tells the aspect language that the public String DBTrans.updateTables(String) join point should be matched only when it's part of a method call.

In some cases, you may use multiple designators to narrow the join point match or create groupings. Regardless, another construct called a *pointcut* is typically used to group the designators. A pointcut can be named or unnamed, just as a class can be named or anonymous. For example, in the following example the pointcut is called updateTable(). It contains a single designator for all calls to the defined join point:

```
Pointcut updateTable() :
  call(public String DBTrans.updateTables(String))
```

The pointcut is used in advice structures, described next.

### Advice

In most AOP specifications, advice code can execute at three different places when a join point is matched: before, around, and after. In each case, a pointcut must be triggered before any of the advice code will be executed. Here's an example of using the before advice:

```
before(String s) : updateTables(s) {
  System.out.println("Passed parameter - " + s);
}
```

Once a pointcut has triggered, the appropriate advice code executes. In the case of the previous example, the advice code executes before the join point is executed. The String argument is passed to the code so it can be used if needed. In most AOP systems, you have access to the object associated with the join point as well as other information specific to the join point itself.

### Aspects

A system that has 10 crosscutting concerns might include 20 or so join points and a dozen or more pointcuts with associated advice. By using AOP, you can reduce code tangling and disorganization rather than create more. With this in mind, the aspect syntax was developed to handle encapsulation of join points, pointcuts, and advice.

Aspects are created in much the same manner as classes and allow for complete encapsulation of code related to a particular concern. Here's an example aspect:

```
public aspect TableAspect {
  pointcut updateTable(String s) :
    call(public String DBTrans.updateTables(String) &&
    args(s);
  before(String s) : updateTable(s) {
    System.out.println("Passed parameter - " + s);
  }
}
```

The TableAspect aspect is an object that implements a concern related to the UpdateTables() method. All the functionality required for this concern is neatly encapsulated in its own structure.

## AOP Language Implementation

The examples presented so far are written in the AspectJ AOP language and follow the Java specification because, as you will see shortly, AspectJ is designed to be used with applications written in Java. Once a concern has been written in an AOP language, a good deal of work must still be done to get the primary and AOP applications to run as a complete system. This task of integrating the crosscutting concern code and the primary application is called *weaving*. Table 2.1 lists the different types of weaving.

**Table 2.1**  AOP Weaving Types

| TYPE | DESCRIPTION | TOOL USED |
|------|-------------|-----------|
| Compile-time | The source code from the primary and aspect languages is weaved before being put through the phases of the compiler where byte code is produced. AspectJ 1.0.x uses this form of weaving. | Compiler |
| Link-time | The weaving occurs after the primary and aspect language code has been compiled into byte code. AspectJ 1.1.x uses this form of weaving. | Linker |
| Load-time | The weaving occurs when classes are loaded by the classloader. Ultimately, the weaving is at the byte-code level. | Classloader under Java |
| Run-time | The virtual machine is responsible for detecting join points and loading and execution aspects. | Virtual machine |

Using Java as an example, at some point in development a number of classes and possibly aspects will represent all the concerns defined for a particular application. The primary application can be compiled into Java byte code using the Javac compiler. Once compiled, the application byte code can be executed within the Java Runtime Environment. Unfortunately, a number of aspects also need to execute. Because the aspects are Java code as well, it isn't unreasonable to think that a compiler can be used to convert the aspect code into pure Java code; the aspects are converted to classes, and pointcuts, join points, and designators are turned into other Java constructs. If this step is performed, the standard Java compiler can also be used to produce byte code from the aspects.

Assume that a compiler is available that will convert both the Java and aspect code into Java byte code during the compilation process. You need a way to incorporate the aspect code into the Java code. In compile-time weaving, the aspect code is analyzed, converted to the primary language if needed, and inserted directly into the primary application code. So, using the previous example, you know that a join point has been defined on the updateTables() method and that a pointcut defined to execute before the updateTables() method actually executes. The compile-time weaver finds the updateTables() method and weaves the advice code into the method. If the aspect is converted to a class, the call within the updateTables() method can reference a method of the new aspect object.

Here's a simple example of what the code might look like after the compile-time weaver pulls together the primary Java code and the aspect defined earlier:

```
public String updateTables(String SQL) {
   //start code inserted for aspect
   TableAspect.updateTable(SQL);
   //end code inserted for aspect
   initializeDB();
   sendSQL(SQL);
}
```

In this example, a call is inserted to the updateTable() method of the tablesAspectClass class created from the TableAspect aspect code defined earlier. This work is handled by a preprocessor before any traditional compilation takes place. Once the aspect has been weaved into the primary application code, the resulting intermediate files are sent to the Java compiler. The resulting system code implements both the primary and crosscutting concerns.

One of the downfalls of a compile-time weaving system is its inability to dynamically change the aspect used against the primary code. For example, suppose an aspect handles the way the updateTables() method connects to the database. A simple connection pool can consist of the details within the aspect. It would be interesting if the aspect could be swapped with another aspect during execution of the primary application based on predefined rules. A compile-time weaver cannot do this type of dynamic swapping, although code can be written in an aspect to mimic the swapping. In addition, compile-time weaving suggests that you need to have the source code available for all aspects, and convenience features like JAR files cannot be used.

A link-time or run-time weaver doesn't weave the aspect code into the primary application during the compile but waits until runtime to handle the weave. A processor is still used to place hooks in the methods/constructor of the primary language as well as other strategic places. When the hooks are executed, a modified runtime system determines whether any aspects need to execute. As you might expect, dynamic weaving is more complicated because of the need to change the system where the application is executing. In a byte-code system where a runtime environment is available, the process isn't as involved as a system like C++, where a compiler produces machine-level code.

# AspectJ

This book covers the use of a byte-code weaving AOP language called AspectJ. The AspectJ language comes from research work performed at the Xerox Palo Alto Research Center by a team of researchers including Gregor Kiczales (project leader), Ron Bodkin, Bill Griswold, Erik Hilsdale, Jim Hugunin, Wes Isberg, and Mik Kersten. The stated goal of AspectJ is to make the methodology of AOP available to a large number of developers. In order to accomplish this goal, AspectJ is built on top of the Java language and works to provide a seamless integration of primary and crosscutting concerns.

In the forthcoming chapters, we'll discuss the AspectJ system in detail. To kick things off, let's look at a simple example along with aspect code and see how the AspectJ weaver accomplishes the task of integrating AOP into standard Java.

## Example Aspect

This example class and related aspect will give you an idea of what writing in AspectJ is all about. Listing 2.1 shows the code for a very simple Java class and main() method. The Simple class has a single attribute and method. A main() method is used to instantiate an object of the class and makes a call to the getName() method.

```java
public class Simple {
  private String name;

  public String getName() {
    return name;
  }
  public static void main(String args[]) {
    Simple simple = new Simple();
    System.out.println(simple.getName());
  }
}
```

**Listing 2.1**  Simple Java application.

Listing 2.2 shows an AspectJ aspect complete with a join point related to the getName() method in the primary code, and a pointcut defining the conditions necessary for triggering advice code found in the before() statement. The purpose of the aspect is to execute code when a call is made to the getName() method of a Simple object.

```
public aspect SimpleAspect {
  pointcut namePC() : call (public String getName());
  before() : MatchAllgetName() {
    System.out.println(thisJoinPoint.getSignature());
  }
}
```

**Listing 2.2** Simple aspect.

If the standard Java compiler is used to compile the Simple class and the SimpleAspect aspect files, the compiler will produce a few errors related to the SimpleAspect aspect. The compiler won't be able to recognize the aspect, pointcut, before, and other statements used in the code. The AspectJ system includes a compiler called ajc that compiles both the aspect code and the primary code. As you will see in detail in Chapter 12, "Error Handling and Common Problems," the ajc compiler is built on top of IBM's Eclipse project compiler, which allows a strict compliance to the Java language and resulting byte code. The ajc compiler adds the ability to compile the AspectJ-specific keyword into byte code and facilitates the weaving of the byte codes into class files. The aspect code is converted from an aspect construct into a class, and the other AspectJ-specific constructs are converted to standard Java. The AspectJ compiler weaves the aspect byte code into the byte code of the primary application byte code and produces appropriate Java class files that can be executed by the Java Runtime Environment.

## What's Next

In this chapter we have looked at the major components necessary for the implementation of concerns that crosscut a primary application. An AOP language consists of a specification and implementation such that concerns can be accurately represented in the primary code without code tangling. We introduced the AspectJ language and showed how the language implements the major components. In Chapter 3, we look at the steps necessary to obtain AspectJ, install it, and verify a successful installation.

# 3

# Obtaining and Installing AspectJ

AspectJ is an implementation of AOP for the Java language built as an extension to the language. A compiler and a set of JAR files take common Java code and AspectJ aspects and compile them into standard Java byte-code, which can be executed on any Java-compliant machine. In this chapter, we will look at:

- Requirements for AspectJ
- Downloading and installing AspectJ
- Testing the AspectJ installation

## Requirements for AspectJ

AspectJ is an extension to the Java language and thus requires Java to be installed on the local machine. Your version of Java must be 1.2 or later, and the full Software Development Kit (SDK) needs to be installed. For the examples in this book, we used the latest version of Java (1.4) with great success. You can download and install Java from java.sun.com.

## Downloading AspectJ

You can find the AspectJ system at www.eclipse.org/aspectj under the Downloads links on the left navigation menu to bring up the page shown in Figure 3.1.

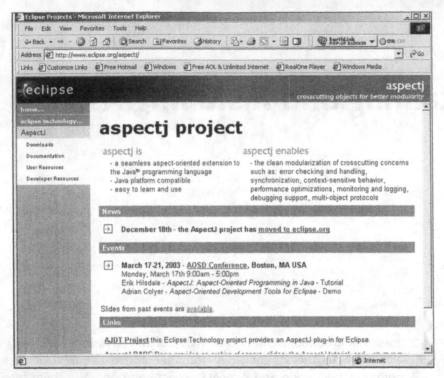

**Figure 3.1** Primary download page at www.eclipse.org/aspectj.

The AspectJ system is divided into three areas:

- **Compiler and Core Tools**—A single JAR file download containing the AspectJ compiler and its support files.

- **Documentation and Examples**—Offline documentation, tutorial, and examples. The documents are the same as those found on the Web site.

- **Development Environment Support**—Extensions to several popular development tools. These extensions let you directly display and manipulate AspectJ components through a specific IDE. More information about these extensions can be found in Chapter 11 "Using AspectJ Tools."

The primary download necessary to begin working with AspectJ is the one found in the Compiler and Core Tools areas. At the time of this writing, there is a single JAR file with a version of 1.1.b2. Click on the link for the file and save the file to your local hard drive. Don't decompress the JAR file; it is a self-extracting Java installer. Once you've downloaded the file to the hard drive, you can install it.

# Installing AspectJ

The process of installing AspectJ on all Java-supported environments is the same, due to the nature of Java. The JAR file downloaded from the Aspect.org Web site is a self-extracting Java installer; you can invoke it either by double clicking the program's icon in a GUI window (My Computer in Windows or a Window Manager window under UNIX) or by executing the following Java command in a Command Prompt or Terminal window:

```
java -jar aspectj-tools-1.1.0.jar
```

This command launches Java, unjars the specified file, and begins executing the file. The installation begins with a splash screen, as shown in Figure 3.2.

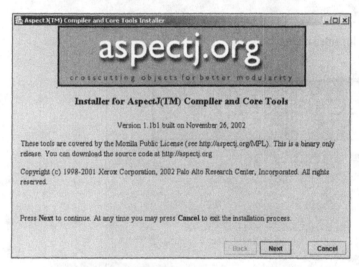

**Figure 3.2** AspectJ installer splash screen.

After you read the information on the splash screen, click the Next button to continue with the installation or click Cancel to exit. The next screen defines your Java home path. Figure 3.3 shows that the system has accurately found an installation of Java.

On the machine where AspectJ was installed in Figure 3.3, a JAVA_HOME environment variable was previously defined. If the installer cannot find a Java installation, use the Browse button to find a root directory for an installation.

After you've entered the correct path into the Java Home Directory control, click Next. The next installer dialog will prompt you for an installation directory for AspectJ; see Figure 3.4. A default path will be provided; you can change it as needed.

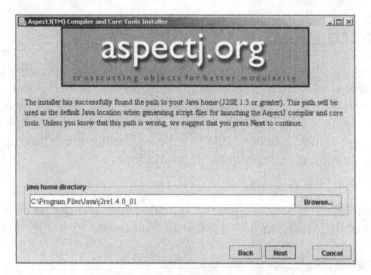

**Figure 3.3** AspectJ Java locator screen.

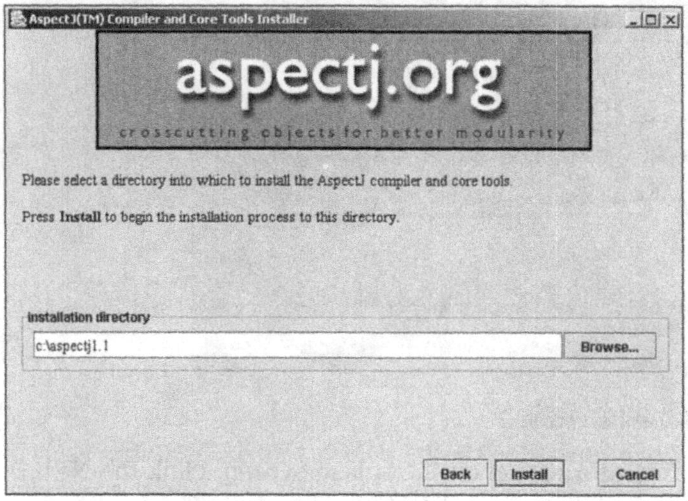

**Figure 3.4** AspectJ installation path screen.

Clicking the Install button will begin the process to copy AspectJ to your system. If you need to make any changes to previous screens, click the Back button before clicking Install. When the installation program finishes putting the necessary system files on the local machine, a Continue screen will be displayed, as shown in Figure 3.5.

Click Next to see the final screen of the installation, shown in Figure 3.6.

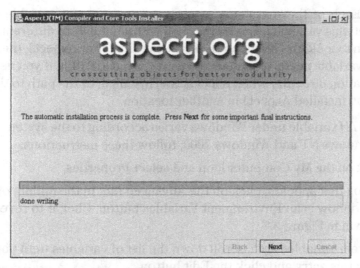

**Figure 3.5**    AspectJ installation Continue screen.

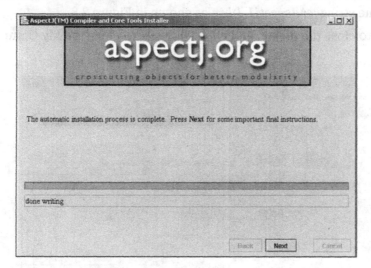

**Figure 3.6**    AspectJ installation final screen.

The final screen shows several final steps you need to perform regardless of the system type on which you are installing the system. These steps include setting up the /bin directory of AspectJ to be visible from the PATH variable and setting up the CLASSPATH for the aspectjrt.jar runtime file.

## Setting *PATH*

When you aren't using a graphical development tool, the AspectJ compiler is launched from a command prompt under Windows or a terminal window under

UNIX/Linux. Each of these systems requires an environment variable called *PATH* to be set; this variable provides the shell with a number of different directories in which to look for commands typed at a prompt. For AspectJ, the *PATH* environment variable needs to include the path c:\aspectj1.1\bin if you used the default installation directory when AspectJ was installed, or the path to the \bin directory if you installed AspectJ in another location.

Setting the *PATH* variable under Windows varies according to the system you're using. For Windows NT and Windows 2000, follow these instructions:

1. Right-click on the My Computer icon and select Properties.

2. In the dialog that appears, click on the Advanced tab. In the middle of the resulting window is an Environment Variables button. Click it to reveal the dialog shown in Figure 3.7.

3. In the System Variables area, scroll down the list of variables until you find Path. Click this entry and click the Edit button.

4. Click in the Variable Value edit line, move to the end of the list of values, and add the string *;c:\aspectj1.1\bin* as shown in Figure 3.8.

5. Click OK to close the dialog, and click OK again to close the My Computer dialog.

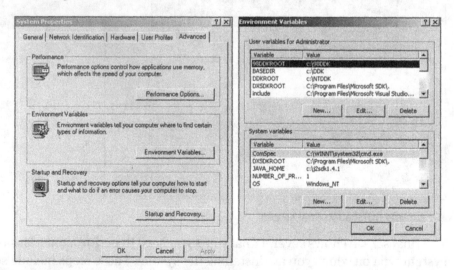

**Figure 3.7** Environment Variables tab in Windows.

For Windows XP, follow these instructions:

1. Click Start and right-click on the My Computer icon.

2. Select the Advanced Tab.

3. Follow steps 2 through 5 in the previous list of instructions for Windows 2000.

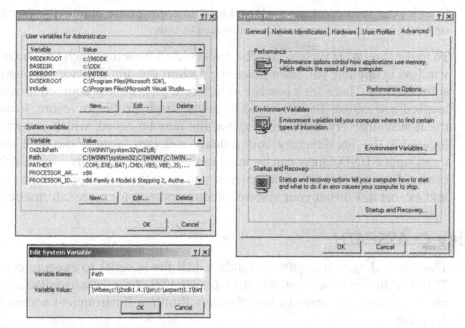

**Figure 3.8**  Editing the *PATH* variable.

For Win95/98/ME, follow these instructions:

1. Locate the autoexec.bat file in the C:\ root directory.

2. Open the file using notepad.exe.

3. Find and edit or add a line for the PATH:

```
PATH C:\WINDOWS;C:\WINDOWS\COMMAND;C:\;C:\DOS;C:\aspectj1.1\bin.
```

4. Save the file.

For all the Windows configurations, the new environment variable will not be available until you open a new command prompt window. All existing command prompt windows will not see the new or changed variable.

In the UNIX/Linux world, things are a little different. A terminal window is actually a shell application that has been executed. Each time a new terminal window is opened, a series of files are sourced and an environment is created. For the most part, a current environment's *PATH* environment variable can be changed for the current session in a terminal window. The *PATH* variable in the current session is changed based on the environment currently being used. For example, if you are using bash, you should be able to execute the following commands:

```
$PATH=$PATH:\apps\aspectj\bin
EXPORT PATH
```

Check your version of the shell and look in appropriate online documentation or UNIX books for the specific command to use.

To make the *PATH* variable see the AspectJ /bin directory each time a terminal window is opened, you must place the path to the /bin directory in one of the sourced files. There are a number of different places these sourced files can be located and called. The file could be .login, .bash_profile, or .cshrc, located in the home directory. At times, a global file may be called, which is commonly located in the /etc directory. Your mileage will vary, because the shell environment under UNIX/Linux can be any number of environments—bash, csh, and others. In some of these environments, you need to set the appropriate variable and export it. Consult your system's documentation for more information.

## Setting *CLASSPATH*

The AspectJ system requires a runtime JAR file in order to execute correctly. This JAR file must be located in the *CLASSPATH* of the Java installation. There are three common ways to give the Java Runtime Environment access to the JAR file:

- The JRE can access JAR files directly if they are in the /jre/lib/ext directory of the current Java system. If you use this access, copy the aspectjrt.jar file to the jdk1.x/jre/lib/ext directory. The aspectjrt.jar file can be found in the \aspectj1.1\lib directory.

- Using the same steps outlined earlier, you can add the path to the aspectjrt.jar file to the *CLASSPATH* environment variable. Be sure to add the entire path, such as c:\aspectj1.0\lib\aspectjrt.jar.

- A common way to use a *CLASSPATH* is through the –classpath command-line flag to the Java compiler. You can use the same command-line flag with the AspectJ compiler. The format of the flag is

```
-classpath c:\aspectj1.1\lib\aspectjrt.jar
```

## Testing the Installation

When you've finished all the installation steps, you should test the complete installation. Our goal for now is to test that the Java compiler, AspectJ compiler, *PATH*, *CLASSPATH*, and Java runtime are all working together nicely; we won't discuss any details of the code.

To test the installation, follow these steps:

1. Open a terminal window or command prompt and change to a working directory.

2. Type the command java. You should receive output from the compiler displaying all the command-line options. If you don't receive this information or you receive text saying the command cannot be found, your PATH environment variable is unable to see the /bin directory of your Java installation. Verify the PATH environment variable, the value entered, and the path to the /bin directory of your Java installation.

3. Type the command ajc. You should receive output from the AspectJ compiler listing all of its command-line options. If you don't receive this information or you receive text saying the command cannot be found, your PATH environment variable is unable to see the /bin directory of your AspectJ installation. Verify the PATH environment variable, the value entered, and the path to the /bin directory of your AspectJ installation.

4. Open a text file called Test.java and enter the code found in Listing 3.1. Compile the code with the command *javac Test.java*. Execute the code with the command *java Test*. A single string should appear on the screen reading "Test Method."

5. Open a text file called TestAspect.java and enter the code found in Listing 3.2.

6. Compile the Test and TestAspect.java files using the AspectJ compiler with the command – *ajc Test.java TestAspect.java*. If you get an error stating the aspectjrt.jar file cannot be found, try the following command:

```
ajc -classpath ".;c:\aspectj1.1\lib\aspectjrt.jar"
Test.java TestAspect.java
```

7. This command uses the –classpath command-line flag to tell the system where the AspectJ runtime JAR file is located. If you still receive an error saying aspectjrt.jar cannot be found, check the AspectJ installation.

8. Execute the code with the command – *java Test.java*.

Figure 3.9 shows the output from this test installation code. If your output looks like that found in Figure 3.9, the AspectJ and Java installations were successful, and you are ready to begin using AspectJ.

```
class Test {

  public void testMethod() {
    System.out.println("Test Method");
  }

  public static void main(String args[]) {
    Test test = new Test();
    test.testMethod();
  }
}
```

**Listing 3.1**  Test.java code.

```
public aspect TestAspect {
  pointcut callTestMethod() : call(public void Test.test*(..));
  before() : callTestMethod() {
    System.out.println("Before Call");
  }
  after() : callTestMethod() {
    System.out.println("After Call");
  }
}
```

**Listing 3.2**   TestAspect.java code.

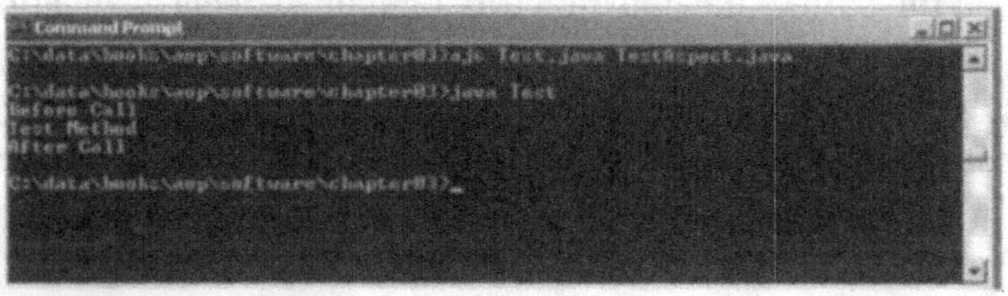

**Figure 3.9**   Installation example execution output.

## What's Next

In Chapter 4, we will take a more detailed look at using the command-line AspectJ compiler. To help with this task, we will discuss a simple Hello World program as we begin to dive deeper into AOP and AspectJ.

# Implementing AspectJ

In most programming books, you find an example of how to use a new language that incorporates the familiar Hello World program. Using a small programming example allows an author to express most of the basics of a new language or paradigm in a compact manner.

In this first chapter on the use of AspectJ, we also use a version of Hello World to illustrate how to use the AOP (aspect-oriented programming) paradigm using AspectJ. The topics we cover include:

- Writing a component
- Identifying join points
- Determining pointcuts
- Giving advice
- Adding an aspect
- Compiling and executing
- Adding new concerns
- Exposing context
- Using inter-type declarations
- Using AspectJ Compiler

# Our First AspectJ Program

In any development cycle for a software application, we must take a clear number of steps, and AspectJ is no different. Unfortunately, the overall coding experience with AspectJ is limited because of its recent introduction into the mainstream of software development. For the most part, though, traditional software development methodologies such as incremental development and object-oriented analysis, design, and programming can be used to develop AspectJ-based applications.

At a basic level, there are three ways to develop an AspectJ application. The first is to begin development using the primary concerns and writing in the component language. This development is followed with the writing of AspectJ code for the crosscutting concerns. The second way to develop an AspectJ application is to add a new concern to existing code using AOP. The third way isn't obvious but it's very important: You add a new primary concern to an application you have already developed (using either of the methods we just listed). By virtue of AspectJ, the new code is automatically crosscut by the existing crosscutting concerns assuming that the code matches defined join points.

## Writing the Component First

Software development is supposed to begin with a discussion of the requirements the customer feels are most important. These requirements are written as a specification document, illustrated in some visual presentation, or defined in a host of other ways. Although not exclusive to aspect-oriented programming, the term *concern* can be applied to the requirements. The concerns are generally separated into "must-have" and "nice-to-have." The must-have concerns have to be implemented in order for the application to provide an appropriate level of functionality to the customer. At the same time, designers and architects look at the must-have concerns and add additional ones to provide important functionality for the operation of the application during execution—functionality such as log caching and connection pools.

In the case of our Hello World program, there is one primary concern. The definition of the concern is:

**Concern 1:** Application shall produce the text "Hello World" to the console.

Obviously, this concern has a single focus and doesn't require implementation across several classes. In fact, just one is required, as shown in Listing 4.1.

```
class Test {
  public void helloWorld() {
    System.out.println("Hello World");
  }

  public static void main(String args[]) {
    Test test = new Test();
    test.helloWorld();
  }
}
```

**Listing 4.1**  Test.java.

The code in Listing 4.1 implements a Test class with two methods. The first method, called helloWorld(), implements the single concern of our system. When called, the method outputs the text *Hello World* to the console. The method is called from the main() method of the Test class. Because the Test class is simple, the compiling and executing is also simple. The command to do the compile is

```
javac Test.java
```

Once compiled, the code is executed with the command

```
java Test
```

The output of the application is also simple:

```
Hello World
```

After you've implemented the primary concern for the system with the component language, it is time to look at any ancillary concerns. When our architects looked at the Hello World application and the requirements from the customer, they decided an additional concern was necessary. The new concern says:

**Concern 2:** All output functions shall log their execution.

## Aspect Code

To aid our discussion in the remainder of the chapter, we listed the AspectJ code necessary to implement our ancillary concern in Listing 4.2.

```
public aspect TestAspect {
  pointcut outputLog() : call(public void helloWorld());
  before() : outputLog() {
    System.out.println("Before Call");
  }
}
```

**Listing 4.2**  TestAspect.java.

## Identifying the Join Point

As you'll learn in Chapter 5, the AspectJ language defines a term called a *join point*. A join point is a well-defined "point" in the execution of a component application. This point can be a method call, the execution of a constructor, or even access to an attribute of a specific class. There are a few exceptions, which we detail in Chapter 5.

Once we've implemented a concern in the component language, we need to perform an analysis to determine where ancillary concerns might crosscut the code. This is a new step in the software development process many of us typically use. We have always had concerns that crosscut the primary functionality of the code, but rarely has this functionality been pulled out and made a focus. We might know from experience that we need to add some level of logging to the code without a written requirement. Our typical reaction to the full development of our primary concerns is to begin the test cycle. Instead, we must turn our attention to the ancillary concerns from the architects and designers. And we must be careful to use AspectJ to implement the ancillary concerns.

Given the concern we have documented and the component code from Listing 4.1, it should be clear that there is one join point in the code where a call is made to the println() method of the System class. Thus, any place in the code where a call is made to println(), a log write should occur. This is a subtle point that you must understand. A join point is a point in the execution of the program. Even though the HelloWorld() method is where the call is made to println(), we should not consider the HelloWorld() method to be the join point for our crosscutting concern because it isn't the true moment in time where the join point occurs. However, since the println() method call occurs within the HelloWorld() method, we could say that the execution of the HelloWorld() method or the call to the method is a join point. The distinction partially falls on the granularity of the moment when the code is executed by the system.

## Determining the Pointcut

After identifying the join points for a specific concern, we need to group them using another new AspectJ term called the *pointcut*, which is outlined in detail in Chapter 6. By combining the join points into a pointcut, the crosscutting of a concern becomes evident. The pointcut acts as a grouping for specific join points. We could easily have two different pointcuts that group 10 join points in different ways. The format of a pointcut is

```
pointcut  name([parameters]): designator(ajoinpoint);
```

For example, the pointcut for handling our ancillary concern is defined in line 2 of Listing 4.2. This sample pointcut illustrates many important characteristics.

First, we have the name() part of the pointcut. The name, which looks like a method, will be used shortly to handle actions performed when a join point is encountered by the Java runtime. Second, the ajoinpoint part of the pointcut is the signature of the join point where something should occur based on our ancillary concern. Finally, and possibly most important, is the designator. The designator is an AspectJ-defined term that indicates when a join point should be associated with a pointcut. In our example, the call designator associates the join point defined by the calling of the public void helloWorld() method with the outputLog() pointcut. When other actions are needed for the join points, a dozen or so designators (described in Chapter 6) are available.

## Giving Advice

The pointcut defines the places within a component—the join points—where a concern crosscuts the code. Of course, this is only half of the implementation of the ancillary concern. The second half of the story is the action that should take place when a pointcut is triggered. The action has a specific term in AspectJ called *advice* (which we cover in detail in Chapter 7).

The three types of advice are:

- After
- Before
- Around

*After* advice tells the system that when a pointcut is triggered, some code should be executed after the join point has executed. *Before* advice tells the runtime to execute designated code just before the join point. *Around* advice executes code defined for the concern instead of the code in the join point.

Based on the definition of our aspect concern, the system should log when an output function is called. Whether this concern means *before* the method call or *after* is certainly open to interpretation. Let's just assume it means before the method call actually takes place. With this in mind, the general form of the advice declaration is as follows:

```
before([parameters]) : pointcut {
    code to execute before pointcut
}
```

The advice signature begins with one of the three types—*before, after, around*—followed by a pointcut declaration. After the signature, a block of code is created that will be executed when the pointcut is triggered. The code declared within an advice block consists of standard Java code. You can make calls to the Java class library or other methods just as you would when writing a traditional Java application. You can find more on this topic in Chapter 7.

To handle the crosscutting concern in our example, let's accomplish the logging of a call to an output method through a single display of text to the console. The advice resembles lines 3 through 5 in Listing 4.2.

Let's take a moment and explain what this code is doing. When our component code is executed, a call will eventually be made to the helloWorld() method. Clearly the exact moment and time when the method call takes place isn't known. The method call is a join point for our example, and when the method call is executed, a match is made against the join point declaration and any pointcut used to group the join point. The advice code associated with any pointcut using the executed join point is executed.

## Adding an Aspect

The code developed so far includes the Test class, which implements the primary system concern, a pointcut defining a specific join point in the component code, and advice to be executed upon a matched join point or combination of join points. The pointcut and advice contain the AspectJ code needed to implement the crosscutting concern previously defined. In one sense, the pointcut could be related to a class attribute and the advice to a class method. This comparison isn't altogether far-fetched because AspectJ includes the concept of an *aspect*, a construct that encapsulates all the code necessary to implement a crosscutting concern. We cover the aspect keyword and concept in depth in Chapter 9, "Aspects."

By using the aspect keyword, we can combine the pointcut and advice code into a single encapsulated module that works as a unit to implement a single crosscutting concern. This encapsulation is important because it allows the crosscutting code to be modularized in the same way as the component Java code. The aspect in Listing 4.2 shows how the pointcut and advice code defined earlier are encapsulated.

From the code in Listing 4.2, you can see that the format of an aspect models that of a class in the Java language. Note that this doesn't have to be the case because the aspect language could be different from the component language. For instance, the component language might be Java but the aspect language could be C++.

## Compiling and Executing the Example

Once all the concerns have been written, we need to compile and execute the code. In Chapter 3, we installed the AspectJ system and tested it to be sure it was operational. The same steps for testing AspectJ should be used when compiling most AspectJ and Java code. To begin with the code in this chapter, either type the code in Listings 4.1 and 4.2 into Java source files with the names Test.java and TestAspect.java, respectively, or download the code from www.wiley.com/compbooks/gradecki.

From a command prompt under Windows or a terminal window under UNIX, execute the AspectJ compiler with the appropriate command:

```
ajc Test.java TestAspect.java
```

The compiler command invokes a batch or script file on the appropriate environment, which in turn invokes the Java runtime to execute the org.aspectj.tools.ajc.Main code found in the \lib\aspectjtools.jar file. This code is the actual AspectJ compiler, and it handles compiling the component Java classes as well as the AspectJ aspects.

If the command works successfully, two class files should be generated in the current directory (or in directories appropriate for any package definition added to the code). Once the class files have been generated, they can be executed just as any other Java application would be. Use the following command to see the result of our implementation of the concerns:

```
java -classpath "./;c:\aspectj1.0\lib\aspectjrt.jar" Test
```

The result of this command is the execution of the Test main() method, which implements the primary concern with appropriate hooks in place for the AspectJ code handling the crosscutting concern. The output from the example code is

```
Before Call
Hello World
```

# Adding a New Concern

Once a system is operational, we must typically make changes to satisfy the requirements of our users. In this section, we add three new concerns and see how they affect the code necessary to build the system:

**Concern 3:** Application shall return the text "Hello World".

**Concern 4:** Application shall log all methods returning text to a log file.

**Concern 5:** Application shall accept name parameter, append to "Hello" text, and display to console.

## The Method for Returning Text

The third concern in our application requires that we add to the component code that returns a text string instead of displaying the text to the console. This is a simple method; Listing 4.3 shows the new method highlighted in bold.

```
class Test {

  public void helloWorld() {
    System.out.println("HelloWorld");
  }

  public String helloWorldReturn() {
    return "Hello World";
  }

  public static void main(String args[]) {
    Test test = new Test();
    test.helloWorld();
    System.out.println(test.helloWorldReturn());
  }
}
```

**Listing 4.3**   New Test.java.

With the new method added to the component, you're probably wondering what the AspectJ code will produce. A quick recompile and execution yields the following result:

```
Before Call
Hello World
```

Is this what we would expect based on the pointcut defined earlier and its related join point? Actually, yes, the pointcut uses a join point defined as

```
call(public void helloWorld());
```

The join point is very specific to the method with a signature public void helloWorld(). The method added to the component code is public string helloWorldReturn(), which is very different from the one defined.

## Logging Return Methods

The second new concern, Concern 4, tells us that all methods returning a text string should also be logged just as those that display text to the console. The pointcut used in our aspect is

```
pointcut outputLog() : call(public void helloWorld());
```

There are two easy ways to add functionality to the aspect to support the new concern. The first way is to change the defined point using wildcards or logical operators. The second way is to add an additional pointcut to handle the new concern. Let's take a look at both methods.

## Using the Same Pointcut

The first way is to change the pointcut by adding a completely new signature or using wildcards in the definition of a pointcut. The first step in the process is to define the join point we are interested in adding to the aspect. The pointcut necessary to support the new concern is

```
call(public string helloWorldReturn())
```

The pointcut uses a join point defined as a call to the helloWorldReturn() method. Clearly the new pointcut is different from the pointcut used to match the public void helloWorld() signature and supports the output we saw when we ran our code earlier. A pointcut can use logical operators like AND and OR to build a set of join points that can be related to one another. Since the two concerns—Concern 2 (All output functions shall log their execution) and Concern 4 (Application shall log all methods returning text)—appear to support the same kind of logging, it makes sense to use the same pointcut. In fact, we could just change Concern 2 to support the logging listed in Concern 4, further supporting the idea of using a single pointcut for both concerns.

By using the OR logical operator, we combine the two join points in the following way:

```
pointcut outputLog() : call(public void helloWorld()) ||
                       call(public string helloWorldReturn());
```

This pointcut is triggered when either the helloWorld() or the helloWorld Return() method is encountered during the execution of the component application. No additional changes are needed in the aspect code to support concerns 2 and 4. To demonstrate the use of the new primary concern, we changed the Test code as shown in Listing 4.4.

```
class Test {
  //methods defined in Listing 4.4

  public static void main(String args[]) {
    Test test = new Test();
    test.helloWorld();

    System.out.println("say - " + test.helloWorldReturn());
  }
}
```

**Listing 4.4**  The code that calls the new primary concern.

After we've compiled and executed the Test code and the modified AspectJ code, the output from the application is as follows:

```
Before Call
Hello World
Before Call
say - Hello World
```

### Join Point Wildcards

Pointcuts can also be created by using join point wildcards. After a quick analysis of the two methods being caught by the pointcut, we find that the only differences between the methods are the return types and the method name. In the case of the method name, the first part of the name is the same, with only the addition of the text *Return* at the end of one of them. AspectJ allows the use of wildcards in most parts of the join point. You can find more information on join point wildcards in Chapter 6. Our example suggests a join point like this one:

```
call(public * helloWorld*())
```

This join point says to match all methods that:

- Are defined as public
- Have any return type
- Have a method name starting with a text string "helloWorld"

## *Adding a Second Pointcut*

It just so happens that both of the crosscutting concerns indicate that logging should occur when specific types of methods are called within the component code. However, if we read Concern 4 closely, we find that the concern also requires that the logging be saved in a log file. Using the pointcut defined earlier using the logical operator, a call to either of the methods results in a message being displayed on the console. Calls to the helloWorldReturn() method should be logged but not to the console.

How do we handle implementing two or more concerns that seem to have identical functionality but would need to be coded differently? This comes down to a design decision similar to the one you must make when designing the primary application. The two concerns we are talking about in this example both require logging but in different respects. One quick design solution would group the two concerns into a single aspect, a logging aspect, with different pointcuts to handle the different join points. The code for handling the logging of the helloWorldReturn() method to a log file would exist in a separate advice. In this example, the concerns don't differ enough in functionality to warrant separate aspects.

The aspect for handling both of these concerns is shown in Listing 4.5.

```
public aspect TestAspect {
  pointcut outputLog() : call(public void helloWorld());
  before() : outputLog() {
    System.out.println("Before Call - log to console");
  }

  pointcut fileLog() : call(public String helloWorldReturn());
  before() : fileLog() {
    System.out.println("Before Call - log to file");
  }
}
```

**Listing 4.5** This aspect handles multiple concerns.

After compiling and executing the aspect shown in Listing 4.5 with the Test component class, the output generated is as follows:

```
Before Call - log to console
Hello World
Before Call - log to file
say - Hello World
```

## A New Primary Concern

The fifth concern we must add to our application is:

**Concern 5:** Application shall accept name parameter, append to "Hello" text, and display to console.

For this concern, we need to add a simple method to the Test class that accepts a single String parameter and outputs a string to the console:

```
public void helloWorldUnique(String name) {
  System.out.println("Hello, " + name);
}
```

Once we've added this new method to the component class, we must perform a quick analysis of the crosscutting concerns and related aspects to be sure the new method will be included in appropriate pointcuts. If we use the aspect in Listing 4.6, then we are in trouble because the new code will not be caught.

We must compare the functionality of the new code against the two concerns currently defined in the system. Concern 2 crosscuts those methods that output text to the console that matches the output of the new code. To handle the new code, the new method's join point must be added to the pointcut. It's probably a safe bet that a wildcard can be used in the outputLog() point to handle all potential helloWorld methods. We've listed the new aspect code in Listing 4.6, with the change in bold. The new component code is shown in Listing 4.7.

```
public aspect TestAspect {
  pointcut outputLog() : call(public void helloWorld*());
  before() : outputLog() {
    System.out.println("Before Call - log to console");
  }

  pointcut fileLog() : call(public String helloWorldReturn());
  before() : fileLog() {
    System.out.println("Before Call - log to file");
  }
}
```

**Listing 4.6**  The parameter method aspect.

```
class Test {
  // unchanged methods omitted

  public void helloWorldUnique(String name) {
    System.out.println("Hello, " + name);
    }

  public static void main(String args[]) {
    Test test = new Test();
    test.helloWorld();

    System.out.println("say - " + test.helloWorldReturn());

    test.helloWorldUnique("Joe");
  }
}
```

**Listing 4.7**  The parameter method component code.

After executing the Test code with the new component method and the new Aspect code, we see the following output:

```
Before Call - log to console
Hello World
Before Call - log to file
say - Hello World
Hello, Joe
```

The first four lines of output relate to our concerns written earlier. The last line is the important one for our new component code. You're probably thinking, "Wait a minute—shouldn't there be six lines of code? An output line for the aspect followed by a line of code from the component?" Yes, that's true; however, if you look back at the aspect in Listing 4.6 and take a good look at the outputLog() pointcut versus the signature of the helloWorldUnique() method, one difference should be noted. The helloWorldUnique() method includes a parameter but the pointcut's join point definition shows an empty parameter list. Go into the code and add two periods in the parameter list of the join point, like this:

```
pointcut outputLog() : call(public void helloWorld*(..));
```

Now when the code is executed, the output is as follows:

```
Before Call - log to console
Hello World
Before Call - log to file
say - Hello World
Before Call - log to console
Hello, Joe
```

The new output is what should be expected for all three calls in the main() method of the application. The double periods in the parameter part of the join point signature act as a wildcard for any number or types of parameters.

## Exposing Context

In the previous example, we added a new method to the component code that included parameters. When we executed the advice code, a simple text message was displayed to the console and the parameter to the join point method was ignored. AspectJ provides the ability to access the parameters of the component method being executed within the advice code, as well as a host of other contextual information.

The parameters of the component are visible by adding an args designator to the pointcut definition as well as by specifying the arguments in the parameter list of the pointcut definition itself. For example, in the method call helloWorldUnique(String), a single parameter is available of the String type. We can create a pointcut definition that indicates our desire to access this parameter when the appropriate component join points are triggered. Here's the code for the pointcut:

```
pointcut uniqueLog(String s) :
              call(public void helloWorldUnique(String)) &&
              args(s);
```

This pointcut looks the same as the others we have built except for two things. First, we have added a parameter in the pointcut signature name. Second, we added another designator called *args*. The purpose of the args designator as used here is to provide the associated advice code with access to the parameters originally passed to the helloWorldUnique() method. There is just one join point in this pointcut definition, and it includes calls made to the method public void helloWorldUnique(String). By including a single parameter type in the method signature, we are stating that only calls with a single parameter should be considered.

The args designator has a single parameter. This parameter is directly related to the single parameter passed to the method defined as part of our join point. The pointcut completely defines a single parameter based on a combination of the join point and the args designator. Therefore, if the pointcut is expecting a String called *s*, there should be a join point defined with a String parameter and an args designator with a variable defined as *s*. Now the pointcut can be used with advice to examine the parameter. For example:

```
before(String s) : uniqueLog(s) {
    System.out.println("Passed value = " + s);
}
```

Notice the use of the parameter to the before advice designator. When the pointcut uniqueLog is triggered, its String parameter defined by the *s* variable is made available to the before() advice body. Within the body of the advice, the *s* parameter is used to display the value of the String passed to the original method. The output from the Test component class and the new aspect is as follows:

```
Before Call - log to console
Hello World
Before Call - log to file
say - Hello World
Passed value = Joe
Hello, Joe
```

When the helloWorldUnique() method is executed, the appropriate advice is triggered and the value passed to the component method is displayed.

# Inter-type Declarations

All of our examples to this point have dealt with the concept of dynamic crosscutting, which provides a way to crosscut the primary code. However, dynamic crosscutting doesn't change the hierarchy of the classes in an application, nor does it change the makeup of any of the classes. If a class doesn't contain a specific attribute or method at runtime, it won't change at runtime either unless AspectJ Introduction declarations are used.

An Introduction declaration is a way to add new functionality to an application by defining new attributes and methods to an established class or set of classes.

In this section, we examine this topic; you can find a more in-depth discussion on inter-type declarations in Chapter 8, "Inter-type Declarations."

To show how the introduction can be used, let's continue with our example Test class and its aspect class. The Test class doesn't support keeping track of the number of times a call is made to the helloWorldUnique() method. This is an important requirement because the helloWorldUnique() method is very expensive when executed in a production environment. Imagine for a moment that the source code for this class wasn't available but the boss just needed to have this information. Rather than having to rewrite the code, we can use AspectJ.

## Adding Class Code

To keep track of the number of times the method is called, let's use a simple integer variable. The Test class doesn't include an integer, so we need to add one using the TestAspect aspect. You can add an inter-type declaration in much the same way you add an attribute or a method to a class. The code for adding a vector to the Test class is

```
private int Test.methodCallCount;
```

This code instructs the compiler to add an integer to the Test class and make the attribute private. Now we need to write some code to access the integer. The code in Listing 4.8 shows a new aspect, including code to use the vector defined earlier.

```
public aspect TestAspect {
  private int Test.count = 0;

  public void Test.incCount() {
    count++;
  }

  public int Test.getCount() {
    return count;
  }

  pointcut uniqueLog(Test t, String s) :
                      call(public void helloWorldUnique(String)) &&
                      args(s) &&
                      target(t);

  before(Test t, String s) : uniqueLog(t, s) {
    t.incCount();

    System.out.println("Count:" + t.getCount());
  }
}
```

**Listing 4.8**  Our inter-type declarations aspect code.

The aspect code in Listing 4.8 includes a new designator called target in the pointcut definition. The target designator is used to provide access to the target object of the method call public void helloWorldUnique(String). The code for providing access to the object is basically the same as the code for accessing the join point's arguments. The primary difference is the addition of the target designator. Notice the order of the object and parameter in both the pointcut and the advice definitions. The order must be the same between the two definitions.

Within the advice code, the target object is accessed using the variable defined in the pointcut and advice–$t$ in the case of our example in Listing 4.9. Since the aspect has added the count integer variable to the Test class as well as appropriate accessor functions, it can access the variable as needed and yet maintain the modularity of the Test class.

The Test class code, shown in Listing 4.9, includes several calls to the helloWorldUnique() method to illustrate the use of the added vector.

```
class Test {
  public void helloWorld() {
    System.out.println("Hello World");
  }

  public String helloWorldReturn() {
    return new String("Hello World");
  }

  public void helloWorldUnique(String name) {
    System.out.println("Hello, " + name);
    }

  public static void main(String args[]) {
    Test test = new Test();

    test.helloWorldUnique("Joe");
    test.helloWorldUnique("Sam");
    test.helloWorldUnique("Fred");
  }
}
```

**Listing 4.9** Our Test class code.

The output from the Test class and its aspect is as follows:

```
Count: 1
Hello, Joe
Count: 2
Hello, Sam
Count: 3
Hello, Fred
```

The aspect was able to successfully add code to the Test class, and the integer and its associated accessor function were used to display the number of times the helloWorldUnique() method was called.

## Aspect Granularity

Looking back at the last primary example code in Listing 4.9 and the various aspects defined in this chapter, you note that each time new methods are added to the primary code, the aspect code also has to change. This is because we based our join points on the calls to methods that contained the System.out.println() method call instead of on the call to the println() method itself. Although this doesn't seem like a big deal, it causes us more work when additional classes and methods are added to the primary code.

Let's assume we still have our crosscutting concern that dictates we need to log all output calls. If we use our previous method of defining join points and point-cuts, we need to write an aspect as shown in Listing 4.10.

```
public aspect MultiPoint {
  pointcut logBasic() : call(public void helloWorld());
  pointcut logReturn() : call(public String helloWorldReturn);
  pointcut logUnique() : call(public void helloWorldUnique(String));

  pointcut logAll() : logBasic() ||
                      logReturn() ||
                      logUnique();

  before() : logAll() {
    //log to database
  }
}
```

**Listing 4.10**  A multiple join point aspect.

In Listing 4.10 we take some liberty by combining several join points into a single pointcut using the OR operator. If we add a new method that uses a println() method call, we have to add another join point definition to the code and append it to the pointcut definition. This approach isn't very efficient.

Fortunately, AspectJ is powerful and allows us to define a join point based on calls to methods in packages we didn't write ourselves. Consider the aspect shown in Listing 4.11.

```
public aspect SinglePoint {
  pointcut logPrintln() : call(* System.out.println(..));

  before() : logAll() {
    //log to database
  }
}
```

**Listing 4.11**  A single join point aspect.

In the new aspect, the join point is now a call to the System.out.println()
method regardless of the type or number of parameters to the method call. If
we add another method to the primary code to satisfy a new concern, our
aspect automatically picks up any calls to the println() method in the new code.
This is a tremendous development savings—provided by the power contained
in the AOP paradigm and the AspectJ language.

# AspectJ Compiler Functionality

The AspectJ compiler is built to allow the use of aspects in a variety of circumstances regardless of whether or not the source code is available to the developer. Suppose you'd like to add an aspect to code contained within a JAR file,
or you'd like to package a useful aspect into its own JAR file for use by other
developers. The compiler allows for these types of scenarios. In this section, we
show you how to:

- Specify source directories
- Weave with JARs
- Specify output to a JAR
- Create and use aspect libraries
- Compile without weaving
- Use incremental compiling

## Specifying Source Directories

When you're developing a software project, it is customary to separate the modules or objects into different files. This separation can be extended to the files
themselves, whereby groups of files are placed in different directories based on
their usage. For example, we might build an application that has a GUI and
includes network and encryption components. We could place the files for each
in these directories:

```
/development/project1/gui
/development/project1/network
/development/project1/encryption
```

To compile the files, we must pass all the code to the AspectJ compiler. We accomplish this by using the –sourceroots compiler flag and separating the directories with a delimiter. On UNIX, we'd compile the directories with the command

```
ajc -sourceroots /development/project1/gui:
/development/project1/network:/development/project1/encryption
```

The compiler moves into each directory and compiles the code found in the directories. As of this writing, all files in the specified directories with extensions of .java and .aj are automatically compiled.

Under UNIX, the delimiter for separating the directories is the : (colon). On a Windows machine, the delimiter is a ; (semicolon).

## Weaving with JARs

The 1.1 release of AspectJ broke with the past 1.0 version by performing all weaving of aspects using byte code instead of at the source level. This means an aspect can be written and applied to binary code even if the source code isn't available. The most common scenario where binary code will be weaved with an aspect is when a JAR file exists with the compiled .class files.

Consider the following two snippets of code:

```
public class GUI1 {
  public GUI1() {
    init();
  }
  private void init() {}
}

public class GUI2 {
  public GUI2() {
    init();
  }
  private void init() {}
}
```

Using another Java compiler, the two classes are compiled and added to a JAR file called gui.jar:

```
javac GUI1.java GUI2.java
jar -cf gui.jar GUI1.class GUI2.class
```

Let's further assume that we have an aspect defined to match on the init() methods:

```
public aspect InitAspect {
  pointcut outputLog() : execution(private void init());
  before() : outputLog() {
    System.out.println("GUI classes Init() method - log to
console");
  }
}
```

We also need a Driver object, which could be defined as

```
public class Driver {
  public static void main(String[] args){
    GUI1 gui1 = new GUI1();
    GUI2 gui2 = new GUI2();
  }
}
```

We want to weave the aspect defined earlier into the gui.jar file as well as include the Driver class so we can execute the code. The following command does the work:

```
ajc -injars gui.jar Driver.java InitAspect.aj
```

The result will be four files:

```
GUI1.class
GUI2.class
Driver.class
InitAspect.class
```

To accomplish the weaving into JAR files, we use the –injars flag. This flag tells the compiler to pull the .class files stored in the specified JARs and use them in the weaving with any provided aspects. Multiple JAR files are passed to the compiler by separating the JARs with : (in UNIX) or ; (in Windows).

## NOTE

The AspectJ compiler assumes and requires that aspects be woven into the code once. Therefore, JAR files that have already been woven should not be passed to the compiler for a second pass with a new aspect.

## Specifying Output to a JAR

It is possible to direct the output from the AspectJ compiler into a JAR file. Consider our earlier example. Suppose we want to weave the InitAspect into the gui.jar file and place the results into a new JAR called weavedgui.jar. The following command does the job:

```
ajc -injars gui.jar -outjar weavedgui.jar InitAspect.aj
```

The JAR weavedgui.jar contains the classes GUI1.class, GUI2.class, and InitAspect.class all weaved together. Note again that the new JAR file cannot be used in a further AspectJ compile.

## Creating and Using Aspect Libraries

Using JAR files creates a more modular and easy-to-handle system. The files also allow components to be shared and used in other projects. When aspects are created and compiled, they can also be combined into a JAR file using the –outjar option. For example, we might have a directory called aspects where only source code for aspects is located. This directory can be compiled and a new JAR file built with this command:

```
ajc -sourceroots aspects -outjar aspects.jar
```

The aspects.jar file contains all the aspects ready to be woven into the system code. Let's say the system code is located in a directory called code. The following command compiles the system, weaves in the aspects contained within the aspects.jar file, and produces a final JAR:

```
ajc -aspectpath aspects.jar -sourceroots code -outjar system.jar
```

This compile command uses a new flag called –aspectpath. This flag is designed to pick up a JAR file containing aspect byte code to be weaved with other Java code. The –sourceroots flag is used to pull all the source code within the code directory. The two pieces of code are weaved and the output placed in a JAR file called system.jar.

## Impeding Weaving

As a convenience function, the AspectJ compiler can be used as a traditional Java compile where the weaving activity is suppressed. The suppression is accomplished by using the –noweave flag. The classes produced by the compiler when weaving is suppressed can be passed back through the compiler for weaving at a later time.

## Using Incremental Compiling

One of the requested options for the AspectJ compiler between versions 1.0 and 1.1 was support for incremental compiling. The compiler now supports incremental compiling through both the command-line version and the various IDE plug-ins presented in Chapter 11, "Using AspectJ Tools."

To use incremental compiling, we need to add the –incremental flag to the compile command line, and the –sourceroots option must also be present. The –incremental flag tells the compiler to perform incremental compiling on the directories specified in –sourceroots. For example, we can perform incremental compiling on the three directories mentioned earlier with the following command:

```
ajc -incremental -sourceroots /development/project1/gui:
/development/project1/network:/development/project1/encryption
```

The compiler performs an initial compile of all the source code and then waits for console input before attempting an incremental compile. The incremental option can also be used with –injars, as shown in Figure 4.1.

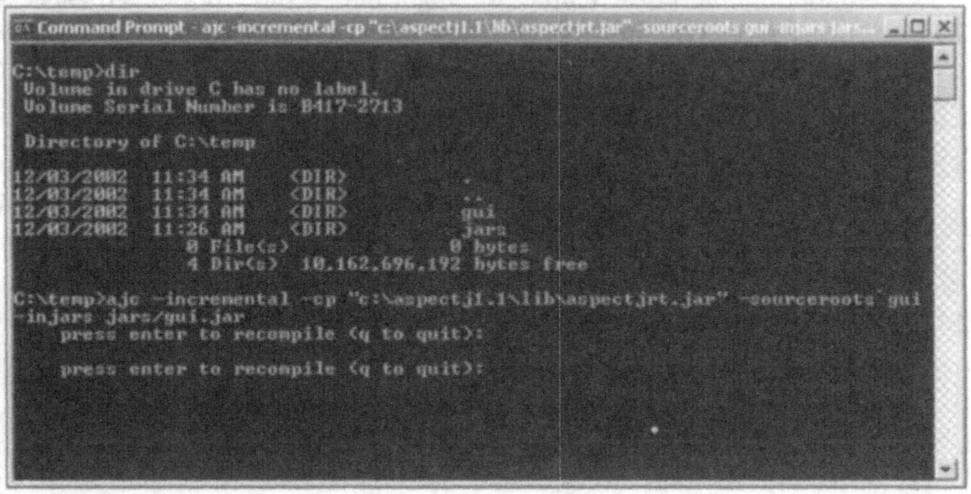

**Figure 4.1** Incremental compiling with a JAR file.

As shown in Figure 4.1, there are three directories: one that contains the application driver source code, one that contains the system aspect and JARs, and one that contains a JAR file. By combining the flags, we ensure that all of the code is compiled; the user is then prompted to press a key to perform an incremental compile.

# What's Next

In this chapter, we looked at all of the major pieces necessary for the creation of a component application and the AspectJ code necessary to support those concerns that crosscut the primary concerns of the system. In the next chapter, we dive into the join points and learn how they can be referenced in an AspectJ aspect.

# CHAPTER 5

# AspectJ Join Points

O nce you become familiar with the concepts surrounding AOP (aspect-oriented programming) and using the AspectJ language, it becomes clear that one of the most important parts of the paradigm is the *join point*. The join point is a well-defined "point" in the execution of a component application. As discussed in the paper "An Overview of AspectJ," the team at PARC went through a number of different join point models before ending up with a model based on well-defined execution points. In this chapter, we explore the concept of a join point in detail and provide several working examples of how to indicate (using AspectJ) the join points upon which crosscutting should occur. The topics in this chapter include:

- The dynamic join point model
- AspectJ join points
- Signatures
- Patterns
- Reflections
- Join point examples

## The Dynamic Join Point Model

To illustrate what join points are and how they are used in writing AspectJ programs for crosscutting a component application, let's use a simple component class. We use this same class throughout this chapter to provide join point examples. Figure 5.1 shows a class hierarchy that implements a hierarchy for products. The Product class is a high-level class containing attributes for the product price. The DVD class represents a DVD and extends Product. The Boxset class extends Product and encapsulates some number of DVD products. Each class has setter and getter methods, and the DVD/Boxset class has a constructor. Listing 5.1 contains the code for the various classes represented in Figure 5.1.

Of particular importance are the count and location attributes in both DVD and Boxset. These attributes and associated methods are used to track product. In themselves, these attributes and methods don't have anything to do with the fundamental DVD and Boxset product. They represent a concern, inventory handling, outside the scope of either class. The concern is crosscutting the core implementation of the classes. As we all know, there are always several ways to code a problem. Some argue that inventory handling should be a primary concern and thus coded with the component language and potentially as part of the Product class. However, I contend that a product doesn't contain inventory information. A product is an entity that contains attributes such as price, title, and size.

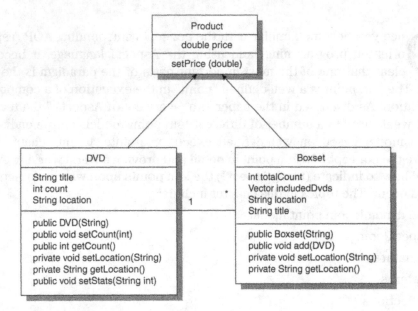

**Figure 5.1** Our sample class hierarchy.

```
public class Product {

  private double price;
```

**Listing 5.1** Our sample class code. (continues)

```
    public void setPrice(double inPrice) {
      price = inPrice;
    }
}

public class DVD extends Product {

  private String title;
  private int count;
  private String location;

  public DVD(String inTitle) {
    title = inTitle;
  }

  public void setCount(int inCount) {
    count = inCount;
  }

  public int getCount() {
    return count;
  }

  private void setLocation(String inLocation) {
    location = inLocation;
  }

  private String getLocation() {
    return location;
  }

  public void setStats(String inLocation, int inCount) {
    setLocation(inLocation);
    setCount(inCount);
  }
}

import java.util.Vector;

public class Boxset extends Product {
  private int totalCount;
  private Vector includedDvds;
  private String location;
  private String title;

  public Boxset(String inTitle) {
```

**Listing 5.1**   Our sample class code. (continues)

```
    includedDvds = new Vector();
    totalCount = 0;
    title = inTitle;
  }

public void add(DVD inDvd) {
  inDvd.setStats(location, 1);
  includedDvds.add(inDvd);
  totalCount++;
}

public void setLocation(String inLocation) {
  location = inLocation;
}

public String getLocation() {
  return location;
}
}
```

**Listing 5.1** Our sample class code. (continued)

We use the defined classes in the following snippet of code to show how the join points are detailed throughout the DVD class:

```
DVD dvd1 = new DVD("Star Wars");
DVD dvd2 = new DVD("Empire Strikes Back");
DVD dvd3 = new DVD("Return of the Jedi");
Boxset set = new Boxset("StarWars Trilogy");
set.setTitle("Great DVD Store");
set.add(dvd1);
set.add(dvd2);
set.add(dvd3);
```

The code begins with the creation of three DVD objects and one Boxset object. All the objects have their title attribute set through the constructor of each individual object. Figure 5.2 illustrates the creation of all the objects along with an execution path for the creation of the Boxset object. The join points for the creation of the Boxset object are as follows:

1. A constructor call join point for the call made to create the Boxset object

2. A constructor call reception (not a join point in AspectJ but noted)

3. A constructor execution join point for when the code within the constructor is invoked

4. A constructor call for the creation of the Vector object within the Boxset constructor

5. A constructor call reception join point for the creation of the Vector object

6. A constructor execution join point for the Vector object

7. A field set join point for setting the totalCount attribute

8. A field set join point for setting the title attribute

Although we haven't shown them here, the Vector object could have join points defined against it as well. Just because we don't have the source code doesn't mean we cannot match the methods/constructors and other join points with the object.

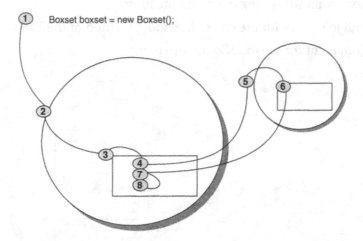

**Figure 5.2** The execution path for creating the Boxset object.

The point that should be most clear from Figure 5.2 is the number of join points available in the execution of just a single line of code. At just about any key location (except for the individual statements), a join point is available.

In Figure 5.3, we see the execution path for a line of code in the previous example, set.add(dvd1);, which adds a whole set of additional join points. The points are as follows:

1. A method call join point for the call to the add() method

2. A method call reception join point for the beginning of code execution within the add() method

3. A method execution join point

4. A method call reception join point for the call to the DVD setStats() method

5. A method execution join point for the beginning of code execution with the setStats() method

6. A method call join point for the call to the DVD setLocation() method call

7. A method execution join point for the beginning of code execution within the setLocation() method call

8. A field set join point for setting the location attribute

9. A method call reception join point for after code execution in the setLocation() method call

10. A method execution join point for the call to the DVD setCount() method call

11. A field set join point for setting the count attribute

12. A method call join point for the call to the add() method of the Vector

13. A field set join point for the totalCount join point.

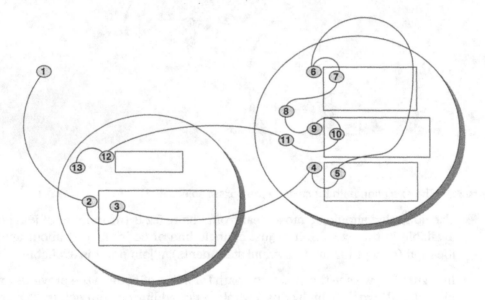

**Figure 5.3** The execution call path for the add() method.

We used some of the specific join points made available in AspectJ in our execution call paths. Note that not all available join points are used in a typical application, nor are all types of designators used. In the next section, we examine the specific join points available in AspectJ.

## AspectJ Join Points

The current version of AspectJ, 1.1, defines a host of join points available to be triggered. These join points are:

**Method call**—A method call join point is defined when any method call is made by an object or a static method if no object is defined, as in the case of the main() method. This join point is defined within the calling object or application. Consider this code example based on the classes we defined earlier:

```
public static void main(String args[]) {
  Boxset set = new Boxset("StarWars Trilogy");
  set.setTitle("Great DVD Store");
}
```

A join point set on the set.setTitle("Great DVD Store"); method is triggered in the context of main() as opposed to the Boxset object. Consider the following pointcut:

```
pointcut TitleChange() : call(public void setTitle(String)) &&
                         target(Boxset);
```

This pointcut defines a group containing a join point defined by a call to the setTitle(String); method. Any place in the code where a call is made to set-Title(String), the pointcut is triggered as long as the target of the call is a Boxset object.

**Constructor call**—A constructor call join point is defined when a constructor is called during the creation of a new object. This join point is defined within the calling object or application if no object is defined. Consider this code example:

```
public static void main(String args[]) {
  Boxset set = new Boxset("StarWars Trilogy");
}
```

A join point set on the new statement triggers a constructor call join point based on the main() method. Here's a pointcut for this example:

```
pointcut constructSet() : initialization(Boxset.new(String));
```

**Method call execution**—A method call execution join point is defined when a method is called on an object and control transfers to the method. The join point is triggered based on the object receiving the method call before any of the code within the method is executed. It is assured that the join point will be triggered upon transfer of execution to the method just before the method code begins to process. For example, consider the following code example:

```
public static void main(String args[]) {
  Boxset set = new Boxset("StarWars Trilogy");
  set.setTitle("Great DVD Store");
}
```

In this example, a method call execution join point could be defined on the setTitle(String) method. When the call is made to the method through the set object, the join point will be triggered based on the set object just before the setTitle() method is to be executed. A corresponding pointcut would be

```
pointcut titleReception() :
  execution(public void setTitle(String));
```

**Constructor call execution**—A constructor call reception join point is the same as the method call reception join point except we are dealing with constructors. The join point is triggered before the constructor code starts to execute.

**Field get**—A field get join point is defined when an attribute associated with an object is read. In our example, a call to the method getLocation() causes a field get join point to be triggered because the attribute is accessed, not because of the actual getLocation() method. A corresponding pointcut would be

```
Pointcut locationGet() : get(public String DVD.location);
```

**Field set**—A field set join point is defined when an attribute associated with an object is written. In our example, a call to the method setLocation(String) causes a field set join point to be triggered. A corresponding point would be

```
Pointcut locationSet() : set(public String DVD.location);
```

**Exception handler execution**—An exception handler execution join point is defined when an exception handler is executed.

**Class initialization**—A class initialization join point is defined when any static initializers are executed for a specific class. If there are no static initializers, there will be no join points.

**Object initialization**—An object initialization join point is defined when a dynamic initializer is executed for a class. This join point is triggered after a call to an object's parent constructor and just before the return of the object's constructor.

# Join Point Signatures

By far, one of the most important parts of a join point is the *signature*. For each of the different join point types, AspectJ defines specific parts to be included in the signature:

**Method call execution**—The format of a method call execution signature is

```
<access_type> <return_value> <type>.<method_name>(parameter_list)
```

For example:

```
public void DVD.setLocation(String)
```

**Constructor call execution**—The format of a constructor call execution signature is

```
<method_access_type> <class_type.new>(<parameter_list>)
                    [throws <exception>]
```

For example:

```
private DVD.new(String)
private DVD.new(String) throws IOException;
```

**Field get**—The format of a field get signature is

```
<field_type> <class_type>.<field_name>
```

For example:

```
double Product.price
```

**Field set**—The format of a field set signature is

```
<field_type> <class_type>.<field_name>
```

**Exception handler execution**—The format of an exception handler execution signature is

```
<exception_type>
```

For example:

```
IOException
```

**Class/object initialization**—The format of an object initialization signature is

```
<method_access_type> <method_name>(<parameter_list>)
```

For example:

```
DVD.new()
```

As we see later in this chapter, we can define signatures for the join points in an example program in numerous ways. Unfortunately, at times there is a need to match more than a single join point with a single signature, as was the case in Chapter 3, when we needed to match helloWorld and helloWorldUnique. Instead of writing two separate signatures, we can use wildcards or patterns.

# Patterns

Using our example code in Listing 5.1, suppose we have a concern that tells us to handle the setting of all attributes in a class in a common format. Looking at the DVD class, we find that there are two set methods: setLocation() and setCount(). Using some of the knowledge we have from Chapter 3, we can create two join points with the code

```
call(public void setLocation(String)
```

and

```
call(public void setCount(int)
```

These two join points are based on the setLocation() and setCount() methods, which are defined as

```
private void setCount(int inCount) {
    count = inCount;
}

private void setLocation(String inLocation) {
    location = inLocation;
}
```

The two join points can be used in a single pointcut by combining the join points using the || symbol. In this scenario, we could define a pointcut so that a trigger would occur when the setLocation() or the setCount() method is called. This certainly works and it isn't much trouble, but more complex join points or a larger number of join points could get messy.

## Type Name Patterns

Fortunately, AspectJ allows the use of name patterns through the * character. The * is actually a special type name and can be used to match all types, including primitive types as needed. In addition, the * can be used to match zero or more characters except for ".". Using this information, we can combine the two join points into one:

```
call(private void DVD.set*(*))
```

Notice the need for two * wildcards. The first wildcard used in the *set** portion tells the system to match all methods that are defined as access private, that return void, that belong to the DVD class, and that have a method name starting with the text "set" followed by any number of additional characters (except the "."). Based on the earlier code for setLocation() and setCount(), these two methods would match so far. However, notice that both of the methods have different parameter types passed to them. Without the second wildcard, this would cause a problem in the join point. The second wildcard tells the system to continue matching methods as long as they have a single parameter of any type. If one of the methods is changed to have zero parameters or more than 1, the signature will not be triggered on that particular join point because it won't match.

In another example, suppose we are interested in all the methods defined within the DVD class that have a single parameter. The signature is

```
call(private void DVD.*(*))
```

This signature matches all private methods defined within the DVD class having a single parameter. This example can be expanded to match all methods regardless of access type:

```
call(* void DVD.*(*))
```

In this signature, we've replaced the access type with a wildcard indicating that join points within the application should be matched regardless of whether they are defined as public, protected, or private. Further, we can eliminate the return type and replace it with a wildcard as well:

```
call(* * DVD.*(*))
```

Here we are matching all methods within the DVD class having a single parameter. If there is no class type defined in a signature, the system will assume you mean any class within the application should be used for matching join points. Next, any class can be used:

```
call(* * *.*(*))
```

In this signature, the class type has been replaced with a wildcard. Now all methods will be matched across all classes used in an example application. However, in all your examples, a single parameter is matched because of the wildcard. This signature will not match methods with two parameters. An additional wildcard is available in AspectJ to handle this situation as well as several others.

AspectJ has a wildcard, "..", which can be used to match any sequence of characters as well as act as a wildcard for parameter counts within matching parameters. Take, for example, the following methods:

```
private void setCount(int inCount) {
      count = inCount;
}

private void setLocation(String inLocation) {
    location = inLocation;
}
private void setStats(String inLocation, int inCount) {
  setCount(inCount);
  setLocation(inLocation);
}
```

To match all these methods, we can use the following signature:

```
call(private void DVD.set*(..))
```

This signature matches all three of the earlier methods, including the one with two parameters. The ".." wildcard, when not used in the parameter part of a call or execution join point, can be used to match any sequence of characters that start and end with a period. As an example of using the ".." wildcard as well as matching types within a package, let's assume there is a package hierarchy defined as

```
com.company.department.room.class1
com.company.department.room.class2
com.company.department.room.class3
```

As we see in the next chapter, a pointcut designator called target is triggered when a class is a target during execution. There will be times when join points need to be defined based on specific classes in a package. As a start, we can specify that a join point be triggered when the class1 class defined earlier is a target in the execution of a program. The signature might look like this:

```
target(com.company.department.room.class1)
```

If we want to target any of the classes within the com.company.department. room path, we can use this signature:

```
target(com.company.department.room.*)
```

This signature matches all three class types: class1, class2, and class3. If we use the * wildcard (as in the signature we just created), the system assumes that there will be no types between room and the actual class. What if we want to match inner class types, such as com.company.department? In that case, we need to use the ".." wildcard. For example:

```
target(com.company..*)
```

This signature matches all class types that begin with the path com.company. If you know all the possible inner types, you could also write the signature as

```
target(com.company.*.*.*)
```

Finally, the wildcards can be used along with package definitions in a signature like the following example:

```
call(public * com.company.department.room.*.*(..))
```

This signature matches all public methods with any number of parameters and any return type belonging to any class defined in the com.company. department.room hierarchy. Using our example classes above, this signature matches any public methods in class1, class2, and class3. Inner classes can also be part of a signature for a method call join point. For example:

```
call(private * com.company.department..*(..))
```

This signature matches all private methods with any return type and part of the com.company.department package hierarchy. The methods can have any type and number of parameters.

# Subtype Patterns

We have seen how a class type can be matched based on a method or a constructor. For example, we can match the constructor call join points with the signature

```
call(DVD.new(..))
```

Only constructors for the DVD class are obtained. Now, let's assume we have the following class:

```
public class SpecialEditionDVD extends DVD {
}
```

The signature defined here will not find the constructors of the SpecialEditionDVD class. We must create a new signature for this specific purpose. AspectJ includes a subtype pattern wildcard, +, which allows a hierarchy of types to be matched instead of just a single class. The signature necessary to match all constructors in the DVD class as well as any derived classes is

```
call(DVD+.new(..)
```

The same subtype pattern can be applied to method join points. For example:

```
call(public String DVD+.set*(String))
```

This signature matches all methods that have a name beginning with *set* throughout the DVD class hierarchy.

# The Throws Pattern

There will be times when a method or constructor must be matched based on the exceptions it is defined to throw. For example, we might have a method defined as

```
public int getInventory(String title) throws PCException8 {
}
```

While we've seen that the call() designator can be used to match the method based on its access type, return value, name, and parameters, AspectJ 1.1 adds the ability to extend the matching to the entire signature. Thus, we might create a join point like

```
call(public int getInventory(String title) throws PCException8)
```

The throws clause can take advantage of wildcards as well. For example:

```
call(public int getInventory(String title) throws *Exception*)
```

This join point matches methods where the word *Exception* appears in the exception class name. The rule behind the match says that the call designator will match methods if the matching method or constructor contains any of the types in the throws clause. In other words, the call designator would match the following method:

```
public int getInventory(String title) throws PCException8, RunExcept {
}
```

The call designator is looking for matching methods where there is at least one exception that has the Exception string in it, and our new signature has at least one. We can negate the matching with a ! character. For example:

```
call(public int getInventory(String title) throws !PCException8)
```

This designator does match our method because it contains a PCException8 exception.

## Type Patterns

Just when creating join points was getting commonplace, another variation was thrown into the mix. All the previously defined join points can be combined using logical operators and (&&), or (||) and not (!). Using our last join point as an example, suppose we're interested in the subtypes of the DVD class hierarchy but not the DVD class itself. To match the constructors in the subtypes only, we can use the following join point:

```
call((DVD+ && ! DVD).new(..))
```

Note the use of the grouping brackets before the new() method. This signature begins by saying we are interested in matching all DVD+ subtypes, including the DVD type with DVD+. The signature continues with an AND logical operator. Thus we are interested in all DVD subtypes, including DVD as well as NOT DVD. Therefore, all subtypes of DVD will be matched but not DVD itself, which is the normal operation for DVD+. Once the type matching is complete, the rest of the signature is included to determine the entire join point matching criteria. All constructors of DVD subtypes will be matched, but not those for the DVD type itself.

There is virtually no limit to the number of logical combinations that you can create. However, the placement of the brackets is very important and dictates how you set up the join point combination.

## Reflection

When a join point is triggered, AspectJ can give the code access to some of the context of the join point. The access is provided through three classes:

**thisJoinPoint**—This variable is bound to the join point object and has a parent type of org.aspectj.lang.JoinPoint.

**thisJoinPointStaticPart**—This variable is bound only to a limited amount of the join point object and doesn't require memory allocation when used.

**thisEnclosingJoinPointStaticPart**—This variable is bound to only the static part of the join point object and has a parent type of org.aspectj.lang.Join point.StaticPart.

Through these variables, a wide variety of information becomes available. For the following list of methods, consider a join point defined as

```
call(public void setCount(int))
```

This join point is based on the DVD class defined earlier in the chapter.

## thisJoinPoint Methods

The methods available in the thisJoinPoint object are as follows:

**String toString();**—This method returns a string representation of the join point. Using this method and the join point from our earlier example produce the string

```
call(void DVD.setCount(int))
```

Notice the addition of the DVD class type to the join point string returned from the method. In the definition of the join point, an implied * wildcard is assumed. A full signature is public void *.setCount(int), thus matching a setCount() method regardless of class type.

**String toShortString();**—This method returns a short string representation of the join point. The output of this method using the above join point is

```
call(DVD.setCount(..))
```

**String toLongString();**—This method returns an extended representation of the join point. For example:

```
Call(public void DVD.setCount(int))
```

**Object getThis();**—This method returns the currently executing object associated with the join point. As the source code for AspectJ suggests, this method shouldn't be used because the this() pointcut designator is more efficient and offers better typing support. The object is made available during the execution of a method. Note that a join point object is available only when you're using a method or constructor execution join point. The following code uses the method and produces the listed output:

```
DVD dvd = (DVD)thisJoinPoint.getThis();
System.out.println(dvd.toString());
```

The output is

```
DVD@172e08
```

which shows that the enclosing join point object was obtained successfully.

**Object getTarget( );**—This method returns the target object associated with a join point. The target object is available on join points such as the method call reception or constructor call reception join points. When a join point or method is called, the getTarget() method returns the object. Note that the target designator should be used for more efficient access to the target object.

**Object[] getArgs( );**—This method returns the actual arguments to the join point. The getArgs() method should be used on the join points associated with execution of a method or constructor. For example, consider the following code based on the join point defined earlier:

```
Object[] args = thisJoinPoint.getArgs();
for(int i=0;i<args.length;++i) {
  System.out.println("Argument:" + i + " is " + args[i]);
}
```

The result of this code when the application has a statement, dvd.setCount(1);, is

```
Argument:0 is 1
```

**Signature getSignature( );**—This method returns an object representing the signature at the join point. The Signature object contains several of its own methods:

**String getName( )**—This method returns the identifier part of the signature.

**int getModifiers( )**—This method returns the modifiers of the signature represented as an integer. The integer returned can be cast to a java.lang.reflect.Modifier and used to determine what type of access modifier the join point uses.

The following code shows an example of using both the getName() and getModifiers() methods:

```
Signature signature = (Signature)thisJoinPoint.getSignature();

System.out.println(signature.getName());
System.out.println(java.lang.reflect.Modifier.toString(
  signature.getModifiers()));
System.out.println("isPublic : " +
  java.lang.reflect.Modifier.isPublic(
  signature.getModifiers()));
System.out.println("isPrivate : " +
  java.lang.reflect.Modifier.isPrivate(
```

```
    signature.getModifiers()));
System.out.println("isProtected : " +
  java.lang.reflect.Modifier.isProtected(
  signature.getModifiers()));
```

The output produced by this code is

```
class DVD
isPublic : false
isPrivate : true
isProtected : false
```

In addition to the Signature class, the output of the getSignature() method can be cast to a more specific subtypes as defined in org.lang.aspectj.reflect. These subtypes, which are discussed in more detail in Chapter 6, are

- AdviceSignature
- CatchClauseSignature
- CodeSignature
- FieldSignature
- InitializerSignature
- MemberSignature
- MethodSignature

**SourceLocation getSourceLocation();**—This method, associated with the thisJoinPoint object, returns an object from the SourceLocation class representing the caller of the join point. If there is no object, the method will return null. Within the SourceLocation class is the method Class getWithinType();, which is called to obtain the calling class.

Consider the following code:

```
SourceLocation sl = thisJoinPoint.getSourceLocation();
Class  theClass = (Class)sl.getWithinType();
System.out.println(theClass.toString());
```

This code produces the following output because the call to the method set-Count() occurs within the DVD class:

```
class DVD
```

**String getKind();**—This method returns a String representing the type of join point that has been triggered. For example:

```
System.out.println(thisJoinPoint.getKind());
```

This code produces the following output because the join points were defined with a call pointcut designator:

```
method-call
```

StaticPart getStaticPart( );—This method returns the static part of the context as described in the next section.

## thisJoinPointStaticPart Methods

The thisJoinPointStaticPart class is defined as a helper class to thisJoinPoint. Through this class, only the static parts of the context are available. The static part can be accessed using the getStaticPart() method described earlier or through the thisJoinPointStaticPart object. The methods available in the static part are

```
Signature getSignature();
SourceLocation getSourceLocation();
String getKind();
String toString();
String toShortString();
String toLongString();
```

The functionality for these methods is identical to those listed in the thisJoinPoint section.

# Example Join Points

In this final section, we present code snippets for each of the major join point types along with example join points.

## Method Call Reception and Execution

The method call reception join point is based on the assumption that a method associated with an object will be called by some other method. As we see in the next chapter, method call reception join points are primarily used in the call() pointcut designator. To get an idea of how to use these join points, consider the Stack class in Listing 5.2.

```
public class Stack {
  static final int DEFAULT_CAPACITY=5;

  private Object [] theArray;
  private int topOfStack;

  public Stack() {
    theArray = new Object[DEFAULT_CAPACITY];
    topOfStack=-1;
```

**Listing 5.2**   A method join point example stack. (continues)

```
  }

  public Stack(int capacity) {
    theArray = new Object[capacity];
    topOfStack=-1;
  }

  public void push(Object x) {
    if (topOfStack+1 == theArray.length)
      doubleArray();
    topOfStack++;
    theArray[topOfStack]=x;
  }

  public void pop() throws Exception {
    if (isEmpty())
      throw new Exception("Stack pop");
    topOfStack--;
  }

  public Object top() throws Exception {
    if (isEmpty())
      throw new Exception("Stack top");
      return theArray[topOfStack];
  }

  public boolean isEmpty() {
    return topOfStack==-1;
  }

  public void clear() {
    topOfStack=-1;
  }

  public int getSize() {
    return topOfStack+1;
  }

  private void doubleArray() {
    int oldArraySize = theArray.length;
    Object [] biggerArray = new Object[oldArraySize*2];

    for (int i=0; i<oldArraySize; i++){
      biggerArray[i]=theArray[i];
      theArray=biggerArray;
    }
  }
}
```

**Listing 5.2**   A method join point example stack. (continues)

```
public static void main(String args[]) {
  Stack stack = new Stack();
  stack.push(new Integer(4));
  try {
    System.out.println(stack.top());
  } catch(Exception e) { System.exit(1); }

  stack.push(new Integer(5));
  stack.push(new Integer(6));
  try {
    System.out.println(stack.top());
    stack.pop();
  } catch(Exception e) { System.exit(1); }
  System.out.println("Empty? : " + stack.isEmpty());
  }
}
```

**Listing 5.2** A method join point example stack. (continued)

Running the code in Listing 5.2 produces the following output:

```
4
6
Empty? : false
```

Let's put together a few situations and determine what the method call join points should look like.

**Situation:** All stack manipulations should be logged to the console.

**Solution:** Implement a join point that takes into consideration all the methods in the Stack class but only the Stack class. The join point might look like this:

```
call(public * Stack.*(..))
```

When put into a simple aspect (as shown in Chapter 3) and using the thisJoinPoint.toLongString() method, the following output is displayed to the console:

```
call(public static void Stack.main(java.lang.String[]))
call(public void Stack.push(java.lang.Object))
call(public java.lang.Object Stack.top())
call(public boolean Stack.isEmpty())
4
call(public void Stack.push(java.lang.Object))
call(public void Stack.push(java.lang.Object))
call(public java.lang.Object Stack.top())
call(public boolean Stack.isEmpty())
6
call(public void Stack.pop())
```

```
call(public boolean Stack.isEmpty())
call(public boolean Stack.isEmpty())
Empty? : false
```

Notice the output from just the Java application is intermixed with output from the toLongString() method. The output can be analyzed against the code in main() to determine if it is doing what it should be doing. This can be very useful when your code is doing more than you expect it to be doing.

*Situation:* The push operation appears to be having problems with the top of the stack. You want to know the size of the stack just before a new object is forced on top of it.

*Solution:* Narrow the scope of the method call join point to only the push() method and obtain the target object of the call. The following join point code will do the trick:

```
pointcut field() : call(* Stack.push(..));
  before() : field() {
    Stack stack = (Stack)thisJoinPoint.getTarget();
    System.out.println(thisJoinPoint.toLongString() +
      " Stack Size:" + stack.getSize());
}
```

Ignoring most of the code in this example, we see the join point has been narrowed to just the Stack.push methods that accept any number of parameters and types. When a join point is found, the code uses the thisJoinPoint object to obtain the signature of the method triggered by the join point as well as the target object that will be handling the join point method. The output produced using the same main() method in Listing 5.2 is as follows:

```
call(public void Stack.push(java.lang.Object)) Stack Size:0
4
call(public void Stack.push(java.lang.Object)) Stack Size:1
call(public void Stack.push(java.lang.Object)) Stack Size:2
6
Empty? : false
```

The output produced shows the full join point method, which could be helpful when there are multiple overloaded methods of the same name. The code could have been calling the wrong method. Following the method name is the size of the stack before the new value is pushed onto it.

*Situation:* The join point could be further narrowed to just when the Stack is doubled in size.

*Solution:* Build a join point specifically for the doubleStack() method. The following join point should do the trick:

```
call(private void Stack.doubleArray());
```

However, when this join point is used along with thisJoinPoint to display the actual method call, nothing appears on the screen based on the code in Listing 5.2. That shouldn't be the case since the signature is accurate. However, notice the default size of the stack. Either it's greater than the number of items pushed onto the stack, or the doubleArray() method was never executed. When you're creating join points, it's important to realize that an accurate signature doesn't mean much if the method is never called.

**NOTE**

In order for the AspectJ compiler to recognize and match call join points, you must present the code where the call is made to the compiler in source-code format and not as a CLASS or JAR file.

## Constructor Call Reception/Execution and Object Initialization

The next class of join points we discuss is the constructor call reception. This join point is matched when a call is made to a constructor. In the course of a normal application, the constructor is called many times, not just by your code but also by the system when a temporary object is needed or a copy must be created.

*Situation:* You are only interested in the constructors of a class.

*Solution:* Calling a constructor isn't the same as calling a method because the object hasn't been created yet. As you know, a special pattern is used to identify a constructor join point. This join point can be used for any and all constructors in a class:

```
call(Stack.new(..))
```

*Situation:* You are only interested in the default constructor of a class.

*Solution:* For this join point, no parameters can be allowed in the signature part of the join point:

```
call (Stack.new())
```

*Situation:* You want to see the constructor that accepts an integer parameter.

*Solution:* Use a join point with the integer parameter specified:

```
call(Stack.new(int))
```

*Situation:* Extensive memory use is occurring in your application, and you suspect that the constructor is being called to create an extraordinary number of objects.

*Solution:* Build a join point that will match all constructors for your class. For the Stack class in Listing 5.2, the following join point will do what is needed. Also included in this join point is an introduction so a running count of objects can be kept:

```
private int Stack.objectCount = 0;

pointcut field() : execution(Stack.new(..));
before() : field() {
    Stack stack = (Stack)thisJoinPoint.getTarget();
    stack.objectCount++;
    System.out.println("Object Count = " + stack.objectCount);
}
```

For this join point, the new() operator is specified in order to match appropriate constructors of the class. The use of a count variable lets us know how many objects are created. The output using this join point is

```
Object Count = 1
4
6
Empty? : false
```

## NOTE

**If the instantiation of the object is presented to the AspectJ compiler as a binary (either CLASS or JAR), the call to the constructor won't be matched. You must pass the source code for the instantiation to the compiler for the match to be successful.**

## Field Get/Set

Nearly all classes have attributes, and those attributes define the state of an object once instantiated. The state of the object changes when the attributes are written with different values. During the course of an application's execution, keeping track of when the attributes change can be important. However, at the same time, it might not be important to know what method is changing the attribute. For these situations, we can use the field get/set join points.

*Situation:* For the Stack class, one of the most widely used attributes is theArray, which holds the values in the stack. Each time the theArray attribute is set, we want to know it.

*Solution:* Add a join point against the attribute in question. For example, the following snippet of code produces a message with the size of the array attribute each time it is accessed:

```
pointcut field() : set(private Object [] Stack.theArray);
before() : field() {
    System.out.println("Attribute theArray set");
}
```

When this join point is used against our example Stack class, the following output is produced:

```
Attribute theArray set
4
6
Empty? false
```

What's important to notice when using an array join point is the fact that each write to the cells of the array is not a trigger for the join point. Only when a value is assigned to the actual variable does the join point get triggered.

*Situation:* At the same time, each of the reads of an attribute can be triggered through a join point. We are interested in identifying when the top of the stack indicator is read by our code.

*Solution:* We can create a specific join point against the topOfStack attribute. For example:

```
pointcut field() : get(private int Stack.topOfStack);
before() : field() {
  System.out.println("Attribute topOfStack read");
}
```

The output produced when this join point is used against our stack code is as follows:

```
Attribute topOfStack read
Attribute topOfStack read
Attribute topOfStack read
Attribute topOfStack read
Attribute topOfStack read
4
Attribute topOfStack read
Attribute topOfStack read
Attribute topOfStack read
Attribute topOfStack read
Attribute topOfStack read
Attribute topOfStack read
Attribute topOfStack read
Attribute topOfStack read
6
Attribute topOfStack read
Attribute topOfStack read
Attribute topOfStack read
Empty? : false
```

Clearly the topOfStack attribute is read quite extensively during the operation of our code. By analyzing the access to the attributes of our objects, we can identify patterns as well as potential efficiency problems.

## Exception Handler Execution

AspectJ allows the capturing of exceptions using exception handler execution join points. Capturing exceptions can be useful for activities such as logging, where all exceptions are written to a log file regardless of whether or not they cause the application to end. Here's an example of a join point for an exception in our Stack class:

```
pointcut field() : handler(Exception);
before() : field(s) {
  System.out.println("Exception Thrown");
}
```

The Stack class main() was changed to attempt a pop() operation on an empty stack. This action throws an exception and causes the join point to grab it, producing the following output:

```
4
5
Empty? : true
Exception Thrown
```

## Class Initialization

When a new object is instantiated, unique static code is executed to facilitate the creation. The developer isn't generally involved in writing the static code, but a join point can be created against it. The static class initialization code will most likely execute only a single time regardless of the number of objects instantiated from the class. For example:

```
pointcut field() : staticinitialization(Stack);
before() : field() {
  System.out.println(thisJoinPoint.getSignature());
}
```

When the stack code is executed, a single stack object is created. The output shows the join point captured:

```
Stack.<init>
4
5
Empty? : true
```

If another stack statement—such as Stack stack2 = new Stack(45);—is added to the stack code, the join point will not be captured a second time.

## What's Next

This chapter has focused on the many different variations of join points that can be defined using AspectJ. In addition, we examined the reflective characteristics available in AspectJ through the thisJoinPoint object and its related classes. In the next chapter, we use the join points in the definition of pointcuts. Pointcuts are the next step in defining code for implementing crosscutting concerns.

# CHAPTER 6

# AspectJ Pointcuts

In the previous chapter, you learned all about the join point. As you know, the join point is a well-defined location within the execution of an application. This might be a method call or an attribute within one specific class or all classes. By itself, the join point isn't of much use, but when combined with a designator and a pointcut definition, the code begins to show how crosscutting concerns affect the execution of the primary application. In this chapter, we cover the AspectJ construct called the pointcut and all its intended purposes. The specific topics include:

- Building a pointcut using the previously defined join points
- Using pointcut designators
- Combining designators
- Understanding pointcut reflection

## Introducing Our Three Classes

For the examples in this chapter, we use three classes. The first, called Product, represents a high-level top class. The code for the Product class is shown in Listing 6.1. A second class, called DVD, extends the Product class and provides implementation for a DVD product. Listing 6.2 contains the code for the DVD class. The third class, called Boxset, is designed to contain any number of DVD objects and represent them as a boxed set. The code for the Boxset class is shown in Listing 6.3. Refer back to Chapter 5, Figure 5.1, to see the UML class diagram for the represented classes.

```
public class Product {

  private double price;

  public Product() {
    price = 0.0;
  }

  public double getPrice() {
    return price;
  }

  public void setPrice(double inPrice) {
    price = inPrice;
  }

  public static void main(String args[]) {
    Product product = new Product();
    product.setPrice(5.00);
  }
}
```

**Listing 6.1**  The Product class.

```
public class DVD extends Product {

  public static final String encoding = "region 0";

  private String title;
  private int count;
  private String location;

  public DVD(String inTitle) {
    super();
    title = inTitle;
  }

  private void setCount(int inCount) {
    count = inCount;
  }

  public int getCount() {
    return count;
```

**Listing 6.2**  The DVD class. (continues)

```
  }

  public void setTitle(String inTitle) {
    title = inTitle;
  }

  public String getTitle() {
    return title;
  }

  public void setLocation(String inLocation) {
    location = inLocation;
  }

  public String getLocation() {
    return location;
  }

  public void setStats(String inLocation, int inCount)
                        throws DVDException {
    setLocation(inLocation, 0);
    if (inCount == 0) {
      throw new DVDException(title);
    } else {
      setCount(inCount);
    }
  }

  public static void main(String args[]) {
    DVD dvd = new DVD("Title");

    try {
      dvd.setStats("store 1", 1);
    } catch(DVDException e) {}

    dvd.setLocation("New Store", 0);
    dvd.setCount(1);

    System.out.println("Location and count = " +
dvd.getLocation());
    dvd.setTitle("Better Title");
    System.out.println("Title = " + dvd.getTitle());

  }
}
```

**Listing 6.2**  The DVD class. (continued)

```
import java.util.Vector;

public class Boxset extends Product {
  private int totalCount;
  private Vector includedDvds;
  private String location;
  private String title;

  public Boxset(String inTitle) {
    includedDvds = new Vector();
    totalCount = 0;
    title = inTitle;
  }

  public void add(DVD inDvd) {
    try {
      inDvd.setStats(location, 1);
    } catch (DVDException e) {
      e.printStackTrace();
    }
    includedDvds.add(inDvd);
    totalCount++;
  }

  public void setLocation(String inLocation) {
    location = inLocation;
  }

  public String getLocation() {
    return location;
  }

  public static void main(String args[]) {
    Boxset boxset = new Boxset("Star Wars");
    DVD dvd = new DVD("Return of the Jedi");
    boxset.add(dvd);
  }
}
```

**Listing 6.3**   The Boxset class.

```
class DVDException extends Exception {
  private String title;

  public DVDException() {
    title = "none";
```

**Listing 6.4**   The DVDException class. (continues)

```
}

public DVDException(String intitle) {
  title = intitle;
}

public String getTitle() {
  return title;
}
}
```

**Listing 6.4** The DVDException class. (continued)

# Building Pointcuts

Once the join points for crosscutting concerns have been identified and written, they need to be put into code using a pointcut. A *pointcut* is an AspectJ construct designed to identify join points and obtain the context surrounding the join point. The pointcut is more than just a container for join points; it directly shows how a concern will crosscut the primary application. The pointcut is valid across all objects instantiated from the classes, and if you have a large number of objects, you should anticipate a large number of matches.

## The Structure of a Pointcut

We can represent the structure of a pointcut in the same way we'd represent a method signature in the Java language. Here's the format of a pointcut:

```
<pointcut> ::= <access_type> <pointcut_name> ( { <parameters> }  )

            : { designator [ && | || ] };
<access_type> ::= public | private [abstract]
<pointcut_name> ::= { <identifier> }
<parameters> ::= { <identifier> <type> }
<designator> ::= [!]Call | execution | target | args |
                cflow | cflowbelow | staticinitialization |
                within | if | adviceexecution |
                preinitialization
<identifier> ::= letter { letter | digit }
<type> ::= defined valid Java type
```

As you have already seen in some of our previous examples and in Chapter 8, you place the pointcut within an aspect construct and use it to match join points in the code. The access type of the pointcut can be either public or private (depending on design considerations) and indicates the scope of the pointcut in the aspect/class. The default access type is package, and thus you must supply the specific access type needed for the pointcut. After the access type is the name of the pointcut. This name is a text string used to represent the pointcut within the aspect/class. The name is analogous to the method name used in a traditional Java class. Within the context of an aspect or class, all pointcuts must have a unique name, which means there is no overloading of pointcuts in AspectJ. If you have to make a small change in a pointcut definition, you have to create a new pointcut.

The name of the pointcut can contain a number of parameters. These parameters, as we discuss later in this chapter, are used to transfer the context pulled from a join point. The context can be transferred to either an advice construct or other join points.

The parameters to the pointcut are followed by a colon and one or more pointcut designators. Our examples in Chapter 5 showed several of the different designators, including call and execution. The designator provides a definition around the join point used in the pointcut. The majority of this chapter covers the various designators and how they are used to build pointcuts. In order for a pointcut to have multiple designators, you must use the common logical operators to create a combination.

Most of the pointcuts defined in this book will be the named variety. Java provides the ability to create unnamed or anonymous structures. AspectJ offers this ability as well, in a construct called the *primitive pointcut*. The primitive pointcut doesn't have a name and merely consists of the join point designators. As we move forward in the chapter, any place where you see a pointcut used with an advice construct, know that you can replace the pointcut with a primitive pointcut.

## Using Designators

As mentioned earlier, the pointcut selects a set of one or more join points to determine its intended action. When the join point is reached in the primary application code, the pointcut will be activated and potentially some amount of code executed. (This code, called the *advice*, is covered in Chapter 7.) In this section, we examine each of the possible pointcuts and provide example code to show how the designator acts in an AspectJ application. All the designators are written in the following format:

```
designator ::= designator_identifier(<signature> |
            <typePattern> | <pointcut>)
<designator_identifier> ::= Call | execution | target | args |
        cflow | cflowbelow | staticinitialization |
```

```
                    within | if | adviceexecution |
                    preinitialization
<typePattern> ::= Java class type
<pointcut> - defined above
```

The "parameter" in the designator is either a join point signature or a join point class type, or another pointcut. As you may recall, we discussed these parameter types in Chapter 5, but to refresh your memory, a join point signature generally represents the signature of a method, a constructor in a class, or a type. There might be a number of different wildcards in the signature, but at some level the join point signature resembles a method call. In the case of a constructor join point, the signature includes the new() call. For a join point class type, the parameter is the name of a class in the application. You can use wildcards with class types as well.

The TypePattern is typically a class in the application with or without wildcards. An example would be DVD or PRODUCT+, as discussed in Chapter 5. Keep in mind that some of the designators require a parameter to be another pointcut construct, either named or primitive. Throughout the remainder of this book, you'll see examples that use these three parameters types.

## A Designator Quick Reference

We describe all the designators in detail in the sections that follow, but we've listed them here for quick reference:

**execution**—Matches execution of a method or constructor.

**call**—Matches calls to a method or constructor.

**initialization**—Matches execution of the first constructor to a class.

**handler**—Matches exceptions.

**get**—Matches the reference to a class attribute.

**set**—Matches the assignment of a class attribute.

**this**—Returns the object associated with a particular join point or limits the scope of a join point by using a class type.

**target**—Returns the target object of a join point or limits the scope of a join point.

**args**—Exposes the arguments to a join point or limits the scope of the pointcut.

**cflow**—Returns join points in the execution flow of another join point.

**cflowbelow**—Returns join points in the execution flow of another join point but not including the current join point.

**staticinitialization**—Matches the execution of a class's static initialization code.

**withincode**—Matches join points within a method or constructor.

**within**—Matches join points within a specific type.

**if**—Allows a dynamic condition to be part of a pointcut.

**adviceexecution**—Matches on advice join points.

**preinitialization**—Matches preinitialization join points.

## Using Logical Operators to Create Designator Combinations

All the designators we've listed can be combined using the standard logical operators:

**&& (and)**—Matches when both arguments to the operator are true.

**|| (or)**—Matches when one or more of the operator arguments is true.

**! (not)**—Matches all join points not matched by the defined pointcut.

When using the logical operators to form designator combinations, take care to order the arguments correctly. If you have any doubt how the system will evaluate the logical combinations, use parentheses to group combinations for the desired outcome.

## Combining Pointcuts

When you're writing pointcuts, it is possible to combine them. For example:

```
pointcut setLoc() :
  call(public void DVD.setLocation(..));
pointcut setStat() :
  call(public void DVD.setStats(String, int));
pointcut localSetLoc() :
  setLoc() && cflow(setStat());

before() : localSetLoc() {
    System.out.println(thisJoinPoint.toLongString());
}
```

Notice how the third pointcut definition includes the previously defined setLoc() and setStat() pointcuts. This makes writing pointcuts very clean and easy to read.

# Method-Related Pointcuts

The first three designators—execution, call, and initialization—are part of a set called the method-related pointcuts. You use these designators to match point-cuts when a method or constructor of a Java class is invoked and/or executed.

## execution

The execution designator is matched by a join point defined on a method or constructor of a class within the primary application. Use this designator when you are interested in the actual execution of a method or constructor. The format is

```
execution(join point signature)
```

Figure 6.1 shows where the match will occur using the execution designator.

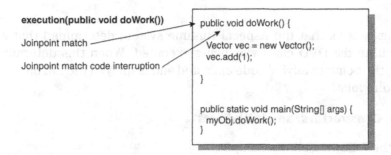

**Figure 6.1** The execution designator.

You can write the join point signature using the full Java signature of a method/constructor or one of the many different combinations of wildcards shown in Chapter 5. Here's an example of an execution pointcut:

```
pointcut Location() :
    execution(public void setLocation(String));
```

This example defines a pointcut that cuts across all objects in the primary application that have a method called setLocation(String). The pointcut matches only when the method defined by the join point begins execution. In this case, we define *execution* as beginning at the moment just before the first statement in the method is to execute and ending after the last statement of the method/constructor.

The execution designator works on class constructors as well as methods. When you're capturing a constructor join point, note that the only difference is the use of the new() pattern. For example:

```
pointcut DVDConstruct : execution (public DVD.new(..));
```

This code will match the pointcut when the default constructor of any DVD object is executed. In either case—the method or the constructor signature— the execution designator will be matched when the application is executing within the scope of the signature's object. At this point, the pointcut only knows about the called object and doesn't know anything about the object or static method that made the originating method/constructor call. This is important because we will use another pointcut designator shortly that will allow us to obtain the context of the pointcut. Consider the pointcut defined earlier and some example advice:

```
pointcut DVDConstruct() : execution (public DVD.new(..));
  before() : DVDConstruct() {
    System.out.println(thisJoinPoint.toLongString());
}
```

The output from the previous pointcut using our DVD example code is

```
execution(public DVD(java.lang.String))
store 1
```

This output tells us that the AspectJ runtime system determined that a constructor within the DVD class was being executed. When this determination was made, the pointcut advice code executed and displayed the full name of the matched join point.

## Execution, Constructors, and Initializers

Consider the following short example:

```
public class Test {
  public  Vector vec = new Vector();

  public Test() {
    vec.add(1);
  }

  public static void main(String[] args) {
    Test test = new Test();
  }
}
```

Here we find a class that creates a private vector and pushes an integer to it. Now consider this aspect:

```
public aspect TestVec {
  pointcut vec(Test t) : execution(Test.new()) &&
                         this(t);
  before(Test t) : vec(t) {
    System.out.println("Size of Vector : " + vec.size());
  }
}
```

This aspect is designed to match the constructor of the Test class and execute advice before the constructor executes. The value output to the screen for the size of the vector in AspectJ version 1.0 is 1. However, in AspectJ 1.1, an exception is thrown. This is because the initializer code—Vector vec = new Vector();—is considered part of the execution of the constructor and is not independent.

Because the initializer code is part of the constructor, we cannot work with any of the attributes or objects created because the constructor has not yet executed. This change between versions 1.0 and 1.1 doesn't affect after advice because the constructor will have already executed before the after advice executes.

## call

The call designator, shown in Figure 6.2, is also matched by a join point defined on a method or constructor. Use this designator when you are interested in the actual *calling* of a method or a constructor as opposed to the *execution* of code within a join point. The format of the designator is

```
call(join point signature)
```

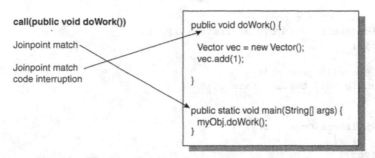

**Figure 6.2** The call designator.

In Figure 6.2 we see that the call designator matches a join point before an execution designator matches the same join point. Of particular importance is the context from which the match occurs. In the case of call, the context is the object making the call. In execution, control has passed to the target object of the method call:

```
call(join point signature)
```

Here's an example of a call designator used in a pointcut:

```
pointcut DVDGetLoc() :
  call(public String DVD.getLocation());
```

This pointcut tells us it will be matched when the getLocation() method of any DVD object is called. The scope of the pointcut remains with the object or static method that performed the actual call. Later in this chapter you learn how to obtain both the caller of the method and the target object of the call. When the match occurs, the system hasn't yet begun any execution of the method or constructor; thus the match point indicates an intention to execute the named signature. The pointcut can be combined with advice, as shown here:

```
pointcut DVDGetLoc() : call(public String DVD.getLocation());
before() : DVDGetLoc() {
  System.out.println(thisJoinPoint.toLongString());
}
```

With the DVD example code and this pointcut, the following output is displayed to the console:

```
call(public java.lang.String DVD.getLocation())
store 1
```

The pointcut has been matched on the call to the getLocation() method. The output from the call designator doesn't look that much different based on the use of the toLongString() context method. However, if we look ahead and use the this designator, we can see that we have full access to the object associated with the match join point. The following code uses the both the execution and call designators along with the this designator:

```
pointcut Stats(Object obj) :
  execution(public void DVD.setStats(..)) &&
  this(obj);

pointcut Stats2(Object obj);
  call(public void DVD.setStats(..)) &&
  this(obj);

pointcut allStats(Object obj) :
  Stats(obj) ||
  Stats2(obj);

before(Object obj) : DVDGetLoc(obj) {
  System.out.println(thisJoinPoint.toLongString());
  if (obj instanceof DVD)
    System.out.println("DVD object");
  else if (obj instanceof Boxset)
    System.out.println("Boxset object");
  else
    System.out.println("Unknown object");
}
```

When executed against the Boxset example code, the following output is produced:

```
call(public void DVD.setStats(java.lang.String, int))
Boxset object
execution(public void DVD.setStats(java.lang.String, int))
DVD object
```

As expected from the designator descriptions, the call designator matches on the call to the setStats() method from the Boxset object, whereas the execution designator matches the join point as it executes within the DVD object.

## initialization

The initialization designator is used to match the constructor called when a new object is instantiated. The designator is designed so that all constructors in a hierarchy chain are called. The format of the initialization designator is

```
initialization (join point signature)
```

Here's an example of the designator used in a pointcut:

```
pointcut Construct : initialization (new(..));
```

This pointcut creates a crosscut through the entire constructor chain of all objects in the system. In our example classes defined earlier in the chapter, the DVD class constructor calls the Product constructor through the use of the super() statement. The pointcut is matched when the DVD constructor is called and when the Product constructor is called. The order of the join points are the Product and then the DVD constructor because the Product constructor is actually the first constructor to execute. This is because the super() statement has a special meaning in the Java language.

The output from our example classes would be different if we changed the join point signature to something along the lines of

```
pointcut DVDconstruct : initialization (DVD.new(..));
```

This pointcut includes a join point that narrows the scope of the crosscut to only the DVD class. The join point for the Product constructor is not recognized. In another example, consider several classes that implement and extend each other:

```
interface NewInterface {}
class Inner1 {}
class Inner2 extends Inner1 {}
class Outer extends Inner2 implements NewInterface {
  public static void main(String[] args) {
    Outer outer = new Outer();
  }
}
```

This initialization designator would match the Outer class:

```
pointcut outerMatch() : initialization(Outer.new());
```

If executed, the matches made by the pointcut would be as follows:

```
Inner1
Inner2
NewInterface
Outer
```

The initialization designator matches all the constructors found in the entire hierarchy of the instantiated object. In our example, the Outer class extends the Inner2 class, which itself extends Inner1. The execution of the code requires that the Inner1 constructor be called first because it is the foundation of all the other classes.

## The Exception-Handling Designator

When an application is executing, there is a very good chance that it will produce an error at some point. A good developer will include exception-handling code in the key parts of the application so that errors can be caught and potentially handled. Let's take a look at the handler designator.

### Handler

The handler designator is designed to capture the execution of exception handlers anywhere in the primary application. The format of the designator is

```
handler(Class Type Pattern)
```

The single join point for the handler designator is a class type pattern. The pattern can consist of a single class, a full class hierarchy, a class with a wildcard, or a combination of classes using logical operators. Here's an example of a pointcut based on one of the exceptions in our example code at the beginning of the chapter:

```
pointcut handle() : handler(Exception)
```

This pointcut is matched when any exception is thrown in the code that has a class type of Exception. For example, the handler designator and pointcut just defined could be used to display where a particular exception is thrown. The code looks like this:

```
before() : handle() {
  System.out.println(thisJoinPoint.toLongString());
}
```

Looking at the class definition for DVD and DVDException in Listing 6.4, note that a single exception exists in the add() method. If the value of the incoming count parameter is 0, an exception is thrown. If we compile and execute the main() method found in the Boxset class, the only output generated is

```
DVDException
        at DVD.setStats(DVD.java:32)
        at Boxset.add(Boxset.java:17)
        at Boxset.main(Boxset.java:36)
```

This output comes from the code in the catch() part of the add() method of the Boxset class. The e.printStackTrace(); statement produces the method tree listed here. But why wasn't the exception caught by AspectJ code? The reason is our pointcut specifically used a class type of Exception. The exception thrown in the DVD code is a call derived from Exception called DVDException. There are a few ways to get the DVDException to match a pointcut, such as the following:

```
pointcut handle() : handler(DVDException);
pointcut handle() : handler(DVD*);
pointcut handle() : handler(Exception+);
```

Each of these pointcuts are matched when the DVDException is thrown. The output looks like this:

```
handler(catch(DVDException))
DVDException
        at DVD.setStats(DVD.java:32)
        at Boxset.add(Boxset.java:17)
        at Boxset.main(Boxset.java:36)
```

When an exception is thrown, it would be great if the exception object could be accessed within the code. It is possible to get access to the exception object by using the args designator, which we discuss later in the chapter. For now, here's an example of how the handler designator looks when combined with the args designator:

```
pointcut handle(DVDException e) : handler(DVDException) &&
                                  args(e);
before(DVDException e) : handle(e) {
  System.out.println(thisJoinPoint.toLongString());
  System.out.println(e.getTitle());
}
```

The result of executing the Boxset code with this new pointcut is

```
handler(catch(DVDException))
Return of the Jedi
DVDException
        at DVD.setStats(DVD.java:32)
        at Boxset.add(Boxset.java:17)
        at Boxset.main(Boxset.java:36)
```

The exception object was successfully passed to the code where the title attribute is output to the console. Since we might not always know if an Exception class is caught or is a derived class, we can use the class wildcard pattern and the instanceof keyword to determine the right class type. For example:

```
pointcut handle(Exception e) : handler(Exception+) &&
                               args(e);
```

```
before(Exception e) : handle(e) {
  if (e instanceof DVDException) {
    System.out.println(((DVDException) e).getTitle());
  }
  System.out.println(thisJoinPoint.toLongString());
}
```

In this pointcut and related advice code, any Exception class will be caught because of the Exception+ class type used in the handler designator. When the exception object is passed to the advice code, the instanceof keyword determines whether or not the join point class is DVDException. If the class is DVDException, the title given to the object is displayed.

## Field-Related Designators

Attributes are one of the most important parts of a class because they define the state of an instantiated object. Any change to an attribute changes the state of the object; therefore, most attributes should be defined as private. To change the state of the object we use an accessor method, or directly change an attribute from within the body of a class method. There are two accessor methods: the setter and the getter. AspectJ allows join points to be created against setter and getter methods using the call and execution designators but also provides an even stronger tool: the get and set designators. These designators allow pointcuts to be defined when an attribute is referenced (get) and assigned (set).

### get

The get designator is matched when a join point based on a class attribute is referenced anywhere in the primary code. The format of the get designator is

```
get(join point signature)
```

The join point signature used in a get designator is that of an attribute in a class. The signature can be very specific, such as a class type and the attribute name. For example:

```
getTitle() : get(private String DVD.title);
```

If we use the same advice code from our previous code examples and execute the Boxset main() method, we get the following output:

```
get(private java.lang.String DVD.title)
DVDException
        at DVD.setStats(DVD.java:32)
        at Boxset.add(Boxset.java:17)
        at Boxset.main(Boxset.java:36)
```

This output is interesting because we executed the Boxset main() method and not the DVD code. However, the Boxset code includes code for creating a new DVD object. When the object is added to the Boxset object, an exception is thrown. The code within the exception is passed the title of the DVD where the exception occurs. This passing of the title is a reference to the title attribute and thus matches the defined pointcut.

If we are interested in an attribute that just happens to have the same name across a number of different classes, we can eliminate the class type from the signature, as shown here:

```
getTitle() : get(private String title)
```

This signature matches all title attributes regardless of the class in which the attribute is defined.

### set

The set designator is matched when a join point based on a class attribute is assigned anywhere in the primary code. The format of the set designator is

```
set(join point signature)
```

The join point signature used in the set designator is the same as that used in the get designator. We can use specific join points or add wildcards to make the signature hit a broad number of join points. Here's an example of a set join point:

```
setTitle() : set(private String title)
```

This pointcut matches all title attributes across classes within the primary code. Consider the following advice:

```
pointcut setTitle() : set(private String title);
    before() : setTitle() {
        System.out.println(thisJoinPoint.toLongString());
    }
```

This pointcut says that we want to match all changes to the title attribute that is declared as private String. Since a specific class isn't defined in the join point, all classes with a title attribute are potential matches. If we use this pointcut against the Boxset code, we obtain the following output:

```
set(private java.lang.String Boxset.title)
set(private java.lang.String DVD.title)
set(private java.lang.String DVDException.title)
DVDException
        at DVD.setStats(DVD.java:32)
        at Boxset.add(Boxset.java:17)
        at Boxset.main(Boxset.java:36)
```

The code in the Boxset example and the output here shows that a title attribute is set in three different objects of the application. The Boxset, DVD, and DVDException classes all have the specified join point defined in the pointcut because they all have separate definitions of the title attribute. Each of the three join point definitions shown in the output are based on different classes. The first is the Boxset, followed by the DVD, and finally the DVDException class. The idea of tracking all changes to an attribute directly instead of relying on catching all methods that change the attribute is a powerful feature. In looking at the Boxset class, you wouldn't know that the DVD and DVDException classes also include a title attribute.

Because the set designator deals with the changing of an attribute, it passes a single argument to the pointcut. The argument represents the value the attribute is being set to, but in order to access the value, we have to use the args designator. Here's an example pointcut for the title attribute using the args designator to grab the new value:

```
pointcut setTitle(String arg) : set(private String title) &&
                                args(arg);
  before(String arg) : setTitle(arg) {
    System.out.println(thisJoinPoint.toLongString());
    System.out.println("New value = " + arg);
}
```

The output based on the Boxset code is

```
set(private java.lang.String Boxset.title)
New value = Star Wars
set(private java.lang.String DVD.title)
New value = Return of the Jedi
set(private java.lang.String DVDException.title)
New value = Return of the Jedi
```

It just so happens that the title in the objects is set by either a specific accessor function or the class constructor. In each case, the value to be assigned to the title attribute is passed into the method or constructor. The join point catches the passed value, and we are able to display the value before it is actually set to the title attribute.

## State-Based Designators

When a join point is executed in the primary application, the pointcut associated with the join point is matched. In several cases throughout this and the previous chapter, we use a variable called thisJoinPoint to access the object where a method is executing. The variable thisJoinPoint allows us to use the methods of the object to send detailed output to the console or to examine attributes of the object. AspectJ includes three designators that provide us with even greater control over access to objects and parameters of join points—as well as more control over when a join point is matched. The designators are this, target, and args.

## *this*

The this designator is typically used in two different cases. The first is in combination with other designators to provide access to the object where the join point is found. The second is to force the join point to be matched only when found in a particular class. The format of the this designator is

```
this(class type pattern or ID)
```

When the signature of the this designator is a class type pattern, the current join point is picked if the currently executing object is an instance of the class. If an ID is used for the signature, the ID will have a class identifier associated with it. This class will be used in the matching process. The ID actually acts as a parameter to the pointcut and will ultimately hold the object when the join point has been matched. In an upcoming section, we see an example of using the ID.

### Using this instead of getThis()

In our first example, we are using the this designator in place of the method call getThis() associated with the thisJoinPoint variable—which happens to be the preferred method according to the AspectJ programmer's guide because of the cost of reflection involved with the getThis() method call. Consider the following pointcut and related code:

```
pointcut DVDGetLoc() :
   execution(public String DVD.getLocation());
before() : DVDGetLoc() {
   System.out.println(thisJoinPoint.toLongString());
   DVD dvd = (DVD)thisJoinPoint.getThis());
   System.out.println(dvd.getCount());
}
```

In this pointcut, the join point is the method getLocation() of the DVD class. When a join point is found, the pointcut is matched and the object associated with the execution of the join point is obtained using the getThis() method. Instead of relying on the getThis() method, the AspectJ language recommends you use the this designator. Using the this designator, our pointcut now looks like the following:

```
pointcut DVDGetLoc(DVD dvd) :
   execution(public String getLocation())
   && this(dvd);
before(DVD dvd) : DVDGetLoc(dvd) {
   System.out.println(thisJoinPoint.toLongString());
   System.out.println(dvd.getCount());
}
```

The new pointcut includes a combination of the execution and this designators. The this designator is defined to pass the object where the execution match occurs through the *dvd* variable. The dvd parameter is used to pass the object associated with the join point getLocation() when it matched in the primary application. Within the advice code, the dvd parameter is passed from the pointcut. Once inside the advice code, the DVD object can be used just as if it were in the primary code. The advice shown here calls the getCount() method to output a value from the object.

### Adding Match Criteria Through this

The second case for using the this designator is to add criteria for the selection of a join point. Consider the following pointcut:

```
pointcut setTitle(String arg) : set(private String title) &&
                                args(arg) &&
                                this(DVD);
before(String arg) : setTitle(arg) {
    System.out.println(thisJoinPoint.toLongString());
    System.out.println("New value = " + arg);
}
```

Note that this code example works only when the object is setting its own fields because of the this && set designators. When the code is executed without the this(DVD) designator, there will be three join point matches for Boxset, DVD, and DVDException. When we add the designator this(DVD), the pointcut will be matched when the title attribute is set by a DVD object only. There is no need to add a parameter to the pointcut signature because we don't return the object for further processing.

### Using Class Type Wildcards

The 1.1 version of AspectJ does not allow the use of wildcards with the this, target, or args designators. This is a change from version 1.0. Refer to the section on the if designator to learn a way around this limitation.

### Combining this Designators

There will be times when you might have a large number of classes in a hierarchy but you are ultimately interested in only two or three of them. When defining a pointcut, you can combine multiple this designators to match just the right classes you are interested in. For example, suppose we want the entire Product hierarchy but not the Boxset class. Using the this designator and wildcards, you'd just list the classes you want to match. Here's an example of the pointcut:

```
pointcut setTitle() :
    set(private String title) &&
    (this(DVD) || this(CD);
```

In this pointcut, two this designators are used to match the classes we are interested in. We've added a fictitious CD class to illustrate the OR. Notice the use of the parentheses to make sure we get a match on either class and that they aren't mixed up in another other combination.

Finally, we can combine the classes within the parameter space of a single this designator. A pointcut using this technique is

```
pointcut setTitle() :
  set(private String title) &&
  this(DVD || CD);
```

### Combining this and call Designators

Before we move on to the target designator, consider this pointcut and advice code:

```
pointcut setTitle(DVD dvd) :
  call(public String DVD.getLocation()) &&
  this(dvd);
before(DVD dvd) : setTitle(dvd) {
    System.out.println(thisJoinPoint.toLongString());
    System.out.println(thisJoinPoint.getKind());
}
```

When this pointcut is used with the DVD code, nothing is produced from the advice code. Here's why: The intent of the call designator is to match when a method call is being made. However, when combined with the call designator, the this designator binds to the caller. We could actually use the call with this to find all calls to DVD.setLocation() that come specifically from the Boxset object:

```
pointcut setTitle(DVD dvd) :
  call(public String DVD.getLocation()) &&
  this(Boxset);
before(DVD dvd) : setTitle(dvd) {
    System.out.println(thisJoinPoint.toLongString());
    System.out.println(thisJoinPoint.getKind());
}
```

## *target*

The target designator works in two situations with the call/execution and set/get designators. The first situation is invoked when the target designator is provided a class type pattern as its parameter. The class type pattern narrows the scope of the call, set, or get designators to any or all classes it matches. In the second situation, the target designator is used much like the this designator to return to the pointcut the object where the call or access of an attribute is about to occur. The format of the target designator is

```
target(class type pattern or ID)
```

### Limiting Scope Using the target Designator

When the target designator is used to limit the scope of a call join point, it is combined with the call, as in the following example:

```
pointcut setTitle() :
  call(public String getLocation()) &&
  target(DVD);
before() : setTitle() {
    System.out.println(thisJoinPoint.toLongString());
    System.out.println(thisJoinPoint.getKind());
}
```

Here we find a call join point based on any getLocation() method in the application combined with a target class of DVD. When executed against the DVD code, the following output is observed:

```
call(public java.lang.String DVD.getLocation())
method-call
store 1
```

### Using the target Designator with set/get

You can also use the target designator with set/get. For example:

```
pointcut setTitle() :
  set(private String title) &&
  target(DVD);
before() : setTitle() {
    System.out.println(thisJoinPoint.toLongString());
}
```

This pointcut tells the system to match all assignments on the title attribute for all classes in the system. If just set(private String title) were matched against the Boxset code, there would be three join point matches. However, with the addition of the target designator and its class type pattern of DVD, a single join point will actually get the match. Note that in the case of the set/get designators and an un-encapsulated member, you can detect which object is accessing the member and target, which enables you to detect whose member is being accessed.

### Returning the Target Object Using the target Designator

Next, let's look at a situation where we don't have to limit the matching but can return the target object of a call join point. Keep in mind, though, that you can also limit and return the object using the target designator. For example:

```
pointcut setLoc(DVD dvd) :
  call(private void DVD.setLocation(..)) &&
```

```
        target(dvd);
    before(DVD dvd) : setLoc(dvd) {
        System.out.println(thisJoinPoint.toLongString());
        System.out.println(dvd.getCount());
    }
```

In this code, we are attempting to catch the setLocation() method on DVD objects—the idea is that if the location is being set, a check should be made of the current count. If the count is 0, maybe the location should not be set. For the example, we just display the value of *count*. Notice how we've used the target designator to obtain access to the object where the call to the getLocation() method executes. Once the join point is matched, the target object is supplied to the pointcut and, subsequently, to the advice code. Running this against the DVD count code returns the following:

```
call(private void DVD.setLocation(java.lang.String, int))
0
store 1
```

### Obtaining Multiple Class Target Objects

Sometimes when using the target designator to return the object of the intended method call, you might want to return several different object types. The most logical way to return an object is by using a wildcard; however, this doesn't work in the current version of AspectJ:

```
pointcut setLoc(Product prod) :
    call(* void DVD.setLocation(..)) &&
    target(prod);
//Note: no + wildcard
```

Let's look at an example to see the problem. Consider the following pointcut:

```
pointcut setLoc(DVD dvd) :
    call(private void DVD.setLocation(..)) &&
    target(dvd);
```

Assume we don't want to just return DVD objects but all the objects in the Product+ hierarchy—including Product, DVD, and Boxset. Here's a possible solution:

```
pointcut setLoc(Product+ prod) :
    call(* void DVD.setLocation(..)) &&
    target(prod);
```

Here we find an attempt to place the + wildcard in the class type defined within the pointcut name parameter. Unfortunately, AspectJ doesn't like this format. We can't use the * wildcard either, or we'll get an error. One solution is to use the Object class. For example:

```
pointcut setTitle(Object prod) :
  set(private String title) &&
  target(prod);
before(Object prod) : setTitle(prod) {
System.out.println(thisJoinPoint.toLongString());
System.out.println(((Product)prod).getPrice());
}
```

In this pointcut, the target designator references the ID in the pointcut name parameter, which is defined as an Object. The same Object definition extends to the advice code, where the incoming object is cast to a Product. Since Boxset and DVD derived from Product, we don't have to worry about the cast unless another class type is introduced in the code that isn't derived from Product. In a case like this, we could add another target designator to limit the scope of this point to the Product hierarchy. For example:

```
pointcut setTitle(Object prod) :
  set(private String title) &&
  target(prod) &&
  target(Product) ||
   target(DVD);
```

The last target designator will allow matches on the join point only when the target of the assignment is a Product class or any of its derived types. Fortunately, there is a simple solution. Consider the following pointcut, which looks very similar to the previous one:

```
pointcut setLoc(Product prod) :
  call(* void setLocation(..)) &&
  target(prod);
```

Here we are requesting the target object of type Product, but since Boxset and DVD are derived classes of Product, we automatically get them in the process. Note that if you are interested in limiting those classes that are making method calls, you should use specific classes in the call designator; however, if you want to limit your results based on the object being called, use classes in the target designator.

### Beware of the Infinite Loop

There is a situation that can develop when you're using an object returned through the this or target designators and you're accessing some of the methods of the object. Consider the following pointcut and advice code:

```
pointcut Location(DVD dvd) :
  call(public String DVD.getLocation()) &&
  target(dvd);
before(DVD dvd) : Location(dvd) {
    System.out.println(thisJoinPoint.toLongString());
    System.out.println(dvd.getLocation());
  }
```

The intended functionality of the pointcut is to match all calls to a getLocation() method of a DVD object. When the match is made, the target object is returned and used in the advice code. The code displays the current value of the Location before the call is made. However, notice that when the System.out.println(dvd.getLocation()); statement executes, another call is made to getLocation() and the pointcut is matched again—which in turn executes our statement and results in the creation of an infinite loop. We can avoid the infinite loop by using a designator called within (discussed later in the chapter). This designator allows a pointcut to be scoped based on a join point within a method or class type. Since an aspect defines a Java type, it can be used with the within designator. Consider the following join point and aspect:

```
public aspect DVDAspect {
pointcut setTitle(DVD dvd) :
    call(public String DVD.getLocation()) &&
    target(dvd) &&
    !within(DVDAspect);
  before(DVD dvd) : setTitle(dvd) {
      System.out.println(thisJoinPoint.toLongString());
      System.out.println(dvd.getLocation());
  }
}
```

The new pointcut matches against the getLocation() method in a DVD object, returns the target object, and checks to make sure that the getLocation() method being picked doesn't reside within the DVDAspect class type. Thus, the call to getLocation() in the advice code will not match the join point.

### Multiple Targets

There will be times when you'll define a pointcut using two different join points. For example:

```
pointcut titleCount() :
  call(public void DVD.setTitle(..)) ||
  call(public void DVD.setCount(..)));
```

This pointcut will be matched when either of the join points is matched. Note that using a && (and) logical operator in this pointcut instead results in the pointcut never being matched because there is no place in the primary code where both the setTitle() and setCount() methods can be executed at the same time. Note that call() && call() can never match without the use of wildcards. For example, call(process*) && call(*Image) would match processImage(). In such cases, you might want to use a match like call(process*Image()). Let's make a small change to the code that will allow us to pull target objects when a join point is matched:

```
pointcut titleCount(DVD dvd) :
  target(dvd) &&
```

```
(call(public void DVD.setTitle(..)) ||
call(public void DVD.setCount(..)));
```

Notice that we used parentheses to make sure that we are matching on one of the join points first and then the target designator to return the object.

When writing a join point, you might encounter situations in which the compiler complains. Here's one such situation:

```
pointcut titleCount(DVD dvd1, DVD dvd2) :
  ((target(dvd1) && call(public void DVD.setTitle(..)) ||
   (target(dvd2) && call(public void DVD.setCount(..))));
```

This join point either matches the setTitle() method and returns the target object, or it matches the setCount() method and returns its target object, but never both. The AspectJ compiler complains about this pointcut because it is expecting two target objects based on the parameters in the pointcut name. However, only a single join point is matched, leaving one target not available.

### args

The last designator in this group is called args, and it has two purposes. The first is to provide the arguments sent to the join point as parameters. The second is to limit the matching on a specific call, execution, or initialization designator. The format of the args designator is

```
args(class type or ID, class type or ID, .., class type or ID)
```

#### Limiting Access with args

In the previous chapter, you learned that a join point will typically represent a method or constructor in our code. Since methods/constructor often contain parameters, you can specify those parameters directly in the join point. For example:

```
pointcut arguments() :
  call(public void setTitle(String));
```

This pointcut will match join points only in which the name is setTitle and the parameter to the method is a String. This pointcut could also be written as

```
pointcut arguments() :
  call(public void setTitle(..)) &&
  args(String);
```

#### Obtaining a Single Argument

A common use for the args designator is to obtain access to the parameters being passed to the join point. For example, the DVD object has a method called setTitle() that accepts a single String parameter. At present, the code does not check the string being set to the parameter. Suppose we want to have a spell-checker run against the incoming value. The following pointcut allows us access to the argument of the setTitle() method:

```
pointcut setTitle(String inTitle) :
  call(public void setTitle(..)) &&
  args(inTitle);
before(String inTitle) : setTitle(inTitle) {
    System.out.println(thisJoinPoint.toLongString());
    System.out.println("Incoming title " + inTitle);
}
```

In this pointcut, the args designator includes an ID related to the parameter of the pointcut name. When the pointcut is matched, the string sent to the setTitle() method is associated with the inTitle ID. The inTitle ID is passed to the advice and printed so we can see that it was truly passed from the join point into the advice code. The output from this code is

```
Location and count = store 1
call(public void DVD.setTitle(java.lang.String))
Incoming title Better Title
Title = Better Title
```

The second and third text lines come from the pointcut being matched when the DVD object calls the setTitle() method. The parameter to the setTitle() method is a String. What happens if the wrong type is put in the args designator? For example:

```
pointcut setTitle(int inTitle) :
  call(public void setTitle(..)) &&
  args(inTitle);
```

Here the inTitle ID is associated with an int instead of a String type. The setTitle() join point tells us to accept any parameter type or count when it finds a setTitle() method. This pointcut will compile just fine, but when woven into the same code as the earlier pointcut, there is no match. This is because even though the join point will be matched, the system is unable to return the String passed to the setTitle() method into the args designator since they aren't identical. Even if we change the ".." wildcard to be an exact match of String, the compiler will still be successful and no match will be found.

### Obtaining Multiple Arguments

Occasionally methods will have more than a single parameter and the types won't be the same. Consider the setStats(String, int) method of the DVD class. In this case, we want to match the join point on this method and return both of the parameters to the advice code. Here's a join point to accomplish this:

```
pointcut setStats(String inTitle, int inCount) :
  call(public void setStats(String, int)) &&
```

```
    args(inTitle, inCount);
before(String inTitle, int inCount) : setStats(inTitle, inCount) {
    System.out.println(thisJoinPoint.toLongString());
    System.out.println("Incoming title " + inTitle);
    System.out.println("Incoming count " + inCount);
}
```

This pointcut is designed to pull both of the arguments to the setStats() method and display them on the console. The output from this pointcut and DVD example code from earlier in the chapter is

```
call(public void DVD.setStats(java.lang.String, int))
Incoming title store 1
Incoming count 1
Location and count = store 1
Title = Better Title
```

Each of the parameters are passed to the pointcut in the order they are found in the join point. Just as in the previous example, if the args IDs are not the same type as the parameters being passed, the join point will not be matched.

### Combining args and target/this Designators

In many of our previous examples, we have used args along with target or this. Here's one such pointcut:

```
pointcut setTitle(String inTitle, DVD dvd) :
    call(public void setTitle(..)) &&
    args(inTitle) &&
    target(dvd);
before(String inTitle, DVD dvd) : setTitle(inTitle, dvd) {
    System.out.println(thisJoinPoint.toLongString());
    System.out.println("Incoming title " + inTitle);
    System.out.println("Count = " + dvd.getCount());
}
```

This pointcut matches the setTitle() method passing into the pointcut the argument of the method as well as the target object. All of this is sent to the advice code to produce the following output based on the DVD class:

```
Location and count = store 1
call(public void DVD.setTitle(java.lang.String))
Incoming title Better Title
Count = 1
Title = Better Title
```

### Using Wildcards with the args Designator

As you might expect, we can also use wildcards in the args designator to enable matching of overloaded methods. Consider the following class:

```
public class UpdateIt {
  public void update(String s, int i, String s2) {
  }

  public void update(String s, int i, double d) {
  }

  public static void main(String args[]) {
    UpdateIt updateIt = new UpdateIt();

    updateIt.update("One", 1, "1");
    updateIt.update("One", 1, 1.0);
  }
}
```

These methods are overloaded based on the type order of the parameters. If we want to build a join point to match the two methods, we can write a pointcut similar to any of the following examples:

```
pointcut updatePC() : call(public void update(..);
pointcut updatePC() : call(* update(String, int, ..);
pointcut updatePC() : call(* update(String, ..);
```

The last two pointcuts use the ".." wildcard in the list of possible parameters for the update method. The second pointcut has the wildcard for the third parameter. In our overloaded methods, this third parameter is where they differ, so the pointcut will be able to match both without a problem. The third pointcut tells the system to match any update method where the first parameter is a String and that has any number or type of parameter after the first.

We now need to extend this example to include the use of the args designator because we are interested in receiving some of the parameters sent to the methods. First, note that there is no way to use the wildcard to send back all of the parameters from the method. The following args designator and pointcut are not valid:

```
pointcut updatePC(..) :
  call(public void update(String, int, ..)) &&
  args(..);
```

This pointcut would imply that when a match is made with the join point, the system would return all of the parameters regardless of the type or count. AspectJ requires that *all* arguments be bound to an actual type and ID. With this in mind, the following pointcut and some advice code return all of the arguments:

```
pointcut updatePC(String arg1, int arg2, Object arg3) :
  call(public void update(String, int, ..)) &&
  args(arg1, arg2, arg3);
before(String arg1, int arg2, Object arg3) :
```

```
updatePC(arg1, arg2, arg3) {
  System.out.println(thisJoinPoint.toLongString());
  if (arg3 instanceof String) {
    System.out.println("It is a String");
  } else {
    System.out.println("It is a double");
  }
}
```

Each of the arguments to the method are bound to the appropriate parameters in the pointcut definition. Notice the use of the third argument. Since we don't know what the argument will be, we have to use the Object class type. The format of this pointcut could cause a problem, though, because the third parameter is an object in one of the methods and a primitive type in another. The result of this pointcut and advice against the UpdateIt class is

```
call(public void UpdateIt.update(java.lang.String, int,
java.lang.String))
It is a String
call(public void UpdateIt.update(java.lang.String, int, double))
It is a double
```

It worked because the system was able to box the double into an Object type during the transfer of the arguments. This example assumes we are interested in all of the objects in the methods that match, but what do we do if we are interested in the last argument only? It could be that the last argument is the only one that will be different based on the business logic of the code. Do we need to pass in the other arguments? The answer is no, as shown here:

```
pointcut updatePC(Object arg3) :
    call(public void update(String, int, ..)) &&
    args(.., arg3);

before(Object arg3) : updatePC(arg3) {
    System.out.println(thisJoinPoint.toLongString());
    if (arg3 instanceof String) {
      System.out.println("It is a String");
    } else {
      System.out.println("It is a double");
    }
}
```

In this pointcut, we changed the args designator to include just a single ID along with the ".." wildcard. This designator tells the system we aren't interested in the number or types of arguments in the first part of the join point—only the very last one. Since the args designator will return only a single argument to the pointcut, only a single parameter appears in the pointcut signature: updatePC(Object arg3). We changed the advice code as well to reflect the single parameter of the pointcut.

When this new pointcut is matched against the UpdateIt code, we receive the same output we did earlier. In this case, we no longer have to specify all of the parameters, nor do we get access to them. We can use the same wildcard for the last part of a join point signature. For example:

```
pointcut updatePC(String arg1) :
    call(public void update(String, int, ..)) &&
    args(arg1, ..);

before(String arg1) : updatePC(arg1) {
    System.out.println(thisJoinPoint.toLongString());
    System.out.println(arg1);
}
```

Here we have switched the placement of the ".." wildcard; it is now the last part of the join point signature because we are only interested in the first argument. Both the pointcut signature and the advice need only the single argument that is returned from the args designator.

## Control Flow-Based Designators

In our examples so far, we have allowed join points to be matched throughout an application without regard to when the join point originated. For example, we were able to catch all calls to the setLocation() method made on a DVD object. The setLocation() method is an accessor function for the Location attribute, and it is defined as public. This means that it can be called by anyone. Looking at the DVD class code at the beginning of this chapter, we can see that the setLocation() method is also called within the setStats() method. It would be interesting if we could localize the matching of the setLocation() method to just the call within the setStats() method. This just so happens to be what the cflow and cflowbelow designators allow. The format of these designators is

```
cflow(pointcut)
cflowbelow(pointcut)
```

These are the first designators where neither an ID nor a join point signature is used as a parameter. Instead, the parameter to these designators is a pointcut definition. This is because these designators come into play when a specific pointcut has been matched. They act as a sort of flag to the system, telling it when a pointcut has been reached and when the pointcut is no longer valid.

### cflow

The cflow designator matches any join points that occur beginning when a call to a specific method takes place until the end of the method. Let's look at an example using the DVD class:

```
pointcut setLoc() :
  call(public void DVD.setLocation(..));
pointcut setStat() :
  call(public void DVD.setStats(String, int));
pointcut localSetLoc() :
  setLoc() && cflow(setStat());

before() : localSetLoc() {
    System.out.println(thisJoinPoint.toLongString());
}
```

The first two pointcuts match join points on the two methods in which we are interested. The setLoc() pointcut represents the call to the setLocation() method, which is our primary focus. The second pointcut, setStat(), is the method that contains a setLocation() call. The use of separate pointcuts for these join points is only partially for convenience. Recall that the cflow designator only takes a pointcut as a parameter. The pointcut can be a named pointcut, as in our earlier example, or just the designator, like cflow(call(public void DVD.setLocation(..));.

The third pointcut in this example combines two conditions. The first is the setLoc() pointcut, which indicates that the setLocation() join point must be matched for this pointcut to be matched. The second condition is the cflow designator using a parameter of setStat(). The cflow indicates that the localSetLoc() pointcut should match when we are currently executing (cflow) within the setStats() method and a setLocation() join point is encountered. If a setLocation() join point is matched but it is outside the execution path starting and ending with the setStat() pointcut, it should be ignored.

When this pointcut is executed against the DVD class, the output obtained is

```
call(public void DVD.setLocation(java.lang.String, int))
Location and count = store 1
Title = Better Title
```

This output should be compared against the original pointcut without the cflow designator:

```
call(public void DVD.setLocation(java.lang.String, int))
call(public void DVD.setLocation(java.lang.String, int))
Location and count = New Store
Title = Better Title
```

Without the cflow() designator, a second setLocation() join point is matched within the main() function as well as in the setStats() method.

### Multiple cflow Designators

If there are several places within your code where the join point in which you're interested can be found, you can use multiple cflow designators. For example:

```
pointcut setLoc() :
  call(public void DVD.setLocation(..));
pointcut setStat() :
  call(public void DVD.setStats(String, int));
pointcut setAll() :
  call(public void Boxset.setAll(..));
pointcut localSetLoc() :
  setLoc() &&
  (cflow(setStat()) ||
  cflow(setAll()));
```

This code contains four pointcuts; we included the first three for use within the fourth. The code says that we are interested in a join point defined against the setLocation() method when a call to the method is made within either the DVD object's setStats() method or the Boxset object's setAll() method. If setLocation() occurs in any other place, it is ignored.

### Combining cflow Parameters

The previous example was based on the desire to match a single join point in two or more methods. The pointcut is built using a join point to be matched ANDed with two or more cflow designators. Let's now turn our attention to a situation in which we want to add depth to the matching process. Consider the following class:

```
public class Flow {
  public void two() {
    System.out.println("two");
  }
  public void one() {
    two();
  }
  public static void main(String args[]) {
    Flow flow = new Flow();
    flow.one();
  }
}
```

In this class, the main() method calls the one() method, which in turn calls the two() method. The two() method displays the value "two" on the console. If we want to match the println() method, the following pointcut will do the job:

```
pointcut callToPrint() :
  call(void java.io.PrintStream.println(String));
```

Now we can easily match this join point within the call to the two() method by adding another pointcut and the cflow designator:

```
pointcut callToPrint() :
  call(void java.io.PrintStream.println(String));
```

```
pointcut getTwo() :
  call(public void two());
pointcut matchPrint() :
  callToPrint() &&
  cflow(getTwo()) &&
  !within(FlowAspect);
```

Now suppose we want to match the println() method call only when the two() method is called by the one() method. How about if we just add another cflow with a pointcut for the one() method as we did in the previous section? Well, this won't do what we want because it tells the system to match the println() method when called from either the one() or two() method.

The solution is to combine the pointcuts for the one() and two() join points in the same cflow. For example:

```
pointcut getPrint() :
  call(void java.io.PrintStream.println(String));
pointcut getTwo() :
  call(public void two());
pointcut getOne() :
  call(public void one());
pointcut matchPrint() :
  getPrint() &&
  cflow(getTwo() &&
  getOne());
```

Here we find the matchPrint() pointcut where a match is made against the println() method and a combination of the one() and two() pointcuts. By combining both getOne() and getTwo() in the same cflow designator, we tell the system to match only when the println() method occurs in the execution flow of both the one() and two() methods. The only way the execution can occur in both methods is when the one() method calls the two() method or the two() method calls the one() method.

## Combining cflow and Other Designators

It is possible to combine the cflow designator with all of the other ones we have discussed so far. For example, suppose we're interested in the setLocation() method when it is called within the setStats() method but we also want to get a copy of the target object and the parameter being passed to setLocation(). The concern we are implementing might require that an inventory-tracking function occur when a DVD is moved from one store to another. Here's what the new pointcut would look like:

```
pointcut setLoc() :
  call(public void DVD.setLocation(..));
pointcut setStat() :
  call(public void DVD.setStats(String, int));
```

```
pointcut localSetLoc(DVD dvd, String place) :
  setLoc() &&
  cflow(setStat()) &&
  target(dvd) &&
  args(place, ..);

before(DVD dvd, String place) : localSetLoc(dvd, place) {
    System.out.println(thisJoinPoint.toLongString());
    System.out.println("Incoming Location = " + place);
    System.out.println("Current Location = " + dvd.getLocation());
}
```

The first thing you notice is the size of the third pointcut, which handles all of the join points we are interested in. Each of the designators in the localSetLoc() pointcut has a job to do, and only when all of the situations line up does the pointcut get matched. Here are the jobs of each designator:

**setLoc() pointcut**—Handles the matching of the setLocation() join point.

**cflow(setStat()) designator**—Handles matching only when the setLoc() pointcut occurs during the execution of setStats().

**target(dvd) designator**—Returns the target DVD object of the setLocation() method.

**args(place, ..)**—Returns the first parameter to setLocation() and ignores all other parameters.

## cflowbelow

In our example, the primary code is in the process of setting a location for a DVD object. If the code had been written so that another setLocation() method call could be made while the current setLocation() method is executing, the pointcut would match again potentially before the first code finished executing. This type of situation can occur when there is a hierarchy of objects, each with a polymorphic version of a single method. In many cases, you don't want to handle all calls to a specific method—just the topmost call.

Consider this pointcut:

```
pointcut setLoc() :
  call(public void DVD.setLocation(..)) ||
  call(public void DVD.setStats(..)) ||
  call(public void Boxset.setLocation(..)) ||
  call(public void Boxset.add(..));
before() : setLoc() {
    System.out.println(thisJoinPoint.toLongString());
}
```

In this pointcut we find a number of join points across both the DVD and Boxset classes, and all of the join points are ORed together, indicating what the set-Loc() pointcut should match when any of the join points are reached. From a concern standpoint, we are interested in knowing when the setLocation() method of any of the DVDs or Boxsets is called. When we execute the code against the Boxset class, we get the following output:

```
call(public void Boxset.add(DVD))
call(public void DVD.setStats(java.lang.String, int))
call(public void DVD.setLocation(java.lang.String, int))
```

If you look at the Boxset code, you notice that the add() method sets the location of the Boxset using a local setLocation() method and the setStats() method of the DVD class using its local setLocation() method. If either the add() or the setStats() method is used, we get a second match of the pointcut when the set-Location() method is called. We really don't want this—we just want to know when the first of any join point listed in the pointcut is reached. The cflowbelow designator can help us with this. Consider this new pointcut using cflowbelow:

```
pointcut setLoc() :
   call(public void DVD.setLocation(..)) ||
   call(public void DVD.setStats(..)) ||
   call(public void Boxset.setLocation(..)) ||
   call(public void Boxset.add(..));

pointcut topSetLoc() :
   setLoc() &&
   !cflowbelow(setLoc());
before() : topSetLoc() {
    System.out.println(thisJoinPoint.toLongString());
}
```

When this new pointcut is executed against the Boxset class, we obtain the following output:

```
call(public void Boxset.add(DVD))
```

Only a single pointcut has been matched. Why? If you follow the code, the add() method calls the setStats() method of the DVD object, which in turn calls the setLocation() method. We only want to know about the add() method in this case. We do this by using the cflowbelow designator, which takes as a parameter a pointcut. Our pointcut topSetLoc() tells the system to first match any of the four join points listed in the setLoc() pointcut. When a match is found, the system should check to see if we are in the execution flow below the current join point. *Below* means not including the current join point. So, when the add() join point is reached, the setLoc() pointcut will match first. The topSetLoc() pointcut will match next, and the system will check to see if the add() method is in the execution flow.

When the setStats() method within the add() method is reached, the setLoc() pointcut will match. The topSetLoc() matches next, and the system checks the execution path of setStats(). Since the pointcut had previously matched, the system remembered that we are still within the execution path of add(), so cflowbelow doesn't match. The same sequence of events occurs in the case of the setLocation() join point.

Let's use an example based on a recursive algorithm. Here's the code for a recursive factorial algorithm:

```
public class Fact {
  public long factorial(int n) {
    if (n == 0) {
      return 1;
    }
    return n * factorial(n - 1);
  }

  public static void main(String args[]) {
    Fact fact = new Fact();
    System.out.println("Fact of 7 = " + fact.factorial(7));
  }
}
```

Next we have a pointcut designed to return just the original call to the recursive algorithm:

```
pointcut getFact(int i) : call(public long factorial(i));
pointcut topGetFact2(int i) :
  getFact(i) &&
  !cflowbelow(getFact(int));
before(int i) : topGetFact2(i) {
  System.out.println(thisJoinPoint.getSignature());
  System.out.println(i);
}
```

In this code, we have two different pointcuts. The first pointcut, called get-Fact(), is based on a join point for the factorial method in the primary code. There are no constraints for this pointcut; therefore, it will be matched each time the primary code calls the method. The topGetFact2() pointcut is a combination built by using the getFact() pointcut and the cflowbelow designator. This cflowbelow designator is built using the getFact() pointcut and will be matched if our current join point is called below the first call that the join point defined in the getFact() pointcut. Since our primary code is recursive, all calls except the first call to the factorial() method will be made below the first one. So, cflowbelow(getFact(int)) will be matched for all getFact() pointcuts except the very first one. The reason for this is the use of getFact(int) in the parameter to cflowbelow, which tells the system to use the join point when first encountered.

The output from the Fact class and our pointcut is as follows:

```
long Fact.factorial(int)
7
Fact of 7 = 5040
```

Next, we might be interested in each of the calls to the factorial join point as well as the original call used to start the recursion. The pointcut would now look like this:

```
pointcut topGetFact2(int i, int j) :
  getFact(i) &&
  cflowbelow(cflow(getFact(j)) && !cflowbelow(getFact(int)));

before(int i, int j) : topGetFact2(i, j) {
  System.out.println(thisJoinPoint.getSignature());
  System.out.println("Current = " + i + " original = " + j);
}
```

The topGetFact2() pointcut has two purposes. The first is to obtain the currently running factorial join point. This step is accomplished using the getFact() pointcut, which matches all factorial method calls and includes a parameter for the integer passed to the method.

The second purpose is to obtain the very first method call to the factorial join point. This step is accomplished using a rather ugly-looking cflowbelow designator. Let's begin talking about this part of the join point by looking at the purpose of the outer cflowbelow. The output for the entire pointcut is as follows:

```
current factorial call parameter value - original call parameter value
```

So if we call factorial(7) , the output looks like this:

```
Current = 6  original = 7
```

With this type of output, there is no purpose for the very first call to factorial. In other words, we don't want to see output like

```
Current = 7 original = 7
```

Therefore, we define the pointcut as

```
getFact(i) && cflowbelow( )
```

This says that we want to know about all calls to the factorial join point but only after the first call to the join point. This combination allows us to bypass the Current = 7 original = 7 output.

Next, we want to be able to pull back the original factorial() method call parameter value. This is accomplished with the code

```
cflow(getFact(j)) && !cflowbelow(getFact(int))
```

This pointcut combination says that we are interested in all calls to the factorial join point, including the first one—which is good because we need the original parameter value. In order to limit which join point call is matched, we created a combination with the inverse of a cflowbelow based on the factorial join point.

The output from the Fact class and this new pointcut is

```
long Fact.factorial(int)
Current = 6 original = 7
long Fact.factorial(int)
Current = 5 original = 7
long Fact.factorial(int)
Current = 4 original = 7
long Fact.factorial(int)
Current = 3 original = 7
long Fact.factorial(int)
Current = 2 original = 7
long Fact.factorial(int)
Current = 1 original = 7
long Fact.factorial(int)
Current = 0 original = 7
Fact of 7 = 5040
```

Finally, suppose we're interested in the current call to the factorial join point as well as the previous. The following pointcut will give us that information:

```
pointcut topGetFact(int i, int j) :
  getFact(i) &&
  cflowbelow(getFact(j));

before(int i, int j) : topGetFact(i,j) {
  System.out.println("Current = " + i + " Previous = " + j);
}
```

The first part of the topGetFact() pointcut pulls all of the calls to the factorial join point and obtains the parameter value passed to the associated method. The second part of the pointcut obtains the previous join point by using the full cflowbelow designator. The output from the Fact class and this pointcut is as follows:

```
Current = 6 Previous = 7
Current = 5 Previous = 6
Current = 4 Previous = 5
Current = 3 Previous = 4
Current = 2 Previous = 3
Current = 1 Previous = 2
Current = 0 Previous = 1
Fact of 7 = 5040
```

# Class-Initialization Designators

When we're defining a class to represent some object in the design of an application, it is likely that each object instantiated from the class must possess certain attributes in order to operate correctly. One or two of these attributes will more than likely have the same value from object to object. An example is a lookup table in which the same values are accessed by all objects in a read-only manner. These type attributes are typically designated as static in a class. The class itself owns the attribute, but all instantiated objects, as well as potentially other objects, can access the attributes provided that the permissions are set correctly. Here's an example of a class with static attributes:

```
public class StaticExample {
  private static int lookup[][];

  private static final int N = 25;
  private static final int M = 25;
}
```

This class code defines three static attributes with scope visibility to the class as well as all objects instantiated from the class. When we execute the Java application that contains this static code, a static initializer built within the Java Runtime Environment executes.

## staticinitialization

AspectJ includes a designator called staticinitialization, which we can use to build a pointcut against a join point for the static initializer of a particular class type. The format of the staticinitialization designator is

```
staticinitialization(class type pattern)
```

The join point matches when the static initializer for the object begins to execute. Consider the following pointcut set against the DVD class:

```
pointcut staticInit() : staticinitialization(DVD);
before() : staticInit() {
  System.out.println(thisJoinPoint.toLongString());
}
```

When we execute this code against the DVD class, the following output is generated:

```
staticinitialization(static DVD.<clinit>)
Location and count = New Store
Title = Better Title
```

The output shows where the join point was matched against the code, clearly showing that the static clinit cliint code was executed. If you remember, the

DVD class is a derived class from Product. The pointcut can be changed slightly to match when the Product and the DVD class static initializers are executed. For example:

```
pointcut staticInit() : staticinitialization(Product+);
before() : staticInit() {
    System.out.println(thisJoinPoint.toLongString());
}
```

The output from this pointcut is

```
staticinitialization(static Product.<clinit>)
staticinitialization(static DVD.<clinit>)
Location and count = New Store
Title = Better Title
```

Notice how the Product static initializer comes before the DVD, as you would expect since Product is the parent class to DVD.

## Program Text-Based Designators

There are times when join points must be limited to specific class types, and the target or this designator can be used for that purpose. However, we don't have much control over where in a class the join points can be matched with these designators. The cflow designator gives us more control, but if the method representing the join point defined in cflow calls another method of the same or different object, a join point can still be matched. This is because the execution flow is still within the scope of the original join point. What we need is a way to limit the scope of a join point to a single method or constructor within an object. The withincode designator handles this type of scoping.

### withincode

The format of the withincode designator is

```
withincode(join point signature)
```

Using our DVD code, suppose we want to match the setLocation() method call. The pointcut is

```
pointcut setLoc() : call(public void setLocation(..));
```

Executing this pointcut against the DVD code produces the following output

```
call(public void DVD.setLocation(java.lang.String, int))
call(public void DVD.setLocation(java.lang.String, int))
Location and count = New Store
Title = Better Title
```

This output tells us that there are two setLocation() calls in the execution of the DVD main() method. One of those setLocation() calls is in the main() method itself, and the other is in the setStats() method. We are interested in only the call within the setStats() method, and we need to build a pointcut to limit the matching scope. At first consideration, the cflow designator appears to be a good match; if we build a pointcut using it and execute the pointcut, a single setLocation() join point will be matched. So, all is well—until the setStats() method is expanded and it calls another method with a setLocation() method within that new method. Remember that cflow limits the scope to the entire execution of the original matched join point regardless of the other methods called.

The solution to this problem is to use the withincode designator. For example:

```
pointcut getLoc() :
  call(public void setLocation(..)) &&
  withincode(public void DVD.setStats(..));
before() : getLoc() {
    System.out.println(thisJoinPoint.toLongString());
}
```

This pointcut tells the system to match all calls to the setLocation() join point but only (using the AND logical operator) when the join point falls within the setStats() method of the DVD class. Note that without the DVD class type attached to the setStats() join point signature, the pointcut could potentially be matched on objects other than DVD that have the setStats() method. The withincode designator is based on the execution of code within the join point selected and doesn't extend to objects created within the matched join point.

### within

What if we had a situation where another object was created local to a method that has been matched by a join point? Would the system be able to tell that our new object is within the scope of a method defined in a withincode designator? Consider the following class:

```
public class Within {

  private int count;

  private class Inner {
    public void updateCount(Within w, int i) {
      w.setCount(i);
    }
  }

  public void setCount(int i) {
    count = i;
  }
```

```
public void one() {
    Inner inner = new Inner();
    inner.updateCount(this, 4);
    System.out.println(count);
}

public static void main(String args[]) {
    Within withinIt = new Within();
    withinIt.one();
}
}
```

In this code, a setCount() public accessor function is used to update a private count attribute. Within the one() method, a private Inner class object is instantiated and the updateCount() method is called using a parameter of the current object and the value 4. The updateCount() method of the Inner class calls the setCount() method. We are interested in a pointcut being matched when the setCount() method is called within the one() method. Here's a possible pointcut definition:

```
pointcut setC() :
    call(public void setCount(int)) &&
    within(public void one());
before() : setC() {
    System.out.println(thisJoinPoint.toLongString());
}
```

The familiar call designator is used to match the setCount() join point anywhere in the code. This is followed by the withincode designator with a join point of the one() method. The question is, will the call to setCount() found in the Inner class's updateCount() method cause the pointcut to the matched? The answer is yes, because an Inner class object was instantiated within the execution path of the one() method. The within designator remains active until the end of the join point.

## Anonymous and Inner-Class within/withincode Join Points

There is currently a limitation for both the within and withincode designators as they relate to inner and anonymous classes. Suppose you have this class:

```
public class test {
private class innertest {
    public inertest() {
        JButton button = new JButton("Button");
        button.addActionListener(
            new ActionListener() {
                public void ActionPerformed (ActionEvent e) {
                    //do something
                }
```

```
            }
        );
      }
    }
  }
```

An aspect created to match join points at the comment //do something won't work when using the designator based on the inner class like this:

```
within(test.innertest)
```

The join points within the anonymous class of the inner class can be matched with the designator

```
within(test)
```

The AspectJ team hopes to clear this limitation in a revision of 1.1.

## Dynamic Property-Based Designators

As we mentioned earlier, you cannot use wildcards with the this, target, and args designators when specifying class information. To overcome this problem, you can use the if designator. The format of the designator is

```
if(BooleanExpression)
```

The if designator matches join points based on some dynamic property used as the condition to the if designator. The dynamic property must, of course, evaluate to a value of true or false. We can take advantage of this designator to match a hierarchy of classes if needed. This example is derived from the initial AspectJ 1.1 readme:

```
pointcut handleMatch() : this (Object) &&
           if (matchThem"com.test.Product.",
              thisJoinPoint.getTarget().getClass().getName()));

static boolean matchthem(String pattern, String className) {
  if (className.indexOf(pattern) >= 0) return true;
}
```

In this pointcut, we match on all objects in the code derived from Object and a dynamic property based on the name of the current object. The name of the current target object and the pattern we are interested in are passed to the matchThem() method. The method checks the pattern against the object name. If the pattern is found, the method returns a true value. If you have more complex patterns, the matchThem() method might be more complex, but all it needs to do is make sure the class name has a specific pattern.

# adviceexecution

AspectJ 1.1 introduced a new designator to the language, called *adviceexecution*, which lets you create a pointcut that will match a join point based on the execution of an advice. The format of the designator is

```
adviceexecution()
```

Consider the following example Java application and aspect code:

```
Primary Code:

public class Test {
  public Test() {
    Database database = new Database();
    database.databaseCall();
  }
  public static void main(String[] args) {
    Test test = new Test();
  }
}
Aspect Code
public aspect DatabaseCallAspect {
  pointcut primary() : call(public void databaseCall());
  pointcut aspects() : adviceexecution() &&
                              within(DatabaseCallAspect);

  before() : primary() {
    System.out.println(thisJoinPoint.getSignature());
  }

  before() : aspects() {
    System.out.println("Call to advice");
  }
}
```

In this example, we make external calls to a database in the primary code. In the aspect code, we have created two pointcuts to match the database call and one to match the execution of the two advice code blocks. When the application and aspect code is woven together and executed, the output is

```
Call to advice
Call to advice
void Database.databaseCall()
```

Here we can see the appropriate database calls are matched as well as the beginning of execution for both aspects.

## preinitialization

We can use the preinitialization designator to match a join point defined before an object is fully instantiated. For example:

```
public aspect DVDAspect {
  pointcut instant() : preinitialization(DVD.new());

  before() : instant() {
    System.out.println(thisJoinPoint.getSignature());
  }
}
```

## Dealing with Interfaces

All of the pointcuts we have discussed are also valid in those cases where interfaces are used to enhance the design of an application. Consider the following interface and two implementations:

```
public interface SimpleInterface {
  public void doSimple(int i);
}

public class SimpleIOne implements SimpleInterface {

  private int count;

  public void doSimple(int i) {
    count = i;
  }

  public static void main (String args[]) {
    SimpleIOne simple1 = new SimpleIOne();
    simple1.doSimple(5);

    SimpleITwo simple2 = new SimpleITwo();
    simple2.doSimple(6);
  }
}

public class SimpleITwo implements SimpleInterface {

  private int count;

  public void doSimple(int i) {
    count = i;
  }
}
```

The two classes, SimpleIOne and SimpleITwo, implement the interface and provide code for the doSimple() method. However, the SimpleIOne class has a main() method where both a SimpleIOne and a SimpleITwo object are created, and the doSimple() method is executed against each of the objects. We can create a join point and associated pointcut to match the doSimple() methods of the two classes quite simply:

```
pointcut simple() : call(public void doSimple(int));
   before() : simple(){
     System.out.println(thisJoinPoint.toLongString());
     System.out.println(thisJoinPoint.getKind());
   }
```

The join point matches all uses of the doSimple(int) method regardless of the class where it is defined. The output from this pointcut and the main() method in the SimpleIOne code is as follows:

```
call(public void SimpleIOne.doSimple(int))
method-call
call(public void SimpleITwo.doSimple(int))
method-call
```

Now, if we were to change the code to match based on the interface itself, the pointcut would be as follows:

```
pointcut simple() :
   call(public void SimpleInterface.doSimple(int));
```

Executing the new pointcut against the SimpleIOne code produces the same output shown earlier since there is no code in the SimpleInterface interface itself. The pointcut is telling us where the interface has ultimately been implemented.

## Anonymous Pointcuts

All of the pointcuts created in this chapter are called named pointcuts because there was a name attached to its definition. AspectJ allows the use of anonymous pointcuts in cases where there isn't a need for a name. Here's an example of an anonymous pointcut:

```
before() : call(public void doSimple(int)) {
  System.out.println(thisJoinPoint.toLongString());
  System.out.println(thisJoinPoint.getKind());
}
```

In this snippet, the same pointcut used in the previous section to find the doSimple() join point is implemented from an interface. The previous pointcut isn't used in a more complex pointcut, so it is a good candidate to become an anonymous pointcut. The output from executing the code is the same as shown earlier.

## Using Aspects in Classes

When writing a number of pointcuts for the implementation of a concern, you should take into account the issue of modularity. For many of our examples, we split the code between primary Java files and files implementing the crosscutting concerns. To show how the cflow and cflowbelow designators work, let's suppose we have a couple of files, called Flow.java and FlowAspect.java. The Flow.java file contains the primary application code, and FlowAspect.java contains the join points, pointcuts, and advice code encapsulated in an aspect. Even though the aspect code is kept in a separate file, the pointcuts and related join points are visible across all of the code compiled to produce an application.

When a concern crosscuts a number of classes in the application code, it might be useful to implement the pointcut in the same source file as the code itself. For example, suppose we defined a pointcut in the Flow.java class that defines a specific join point in the Flow class. We defined another pointcut in a class called Flow2.java that matches some other method specific to the Flow2 class. This is followed by an aspect defined in another file called FlowAspect.java. The pointcut has to reference the pointcuts in each of the files to be effective. For example, assume we have a pointcut called flowPC() in the Flow class and a pointcut called flowPC2() in the Flow2 class. We could define a third pointcut referencing both of the pointcuts:

```
public Aspect FlowPCDs() :
    call(Flow.flowPC()) &&
    execution(Flow2.flowPC2());
```

In order for the compiler to find the appropriate pointcuts, we must provide the full class definition. By putting pointcuts into the class where the pointcut's join point is found, we create another level of encapsulation.

## Creating Factory Objects

Using the Factory design pattern is a common coding technique. The following example application is designed to allow the creation of two different objects called Factory1 and Factory2. If a user of the Factory class needs one of these objects, the user should get an instance of the Factory and request an object of the correct type. If an application uses a new() method, we might build an aspect to produce an error:

```
public class Factory {

    static public Object makeInstance(int i) {
        if (i == 0) {
            return (Object) new Factory1();
        } else {
```

```
        return (Object) new Factory2();
      }
    }

    public static void main(String args[]) {
      Factory1 factory1 = (Factory1)Factory.makeInstance(0);
      Factory2 factory2 = (Factory2)Factory.makeInstance(2);

      Factory1 badFactory1 = new Factory1();
    }
  }
  public class Factory1 {
    public Factory1() {
    }
  }
  public class Factory2 {
    public Factory2() {
    }
  }
```

Next we have the aspect that accomplishes two tasks. The first is determining when an object is created properly through the makeInstance() method of the Factory class. We accomplish this by using a call designator with a signature of Factory.makeInstance. To find examples of using just a new() method to produce a new Factory1 or Factory2 object, we must create a combination pointcut. The first part is matching a call to the new() method of any Factory class. This is done using the call(Factory*.new()) designator. However, we don't want to include calls in the makeInstance() method of the Factory class because that's where the good objects are created. To keep the pointcut from matching the new() calls in makeInstance(), we can use the cflow designator with a NOT operator.

Finally, say we don't want to match on any calls to instantiate the Factory class itself. The resulting pointcuts and example advice is shown here:

```
public aspect FactoryAspect {
  pointcut buildFactory() : call(Factory.new());

  pointcut factory() : call(* Factory.makeInstance(..));

  pointcut notFactory() :
    call (Factory*.new()) &&
    !cflow(factory()) &&
    !buildFactory();
  }

  before() : factory() {
    System.out.println(thisJoinPoint.getSignature());
  }
```

```
before() : notFactory() {
   System.out.println(thisJoinPoint.getSignature() + " BAD!");
}
}
```

When the main() method of the Factory class is executed with the aspect woven into the code, the following output occurs:

```
Object Factory.makeInstance(int)
Object Factory.makeInstance(int)
Factory1() BAD!
```

## Catching Java Library Calls

A very common question about AspectJ is how to match join points on code found in a package that wasn't written by the developer. A good example is the class libraries provided by Java—especially the GUI classes. We use the following example to illustrate matching on package methods:

```
import java.io.*;
import java.awt.*;
import java.awt.event.*;
import javax.swing.*;

public class Gui extends JFrame {

   JTextArea displayArea;
   JButton sendButton;

   public Gui() {
      super("GUI");

      Container c = getContentPane();

      sendButton = new JButton("Send Search");
      sendButton.addActionListener(
         new ActionListener() {
            public void actionPerformed(ActionEvent e) {
               sendData();
            }
         }
      );
      c.add(sendButton, BorderLayout.NORTH);

      displayArea = new JTextArea();
      c.add(new JScrollPane(displayArea), BorderLayout.CENTER);

      setSize(150,150);
```

```
        show();
    }

    private void sendData() {

    }

    public static void main (String args[]) {
      Gui gui = new Gui();
      gui.displayArea.append("New String");
    }
}
```

This example builds a GUI and displays a button and text area. After the GUI is instantiated, the code adds a small text string to the text area. When a user clicks the button, the sendData() method is called. Our goal is to match on the calls to the constructor for the JTextArea, to the add() method of the GUI container, and to the sendData() method. The following shows an aspect with the necessary pointcuts:

```
public aspect GuiAspect {
    pointcut textArea() : call(javax.swing.JTextArea+.new(..));
    pointcut container() : call(* java.awt.Container.add(..));
    pointcut senddata() : call(private void Gui.sendData());

    before() : textArea() {
       System.out.println(thisJoinPoint.getSignature());
    }

    before() : container() {
       System.out.println(thisJoinPoint.getSignature());
    }

    before() : senddata() {
       System.out.println(thisJoinPoint.getSignature());
    }
}
```

Once the aspect is woven in the primary code, the application displays a GUI on the screen. When a user clicks the button, the application generates the following output:

```
void java.awt.Container.add(Component, Object)
javax.swing.JTextArea()
void java.awt.Container.add(Component, Object)
void Gui.sendData()
```

Note the use of the entire signature for the join points. This is a requirement when you're matching join points in a package.

## Access to Final Attributes

Many classes use constants or final attributes in their class definitions. For example:

```
public class Test{
    public static final String WARNING = "This is a warning";
}
```

Currently no designator is available that will allow a match to occur when a final attribute is used.

## Patterns with Exceptions

There might be times when you need to match methods with a listing of thrown exceptions. It is possible to list the exceptions in the various designators. For example:

```
call(* *(..) throws IOException)
```

This call designator selects all the methods declaring that they threw IOExceptions.

# What's Next

In this chapter, we provided an in-depth overview of the pointcut and discussed how you can use designators along with join points to implement the crosscutting of concerns. Several of our examples have shown the use of pointcuts in action on real code. The join point identifies the place where a pointcut should be matched in the execution of the primary application. The advice, which we cover in the next chapter, is executed when the pointcut is matched and provides the code necessary to implement the crosscutting concerns.

# CHAPTER 7

# Advice

C hapter 6 discussed pointcuts, which are vital for assembling and naming interesting "points" in the execution of an application. The natural complement to a pointcut is *advice*—code that executes when the application reaches a join point. If you've been reading this book chapter by chapter, you've seen dozens of pieces of advice. For instance, in this example the advice is shown in bold:

```
pointcut DVDConstruct() : execution (public DVD.new(..));
before() : DVDConstruct() {
    System.out.println(thisJoinPoint);
}
```

We've shown you so much advice without fully introducing the concept because advice is such a vital part of AspectJ. We've used it to demonstrate that join points were reached, that pointcuts selected the right join points, and that pointcuts can expose join point context. This chapter delves into advice in its own right. We'll explore:

- How to define advice
- How to use join point context in advice
- Advice and exceptions
- The different types of advice (before, after, and around)
- How to use the special proceed syntax available in around advice
- Advice precedence

Along the way, we'll show you some examples of how advice can implement crosscutting concerns. We'll only be able to scratch the surface, because almost everything you do in AspectJ builds on advice. However, we hope this chapter will spark your thinking about the sorts of concerns AspectJ can implement.

# How to Define Advice

If you've read some of the earlier examples in the book, you can probably put together working advice. However, we'll begin from scratch and explore the different parts of advice using an example.

## Adding Information to System.out.println()

Let's start with motivation. For simple programs, System.out.println is a great way to display output to the user or to check on the flow of an application. We'll use it heavily to demonstrate that our advice works as planned.

However (as you're probably aware), using more than one or two occurrences of System.out.println can be confusing. There's no way to tell where the printout came from, when it happened, or anything else about its context. To remedy this problem, JDK 1.4 introduced logging classes. Users of JDK 1.3 can rely on third-party logging frameworks. Either solution introduces complexity. Let's look at what AspectJ can do to help you address System.out.println's limitations.

With what you know of pointcuts, it should be easy to identify and advise calls to System.out.println. First let's set up some test code so you'll know when you've succeeded (see Listing 7.1).

```
public class PrintTest {

    public PrintTest() {
        System.out.println("In constructor.");
    }

    public void test1(){
        System.out.println("In test1");
    }

    public void test2(){
        System.out.println("In test2");
```

**Listing 7.1**  A class that uses printlns. (continues)

```
    }

    public static void main(String[] args){
        System.out.println("In main.");
        PrintTest t = new PrintTest();
        t.test1();
        t.test2();
    }
}

//output
In main.
In constructor.
In test1
In test2
```

**Listing 7.1**    A class that uses printlns. (continued)

# The advice

In order to add a little context to the printlns, let's find out the name of the class that made the call to System.out.println. Here's the advice you can use:

```
before(Object caller) : logCalls(caller) {
    System.out.print(getClassName(caller) + ":");
}
```

Essentially, this advice says, "Before log calls, issue an additional print statement stating the class name of the caller."

## Analysis of Println Advice

Let's break down the advice. First comes the type of the advice:

```
before(Object caller) : logCalls(caller) {
    System.out.print(getClassName(caller) + ":");
}
```

The word *before* specifies the type of advice you're defining—the other options are *after* and *around* (more about them later). In this case, *before* means the advice will execute before the join points it affects.

Next come the formal parameters of the advice (if any):

```
before(Object caller) : logCalls(caller) {
    System.out.print(getClassName(caller) + ":");
}
```

As you saw in Chapter 6, pointcuts can expose variables that represent well-defined pieces of the execution context of a join point. Advice makes use of this context by binding it into formal parameters. We'll get into that topic in detail later in this chapter. For now, understand that the advice can refer to an object exposed by the logCall pointcut via the identifier "caller."

After the advice type and parameters comes the pointcut:

```
//within aspect AddSourceInfo
before(Object caller) : logCalls(caller) {
    System.out.print(getClassName(caller) + ":");
}


public pointcut logCalls(Object caller) :
            call(public void print*(*)) &&
            target(PrintStream) &&
            this(caller) &&
            ! within(AddSourceInfo);
```

Advice is always defined relative to a pointcut. The pointcut selects the join points that the advice runs at. The logCalls pointcut begins by using call() to identify calls to any methods starting with *print* on objects of type PrintStream. this(caller) exposes the currently executing object (the one that made the call to println). Finally, ! within(AddSourceInfo) excludes any calls to println made from within the aspect itself.

Now you define the body of the advice:

```
before(Object caller) : logCalls(caller) {
    System.out.print(getClassName(caller) + ":");
}


private String getClassName(Object o){
    if(o == null){
        return "unknown";
    }
    String name = o.getClass().getName();
    //remove package name for shorter output
    name = name.substring(name.lastIndexOf('.') + 1);
    return name;
}
```

The body of the advice acts like a method body. It can use its formal parameters much like methods use their parameters, and it can call other methods to help it do its work. The main differences between advice bodies and method bodies are that advice bodies are restricted in their return values (more on that later) and advice bodies have implicit access to special AspectJ constructs such as thisJoinPoint and proceed().

If you compile AddSourceInfo and weave it into PrintTest, you get the following output:

```
In main.
PrintTest:In constructor.
PrintTest:In test1
PrintTest:In test2
```

It looks like a success. The pointcut has identified calls to print*. The advice has added the additional information before each call. Only the call from main()was missed. However, that's a limitation of the pointcut, not the advice. Because the pointcut relies on this() to identify the caller, it does not pick out any calls coming from code where there is no currently executing object. This excludes any calls from static methods, which isn't acceptable. Let's see how to include the calls from main().

### Refactoring the Println Advice

If you examine the API for thisJoinPointStaticPart (introduced in Chapter 5, "Join Points") you find a method called getSourceLocation().Replace the body of the advice with the following:

```
before(Object caller) : logCalls(caller) {
    System.out.print(
        thisJoinPointStaticPart.getSourceLocation() + "-"
    );
}
```

Recompile (and reweave), and the output now looks like this:

```
PrintTest.java:23-In main.
PrintTest.java:11-In constructor.
PrintTest.java:15-In test1
PrintTest.java:19-In test2
```

That looks perfect. It even has line numbers! Now that you aren't using the caller parameter of the advice, you can delete it, along with the parts of the log-Calls pointcut that exposed it. The final aspect appears in Listing 7.2.

```
public aspect AddSourceInfo {

    public pointcut logCalls() :
            call(public void print*(*)) &&
            target(PrintStream) &&
            ! within(AddSourceInfo);
```

**Listing 7.2**   The final form of the AddSourceInfo aspect. (continues)

```
before() : logCalls() {
    System.out.print(
        thisJoinPointStaticPart.getSourceLocation() + "-"
    );
}
```

**Listing 7.2**  The final form of the AddSourceInfo aspect. (continued)

## Formal Definition

Now that you've seen a detailed example, let's look at the formal syntax for an advice definition:

```
Advice ::= [ReturnType] TypeOfAdvice "("[Formals]")"
               [AfterQualifier] [throws TypeList] ":"
               Pointcut "{" [AdviceBody] "}"


TypeOfAdvice ::= before | after | around
ReturnType ::= TypeOrPrimitive ;(applies only to around advice)
AfterQualifier ::= ThrowsQualifier | ReturningQualifier
;(applies only to after--defined later)
Formals ::= ;(as a Java parameter list)
Pointcut ::= ;(see Chapter 6)
AdviceBody ::= ;(as a Java method body—with differences discussed
later)
```

This is a simplified treatment that emphasizes AspectJ's contributions rather than those areas where it overlaps with Java. Don't worry about the special syntax for around and after advice—we'll deal with those permutations in the sections about those types of advice.

Unlike pointcuts, which can appear in classes as well as aspects, advice can appear only within the body of an aspect. Unlike methods, fields, or other type members, advice does not have an associated identifier. This is natural, because you never need to refer to the advice by name within your code. However, the lack of an identifier can make things confusing when you're trying to talk or write about advice. Often you can solve this issue by using well-named pointcuts with your advice. For instance, you could refer to the advice developed in the AddSourceInfo example as "the advice that executes before log calls" (logCalls() being the name of its pointcut).

The lack of an identifier also makes it difficult to distinguish one bit of advice from another when reading an advice signature. (This can happen, for instance, if you use thisJoinPoint.getSignature to get information about advice-execution join points). There is also no way to pick out and advise the execution of a single piece of advice. The preferred way to use the adviceexecution() pointcut is to pair it with within(*YourAspect*), thus limiting its scope to advice appearing in the body of *YourAspect*.

# Issues Common to All Types of Advice

Before we consider the different types of advice in detail, let's examine features common to all three types of advice.

## Passing Context to Advice

The previous section included a simple example of passing context to advice. This section examines another example and considers some of the issues raised by passing context to advice.

### Example: Employee Raises

This section introduces an example application that will make several appearances throughout the book: a simple personnel management system. At the heart of the system is the Employee class, shown in Listing 7.3.

```
package personnel;

import java.text.NumberFormat;
import java.io.PrintStream;

public class Employee {
    private int salary;
    private String name;
    private Manager manager;
    private NumberFormat formatter =
        NumberFormat.getCurrencyInstance();

    public Employee(String name, int startingSalary) {
        this.name = name;
        salary = startingSalary;
    }

    public void raiseSalary(int increment){
        salary += increment;
    }

    public void costOfLivingAdjustment(){
```

**Listing 7.3**   The Employee class enables some basic actions. (continues)

```
        salary += 125;
    }

    public int getSalary(){
        return salary;
    }

    public String getSalaryDisplay(){
        return formatter.format(salary);
    }

    public String toString(){
        String type = getClassName();
        return type + " " + name + ":"
        + getSalaryDisplay();
    }

    public personnel.Manager getManager() {
        return manager;
    }

    public void setManager(personnel.Manager manager) {
        this.manager = manager;
    }

    public java.lang.String getName() {
        return name;
    }
    public void setName(java.lang.String name) {
        this.name = name;
    }

    public String getClassName(){
        String name = getClass().getName();
        name = name.substring(name.indexOf('.') + 1);
        return name;
    }
}
```

**Listing 7.3** The Employee class enables some basic actions. (continued)

To give motivation to the examples, assume that you're customizing the personnel management application for a particular department within a company. As you might imagine, raises are an interesting event in this application. Raises mean more money for the employee, less money for the company, new tax calculations, different 401(k) contributions, and so on. Because raises have such far-reaching consequences, the department would like to have a record of them.

You know how well AspectJ handles logging, so let's use advice to perform this task. Listing 7.4 shows both the logging aspect and example code that exercises it.

```
public class Example {
    public static void main(String[] args){
        raiseAndCheck("Rebekah", 5000);
        raiseAndCheck("Omar", 6000);
        raiseAndCheck("Philipe", 7000);
    }

    private static void raiseAndCheck(String name,
                                        int raise){
        Employee e = new Employee(name, 50000);
        e.raiseSalary(raise);
        System.out.println("After raise: " + e);
    }
}
public aspect LogRaises {

    pointcut raises() : call(void raiseSalary(int)) &&
                        target(Employee);

    before() : raises() {
        System.out.println("Raise occurred.");
    }
}

//output--notice output from AddSourceInfo as well as LogRaises
LogRaises.java:10-Raise occurred.
Example.java:18-After raise: Employee Rebekah:$55,000.00
LogRaises.java:10-Raise occurred.
Example.java:18-After raise: Employee Omar:$56,000.00
LogRaises.java:10-Raise occurred.
Example.java:18-After raise: Employee Philipe:$57,000.00
```

**Listing 7.4**  Basic logging of raises.

By now you're probably familiar with using AspectJ to do this sort of logging. The only thing worth mentioning so far is that you can weave in the AddSourceInfo aspect to see which printlns come from where. (In fact, this aspect is so useful in interpreting the examples that we leave it in for many of the examples throughout the chapter.)

### Passing in the Employee and Amount as Formal Parameters

The output from LogRaises isn't very useful. A raise log without data about whose salary was raised and the amount of the raise is fairly useless. So, let's pass that information into the advice as formal parameters.

First the pointcut must be modified to expose the context:

```
pointcut raises(Employee emp, int amount) :
                call(void raiseSalary(int)) &&
                target(emp) && args(amount);
```

Then you modify the advice to accept the employee and amount as formal parameters:

```
before(Employee emp, int amount) : raises(emp, amount) {
        System.out.println(emp + " to receive raise of " +
        amount);
}
```

The output looks like this:

```
LogRaises.java:11-Employee Rebekah:$50,000.00 to receive raise of
5000
Example.java:16-After raise: Employee Rebekah:$55,000.00
LogRaises.java:11-Employee Omar:$50,000.00 to receive raise of
6000
Example.java:16-After raise: Employee Omar:$56,000.00
LogRaises.java:11-Employee Philipe:$50,000.00 to receive raise of
7000
Example.java:16-After raise: Employee Philipe:$57,000.00
```

Now that you've seen context binding in action, let's consider the technical details.

## Formal Parameters

Formal parameters pass join point context to advice in an explicit and type-safe fashion. Most of the information that can be passed in as advice parameters can also be extracted via reflection. Each type of access has advantages and disadvantages. We'll discuss which to use when in the section "Reflective Access to Join Point Context."

### Context Available as Formals

Chapter 6 discussed in detail how to pull context out of join points with pointcuts. To review, advice can use four types of context:

- **Arguments**—(Selected with args().) These can be actual method or constructor parameters. They can also be less formal types of arguments, specifically exceptions passed to handler blocks and field assignment values.

- **The currently executing object**—(Selected with this().) Remember that this context is not available during the execution of a static method.

- **The target of a method/constructor call or field reference**—
(Selected with target().)

■ **The return value or thrown exception from a join point**—(Selected with returning() or throwing().) This type of context can only be accessed by after advice of the correct type.

### The Left-Right Rule

It's important to remember that every named parameter on the *left* side of the colon must match a piece of context exposed by the pointcut on the *right* side of the colon. Consider the raise logging advice discussed earlier:

```
before(Employee emp, int amount) : raises(emp, amount) {
    System.out.println(emp + " to receive raise of " +
    amount);
}
```

Here Employee *emp* on the left side matches raises(*emp*, amount) on the right side. The same does not necessarily apply in the other direction—the right side can expose more context than is used by the left side. The Left-Right rule applies to pointcuts as well as advice. For example, in the definition of the raises pointcut, Employee *emp* on the left matches target(*emp*) on the right.

Unlike method parameters, the order in which the parameters appear doesn't matter; AspectJ will match up the identifiers for you. You could swap the order of the parameters without affecting the program:

```
before(int amount, Employee emp) : raises(emp, amount) {
    System.out.println(emp + " to receive raise of " +
    amount);
}
```

### Parameter-Context Mismatches

Sometimes you can construct a pointcut that seems to match all the required parameters but actually doesn't. Let's say you wanted to add cost of living increases to the raises pointcut:

```
pointcut raises(Employee emp, int amount) :
            call(void raiseSalary(int)) &&
            target(emp) && args(amount) //amount bound
            ||
            call(void costOfLivingAdjustment())
            && target(emp);//amount not bound
```

In this pointcut, args(amount) appears on one side of the || but not on the other. The compiler will complain. Chapter 6 has more examples of this behavior.

### Formal Parameters Are Like Method Parameters

If you're experienced with the Java language, you should find it natural to work with advice parameters. After you enter the body of the advice, the advice parameters behave just like method parameters. The advice body can call methods on the parameters, pass them to other methods, or store them in a data structure. Like method parameters, advice parameters are local to the advice. In other words, if you reassign a parameter, it will have no effect outside the advice. However, you can change the state of the parameters and have the change reflected outside the advice.

**Reassignments.** To illustrate this, consider some malicious aspect code. Here an unscrupulous programmer attempts to reassign the target of a raise:

```
before(Employee emp): raises(emp, int){
    emp = new Employee("me", 60000);
}
```

First (as discussed in the previous section), note that the advice doesn't need to use the *amount* context exposed by the raises pointcut. This snippet illustrates the preferred method of indicating that you don't wish to bind a piece of context: replace the identifier with the type of the context (replace the identifier "amount" with type "int" in the pointcut).

Recompiling with this piece of advice yields output like the following:

```
LogRaises.java:7-Employee Rebekah:$50,000.00 to receive raise of
5000
Example.java:16-After raise: Employee Rebekah:$55,000.00
...
```

In other words, the advice does not affect the actual raises. The effect of "emp =" lasts only until the end of the advice body. It's possible to do what this malicious advice attempts (change the target of a method call), but only with *around* advice—and the syntax is more complicated.

**State changes.** It's much easier to affect join point context by changing the state of formal parameters. Consider the following advice:

```
before(Employee emp): raises(emp, int){
    emp.costOfLivingAdjustment();
}
```

This advice adds a cost of living adjustment to the employee's base pay before any raise. You can see from the output that this advice *does* affect the employees in Example:

```
LogRaises.java:7-Employee Rebekah:$50,125.00 to receive raise of
5000
Example.java:16-After raise: Employee Rebekah:$55,125.00
LogRaises.java:7-Employee Omar:$50,125.00 to receive raise of
6000
Example.java:16-After raise: Employee Omar:$56,125.00
...
```

If you inspect the output closely, you can see that the advice we just looked at takes effect *before* the advice that logs the raise attempt. That's interesting: Does the cost of living adjustment count as part of the raise? If so, shouldn't it be applied *after* the log? AspectJ allows the programmer to control the order of advice execution through advice precedence, which we'll discuss toward the end of the chapter. For the moment, remove both of these pieces of advice.

### Object-typed Parameters and Boxing

Suppose you want to write a pointcut that encompasses widely varying join points. For instance, say you're debugging Employee and you want to track changes in state. The aspect in Listing 7.5 uses the set() pointcut to log any assignments to a field of Employee.

```
public aspect TrackSets {

    before(Object newValue) :
        employeeFieldSets(newValue){

        String name =
            thisJoinPoint.getSignature().getName();
        System.out.println("The new value of " +
            name + " is " + newValue);
    }

    pointcut employeeFieldSets(Object newValue):
        set(* *) && target(Employee) &&
        args(newValue);
}

//output
TrackSets.java:14-The new value of formatter is
java.text.DecimalFormat@67500
TrackSets.java:14-The new value of name is Rebekah
TrackSets.java:14-The new value of salary is 50000
LogRaises.java:7-Employee Rebekah:$50,000.00 to receive raise of
5000
TrackSets.java:14-The new value of salary is 55000
Example.java:16-After raise: Employee Rebekah:$55,000.00
...
```

**Listing 7.5** Object boxing in action.

The pointcut employeeFieldSets uses set(* *) to target all field sets, and then narrows the selection to those join points where the target is an Employee (target(Employee)). It exposes the argument of the field assignment with args(newValue). The advice accepts the args context through its one formal parameter: Object newValue.

The output shows that the pointcut works as described. Formatter is set to a DecimalFormat, name is set to the String "Rebekah", and salary is set to 50000. But Salary is an int field—how did it enter the advice through a formal parameter with the type of Object? If you read Chapter 6, you might remember that AspectJ automatically boxes primitives to their wrapper types. In other words, when it entered the advice, the "50000" you saw in the output was an object of type java.lang.Integer. This boxing behavior is convenient for situations when context must reflect both object and primitive types.

## Reflective Access to Join Point Context

In addition to formal parameters, advice can also use special implicit variables provided by AspectJ to inspect and manipulate join point context. Chapter 5 introduced these objects in detail and explored their API and uses. To review, there are three special variables:

- **thisJoinPoint**—Can access some of the information available through formal parameters using getTarget(), getThis(), and getArgs(). It can also provide information about the signature, location, and kind of the join point.

- **thisJoinPointStaticPart**—Can access less information (signature, kind, and location) but does not require memory allocation at each use.

- **thisEnclosingJoinPointStaticPart**—Is the same as thisJoinPointStaticPart, except that it binds to the join point enclosing the current join point.

### When to Use Reflective Access

As you saw in the first example in the chapter, there are times to use one type of access and times to use the other. Reflective access obviously wins when it provides information that formal parameters cannot (for instance, the line-numbers from getSourceLocation() are very helpful). Another example is getArgs(). The reflective version returns an Object array, allowing for easy access to the full parameter list of a join point. In contrast, formal parameters would require the pointcut to name each possible argument. For uses such as broad logging, reflective access can simplify the code.

On the downside, reflective access can be slower and more memory intensive than similar access through formal parameters. This may or may not have a significant impact on your application, but for certain types of pointcuts, it can introduce a considerable overhead.

### When to Use Formals

Formal parameters clarify the intent of the advice to fellow programmers. After you become familiar with the syntax of AspectJ, context exposure using point-cuts seems expressive. Using the reflective objects, by contrast, involves a degree of obfuscation. Furthermore, the compiler cannot help you catch your mistakes as easily. Casting the result of getTarget() to an Employee will only fail at runtime; using target(anEmployee) will limit the pointcut to those join points where the target is an employee. For these reasons, it's usually better to access context through formal parameters.

## Advice and Exceptions

AspectJ places restrictions on exceptions thrown from advice. These restrictions are similar to the restrictions placed on overriding methods in traditional Java. The rationale is the same: If a class calls System.out.println, it doesn't expect the method to throw a SQLException. Java's exception-handling policy mandates that checked exceptions must be declared in throws clauses. For that reason, you can't subclass PrintStream and throw a SQLException in your version of println. To maintain compatibility with the Java language, AspectJ must enforce similar restrictions on advice. Listing 7.6 (additions to AddSourceInfo) contains troublesome advice that might violate these rules.

```
before(Object msg) : logCalls() && args(msg){
    writeToDatabase(msg);
}

private void writeToDatabase(Object message)
    throws SQLException
{
    if(Math.random() > .5){
        throw new SQLException("DB unavailable.");
    }
}
```

**Listing 7.6** An addition to AddSourceInfo that causes problems.

If you compile the code in Listing 7.6, the compiler complains that the SQLException is not handled by the advice. You can address this issue by adding a throws clause to the advice declaration:

```
before(Object msg) throws SQLException :
        logCalls() && args(msg) {...}
```

However, the advice still violates Java's exception policy because a println should not throw a SQLException. Unfortunately, there's no easy way around this problem. Because PrintStream.println does not declare *throws SQLException*, any advice that applies to that method cannot throw it either. To solve this problem, advice must catch and handle the exception, or it can use AspectJ's exception-softening capabilities (see Chapter 8, "Inter-type Declarations").

### The Rules

To be explicit, the rules for advice and exceptions are

- Advice must declare any checked exceptions it can throw in a throws clause (just like a method).

- Advice cannot throw an exception that would be illegal for one of its join points to throw. (This means that all RuntimeExceptions are legal.)

#### What Can a Join Point Throw?

For cases such as the example in Listing 7.6, figuring out what exceptions are legal is a snap. Method and constructor-based join points can only throw exceptions that appear in their throws clauses. Other join points have less obvious rules. Here are the exceptions that each type of join point can throw:

- Method and constructor call and execution join points can throw exceptions declared in the relevant throws clause.

- Object initialization join points can throw exceptions declared in every constructor in the class.

- Field access and static initialization join points cannot throw any checked exceptions.

- Handler join points can throw any exceptions that may be thrown from the body of the specified handler. In other words, advice that applied to the following handler block could throw a SQLException but not an IOException:

```
catch(Exception e){
    if(someCondition){
        throw new SQLException("Database not up.");
    }
}
```

## Types of Advice: An Overview

Now that we've covered topics that apply to all types of advice, we'll discuss the three different types of advice. We'll postpone a consideration of advice precedence until the end of the chapter, because that discussion requires familiarity with the operation of different advice types.

The types of advice are distinguished by when they run relative to the join points they affect:

- **Before** advice runs *before* each affected join point. It's the simplest type of advice.

- **After** advice runs *after* the join point and comes in three flavors:

  - **Unqualified** after advice runs no matter what the outcome of the join point.

  - **After returning** advice runs only if the join point returned normally (and it can perform additional matching based on the type of the value returned).

  - **After throwing** advice executes if the join point ended by throwing an exception (and it can perform additional matching based on type of the exception thrown).

- **Around** advice is the most intrusive. It runs *instead of* the join point and has the ability to invoke the join point (if it chooses) using the special proceed() syntax.

**NOTE**

**The distinction is subtle, but around advice runs instead of the join point and any advice of lower precedence that affects the join point. The advice of lower precedence may be thought of as part of the join point for the purpose of advice of higher precedence. See the section "Advice Precedence" for further details.**

Certain types of advice fit some concerns better than others. For instance, it's too late to prevent a join point from happening if you use after advice. As another example, around advice is your only choice if you need to alter a join point's arguments. The next three sections will explore the types of advice and offer examples of their use.

## Before Advice

Most of the advice you've seen so far has been before advice. We've used it because it's the simplest. It doesn't have additional matching criteria (like after), nor does it have the power to alter join point context (like around). It simply runs before the join point in question. Its syntax is as follows:

```
BeforeAdvice ::= before "(" [Formals] ")"
                 [throws TypeList] ":"
                 Pointcut "{" [AdviceBody] "}"
```

# Uses

Before advice excels at pre-conditions. Any time you think to yourself, "Before X happens, I must do Y," action Y represents a good concern for before advice. Two common before concerns are argument checking and setup code. In another example, the first aspect in the chapter uses before's time-of-execution to ensure that before a call to println happens, another print prepends information to the print stream.

The lazy-initialization pattern represents a more complicated example of the sort of concern that before can address. Most OO programmers have used this pattern. Lazy initialization defers the initialization of a field until just before it's used. This pattern can postpone or eliminate expensive set-up code that may not need to run in all circumstances. In OO languages, the pattern is accomplished by encapsulating the field—the accessor method initializes the field if it has not already been initialized.

As an example, examine Listing 7.7. The listing shows a simple class that uses a (expensive to construct) Connection to an external resource.

```
public class DataAccessor {

    Connection conn;

    public void getRecords(){
        conn.fetch("some-arg");
    }

    private Connection obtainConnection(){
        return new Connection();
    }

    public static void main(String[] args){
        new DataAccessor().getRecords();
    }
}
//output (without further modification)
Exception in thread "main"
java.lang.NullPointerException
    at lazy.DataAccessor.getRecords(DataAccessor.java:9)
    at lazy.DataAccessor.main(DataAccessor.java:17)
```

**Listing 7.7**  The DataAccessor class is a candidate for lazy initialization.

From the NullPointerException in the output, you can see that conn has not been initialized before use. Suppose that you want to initialize it, but not until a method uses it. To do so using OO techniques, you'd write an accessor like this:

```
private Connection getConnection(){
    if(conn == null){
        conn = obtainConnection();
    }
    return conn;
}
```

The method getRecords() (and any other user of the field) could use conn in the following manner:

```
public void getRecords(){
    getConnection().fetch("some-arg");
}
```

The disadvantage of this pattern is that you must remember to use it everywhere. If even a single method forgets to go through the accessor, the result may be an exception like the one shown in Listing 7.7.

Using before advice to initialize the field allows the weaver to do your remembering for you. Listing 7.8 shows an aspect that uses before advice to ensure that the conn field is initialized before any code uses it.

```
public class DataAccessor {

    Connection conn;

    public void getRecords(){
        conn.fetch("some-arg");
    }

    public static void main(String[] args){
        new DataAccessor().getRecords();
    }

    public static aspect LazyInit {

        before(DataAccessor targ) :
            get(Connection conn) &&
```

**Listing 7.8** An aspect provides lazy initialization using before advice. (continues)

```
        target(targ) && ! within(LazyInit) {

        if(targ.conn == null){
            targ.conn = obtainConnection();
        }
    }

    private Connection obtainConnection(){
        return new Connection();
    }
    }
}
//output
Connection.java:6-Fetching with arg: some-arg
```

**Listing 7.8**  An aspect provides lazy initialization using before advice. (continued)

The aspect appears as a static inner aspect of DataAccessor because it affects the class in an intimate way. For small-scope aspects such as this, including them as static inner aspects allows them to stay near code they affect.

The before advice uses an anonymous pointcut to select all accesses to the field conn (get(Connection conn)). It then limits itself to those field sets that have a target of DataAccessor and do not appear within the aspect itself (target(targ) && ! within(LazyInit)). Using the target pointcut also exposes the DataAccessor instance to the advice, allowing the advice to assign a new value to its conn field (targ.conn = obtainConnection()). As you can see from a message in the output, the fetch executes on the (initialized) Connection. Because the only initialization code appears in the before advice, the output signals that the advice has executed successfully.

Using AspectJ to lazily initialize a class with a single field access is probably overkill—especially when proven idioms exist in the OO realm. However, the weaver will not forget to advise the contents of a new method that someone adds to DataAccessor in five months. Furthermore, you've removed the responsibility for Connection initialization from the DataAccessor class. If you need to change the way the DataAccessor gets its connection, you need only change the LazyInit aspect. This structure allows additional flexibility.

### Stopping Unwanted Join Points

In addition to paving the way for join points by setting up state, before advice can also stop join points from executing if conditions aren't right. It does so by throwing an exception. This capability allows for flexible pre-condition checks.

To illustrate this capability, let's return to the personnel management application. For reasons of their own, management has decided only to allow raises of a minimum amount. Translating this requirement into technical terms, you decide to stop the execution of the raiseSalary method if the amount doesn't meet the minimum ($6000). Listing 7.9 shows the example code that exercises the new capabilities.

```
public class Example {
    public static void main(String[] args){
        raiseAndCheck("Rebekah", 5000);
        raiseAndCheck("Omar", 6000);
        raiseAndCheck("Philipe", 7000);
    }

    private static void raiseAndCheck(String name,
                                     int raise){
        Employee e = new Employee(name, 50000);
        try {
            e.raiseSalary(raise);
        } catch (Exception ex) {
            System.out.println("Raise failed with " + ex);
        }
        System.out.println("After raise: " + e);
    }
}
//output--indicates all raises are applied
LogRaises.java:7-Employee Rebekah:$50,000.00 to receive raise of
5000
Example.java:16-After raise: Employee Rebekah:$55,000.00
LogRaises.java:7-Employee Omar:$50,000.00 to receive raise of
6000
Example.java:16-After raise: Employee Omar:$56,000.00
LogRaises.java:7-Employee Philipe:$50,000.00 to receive raise of
7000
Example.java:16-After raise: Employee Philipe:$57,000.00
```

**Listing 7.9**   The example will signal any exceptions to the console.

Astute readers may be asking themselves at this point why the example application takes care of checking the Employee's state and handling the resultant exception. Couldn't you do it with advice? The answer is that you can—and you will, in the section about after advice. (Feel free to skip ahead if you're interested.)

To implement the policy, you need to get access to the amount of a raise. Perhaps you could reuse the pointcut defined when logging the raises.

To accomplish this end, move the raises pointcut into its own aspect. You can see the result in Listing 7.10.

```
public aspect Raises {

    public pointcut raises(Employee emp, int amount) :
                    call(void raiseSalary(int)) &&
                    target(emp) && args(amount);

}
```

**Listing 7.10**   The Raises aspect now defines the raises pointcut.

Defining the raises pointcut in a separate aspect allows any aspect to reference (and thus reuse) the pointcut. Because you've already written two aspects that need it, this seems like a sensible choice. (Note that the pointcut has not changed since we first saw it.)

The aspect that enforces the minimum raise policy appears in Listing 7.11.

```
public aspect MinimumRaisePolicy {

    private static final int MIN_INCREMENT = 6000;

    before(int increment) :
        Raises.raises(Employee, increment){

        if(increment < MIN_INCREMENT){
            throw new IllegalArgumentException("Raise of " +
            increment + " is less than department minimum.");
        }
    }
}
//output from Example's main method
Example.java:19-Raise failed with java.lang.IllegalArgumentException: Raise
of 5000 is less than

  department minimum.
Example.java:21-After raise: Employee Rebekah:$50,000.00

LogRaises.java:7-Employee Omar:$50,000.00 to receive raise of
  6000
Example.java:21-After raise: Employee Omar:$56,000.00

LogRaises.java:7-Employee Philipe:$50,000.00 to receive raise of
  7000
Example.java:21-After raise: Employee Philipe:$57,000.00
```

**Listing 7.11**   This aspect throws an exception if the raise amount is lower than the minimum.

At each raise join point, the advice in MinimumRaisePolicy executes. The advice inspects the amount of the raise (passed into the advice as a formal parameter) and throws an exception if the amount is too low. The output indicates that the advice operates correctly. On the first line, a printout from the exception handler block indicates that the $5000 raise caused an exception. The next line indicates that Omar's raise met the criteria and proceeded successfully.

### Logging Failure: An Unintended Side Effect

If you look more closely at the output, you'll notice a side effect of the new aspect: Rebekah's raise was not logged. MinimumRaisePolicy's advice suppressed the advice from LogRaises: The new advice executed before the advice written earlier. When MinimumRaisePolicy threw an exception, it prevented LogRaises' advice from executing just as effectively as it prevented the actual raise. This sort of situation can arise whenever two pieces of advice apply to the same join point. Fortunately, AspectJ allows you to specify which advice takes precedence. The final section of the chapter, "Advice Precedence," covers this topic in detail.

For the moment, you can solve this problem by adding the following line to the Raises aspect:

```
declare precedence : LogRaises, *;
```

This line uses a declare form (more on that topic in Chapter 8) to specify that LogRaises' advice takes precedence over advice defined in any other aspect (hence the *). Now the output correctly logs the failed raise:

```
LogRaises.java:7-Employee Rebekah:$50,000.00 to receive raise of
5000
Example.java:19-Raise failed with
  java.lang.IllegalArgumentException: Raise of 5000 is less than
  department minimum.
Example.java:21-After raise: Employee Rebekah:$50,000.00
```

### Is an Exception Appropriate?

We set ourselves up to succeed with this example by inserting a catch block into the example code. If we had not, the IllegalArgumentException would have terminated the main method of the Example class. Because IllegalArgumentException is an unchecked exception, there's no automatic way for a caller to know that it should be caught. (Keep in mind that you could not convert it to a checked exception without modifying Employee—see the section on advice and exceptions.) These issues shouldn't scare you away from using exceptions to halt join points; however, throwing one may not be the right action to take. In these cases, around advice can implement a more flexible response.

### Increased Modularity with Advice

Despite the issues we've raised, adding this business rule as an aspect rather than putting it directly into the component code has led to an increase in modularity. The Employee class does not involve itself in the distinction between legal and illegal raises. You've separated the concern of "raise legality" from the concern of "applying the raise." By separating the concerns, you can alter or replace each of them in isolation. Employee could be deployed in a different department, incorporated into a system with no departmental policy, or used in a situation with completely different rules about what defines an allowable raise. For instance, a different departmental policy aspect could request that a Manager object pre-authorize the change in salary.

# After Advice

The overview earlier in the chapter shed a little light on the three different types of after advice. This section will illuminate the issue further using examples.

## After (Unqualified)

Unqualified after advice (after advice without an additional throwing or returning qualifier) executes after the join points it affects, regardless of the outcome. Because of this guarantee, unqualified after advice behaves as if it were called from a finally block:

```
try{
    //original join point
}
finally{
    //unqualified after advice
}
```

Sometimes this is the desired behavior, but often it's not. For instance, if you're attempting to notify the Payroll system that an employee just got a raise, you probably wish to notify the system only if the raise was successful. In that case, after returning and throwing offer more precise matching of advice to circumstance.

### Mandatory Cleanup Using After Unqualified

In some situations it makes sense to execute advice regardless of the outcome. Users of JDBC will no doubt spot one: In order to conserve database resources, database connections must be closed as soon as their users are through with them. Connection pooling has helped with this situation, but (similarly) the connection must be returned to the pool after use. Let's look back at the DataAccessor class and see if after advice can help you remember to close connections.

Listing 7.12 simulates an open/closed state on the Connection object (we've avoided using the actual JDBC classes for simplicity).

```
public class Connection {
    private boolean isOpen;

    public void fetch(String arg) {
        if(! isOpen){
            throw new IllegalStateException("closed");
        }
        System.out.println("Fetching with arg: " + arg);
    }

        public void riskyFetch() {
            throw new RuntimeException("Bad fetch.");
        }

    public void open(){
        System.out.println("Opening.");
        this.isOpen = true;
    }

    public void close(){
        System.out.println("Closing.");
        this.isOpen = false;
    }
}
//changes to DataAccessor
public void getOtherRecords(){
    conn.riskyFetch();
}

public static void main(String[] args){
    DataAccessor accessor = new DataAccessor();

    accessor.getRecords();
    accessor.getOtherRecords();
}

//output from DataAccessor's main
Exception in thread "main" java.lang.IllegalStateException:
closed
        at lazy.Connection.fetch(Connection.java:8)
        at lazy.DataAccessor.getRecords(DataAccessor.java:9)
        at lazy.DataAccessor.main(DataAccessor.java:13)
```

**Listing 7.12** Connection maintains open/closed state.

Whoops. It looks like you'll need some before advice to open the connection as well as after advice to close it. Listing 7.13 contains the advice for the aspect you'd like to write.

```
public aspect ConnectionState {

    pointcut connectionUses(DataAccessor user):
            /* How should you define this pointcut? */ ;

    after(DataAccessor user) : connectionUses(user){
        user.conn.close();
    }

    before(DataAccessor user) : connectionUses(user){
        user.conn.open();
    }
}
```

**Listing 7.13**  The ConnectionState aspect opens the connection before use and closes it afterward.

As you can see, the aspect is incomplete. To figure out when to open and close the connection, you need to construct a pointcut. The pointcut should encapsulate the idea of connection use. In other words, it should pick out join points that use the connection so that you can open before those join points and close afterward. Unfortunately, selecting when an object is used is a tricky thing. An object can begin use when a client calls one of its methods. Picking out when it leaves use is harder. As humans, we have an intuitive sense of *leaves use* because we can see the intent of the program. However, we want to eliminate the human factor in this example.

There are several ways to write the sort of pointcut you're looking for. One of the simplest is also the most arbitrary. You can specify that the connection will be used by every public method on DataAccessor, and that its use will end once the method terminates:

```
pointcut connectionUses(DataAccessor user):
        this(user) && execution(public * *(..));
```

The pointcut glosses over some potential issues (for instance, what if DataAccessor gives its connection to another class to use?). However, it covers most cases reasonably well. With the new aspect in place, you can execute DataAccessor's main again and inspect the results:

```
Connection.java:14-Opening.
Connection.java:10-Fetching with arg: some-arg
Connection.java:19-Closing.
```

```
Connection.java:14-Opening.
Connection.java:19-Closing.
Exception in thread "main" java.lang.RuntimeException: Bad fetch.
    at lazy.Connection.riskyFetch(Connection.java:24)
    at lazy.DataAccessor.getOtherRecords(DataAccessor.java:13)
    at lazy.DataAccessor.main(DataAccessor.java:20)
```

The first line of the output indicates that the pointcut has correctly matched DataAccessor's fetch() method and that the before advice opened the connection. The fetch method can now execute without an exception. Immediately after fetch(), the after advice executes, closing the connection. Then the connection is reopened for riskyFetch(). Immediately afterward, it's closed. The stack trace at the end of the output shows that riskyFetch() threw an Exception, which was correctly propagated to the main method. Because you saw the *Closing* printout, you know the connection was closed despite the exception.

### Automated Clean Up Saves Code

In order to get the same behavior from a non-aspect-aware system, you would need to insert try-catch-finally blocks into all the methods on DataAccessor that used the connection. Doing so reduces readability, increases tedium, and prevents easy modification of behavior (what if the connection must be returned to a pool instead of closed?). With a little unqualified after advice, the policy of closing connections after every method (regardless of outcome) becomes clear.

### Will After Always Execute?

Despite the guarantee that unqualified after advice will execute regardless of whether the join point returns normally, in some situations advice precedence can prevent it from happening. Be sure to study the section on advice precedence carefully, because the effects of advice on other advice can be counterintuitive at first.

## After Throwing

In many cases, the guarantees of unqualified after advice don't fit the situation. For the next example, let's return to employee raises. Once an employee has received a raise, certain consequences follow: Budgets need updating, the payroll system needs to recalculate the employee's paycheck, the employee needs to get an email informing them of their new salary, and so on. Alternatively, if a raise fails, the employee's manager may need to be notified (perhaps there's something the manager can do to resolve the problem). After advice fits these post-effect needs perfectly, but it must know which situation applies—did the raise succeed or fail? After returning and after throwing advice execute only in the case of failure or success, respectively. This allows aspects to tailor their advice to the post–join point situation.

Let's begin with failure. If a raise fails, you want to log its failure. You can use after throwing to accomplish this.

### Logging All Failed Raises: After Throwing

Listing 7.14 shows a piece of after advice that will execute only if a raise fails.

```
public aspect FailedRaisePolicy{

    after(Employee emp, int amount) throwing :
        Raises.raises(emp, amount){

        System.out.println("Raise of " + amount +
            " failed on " + emp);
    }
}

//changes to example class--no need to log exceptions
//anymore
private static void raiseAndCheck(String name,
                                    int raise){
    Employee e = new Employee(name, 50000);
    try {

        e.raiseSalary(raise);
    } catch (Exception ex) {/*logged by advice*/}
    System.out.println("After raise: " + e);
    System.out.println();//space out the output
}

//output
LogRaises.java:7-Employee Rebekah:$50,000.00 to receive raise of
  5000
FailedRaisePolicy.java:10-Raise of 5000 failed on Employee
  Rebekah:$50,000.00
Example.java:19-After raise: Employee Rebekah:$50,000.00

LogRaises.java:7-Employee Omar:$50,000.00 to receive raise of
  6000
Example.java:19-After raise: Employee Omar:$56,000.00
LogRaises.java:7-Employee Philipe:$50,000.00 to receive raise of
  51000
[...]
```

**Listing 7.14** FailedRaisePolicy uses after throwing to detect an exception thrown from a raise join point.

Again, the aspect reuses the pointcut from Raises. After each raise that throws an exception, the advice executes, printing a message.

## NOTE

**In order to get the advice to execute after the failures, you must alter the precedence situation. The revised line in the Raises aspect reads declare precedence : LogRaises, FailedRaisePolicy, *;. This means FailedRaisePolicy comes second only to LogRaises when determining precedence.**

### Using the Thrown Exception

If you examine the output, it looks like you lost information: You no longer know why a raise failed. Fortunately, AspectJ allows you to pass the thrown exception into the after advice. Listing 7.15 illustrates the syntax.

```
public aspect FailedRaisePolicy{

    after(Employee emp, int amount)
        throwing (Exception e) :
        Raises.raises(emp, amount){

        System.out.println("Raise of " + amount +
            " failed on " + emp + " because of " + e);
    }
}

//output
LogRaises.java:7-Employee Rebekah:$50,000.00 to receive raise of
5000
FailedRaisePolicy.java:11-Raise of 5000 failed on Employee
  Rebekah:$50,000.00 because of
  java.lang.IllegalArgumentException:
  Raise of 5000 is less than department minimum.
Example.java:19-After raise: Employee Rebekah:$50,000.00

LogRaises.java:7-Employee Omar:$50,000.00 to receive raise of
  6000
Example.java:19-After raise: Employee Omar:$56,000.00

[...]
```

**Listing 7.15**  After throwing advice can access the thrown exception.

The bold text shows how to turn the exception thrown from the join point into an extra formal parameter. The output shows that the exception arrives successfully at the advice. Now someone inspecting the log knows why a given raise failed.

## Notifying the Manager: After Throwing(...)

To spice up the example, let's say you want to notify an employee's manager of specific failures. Currently, there's only one cause of failure: Employees cannot receive raises of less than $6,000. So, before you can selectively notify the manager, let's introduce another error condition.

### Adding a New Error Condition

Imagine that HR has strict rules about maximum salaries. Any salary greater than $100,000 needs special authorization. Because this rule is similar to the earlier raise rule, it should be easy to build this aspect. Listing 7.16 contains the code. (Keep in mind that you're just setting the stage for later notification advice.)

```
public aspect MaxSalaryPolicy {

    private static final int MAX_SALARY = 100000;

    before(Employee emp, int amount) :
        Raises.raises(emp, amount){

        int newSalary = emp.getSalary() +
                        amount;

        if(newSalary > MAX_SALARY){
            throw new SalaryCapException("New salary "
                    + newSalary + " exceeds maximum.");
        }
    }

}

//change to Example.main()
public static void main(String[] args){
    raiseAndCheck("Rebekah", 5000);
    raiseAndCheck("Omar", 6000);
    raiseAndCheck("Philipe", 51000);//over cap
}

//output
LogRaises.java:7-Employee Philipe:$50,000.00 to receive raise of
  51000
Example.java:19-Raise failed with raises.SalaryCapException: New
  salary 101000 exceeds maximum.
Example.java:21-After raise: Employee Philipe:$50,000.00
```

**Listing 7.16** An aspect that introduces a new error condition.

If a caller attempts to raise the employee's salary beyond $100,000, the new advice throws a SalaryCapException (SalaryCapException extends Runtime-Exception so that the advice does not violate the throws contract of raiseSalary()).

### Detecting the New Error

In addition to passing the thrown exception into the advice, adding a formal parameter to the throwing clause narrows the scope of the advice. The advice executes only on those join points that throw an exception of the specified type. In other words, if you use after() throwing(SalaryCapException e), you will effectively write advice that executes only if the new error condition occurs. Listing 7.17 contains a new piece of advice that uses this facility.

```
//new after advice added to FailedRaisePolicy
after(Employee emp)
    throwing (SalaryCapException e) :
    Raises.raises(emp, int){

    emp.getManager().notify("Raise failed for " +
        emp.getName() + "--see log.");
}

//changes to Example--give everyone a Manager to notify
private static Manager shelly =
    new Manager("Shelly", 80000);

public static void main(String[] args){
    raiseAndCheck("Rebekah", 5000);
    raiseAndCheck("Omar", 6000);
    raiseAndCheck("Philipe", 51000);
    }

private static void raiseAndCheck(String name,
                                  int raise){
    Employee e = new Employee(name, 50000);
    e.setManager(shelly);

    try {

        e.raiseSalary(raise);
    } catch (Exception ex) {}
    System.out.println("After raise: " + e);
    System.out.println();//space out the output
}

//output
```

**Listing 7.17** After throwing can execute based on which exception was thrown. (continues)

```
LogRaises.java:7-Employee Rebekah:$50,000.00 to receive raise of
  5000
FailedRaisePolicy.java:19-Raise of 5000 failed on Employee
  Rebekah:$50,000.00 because of
  java.lang.IllegalArgumentException:
  Raise of 5000 is less than department minimum.
Example.java:25-After raise: Employee Rebekah:$50,000.00

LogRaises.java:7-Employee Omar:$50,000.00 to receive raise of
  6000
Example.java:25-After raise: Employee Omar:$56,000.00

LogRaises.java:7-Employee Philipe:$50,000.00 to receive raise of
  51000
Manager.java:12-Shelly notified of:
Manager.java:13--->Raise failed for Philipe--see log.
FailedRaisePolicy.java:19-Raise of 51000 failed on Employee
  Philipe:$50,000.00 because of raises.SalaryCapException: New
  salary 101000 exceeds maximum.
Example.java:25-After raise: Employee Philipe:$50,000.00
```

**Listing 7.17** After throwing can execute based on which exception was thrown. (continued)

The important parts of Listing 7.17 are highlighted. Each employee now has a manger with a simple notify(String) method. The new after advice specifies throwing(SalaryCapException e) instead of throwing (Exception e). From looking at the output, you can see that Shelly was only notified of the raise failure for the Philipe (the over-the-limit raise). Notice that the first advice (the one that simply logs the failure) still takes effect. It detects both exceptional terminations, because both IllegalArgumentException and SalaryCapException subclass Exception. If the join point had failed with an Error then neither advice would have executed.

## After Returning

Let's look at an example of how you might use after returning to implement the opposite sort of concern: notifying the payroll system of a *successful* raise. Listing 7.18 contains the code for a simple aspect that informs the legacy payroll system of a raise event.

```
public aspect NotifyPayroll {

    after(Employee emp) returning :
        Raises.raises(emp, int){
```

**Listing 7.18** NotifyPayroll uses after returning to send information about successful raises. (continues)

```
        getPayrollServer().recalculatePaycheck(
            emp.getName(), emp.getSalary()
        );
    }

    private PayrollServer getPayrollServer(){
        return new PayrollServer("PayrollServer1");
    }
}

//output
LogRaises.java:7-Employee Rebekah:$50,000.00 to receive raise of
  5000
FailedRaisePolicy.java:19-Raise of 5000 failed on Employee
  Rebekah:$50,000.00 because of
  java.lang.IllegalArgumentException:
  Raise of 5000 is less than department minimum.
Example.java:25-After raise: Employee Rebekah:$50,000.00

LogRaises.java:7-Employee Omar:$50,000.00 to receive raise of
  6000
PayrollServer.java:12-PayrollServer1
PayrollServer.java:13-Recalculating paycheck for Omar
PayrollServer.java:15-New salary : 56000
Example.java:25-After raise: Employee Omar:$56,000.00

LogRaises.java:7-Employee Philipe:$50,000.00 to receive raise of
  51000
Manager.java:12-Shelly notified of:
Manager.java:13--->Raise failed for Philipe--see log.
FailedRaisePolicy.java:19-Raise of 51000 failed on Employee
  Philipe:$50,000.00 because of raises.SalaryCapException: New
  salary 101000 exceeds maximum.
Example.java:25-After raise: Employee Philipe:$50,000.00
```

**Listing 7.18**  NotifyPayroll uses after returning to send information about successful raises. (continued)

The after advice in NotifyPayroll specifies *returning* and therefore executes only when the raise completes successfully. The output indicates that only news of Omar's (successful) raise reached PayrollServer.

## Using the Return Value

Like after throwing, after returning can pass an extra formal into the advice body by using the form "returning (*SomeType t*)". Again, the advice will execute only if the type of the join point's return value matches *SomeType*. If you specify "returning (Object o)", the advice will match *all* types, including primitives and void returns. Primitives are boxed to Java wrapper types just like other formals. Void returns results in the formal containing null. You can see this if you change the advice a little (as a demonstration):

```
after(Employee emp) returning (Object o):
    Raises.raises(emp, int){

    System.out.println("Returned " + o);
    getPayrollServer().recalculatePaycheck(
        emp.getName(), emp.getSalary()
    );
}
//output
LogRaises.java:7-Employee Omar:$50,000.00 to receive raise of
  6000
NotifyPayroll.java:10-Returned null
PayrollServer.java:12-PayrollServer1
PayrollServer.java:13-Recalculating paycheck for Omar
PayrollServer.java:15-New salary : 56000
Example.java:25-After raise: Employee Omar:$56,000.00
```

### What Constitutes the Return Value?

Now that you know how to inspect the return value of a join point, you can ask, "What is the return value?" Method execution and call join points return the value returned by the relevant method (barring any around advice). The return values of other join points are not so intuitive. Here is a list of other join points and their return values:

**Object construction/initialization.** Most of the join points involved in the construction of a new object (including initialization, static initialization, and constructor execution) return null. The important exception to this rule is that (outermost) constructor calls return the object that was constructed. This makes sense, because the object construction process does not complete until the constructor returns. Returning the object any earlier would return the object in the middle of creation.

**Field access.** Field get join points return the value of the field after the field access completes. In other words, for the following snippet

```
Employee.salary = 100;
someLocalVariable = Employee.salary;
```

the get join point for Employee.salary would return 100.

**Field assignment.** These join points do not return a value. (This is a change from AspectJ 1.0.x, in which assignment join points returned the new value of the field.)

**Handler.** Handler join points cannot be the targets of after returning advice. This limitation may be addressed in future releases of AspectJ, but some thorny issues surround the definition of what it means to return from a handler block. As an exercise, consider the following:

```
//is this a return?
catch(Exception e){
    doSomething();
}
//or is this?
catch(Exception e){
    doSomething();
    return -1;
}
```

### Illegal Matches

Like many areas, after returning/throwing advice allows you to specify a combination of parameters and pointcuts that does not match any join points in your system. For example, the following advice (in the NotifyPayroll aspect) could never run:

```
after() returning (int neverHappens):
        Raises.raises(Employee, int){

    System.out.println("***Never happens.");
}
```

Because none of the join points selected by raises returns an int, this advice cannot execute after anything. However, as of this writing, AspectJ will allow it the advice to compile.

# Around Advice

Around advice is both the most complicated and the most powerful type of advice. Its name suggests that it runs both before and after the join point. Although this can be true, with around advice, the join point may not run at all. Around advice actually runs *instead* of the join point. (Keep in mind that the join point includes any advice of lower precedence that plans to run at the join point.) Around offers the special proceed() form so the advice can invoke the original join point when (and if) it chooses. Because it has control over the underlying join point, around advice can implement invasive changes in your code. You can do such things as replace a field access with a method call, change the target of a method, or alter a constructor's arguments.

# Replacing getProperty() Calls

Let's begin with a simple example. Most programmers who've worked with Java have used java.util.Properties to get basic runtime configuration information. Imagine you're using a properties object to provide messages for an application. Look at the example code and output in Listing 7.19.

```
public static void main(String[] args) {

    Properties props = new Properties();
    props.setProperty("msg1", "Hello");

    System.out.println("Value of msg1 " +
        props.getProperty("msg1"));

    System.out.println("Value of msg2 " +
            props.getProperty("msg2"));
}

//output
Value of msg1 Hello
Value of msg2 null
```

**Listing 7.19**   Properties returns null if a property isn't defined.

Because the marketing department gives regular demonstrations of the unfinished application to the customer, it doesn't want an unfriendly *null* to appear where instructions should be. So, marketing asks you to provide a reasonable default. Rather than manually modifying tens of calls to getProperty, you decide to use AspectJ. With around advice, you can make some intelligent decisions based on whether the returned value from the Properties object was null. Listing 7.20 contains the pointcut and advice you use.

```
pointcut getProp(String key, Properties p) :
    call(String getProperty(String)) &&
    target(p) && args(key) &&
    ! within(NullPropertyHandler);

String around(String key, Properties p) :
    getProp(key, p){

    String result = p.getProperty(key);
```

**Listing 7.20**   Around advice can return a value other than the one originally intended. (continues)

```
    if(result == null){
        return "Instructions go here.";
    }
    else {
        return result;
    }
}

//output
Value of msg1 Hello
Value of msg2 Instructions go here.
```

**Listing 7.20**  Around advice can return a value other than the one originally intended. (continued)

The getProp() pointcut should not contain any surprises. It selects all calls to getProperty where the target is a Properties object. Both the target and the key are exposed so that you can replace the call.

The advice contains a few new elements. Specifically, it declares a return type and returns a value. These elements are necessary because the advice replaces a method call. In order to integrate with the target code, the advice must observe the same contract as the join point it replaces. Because all join points technically return results (even if the result is null or void), around advice must return them as well.

## NOTE

**Experienced AspectJ users may wonder why the example doesn't use proceed(). Don't worry; we'll refactor it in a moment.**

The body of the advice is straightforward. When a getProperty call is encountered, the advice executes. It makes a different call to getProperty with the same argument. If the result is null, it returns a default result instead. The output confirms that the advice behaves correctly: The property msg1 maps correctly, and the value of the property msg2 becomes the default.

### Implications of Replacing Join Points

Around advice can be confusing. Imagine the following code in a system with NullPropertyHandler applied:

```
if(props.getProperty("baz") == null){
    doSomething();
}else{
    doSomethingElse();
}
```

Because of the advice in NullPropertyHandler, getProperty will *never* return null. Therefore, doSomethingElse() will never execute, even if the property baz has no mapping.

As tools support for AspectJ grows, it should be increasingly apparent when advice affects a call such as getProperty. As an example of a tool-based reminder, examine Figure 7.1, which shows the Properties example in the graphical structure browser. Location 1 shows a list of all the method call sites affected by the around advice. Double-clicking on a call site opens the affected source in the right pane (location 2).

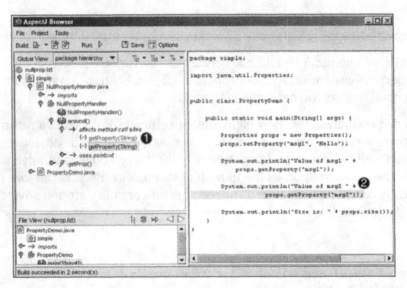

**Figure 7.1**    The AspectJ browser shows which methods are affected by NullPropertyHandler's advice.

Despite increased tool support, replacing join points entirely can still be confusing—proceed with care.

## Returning from Before and After

Having seen a return from around advice, you may wonder whether before and after advice can return values. The answer is no. Before and after advice behave like void methods. They can contain a return statement, but it serves only to forward control flow out of the advice. As an example, you can rewrite one of the raise advices like this:

```
//old
before(int increment) :
    Raises.raises(Employee, increment){
```

```
        if(increment < MIN_INCREMENT){
            throw new IllegalArgumentException("Raise of " +
            increment + " is less than department minimum.");
        }
    }

    //new, with return
    before(int increment) :
        Raises.raises(Employee, increment){

        if(increment >= MIN_INCREMENT){
            return;
        }
        throw new IllegalArgumentException("Raise of " +
        increment + " is less than department minimum.");
    }
```

## Proceed()

In the introduction to this section, we hinted at proceed()—the syntax that allows around advice to execute the original join point. If you think about NullPropertyHandler's advice, you'll see that we spent considerable effort recreating the original call. We had to get the target object and then execute the method we knew we were replacing. For our simple example, it worked. For more complicated pointcuts that select many method calls (or even different kinds of join points), it would be difficult to manually re-create the original join point. The proceed() form solves this problem by shifting the burden of invoking the original join point onto AspectJ. In the next example, you'll rewrite Null-PropertyHandler to use proceed()—Listing 7.21 contains the code.

```
public aspect NullPropertyHandler {

    pointcut getProp() :
        call(String getProperty(String));

    String around() : getProp(){

        String result = proceed();

        if(result == null){
            return "Instructions go here.";
        }
```

**Listing 7.21** Proceed() invokes the original join point. (continues)

```
        else {
            return result;
        }
    }


}
//output
Value of msg1 Hello
Value of msg2 Instructions go here.
```

**Listing 7.21**  Proceed() invokes the original join point. (continued)

The first thing you may notice is what's missing: The pointcut and advice no longer have to worry about the target and arguments of the original method call. The pointcut does not expose them, and the advice does not take them as formal parameters.

Instead of making the method call within the advice, the advice now uses proceed(). The proceed form acts like a method call: It takes as parameters any formals passed to the advice (in this case, none) and returns a value typed to the return type of the advice. (In this example, proceed() returns a String.)

**NOTE**

**The getProp() pointcut also omits the !within(NullPropertyHandler) pointcut. There's no need to include it, because the aspect does not advise proceed(). Using proceed() does not count as a new occurrence of the join point—only a modification of the control flow that leads to the original join point.**

The rest of the advice remains unchanged. It inspects the return value of proceed() (in this case, the result of the original call to getProperty) and returns either the normal or the default value as before. As you'll notice, the output is equivalent.

## More on Return Values

Now that you've seen around and proceed in action, it's worth exploring some of the subtleties of around's return capabilities.

### Compatibility with Join Points

The return type of around advice must be compatible with the return type of the join points it replaces. In other words, you could declare the advice in Null-PropertyHandler like this

```
    Object around() : ...
```

because Object is a supertype of String. Therefore, the return type of the advice is compatible with the return type of the original. However, you couldn't declare the return type as "int", because the only join point affected has a return type of String. Around advice that only affects void-returning pointcuts may declare a return type of void.

If you declare a wider return type (such as Object), AspectJ will do you the favor of casting the return value back to the appropriate type after the advice executes. Naturally, this means that if you return the wrong type, you'll get a ClassCastException at runtime. For instance, if you changed the advice to

```
Object around(...) : ... {//omitting the details

//matches at compile time--Integer is an Object
    return new Integer(-1);
}
```

your output would be

```
Exception in thread "main" java.lang.ClassCastException:
    java.lang.Integer
        at simple.PropertyDemo.main(PropertyDemo.java:14)
```

Although the return was legal at compile time, it was illegal at runtime. In addition to casting, AspectJ will also unbox wrapper types when appropriate. That means the following pieces of around are functionally equivalent:

```
//Object-typed return
Object around(): call(int size()) {
    return new Integer(-1);
}
//int-typed return
int around(): call(int size()) {
    return -1;
}
//example code
System.out.println("Size is: " + props.size());

//output--in either case
Size is: -1
```

You may wonder why you'd need to type around's return to Object when you can use the exact type (such as int). For advice that applies to a single method, precision is indeed better. However, imagine the following pointcut:

```
pointcut allMethods(): call(* *(..));
```

You might need such a pointcut if you were providing security or comprehensive logging. In this case, the only return type that matches *all* the join points is Object.

### The Return Value of Proceed()

As stated in the example, proceed() returns a value that's typed to the return type of the advice. In other words, you could rewrite the NullPropertyHandler advice like this:

```
Object around() : getProp(){
    String result = (String)proceed();
    //...
}
```

The cast becomes necessary because the return type of proceed is now Object (to match the return type of the advice).

If you're dealing with heterogeneous return types, AspectJ will box the return value of proceed() just as it does with after advice. As a short example, look at the following advice applied to the Properties example:

```
pointcut allMethods():
    call(* *(..)) && target(Properties);

Object around() : allMethods(){
    Object result = proceed();
    System.out.println("Result of "
        + thisJoinPoint.toShortString()
        +" was: " + result);
    return result;
}
//output
Result of call(Properties.setProperty(..)) was: null
Result of call(Properties.getProperty(..)) was: Hello
Value of msg1 Hello
Result of call(Properties.getProperty(..)) was: null
Value of msg2 Instructions go here.
Result of call(Hashtable.size()) was: 1
Size is: 1
```

As you can see, proceed() returns null for void methods (see the first printout). The call to proceed() also boxes primitives (see the result of the call to int size()). For more details about return values, see the earlier section on after returning advice.

## Altering Context with Proceed()

So far, you've only altered the return value of a join point. That represents significant power. However, around advice can also change the context in which a join point executes. With proceed(), you can alter the arguments and target of a join point as well.

As an example, let's return to the employee management system. Let's say that constant outages on the payroll server plague the NotifyPayrollAspect. Raises are being denied because the servers are occasionally down. To remedy this situation, you'd like to retry the payroll notification with several of the company's payroll servers before giving up.

### Setting Up the Outages

The code you've written so far does not use an actual server—only a local object that couldn't possibly be down. To simulate the fictional problems experienced by the system, you'll use advice again. Check out Listing 7.22 for the code.

```
public aspect NetworkCalls {

    pointcut callsToServer(PayrollServer server) :
        call(public * PayrollServer+.*(..)) &&
        !call(new(..)) && !call(* get*()) &&
        target(server);

}


public aspect OutageSimulator {

    before() :
        NetworkCalls.callsToServer(PayrollServer){

        if(Math.random() > .5){
            throw new UnavailableException();
        }
    }
}

//output
LogRaises.java:7-Employee Omar:$50,000.00 to receive raise of
  6000
FailedRaisePolicy.java:19-Raise of 6000 failed on Employee
  Omar:$56,000.00 because of raises.UnavailableException
Example.java:25-After raise: Employee Omar:$56,000.00
```

**Listing 7.22** An aspect simulates server unavailability.

The definition of the pointcut (calls to any public method except the constructor) appears in a different aspect because you'll reuse it later. The advice in OutageSimulator throws an UnavailableException on 50 percent of these join points. You can see from the output that the simulated outage affected poor Omar—his representation as an Employee object now has a higher salary. Until the payroll server gets word of it, however, he won't see a dime.

You need to notice two points before we move on to the main example. First, AspectJ excels at simulating error conditions such as these. Often, when you're testing exception-handling code it's difficult to provoke an actual error. AspectJ gets around this problem by letting you simulate failures at any join point. Second, the only calls to the PayrollServer in this code come from the NotifyPayroll aspect. Aspects can advise each other. Anyone who has written advice that affects itself and ended up with a StackOverflowError will remember this, but it's worth keeping in mind in case you're tempted to think that aspects only affect component code.

### Retrying the Call with Around Advice

To get Omar his raise, you need to retry the failed method call on several different servers. You do this by using proceed() with different arguments. Look at the advice in Listing 7.23.

```
public aspect RetryNotifications {

    /**
     * In reality the server choices might
     * come from polling the network.
     */
    private PayrollServer[] servers =
        new PayrollServer[]
        {
            null,//placeholder for original target
            new PayrollServer("PayrollServer2"),
            new PayrollServer("PayrollServer3"),
            new PayrollServer("PayrollServer4"),
        };


    void around(PayrollServer original) :
        NetworkCalls.callsToServer(original){

        servers[0] = original;

        int count = 0;
        while(true){
            PayrollServer current = servers[count];
            try{
                System.out.println(
                "Attempting to send update to " +
                current.getName()
```

**Listing 7.23** RetryNotifications uses proceed() to try different servers in the event of failure. (continues)

```
            );
            proceed(current);
            return;//if successful
        }
    catch(UnavailableException e){
        System.out.println("Network failure");
        if(++count >= servers.length){
            System.out.println("Alternates failed.");
            throw e;
        }
        //continue
    }

    }//while
  }//advice
}

//change to NetworkCalls
declare precedence : RetryNotifications, *;

//output
LogRaises.java:7-Employee Omar:$50,000.00 to receive raise of
  6000
RetryNotifications.java:29-Attempting to send update to
  PayrollServer1
RetryNotifications.java:37-Network failure
RetryNotifications.java:29-Attempting to send update to
  PayrollServer2
PayrollServer.java:12-PayrollServer2
PayrollServer.java:13-Recalculating paycheck for Omar
PayrollServer.java:15-New salary : 56000
Example.java:25-After raise: Employee Omar:$56,000.00
```

**Listing 7.23** RetryNotifications uses proceed() to try different servers in the event of failure. (continued)

There are several things to notice in the example. The around advice declares a return type of void, because the NetworkCalls.callsToServer pointcut only selects join points with void return values. More important, the call to proceed() passes in a single argument of type PayrollServer. This requires some explanation.

Recall the pointcut that the advice uses:

```
pointcut callsToServer(PayrollServer server) :
    call(public * PayrollServer+.*(..)) &&
    !call(new(..)) && !call(* get*()) &&
    target(server);
```

The advice accepts the target of the join point as a formal parameter:

```
void around(PayrollServer original) :
    NetworkCalls.callsToServer(original){...}
```

Because the advice takes the target as a parameter, AspectJ requires that the join point invoked by proceed() receive a target of the same type. When proceed(current) executes, the join point call will happen with whatever target *current* references at the time. In other words, the advice will retry the method call on different servers until it succeeds (or runs out of options). In the output shown, the advice retries the call to recalculatePaycheck on Server2 when Server1 fails. Because the call to Server2 succeeds, the around advice returns, and execution continues normally. Omar gets his raise.

### Implications of Changing Targets with Around

In this case, switching the targets of a method call had few implications for the behavior of the system. Relatively speaking, the system behaves just as it did before the advice was applied (except it tolerates a higher degree of server unavailability). Despite this fact, the implications for how you think about programming are profound. A single method call has been (potentially) converted into several method calls—each with a different target.

You can imagine even wilder alterations. Remember the malicious (but ineffective) advice that redirected raises?

```
before(Employee emp): raises(emp, int){
    emp = new Employee("me", 60000);
}
```

It could work with around advice:

```
void around(Employee emp) : Raises.raises(emp, int){
        proceed(new Employee("me", 50000));
}
//output
LogRaises.java:11-Employee me:$50,000.00 to receive raise of 5000
```

In practice, this advice yields somewhat nonsensical results, but it serves for illustration.

## Altering This and Arguments

In addition to the target of a join point you can change two other pieces of context: the arguments and (in limited circumstances) the currently executing object (*this*).

## Changing This

You may wonder how much sense it makes to change the currently executing object. It depends what sort of join point you're using. For method execution join points, changing *this* acts like changing *target* for call join points. For instance, if you alter the callsToServer pointcut use execution() and this() instead of call() and target(), you get identical results:

```
pointcut callsToServer(PayrollServer server) :
    execution(public * PayrollServer+.*(..)) &&
    !execution(new(..)) && !execution(* get*()) &&
    this(server);
//output
LogRaises.java:7-Employee Omar:$50,000.00 to receive raise of
  6000
RetryNotifications.java:29-Attempting to send update to
  PayrollServer1
RetryNotifications.java:37-Network failure
RetryNotifications.java:29-Attempting to send update to
  PayrollServer2
PayrollServer.java:12-PayrollServer2
PayrollServer.java:13-Recalculating paycheck for Omar
PayrollServer.java:15-New salary : 56000
Example.java:25-After raise: Employee Omar:$56,000.00
```

This works because it makes sense to execute the method on another object. *This* becomes a surrogate *target*.

For almost every other type of join point, changing *this* makes less sense. Think of a method call that happens in Employee. The employee sends a notify message to their boss:

```
//in the (fictional) requestRaise() method
getManager().notify("I want a raise.");
//...method continues
```

The method call join point for that line has the following context:

- **This**—The Employee object (in the middle of execution)
- **Target**—The Manager
- **Arguments**—The String "I want a raise."

When the weaver replaces the call join point with around advice, the around advice can sensibly change the arguments and target of the join point—the notify call hasn't happened yet. However, changing the currently executing object would mean changing something that has already happened. The Employee object has already begun the execution of its requestRaise method. There's no way for AspectJ to go back in time and change the object that's about to make the notify call.

## Changing Arguments

Changing arguments is perhaps the simplest of context manipulations. To demonstrate its effects, let's return to the example that opened the chapter. There you relied on the fact that System.out.print would (in practice) prepend a string onto a subsequent println. If you were affecting a different sort of logging call, this behavior might not hold true. You really want to tack the location information onto the message itself. With around advice, you have that tool:

```
void around(Object msg) : logCalls(msg) {
    String location =
    thisJoinPointStaticPart.getSourceLocation() + "-";
    String newArg = location + msg;
    proceed(newArg);
}

public pointcut logCalls(Object msg) :
        call(public void print*(Object)) &&
        target(PrintStream) && args(msg) &&
        ! within(AddSourceInfo);
```

To get the new version to work, you must modify its pointcut to expose the argument to the print* method. You also limit the join points to those where the method accepts a single argument of type Object (using the pointcut print*(Object)). Doing so avoids advising calls where the argument is a primitive—(more on that in the next section).

With the modified pointcut, the advice uses a slightly different strategy: It gets the location from thisJoinPoint (as before) and concatenates it with the original argument. Then the advice uses proceed() to invoke the original join point with the new argument. The resulting output matches the original output of the aspect.

## *More on Proceed()'s Parameters*

The compiler does its best to ensure that you pass the correct type and number of arguments to proceed(). For example, in the println example you could not write

```
proceed(-1);//wrong type of argument
```

nor
```
proceed(location, msg);//wrong number of arguments
```

The exact rule is that proceed()'s parameter list matches the parameter list of the advice. If the advice takes two Strings as formal parameters, proceed() must receive two Strings as parameters. By employing this rule, AspectJ can catch many problems at compile time. However, because AspectJ allows broad typing of exposed context, you can end up causing a runtime exception if you're not careful. As an example, let's look back at the logCalls pointcut you altered in the previous section. If you do not restrict the join points to those print methods that take an Object, the pointcut will match methods such as println(int). Look at the results:

```
//advice declaration
void around(Object msg) : logCalls(msg) {
//...
}

//new pointcut—Object formal will accept boxed int...
public pointcut logCalls(Object msg) :
        call(public void print*(*)) && //matches primitives
        ... args(msg) ...;

//new line in PrintTest.main
System.out.println(1);//line 27

//output
Exception in thread "main" java.lang.ClassCastException:
java.lang.String can not be converted to int
org.aspectj.runtime.internal.Conversions.intValue(Unknown ...
println_decorator.PrintTest.main(PrintTest.java:27)
```

Because the around advice takes an Object-typed parameter, AspectJ boxes the int as an Integer. In this particular advice, proceed() takes only a single parameter of type Object. Therefore, the compiler allows the advice to pass the enhanced message ("SomeLocation:xx-1") to proceed because the String is an Object. However, the new pointcut will select the call to System.out.println(1) at line 27. This join point expects an int. When the join point gets the new argument (a String), AspectJ cannot convert it to the expected int and so throws a ClassCastException.

# Advice Precedence

Sometimes you can write advice as if it's the only advice in the world. When several pieces of advice affect the same join point, however, they can begin to affect each other as well. So far you've seen several situations where you needed to change the precedence of advice in order to get it to run properly. In the first case, an exception thrown from MinimumRaisePolicy prevented advice in LogRaises from logging the raise. As we explained at the time, this happened because the new advice took *precedence* over the old advice. This section explores AspectJ's precedence rules and how you can make them work in your favor.

## Why Does Precedence Matter?

Precedence affects both *when* advice executes and *whether* it executes at all. AspectJ allows programmers to control the precedence of advice because there's no way for the weaver to automatically know which advice should take precedence. For example, earlier you changed the precedence of your aspects because you wanted to log all raise attempts whether they failed or not. But suppose you did not want to clutter the log files with raise attempts that fell through. In that situation, you would want the MinimumRaisePolicy to take precedence over LogRaises.

To understand how advice affects other advice, it's important to understand how AspectJ determines precedence and how advice reacts to it. There are two phases to the precedence system in AspectJ:

1. The weaver determines the total precedence order for a given join point.

2. Advice executes at runtime according to the precedence order—possibly disrupting the execution of advice of lower precedence.

## Determining Precedence

AspectJ determines precedence one join point at a time. In other words, if two pieces of advice never operate on the same join point, their relative precedence won't ever be determined. If (as in the personnel management system) two pieces of advice *do* share a join point, the weaver assigns relative precedence based on whether they reside in different aspects or in the same aspect.

### Inter-Aspect Precedence

If pieces of advice reside in different aspects, three main situations determine precedence:

1. **Aspects may take precedence over other aspects using precedence declarations**. We discuss this matter in detail in Chapter 8, which covers inter-type declarations. To summarize, all advice declared in A precedes all advice declared in B if the following statement appears in an aspect:

```
declare precedence : A, B;
```

2. If an aspect extends another aspect, **advice in the subaspect receives higher precedence than advice in the superaspect**. This allows sub-aspects to override their parents' behavior.

3. If **neither of the previous cases applies**, then the relative precedence of advice between the aspects remains undefined. They will execute in a definite order, but not one that can be set or determined by the programmer.

## Intra-Aspect Precedence

If two pieces of advice are defined in the same aspect, their precedence is determined by their order and type. There are two main situations:

- **One of the pieces of advice is after advice**. In this case, the advice defined later in the file takes the higher precedence.

- **Neither advice is of the after type**. In this case, the advice defined earlier in the file takes precedence.

For example, let's say you have three pieces of advice in this order:

```
Before1
Before2
After
```

The weaver makes three judgments of relative precedence:

```
Before1 vs. Before2
Before1 vs. After
Before2 vs. After
```

Based on rule 2 from our list, Before1 > Before2 (read > as *takes precedence over*). Based on rule 1, After > Before1 and After > Before2. When combined, the relative precedence looks like this:

```
After > Before1 > Before2
```

If you're asking yourself why the rules are so complicated, you're not alone. At first glance, it seems that an easier precedence rule (earlier advice always takes precedence over later) would serve the language better. It turns out that prior to the 1.0 release of AspectJ, this *was* the precedence rule. However, it also led to confusion. The problem is that after advice of a higher precedence executes *after* advice of lower precedence. This order makes sense, because it gives higher priority after advice the last word on the join point. So, the simpler precedence rule led to a counter-intuitive result. For the following set of advice affecting a common join point,

```
Before1
Before2
After1
After2
```

the older precedence rule led to the following execution order:

```
Before1
Before2
After 2
After 1
```

Many users complained about this effect and asked that it be changed. The AspectJ team obliged. The end result is that if you're trying to manually compute precedence order (or write an AspectJ compiler), your life is more difficult. On the other hand, if you're just writing advice, you're less likely to be tripped up by the resulting execution order.

### Circular Relationships

It's possible to define advice that forms a circular precedence relationship. The weaver will report these errors. A simple example of circular precedence arises when the following precedence declarations appear in the same weaving:

```
declare precedence : A, B;
declare precedence : B, C;
declare precedence : C, A;
```

The same sort of circular error can arise within advice defined in a single aspect. Fortunately, because AspectJ handles precedence on a per-join-point basis, if C does not apply to the same join points as both A and B, the circularity problem never arises. AspectJ's documentation suggests that you can use circularity to ensure that two aspects never affect the same join point. (See Chapter 8 for further details about circularity in precedence relationships.)

## Runtime Execution

The order of advice execution is determined by precedence. However, as we alluded in the section on intra-aspect precedence, the advice with the highest precedence does *not* always execute first. The following list describes the way in which precedence affects each type of advice. In all cases, *the advice with the next precedence* is understood to include the original join point if no further advice affects the join point:

- **After** advice defers execution. Instead of running immediately, after advice forwards control to the advice with the *next highest precedence*. When that advice finishes executing, the after advice runs its body if its subtype matches the outcome of the join point. (In other words, after throwing executes only if the next advice—or the join point—throws an exception.)

- **Before** advice executes its body. If the advice terminates normally, it forwards control to advice with the next highest precedence. If the before advice throws an exception, it will prevent any advice of lower precedence from running.

- **Around** advice also executes its body. It has the option of running the next advice by calling proceed(..). If it throws an exception or otherwise terminates before calling proceed(..), advice of lower precedence (and the join point) will not run.

These rules seem complicated, but they lead to a coherent result. A given piece of advice treats advice of lower precedence as if it were part of the join point. This makes sense conceptually: A method call is not just a method call, it is a method call plus any advice that attaches to it. If the call doesn't happen, neither does the advice. This conceptual model can help you prevent undesirable situations, such as log entries for methods that never execute.

The next section walks through a fictional join point to help you get a feel for precedence in action. For the purposes of this chapter, we'll call the set of lower precedence advice (and the computation under the join point) the *viewable join point*.

## An Example of Precedence Effects

Let's consider a sample join point festooned with some advice (see Figure 7.2).

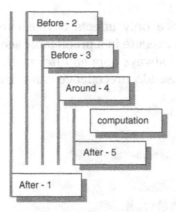

**Figure 7.2** Advice arranged from left to right in order of precedence and from top to bottom in order of execution.

Each piece of advice bears a number according to its precedence. The gray bars indicate the viewable join point for that advice. When the flow of control enters the (whole) join point, the following steps occur:

1. Execution begins with the advice that has the highest precedence. This is After-1 in the figure. Because after advice defers execution, control passes to the advice with the next highest precedence: Before-2.

2. Before-2 executes its body and then forwards control to the advice that has the next highest precedence. If it threw an exception, advice 3-5 and the computation would not execute. After-1 would still execute if its subtype were throwing or unqualified.

3. Before-3 executes in the same manner as Before-2.

4. Around-4 executes. If it calls proceed(), the computation and After-5 get a chance to run.

5. After-5 defers execution and runs the computation. When the computation returns (depending on the type of the after advice), After-5 may run.

6. After-1 gets a chance to execute. Suppose its type is after throwing. Because all the other advice represents its viewable join point, any of the other pieces of advice could trigger After-1's execution by throwing an exception. On the other hand, the computation itself could throw an exception, and if Around-4 caught the exception and returned normally, After-1 would not execute.

This model takes some getting used to, but once you've mastered thinking about precedence this way, you'll find its effects predictable.

## Pseudo Precedence

It's important to remember that precedence only affects advice execution around a single join point. Often join points execute in a predictable sequence. For instance, method execution join points always happen *after* method call join points. As a result, an extra layer of pseudo precedence can affect how advice executes, as illustrated in Figure 7.3.

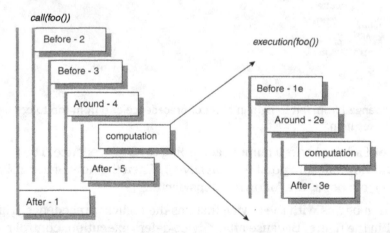

**Figure 7.3** All the advice on the call join point has pseudo precedence over the execution advice.

In the figure, the computation from the earlier example turns out to contain an execution join point for the same method. Because call join points happen before execution join points, all the advice on the left half of the figure takes effect as if it had a higher precedence than the advice on the right. Pseudo precedence is intuitive—if a method call does not happen, then the method execution can't happen either. Despite being intuitive, its effects are worth remembering if your advice does not execute in the expected order.

# What's Next

Looking back over the personnel management application, you've implemented quite a few crosscutting concerns. Raises are logged and checked for adherence to department policy, and the payroll system is automatically notified afterward. If the payroll server is unavailable, you retry the notification on other servers. None of these concerns required modifications to the code for Employee. As far as this chapter is concerned, you could have purchased a JAR containing Employee and Manager from a component vendor.

With advice, you can effectively compose join points. In other words, without changing the source for the original join point, you can add pre and post effects, handle failures, and even alter the join point's arguments or target. AspectJ's advice-weaving capabilities allow almost any join point to be effectively altered from the outside in a predictable and structured way. As a result, you've been able to alter the definition of a raise to include each new concern without changing its basic meaning. Maintainers of the code can now modify each concern without modifying the core raise code and without affecting the other concerns. Because of this situation, flexibility, and cohesion increase.

This chapter has focused on the natural complement to the pointcut: advice. We considered accessing context, exceptions, and advice precedence. We looked at each type of advice (before, after, and around) and showed which sorts of crosscutting concerns you can implement with each. The next chapter focuses on inter-type declarations. These static changes to the type structure of AspectJ programs increase the power and flexibility of advice. By altering Java's type system inter-type declarations allow for more powerful and more modular aspects. Once you've read the next chapter, you'll have a good idea of the full capabilities of AspectJ.

# CHAPTER 8

# Inter-type Declarations

So far, this book has concentrated on dynamic crosscutting—AspectJ's ability to define and advise points in the dynamic execution of a program. We've defined join points, selected them with pointcuts, and executed code at them with advice. These features are revolutionary, so they get a lot of attention. Inter-type declarations—(alterations to classes and inheritance hierarchies from outside the original class definitions) aren't as groundbreaking. Even though they keep a lower profile, AspectJ's inter-type declarations are crucial to the language. Because they support a more flexible type system, they allow aspects to capture crosscutting concerns in an encapsulated way.

As their name suggests, inter-type declarations are declarations about a program's structure that occur between types. For instance, you can use an aspect to add new methods to a class, or declare that a class extends a new superclass. Here are the types of changes possible with inter-type declarations:

- Add members (methods, constructors, fields) to types (including other aspects)
- Add concrete implementation to interfaces
- Declare that types extend new types or implement new interfaces
- Declare aspect precedence
- Declare custom compilation errors or warnings
- Convert checked exceptions to unchecked

Inter-type declarations are described as static crosscutting because they affect the static type hierarchy of programs. Subject to a few new scoping rules, the rest of the system will treat the new program structure as if it had been declared naturally. Although inter-type declarations give aspects the ability to alter classes from the outside, the end result fits neatly into Java's type system. In other words, you know much of this territory already. Familiar rules for overriding methods, shadowing instance variables, and the like apply predictably to AspectJ programs. If something seems as though it would work a certain way in a pure Java program, it probably works similarly in AspectJ. There are some important additions and exceptions to this general principle, which we'll cover in the sections ahead.

On the surface, adding a method or a new interface to a class doesn't seem impressive. When the new method or interface interacts with advice, however, the results can be astounding. It's difficult to get a sense of how inter-type declarations and aspects can cooperate without seeing the process in operation. So, you might have to wait until you're familiar with the basics before you understand why you'd add a new method to a class from the outside, rather than adding it on the inside.

We begin the chapter by looking at examples of inter-type method declarations. Then we'll dive into the mechanics of inter-type members and illustrate how to use declare parents to affect type structure. Once you have a grasp of these features, we'll explore AspectJ's ability to add concrete behavior to interfaces. This topic will open the door to further consideration of idioms and usage. We'll conclude with a look at aspect precedence, exception softening, and custom compilation messages—important but less far-reaching forms of static crosscutting.

## Simple Examples of Inter-type Declarations

Before we dive too deeply into the mechanics, let's look at some examples of how to use inter-type declarations.

**NOTE**

**Many of the examples in this chapter rely on simple component code introduced in Chapter 7, "Advice"—namely, classes representing different types of employees in a personnel management system. Please refer to Chapter 7 or the online code samples to see the full source code for these components.**

### Adding a Method to a Class

Good components encapsulate just enough behavior and state to accurately represent their primary abstraction. An Employee class should encapsulate things like the employee's name, salary, history at the company, and so on. Unfortunately, crosscutting concerns interfere with this simple dictum. Glue code and non-central concerns can obscure the ideal class and prevent programmers from understanding its role in the system.

Representing classes in another format is a perfect example of this sort of crosscutting requirement. Suppose business concerns dictate that the personnel system must integrate with a third-party system via XML. To facilitate the integration, programmers must render each major class in the personnel system to an XML representation. In a traditional OO environment, this concern might dictate that you add the method in Listing 8.1 to the Employee class.

```
/* the conversion method */
public void toXML(PrintStream out){
    out.println("<employee>");
    out.println("  <name>");
    out.println("  " + getName());
    out.println("  </name>");
    out.println("  <salary>");
    out.println("  " + getSalary());
    out.println("  </salary>");
    out.println("</employee>");
}

/* some demo code */
public static void main(String[] args){
    Employee bill = new Employee("Bill Grimes", 35000);
    System.out.println("Bill as XML: ");
    bill.toXML(System.out);
}

/* output */
Bill as XML:
<employee>
  <name>
  Bill Grimes
  </name>
  <salary>
  35000
  </salary>
</employee>
```

**Listing 8.1** The toXML() method implements a crosscutting concern.

A good encapsulator must ask, "Does this behavior really belong to an Employee?" The answer lies in a gray area, but our intuition suggests that toXML() belongs together with other XML integration code rather than with code concerned with raises, payrolls, or managers. Accordingly, an OO programmer might write a separate conversion class (see Listing 8.2).

```java
public class EmployeeXML{
    private Employee emp;

    public EmployeeXML (Employee emp) {
        this.emp = emp;
    }

    public void toXML(PrintStream out){
        out.println("<employee>");
        out.println("  <name>");
        out.println("  " + emp.getName());
        //...etc.
    }
}
```

**Listing 8.2**  A separate converter class provides an OO solution.

However, adding multiple converter classes becomes tedious and introduces another class hierarchy that's tightly coupled to the Employee hierarchy. Inter-type declarations provide an alternative that combines the simplicity of the first solution with the modularization of the second. Check out Listing 8.3.

```java
public aspect XMLInterface {

    /**
     * Exercises the newly introduced capabilities.
     */
    public static void main(String[] args){
        Employee bill = new Employee("Bill Grimes", 35000);
        System.out.println("Bill as XML: ");
        bill.toXML(System.out);/* 4 */
    }

    /**
     * Adds a new public method to Employee.
     */
    public void /*1*/ Employee.toXML(PrintStream out){
        out.println("<employee>");
        out.println("  <name>");
        out.println("  " + getName());/* 2 */
        out.println("  </name>");
        out.println("  <salary>");
```

**Listing 8.3**  Introduction provides something more compact. (continues)

```
        out.println("   " + getSalary()); /* 3 */
        out.println("   </salary>");
        out.println("</employee>");
    }


}
/* output of main method */
Bill as XML:
<employee>
  <name>
  Bill Grimes
  </name>
  <salary>
  35000
  </salary>
</employee>
```

**Listing 8.3**    Introduction provides something more compact. (continued)

The XMLInterface aspect uses inter-type declaration to add the toXML()
method to the Employee class. Let's break down the example. The aspect
includes two elements: a main method and the inter-type declaration. The syntax of an inter-type method declaration resembles that of a traditional method
declaration. The main difference occurs at location 1: Instead of toXML(),you
write Employee.toXML(). This declares the method as part of the Employee
type rather than the enclosing type. Notice that the body of the method has not
changed since it was moved from Employee.java. In particular, at locations 2
and 3 the new method references other public methods of the Employee class.

As you can see from the main method at location 4, client code can call the
inter-type member just as if it were a normal method. The output of the main
method is identical to the output in the first listing. In almost every respect, the
inter-type method behaves like a normally declared method.

## Is Member Introduction a Good Idea?

You've kept a tangential method out of the Employee class. Does this justify a
feature with the power of member introduction? After all, now it's more difficult to look at the source code for Employee and see all of its behavior. Isn't this
a drawback?

### Tool Support

The use of aspect-oriented development tools can alleviate concerns about
overlooking inter-type members. Tools such as the graphical structure browser

that ships with AspectJ provide an aspect-aware view of the code. Figure 8.1 shows a screenshot of the toXML() example.

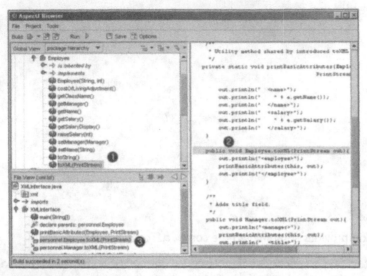

**Figure 8.1**  The structure browser shows toXML() as a member of Employee.

At location 1, the structure browser displays the toXML() method as part of the Employee class alongside traditional members such as setName() and toString(). Double-clicking on the method brings up the source for the inter-type declaration in the right-hand pane (location 2). At location 3, the browser displays the inter-type declaration of toXML() as part of the aspect declares it. As with other AspectJ constructs, the structure browser makes inter-type declarations visible and easy to navigate. (For more information about AspectJ's development tools, see Chapter 11, "Using Aspect J Tools," which includes examples of structure browser functionality as well as demonstrations of its integration into several IDEs.)

Of course, if you don't use an aspect-aware browser, you may miss Employee's new behavior. However, as IDEs have become increasingly necessary for high productivity in any language, the use of graphical tools to browse code has become standard practice among programmers. Relying on AspectJ-specific tools to provide high productivity in AspectJ will be no different.

## More Flexible Code Structure

In addition to being as visible as normal members, inter-type declarations allow more flexibility in the grouping of behavior. Consider Listing 8.4, which refactors the aspect and adds more introductions.

```
public aspect XMLInterface {

    /**
     * Exercises the newly introduced capabilities.
     */
    public static void main(String[] args){
        Employee bill = new Employee("Bill Grimes", 35000);
        System.out.println("Bill as XML: ");
        bill.toXML(System.out);

        Manager boss = new Manager("Big Boss", 90000);
        boss.setTitle("Head Cheese");
        System.out.println("Boss as XML: ");
        boss.toXML(System.out);

        Programmer jenny =
            new Programmer("Jenny Suza", 70000);
        jenny.setLanguage("Java/AspectJ");
        System.out.println("Jenny as XML: ");
        jenny.toXML(System.out);
    }


    /**
     * Utility method shared by introduced toXML methods.
     */
    private static void printBasicAttributes(Employee e,
                                    PrintStream out){

        out.println("  <name>");
        out.println("    " + e.getName());
        out.println("  </name>");
        out.println("  <salary>");
        out.println("    " + e.getSalary());
        out.println("  </salary>");
    }

    public void Employee.toXML(PrintStream out){
        out.println("<employee>");
        printBasicAttributes(this, out);
        out.println("</employee>");
    }

    /**
     * Adds title field.
     */
    public void Manager.toXML(PrintStream out){
        out.println("<manager>");
```

**Listing 8.4**  Introduction allows grouping of similar functionality. (continues)

```
            printBasicAttributes(this, out);
            out.println("  <title>");
            out.println("    " + getTitle());
            out.println("  </title>");
            out.println("</manager>");
    }

    /**
     * Adds language field.
     */
    public void Programmer.toXML(PrintStream out){
        out.println("<programmer>");
        printBasicAttributes(this, out);
        out.println("  <language>");
        out.println("    " + getLanguage());
        out.println("  </language>");
        out.println("</programmer>");
    }

}
/* output */
Bill as XML:
<employee>
  <name>
    Bill Grimes
  </name>
  <salary>
    35000
  </salary>
</employee>
Boss as XML:
<manager>
  <name>
    Big Boss
  </name>
  <salary>
    90000
  </salary>
  <title>
    Head Cheese
  </title>
</manager>
Jenny as XML:
<programmer>
  <name>
    Jenny Suza
  </name>
```

**Listing 8.4** Introduction allows grouping of similar functionality. (continues)

```
   <salary>
      70000
   </salary>
   <language>
      Java/AspectJ
   </language>
</programmer>
```

**Listing 8.4**   Introduction allows grouping of similar functionality. (continued)

In the expanded version, the aspect takes responsibility for the XML rendering of *all* the model objects. By doing so, it causes all the XML conversion code to localize in a single place. Because of the aspect, it's easy to scan all the implementations of toXML at once and to refactor them together. For the example, we deliberately chose simple XML renderings of the objects. However, if the XML was convoluted or proprietary to a third-party system, keeping the XML code out of the component code would make even more sense. An appropriately coupled Employee class shouldn't need to know about the entity names the third-party system uses.

**NOTE**

**For the record, many XML binding tools could provide an elegant solution to rendering an Employee as XML. Similarly, EJB provides solutions to many common crosscutting concerns found in enterprise middleware. The intent of our examples isn't to suggest that AspectJ provides the best solution for *all* crosscutting concerns, but rather to show how AspectJ can help with common ones. Once you're familiar with what it can do, you'll be in a better position to evaluate which tool provides the superior solution. You may also discover new crosscutting concerns that no special tool addresses.**

AspectJ gives users the choice of how they would like to organize and group their functionality. As the previous example suggests, in some situations common behavior belongs together in an aspect rather than in each individually implementing class. With AspectJ, that option is open. You can make intelligent decisions about how to structure your code so it makes the most sense.

## Inter-type Declarations and Coupling

Of course, now that you've added public methods to the entire employee hierarchy, any class that calls the methods becomes dependent (indirectly) on the XMLInterface aspect. This may be acceptable if XML rendering is an important behavior used in many parts of the system. However, such a situation can lead to less modularity. One of the potential benefits of AspectJ is pluggability. With some care, AspectJ will let you design a system that supports layers of behavior you can compose at build time. Having too much interdependence between components and aspects can hinder this type of design.

However, AspectJ's scoping rules allow for inter-type members that other code can't see. This behavior allows the aspect to control how much other code can depend on behavior it introduces onto a type. The next section explores how to use such private inter-type behavior to help an aspect do its job.

## Introduction and Advice

So far, the power of the advice you've written in this book has been limited. One of the reasons is that we just covered inter-type declaration in the last few pages. The utility and elegance of advice increases exponentially once it cooperates with inter-type declarations.

The next example illustrates this fact. It assumes the Employee class has been crosscut by the need to persist its state to a database. To cooperate with a third-party persistence framework, the Employee must implement a store() method that takes care of the details of writing its state to a database. (Readers experienced with EJBs that use bean-managed persistence will recognize the pattern.) As an additional requirement, because database access costs precious time, Employee must be careful to persist data only when its state has changed. Pre-AOP, one of the only ways of doing this was to manually update a *dirty* flag whenever a field changed. To manually maintain a dirty/clean state, you could add the following code to the Employee class:

```
/* manually adding an update to the dirty flag */
public void raiseSalary(int increment){
    dirty =true;
    salary += increment;
}


/**
 * Uses the dirty flag to avoid expensive
 * database updates.
 */
public void Employee.store(){
    if(dirty){
        //update row in database
    }
    dirty = false;
}
```

There is a problem with this approach: Persistence code tangles with Employee code. If many classes persist themselves, inserting code that updates the dirty flag become boring and error-prone. Certainly Employee cannot be reused with a different persistence strategy.

If you have read Chapters 6 and 7 (covering pointcuts and advice), you may spot a way to capture state-change events. Here is some advice that will execute whenever the state of an Employee changes:

```
private pointcut stateChange(Employee emp) :
    set(* Employee.*) &&
    target(emp);

after(Employee emp) : stateChange(emp){
    //now what?
}
```

The pointcut picks out join points that will change the state of the Employee. Note that you can define state change events however you like—execution of any set* methods is another way of doing it. In this case, we chose field assignments. With this pointcut and advice, every time a field on Employee changes, you have the opportunity to record that the object has become dirty.

Inter-type declaration provides the perfect way to store state about an object without tangling the state into the object itself. With a few inter-type declarations, you can easily manage a dirty flag without polluting the original class. Listing 8.5 contains the full Persistence aspect.

```
public aspect Persistence {

    /**
     * 1 Adds a dirty flag to the Employee type.
     */
    private boolean Employee.dirty = false;

    /**
     * 2 Note that we have to exclude sets to
     * the dirty flag--a good reminder that
     * inter-type members are full citizens
     * of the modified type.
     */
    private pointcut stateChange(Employee emp) :
        set(* Employee.*) &&
        ! set(boolean Employee.dirty) &&
        target(emp);

    /* 2 */
    after(Employee emp) : stateChange(emp){
        emp.dirty = true;
    }
```

**Listing 8.5**   Introduction allows an aspect to add state directly to an object. (continues)

```
/**
 * 3. This inter-type method uses the dirty
 * flag to avoid expensive database
 * updates.
 */
public void Employee.store(){
    if(dirty){
        System.out.println("Storing : " +toString());
    }
    else{
        System.out.println("Employee does not need " +
                            "to be stored.");
    }
    dirty = false;
}

/**
 * Exercises the persistence functions
 * of the modified Employee class.
 */
public static void main(String[] args){
    Employee janet = new Employee("J. Smythe", 99000);
    janet.store();//new employee, should store
    janet.store();//no changes
    janet.raiseSalary(2300);
    janet.store();//should store
}

}
/* Output */
Storing : Employee J. Smythe:$99,000.00
Employee does not need to be stored.
Storing : Employee J. Smythe:$101,300.00
```

**Listing 8.5** Introduction allows an aspect to add state directly to an object. (continued)

The first thing to notice about the example is at location 1. The Persistence aspect adds a private member variable to the Employee class that serves as a dirty flag. Like declaring a method, declaring a member variable on another type resembles the standard Java declaration. Again, the aspect must qualify the member with the target of the declaration ("Employee.dirty" instead of just "dirty"). Because it declares the member as private, the aspect ensures that only code *in the aspect* can access and use it. Thus code in the Employee class remains unaware of the dirty flag's existence and could even declare a dirty variable of its own if it wanted to.

You saw the pointcut and advice at location 2 earlier. However, this version makes a couple of changes. The stateChange pointcut excludes field assignments to the dirty flag because they do not reflect changes to persistent state (and would result in recursive advice calls). As we've said before, aspects can affect aspects, and inter-type declared members are no exception. Now that you've added the dirty flag, you also know what to do in the after advice—you set the dirty flag of the changed Employee to true.

The store() method at location 3 uses the dirty flag just as it did without aspects, resetting the flag to false after the database update completes. The main method exercises the new behavior of the Employee class. As the constructors for Employee execute, they initialize member variables, triggering the after advice and setting the dirty flag. Thus the first call to store() saves the object's state. Calling store() again has no effect, because none of Janet's fields have changed. Finally, calling raiseSalary() and then store() results in a database update, because raiseSalary() reassigns the value of one of Janet's fields.

Notice that if you had defined state changes as execution(* void Employee.set*(..)), you might not have captured this last event. Pointcut composition takes careful thought.

### Thoughts on the Example

Inter-type declarations help aspects do their job by giving them the ability to add necessary behavior onto the types they affect. This ability allows aspects to form coherent modules of behavior. The Persistence aspect stores dirty state directly on the object it affects, where other code in the aspect (such as the store method) can use it easily. At the same time, it prevents unrelated code from accessing the state and keeps Employee from having to know about its participation in the persistence strategy.

Because Employee could be recompiled without this Persistence aspect, it could be reused in other persistence environments. In this way, AspectJ expands on Sun's famous promise of "Write once, run anywhere." Sun's promise means "Write your application once, run it on any OS." With careful design, AspectJ can promise, "Write modules once, run them in any application." (We'll look more at the topic of reuse and modularization later in this chapter and in Chapter 13, "Aspect-Oriented Examples: Patterns and Reuse.")

## Inter-type Members: The Mechanics

As you saw in the earlier examples, declaring members from other types can be simple. This section details the mechanics of external member declarations and explores things like member conflicts and scoping in more detail. First we'll look at the syntax of inter-type members; then we'll cover technical details relating to them.

# Types of Inter-type Members

You can declare the following sorts of members using inter-type declarations:

- Concrete methods
- Abstract methods
- Constructors
- Fields

The next sections detail the syntax for each form.

## Concrete Method

You can add a concrete method to any type (including an interface). The syntax is:

```
ConcreteInterTypeMethod ::=
    Modifiers ReturnType TargetType "." Id "(" Formals ")"
    [ThrowsClause] "{" MethodBody "}"

Modifiers ::= ;(as Java modifiers--see below)
ReturnType ::= ;(as Java)
TargetType ::= ;(any legal AspectJ type. Defines the type to add
the member to.)
Id ::= ;(as a Java identifier. Defines the name of the added
method.)
Formals ::= ;(as Java formal parameters)
ThrowsClause ::= ;(as Java throws clause)
MethodBody ::= ;(as Java method body--see below.)
```

You can add any modifiers to the inter-type member that would be legal if the member appeared on target type (static, synchronized, and so on). The only modifiers that act differently are the access modifiers (discussed in their own section).

The body of the inter-type method implements the method and functions as if the method appeared in the target type—with some important restrictions (see the section "Access Control"). Here are some examples:

```
public void Employee.toXML(PrintStream out){
    out.println("<employee>");
    printBasicAttributes(this, out);
    out.println("</employee>");
}

public static double Employee.calculateTax(int salary){
    return salary * .35;
}
```

## Abstract Method

You can also add an abstract method to any abstract type or interface:

```
AbstractInterTypeMethod ::=
    abstract Modifiers ReturnType AbstractTargetType "." Id
    [ThrowsClause] "(" Formals ")" ";"

AbstractTargetType ::= ;(any legal AspectJ type. Must be an
interface or an abstract class. Defines the type to add the
member to.)
```

(Note that the abstract modifier can come before or after the other modifiers.) Just as in Java, concrete subtypes of AbstractTargetType must implement the added abstract method. The concrete subtype can do this with a normal or an inter-type implementation. Here's an example:

```
public abstract void AbstractXMLSupport.toXML(PrintStream out);
```

## Constructor

You can add a constructor to a concrete or abstract class using the special *new* identifier (this identifier matches the join point signature for constructors). Unlike other inter-type member declarations, this one cannot be applied to interfaces or aspects:

```
InterTypeConstructor ::=
    Modifiers ConstructorTargetType "." new "("
    Formals ")" [ThrowsClause] ";"
ConstructorTargetType ::= ;(any concrete or abstract class)
```

For example:

```
public Employee.new(String name, int salary, Manager mgr){
    this(name, salary);
    setManager(mgr);
}
```

## Fields

Aspects can add fields to any type with the following forms:

```
InterTypeField ::= Modifiers TypeOfField TargetType.Id [FieldInitializa-
tion];
TypeOfField ::= ;(any legal AspectJ type)
FieldIntialization ::= "=" Expression ";"
```

The following examples illustrate the use of standard Java modifiers with field introductions:

```
static String[] Programmer.possibleSkills =
        new String[]{"coding", "refactoring"};

private volatile int Employee.someVolatileValue;
```

Note that, unlike normal Java (and AspectJ 1.0), you can only make one inter-type field declaration per line. In other words, the following declaration is illegal:

```
boolean Employee.dirty, Department.dirty;
```

Inter-type members act as full members of the target types. However, the declaration itself belongs as a member to the aspect that declared it.

## Targets of Inter-type Declarations

It's worth remembering that aspects and interfaces are also types, and as such can be affected by inter-type declarations. This section explains some of the consequences of declaring members onto different types.

### Classes

Adding members to classes represents the base case for inter-type declarations. Inter-type methods on classes can be overridden, shadowed, and called as normal. An easy-to-overlook consequence is that if an aspect adds a method to a class, subclasses get the method as well. In other words, if you add terminate() to Employee, terminate() can be called on a Manager, which extends Employee, as well.

### Interfaces

AspectJ can add concrete state and behavior to interfaces, allowing for rootless type hierarchies. This feature enables such interesting behavior that we give it a full section later in the chapter. For the moment, remember that you can add concrete methods and instance variables onto an interface. This will cause any class that implements the interface to exhibit the behavior. For examples, see the section on interfaces later in the chapter ("Interfaces with Concrete Members").

### Aspects

All aspects define Java types. In addition to specifying crosscutting behavior, they can have state, define instance methods, and possess other class-like behavior. Just like other types, they can also be the targets of inter-type declarations. The only plausible examples for inter-type declarations onto aspects that we can think of involve aspects managing and crosscutting other aspects.

Rather than entering that sticky territory, Listing 8.6 simply demonstrates the possibility.

```
public aspect Target {
    //method to be added by other aspect

    public static void main(String[] args){
        Target.aspectOf().addedMethod();
    }
}

aspect Introducer{
    public void Target.addedMethod(){
        System.out.println("HI! You've met my method.");
    }
}
/* Output: */
HI! You've met my method.
```

**Listing 8.6**   Aspects are legal targets for introduction.

### TypePatterns

In AspectJ 1.0, inter-type declarations could affect more than one class by using type patterns. In 1.0, the following modification to the Persistence aspect added the dirty flag to both the Department and Employee classes:

```
private boolean (Employee || Department).dirty = false;
```

AspectJ 1.1 disallows this sort of inter-type declaration because it leads to problems. Experienced readers may guess that there is an alternative—declaring the member on an interface and making the target classes implement the interface. Again, see the section on interfaces for examples.

## Access Control

Inter-type members pose interesting questions regarding access control. Can the new code access private state? Who can see the new member? Is it a good idea for them to see it? Fortunately, AspectJ's access-control rules resolve these questions in a way that's understandable and that allows for full aspect-encapsulation. A single rule describes the lion's share of differences between standard Java access rules and AspectJ access rules:

Access modifiers on inter-type members are scoped with regard to the aspect that declares them, not the target type.

As explained in the persistence example, this means privately declared members such as

```
private boolean Employee.dirty = false;
```

can only be seen/used by code in the aspect that declared them. This rule prevents other code (even that of Employee) from accessing persistence members it should have no knowledge of. One consequence of the rule is that you can't add a private method or field that's usable by the target type (Employee can't access its aspect-declared dirty field directly). This limitation makes sense because private members are supposed to represent hidden implementation details. Scattering them among different files would reduce source cohesion without adding any viewable behavior.

Standard Java has three access levels besides private: public, protected, and package (default). Inter-type members with package access can only be seen by code in the package of the aspect that declared the member. Java's protected level is not supported for inter-type declaration. Finally, as you saw in the toXML example, the public access level allows inter-type members to form part of the public interface of a type.

## What Can an Inter-type Member See?

The access control rule also governs what the added code can see. Because inter-type code is scoped via the aspect that declared it, it can usually view the only the public interface of the target type. In other words, the new store() method can view the public setters and getters of Employee but not the corresponding private variables:

```
public void Employee.store(){
    if(dirty){
        System.out.println("Storing : " +toString());

        /* this ok, getName() is a public method */
        System.out.println("  Writing : " + getName());

        /* will not compile, as inter-type code
         * can only access private members declared
         * by the same aspect
         */
        //System.out.println("  Writing : " + salary);
        //[...]
}
```

## Getting More Access

If Employee was in the same package as Persistence, the store() method would have a little more leeway: It could access any package or protected members defined by Employee. This follows Java's access rules. Code that resides closer to other code has more privileges than code that is further away.

If inter-type members need to use private instance variables of the target type to do their job, you may need to ask whether they should be defined in the target type directly. Of course, there *are* situations (debugging and performance tuning come to mind) when a mechanism to bypass access rules can be convenient. For these situations, you can mark the declaring aspect with the special *privileged* modifier. Inter-type members from a privileged aspect can access almost anything. The previous code snippet would compile in its entirety if the Persistence aspect were declared privileged.

# Conflicts Between Members

The ability to define members on a type from anywhere in the system leads to the potential for conflicts between members with the same name. AspectJ does its best to resolve these conflicts gracefully. However, it's possible to define members that directly conflict. For instance, you can't put two public toString() methods on the same class. This section details some of the gray area cases.

## Non-Conflicting Scopes

In standard Java, you could declare a private method named compute() onto both the Employee and Manager classes. These two methods would not affect each other. Each class could count on being able to execute its own copy. Because each method is private, they reside in *non-conflicting scopes*.

AspectJ attempts to preserve this behavior with inter-type declarations. For example, if you privately declared a compute() method onto Employee from two different aspects, each aspect would use its own version without conflicts. Listing 8.7 illustrates this principle.

```
public aspect Caching {
        /* 1 */
    private void Employee.compute(){
        System.out.println("Computing for Cache.");
    }

    public static void main(String[] args){
        new Employee("C. Calson", 35000).compute();
        /* calls the next aspect just for demonstration */
        Tracing.main(new String[0]);
    }
```

**Listing 8.7** Private Inter-type members don't conflict. (continues)

```
}

public aspect Tracing{
    /* 2 */
    private void Employee.compute(){
        System.out.println("Computing for Trace.");
    }

    /* accesses the method for demonstration
     * purposes
     */
    public static void main(String[] argv){
        new Employee("T. Thompson", 35000).compute();
    }
}
/* Output */
Computing for Cache.
Computing for Trace.
```

**Listing 8.7** Private inter-type members don't conflict. (continued)

In the example, two aspects (Caching and Tracing) each declare a private helper method onto the Employee class (locations 1 and 2). Each aspect also has a static main method that uses compute(). As you can see from the output, each aspect sees its own copy of the method. If both of the aspects declared compute() as public, the compiler would signal an error:

```
//from Caching
public void Employee.compute(){
    System.out.println("Computing for Cache.");
}
//from Tracing
public void Employee.compute(){
    System.out.println("Computing for Trace.");
}
/* compiler error - conflict between publicly visible versions
of compute()
*/
```

## Conflicts and Precedence

Although two public inter-type declarations of compute() result in a conflict, AspectJ allows you to resolve the conflict with aspect precedence (covered later in this chapter). If you add the following line to Caching, its version of compute() will supplant Tracing's version:

```
declare precedence : Caching, Tracing;
/* New Output */
```

```
Computing for Cache.
Computing for Cache.
```

As a result of precedence declaration, Caching has precedence over Tracing. This causes the main method in both aspects to use Caching's version of compute(). This behavior applies to subaspects as well. Since subaspects take precedence over their parents, all inter-type members from a subaspect will supplant inter-type members from its parents in cases of conflict.

## Aspect Versus Target Members

Although inter-type members act as if they are defined directly on the type, they can also see static members of the enclosing aspect. Inter-type code cannot see instance members of the enclosing aspect because there's no way to determine which instance they should access. (See Chapter 9, "Aspects," for information about aspect instantiation.) As an example, let's say you temporarily add an informative println to the store() method that displays statistics about how the aspect is being used:

```
//In Persistence...
public void Employee.store(){
    displayStats();
    if(dirty){
    //[...]

private static void displayStats(){
    System.out.println("The Persistence aspect has ");
    System.out.println("these interesting stats: ...");
}
/* Output from a call to store */
The Persistence aspect has
these interesting stats: ...
Storing : Employee J. Smythe:$99,000.00
   Writing : J. Smythe
```

Employee's store() can access the static displayStats() method of the Persistence aspect. Think of this ability as a convenience that AspectJ provides for inter-type code. Despite being able to access static members of the enclosing aspect, members of the target type with the same name always take precedence. If the Employee class were to define a displayStats() method of its own

```
public void displayStats(){
    System.out.println(getName() +" has " +
                        "these interesting stats: ...");
}
```

the inter-type method would use it instead:

```
/* Output */
J. Smythe has these interesting stats: ...
Storing : personnel.Employee J. Smythe:$99,000.00
   Writing : J. Smythe
```

### *Inter-type Declarations and Inheritance*

Because inter-type methods are first-class citizens of the target types, they are subject to Java's inheritance rules. Public/default methods on subtypes override corresponding methods on supertypes. This happens regardless of whether the overriding method is natural or inter-type. You already saw this behavior in the toXML example, where both programmers and managers overrode the default XML representation of Employee. (Turn back to Listing 8.4 to review the example.)

# Declare Parents

The next two sections illustrate how to leverage interfaces with concrete members. The mechanics of adding members to interfaces with inter-type declaration is largely the same as adding them onto, say, abstract classes. However, a few details are particular to interfaces. Furthermore, adding behavior to interfaces opens several new avenues of design in AspectJ. For these reasons, we've separated the material on interfaces into its own section. Before covering interfaces, however, we'll detour through the *declare parents* form; it becomes instrumental in using interfaces to their full potential.

In addition to allowing you to add individual members to types, AspectJ enables you to add supertypes and interfaces to any type (with some restrictions). Let's look at a basic example.

## Adding a Simple Interface

Suppose you wanted to make Employee Comparable, but you knew different applications that used the class would want different implementations of the method. (One department could compare employees by name, another by salary.) This requirement necessitates an aspect-oriented solution. Listing 8.8 demonstrates how to make Employee implement the Comparable interface without modifying the original class.

```
public aspect EmployeeComparable {

    /* 1
     * ensures that the Employee class
     * implements the Comparable interface
     */
    declare parents : Employee implements Comparable;
```

**Listing 8.8** Adding a simple interface to a class. (continues)

```
/* 2
 * Implements the required method from
 * Comparable.
 */
public int Employee.compareTo(Object o){
    Employee e = (Employee)o;
    return getName().compareTo(e.getName());
}

public static void main(String[] args){
    //not in order
    Employee[] employees = new Employee[]{
        new Employee("Fatima", 55000),
        new Employee("Arthur", 38000),
        new Employee("Belle", 42000)};
    Arrays.sort(employees);

    for(int i=0; i <employees.length; i++){
        System.out.println(employees[i]);
    }
}
}
/* Output -notice that they are in alphabetical order*/
Employee Arthur:$38,000.00
Employee Belle:$42,000.00
Employee Fatima:$55,000.00
```

**Listing 8.8**  Adding a simple interface to a class. (continued)

The example does two major things. At location 1, it uses declare parents to specify that Employee implements the Comparable interface. This declaration has the same effect as writing "implements Comparable" in the class definition of Employee. One consequence is that the class must now implement the compareTo(Object) method. Fortunately, with inter-type declaration, you can add the method at the same time (location 2). Now Employee can be sorted with ease (see the main method and the output).

# Declare Parents: The Mechanics

Declare parents has two subcases: implementing new interfaces and extending new classes. Generally, it's less problematic to implement new interfaces than to extend new classes, so we'll cover that case first.

## Implementing New Interfaces

As you saw in the example, adding a new interface to a class means using the following syntax:

```
InterfaceDeclaration ::=
    declare parents ":" TypePattern implements
    TypeList ";"

TypePattern ::= ;(AspectJ type pattern--see Chapter 6 for examples)
TypeList ::= Type {"," Type}
```

The types in TypeList should represent valid interface types. By using a type list, declare parents can add multiple interfaces at once:

```
declare parents : Employee implements Comparable,
                                       Cloneable,
                                       Serializable;
```

As with most inter-type declarations, using declare parents results in behavior that's almost identical to putting the implements declaration directly in the affected class. To be fully legal, the affected type must now implement all the methods of the specified interfaces. The type can declare these members itself or aspects can introduce them.

## Extending New Classes

To change the superclass/superaspect of a type, you can use the following syntax:

```
SuperclassDeclaration ::=
    declare parents ":" TypePattern extends
    TypeList ";"
```

You may wonder why a *list* of types is allowed. It may have been a convenience to the implementers—although you can add more than one class to the list, they must belong to the same inheritance hierarchy:

```
declare parents : SuperProgrammer extends
                  Programmer,
                  //Manager,-- conflicts with Programmer
                  Employee;//redundant
```

This declaration amounts to the same thing as

```
declare parents : SuperProgrammer extends Programmer;
```

The classes in the type list must be compatible with the original supertype of the target. This means aspects have relative freedom if the target extends Object, but must tread carefully if the target already has a superclass. For instance, a parents declaration could make a Collection extend AbstractList instead of AbstractCollection (because AbstractList extends AbstractCollection), but could not make it extend AbstractMap (no relation to the original superclass). The next section gives an example of when you might want to extend new classes.

## Type Patterns

Unlike inter-type members, which cannot target type patterns, type patterns used with declare parents can have powerful effects. Let's look at some uses cases. Suppose you wanted to add behavior to some test classes you had written for a third-party testing framework (such as JUnit). You might decide to create a custom base class to support common behavior. The following line could add the base class to all classes ending in *Test*:

```
declare parents: *Test extends CustomTestCase;
```

The next declaration selects nearly the same set of classes:

```
declare parents: (TestCase+ && !TestCase)
    extends CustomTestCase;
```

Here you specify that any class that extends JUnit's TestCase (but not TestCase itself) also extends CustomTestCase—this picks up any classes that did not participate in the naming convention but did extend the JUnit's base class.

Superclass declarations can help you adjust inheritance hierarchies, especially when you're using well-known base classes. However, this form can run aground due to limitations on the code AspectJ controls. For instance, you might want to specify that every class in the personnel package should extend a new base class (let's call it Root) that defines useful behavior you need everywhere. You could try this with a line such as the following:

```
declare parents : personnel..* extends Root;
```

However, the compiler will complain that some classes already have a base class: notably, your custom exceptions. There's not much you can do to get around this problem because you can't affect the parents of Exceptions (short of weaving your aspects into java.lang). AspectJ provides a more elegant situation, however—interfaces with concrete members—which we'll cover in a minute.

### Type Patterns and Traditional Interfaces

Before we discuss interfaces with concrete members, let's look at interfaces without inter-type members. As you might guess, you can use type patterns effectively with traditional interfaces. For instance, you can make all the classes in a package serializable with a single line:

```
declare parents : personnel..* implements Serializable;
```

This way you can send any type in the package over a network.

# Interfaces with Concrete Members

We've been hinting at AspectJ's powers with regard to interfaces for most of the chapter. This section will end the suspense. AspectJ allows aspects to use inter-type declaration to add concrete methods and non-public/static fields to interface types. This represents an important divergence from Java's type system. In standard Java, interfaces support interface inheritance but not implementation inheritance. Thus a concrete class that implements an interface must either implement or inherit the implementation for every method on the interface. This obligation may entail a lot of effort, but often there are ways to avoid some of the work. For example, Java2's collections framework comes with both interfaces (Collection) and abstract base classes (AbstractCollection). These abstract classes implement some of the methods of the interface in order to "minimize the effort required to implement this interface" (http://java.sun. com/j2se/1.4/docs/api/java/util/AbstractCollection.html). However, sometimes abstract classes cannot do the trick. For instance, it's impossible to use abstract classes when the class must extend something else.

AspectJ does away with the problems of Java's interfaces by allowing interfaces to support concrete as well as abstract behavior. This way, AspectJ programs can support a sort of multiple inheritance. Interfaces that receive concrete members work a little like mixin classes in other languages: They cannot be instantiated directly and do not support constructors. Because of these restrictions, they remain true to Java's conception of interfaces as perspectives or views on the classes that implement them.

Interfaces are crucial to AspectJ's quest for modularity. Using them, an aspect can define a protocol for classes that it affects and then interact with its targets only through that protocol. By allowing concrete members on interfaces, AspectJ allows the protocol to support behavior without forcing the affected components to implement the behavior. The next example explores this idea.

## Refactoring the Persistence Solution

Early in the chapter, you integrated the Employee class with a persistence framework. You added a flag to indicate when a store operation was necessary. If you're particularly attuned to software reuse, you might wonder if you'll have to do this for each affected class. The answer is no—if you use power of AspectJ's interfaces. Listing 8.9 contains the code for a new Persistence aspect that uses an interface.

```
/* The basic definition of a persistable object */
public interface PersistentObject{
    public void store();
}

public aspect InterfacePersistence {

    /* 1
     * Declares a private member variable on
     * the PersistentObject interface
     */
    private boolean PersistentObject.dirty = false;

    /* 2
     * This concrete method
     * decides whether or not to store
     * based on the private dirty flag
     */
    public void PersistentObject.store(){
        if(dirty){
            System.out.println("Storing : " + toString());
        }
        else{
            System.out.println("This PersistentObject " +
            "does not need to be stored.");
        }
        dirty = false;
    }

    /* 3
     * This declare parents applies the
     * PersistentObject interface to Employee
     * and department.
     */
    declare parents : (Employee || Department)
            implements PersistentObject;

    /* 4
     * The pointcut and advice now operate
     * on the interface type rather than
     * the affected classes directly
     */
    pointcut stateChange(PersistentObject po) :
        (set(!transient * *.*) &&
```

**Listing 8.9**   Concrete interfaces allow aspect-oriented behavior to be applied to multiple types.
(continues)

```
          ! set(boolean PersistentObject.dirty))
          && target(po);


    after(PersistentObject po) : stateChange(po){
        po.dirty = true;
    }

    /* Exercises both affected classes */
    public static void main(String[] args){
        Employee janet = new Employee("J. Smythe", 99000);
        janet.store();//new employee, should store
        janet.store();//no changes
        janet.raiseSalary(2300);
        janet.store();//should store

        System.out.println("Now trying a department:");
        Department hr = new Department("Human Resources");
        hr.store();//new, should store
        hr.store();//no changes
        hr.setBudget(1000000);
        hr.store();//should store
    }
}
/* Output */
Storing : Employee J. Smythe:$99,000.00
This PersistentObject does not need to be stored.
Storing : Employee J. Smythe:$101,300.00
Now trying a department:
Storing : Department Human Resources budget: 0
This PersistentObject does not need to be stored.
Storing : Department Human Resources budget: 1000000
```

**Listing 8.9**  Concrete interfaces allow aspect-oriented behavior to be applied to multiple types. (continued)

Let's look at the example step by step. First, notice the PersistentObject interface. The first file in the example defines this interface exactly as in standard Java. Even though AspectJ allows inter-type declarations onto interfaces, it does not support directly defining concrete methods and fields in the body of the interface. (We'll talk more about this under the section, "An Idiom for Bodies.")

The aspect itself has several sections. Sections 1 and 2 use inter-type declarations to add the dirty flag and the store() method directly to the PersistentObject interface (instead of the Employee class). Note that the store() method can access and write to the private variable *dirty* that belongs *to the interface*.

The declare parents at location 3 uses a type pattern to make Employee and Department implement PersistentObject. The stateChange pointcut and advice at location 4 can now refer to the types they affect through PersistentObject. Notice that the stateChange pointcut now affects *all* (non-transient) field sets where the target is a PersistentObject—not just those defined by Employee.

The main method demonstrates the effects of the aspect. Both Department and Employee now act as persistent objects with optimized writing behavior.

### Thoughts on the Example

Consider that *both* Employee and Department exhibit persistent behavior without modifications to their class. Further consider that the "don't update unless dirty" behavior applies to both objects (and any new objects marked with the PersistentObject interface). Now compare this behavior to the Java solution of declaring a dirty flag on each persistent object, manually updating it at each state change, and checking the flag before writing, and you'll get a sense of how much code you can save with AspectJ.

Experienced developers may see problems remaining with this example. In a real system, each class would need its own store() method—or at the very least you'd need a better general-purpose implementation. Furthermore, you need to customize the pointcut that defines state changes. Changes to instance variables are not necessarily reliable indicators of state changes. Look at the following methods from Department:

```
public void removeEmployee(Employee emp){
    employees.remove(emp);
}
public void addEmployee(Employee emp){
    employees.add(emp);
}
```

These methods clearly change the state of the department. However, because they don't set instance variables, their use will not dirty the object. Chapter 13, "Aspect-Oriented Examples: Patterns and Reuse" further expands this example to solve these problems and provide a more reusable persistence solution.

## Interfaces with Concrete Members: The Mechanics

As you can see in Listing 8.9, the syntax of declaring members onto interfaces does not vary from the syntax for declaring members on any other type. The only thing you cannot declare on an interface is a constructor. This limitation keeps the notion of an interface separate from that of a class and also ensures that object construction remains predictable. Access rules function the same way for interfaces as for other types. Multiple aspects can declare members on an interface, and they can also use declare parents to affect the inheritance hierarchy of an interface.

Despite these major similarities, there are a few tricky issues regarding initialization and conflicts when dealing with interfaces that have concrete members. The next two sections detail these issues.

## Conflicts

All languages that support multiple inheritance must deal with the issue of conflicts between inherited behavior. Much ink has been spilled about the issue of the *diamond problem* (a particular variety of conflict). Many articles contend that Java programs are simpler without multiple inheritance and that the headaches aren't worth the benefits. Let's look at examples of how these problems might arise and what AspectJ does to solve them.

### The Diamond Problem

The diamond problem poses this question: "What happens if you build a class that inherits from two different parents that have a method with the same name?" Listing 8.10 shows an example of how this problem might arise.

Figure 8.2 illustrates the hierarchy graphically.

```
interface ThreeDimensional {}
interface Persuadable {}
public class Person implements ThreeDimensional,
                               Persuadable{}


public aspect MultipleInheritance {

    public void ThreeDimensional.manipulate(){
        System.out.println("Rotating object");
    }

    public void Persuadable.manipulate(){
        System.out.println("Persuading someone");
    }
}
```

**Listing 8.10**  Person implements two conflicting interfaces.

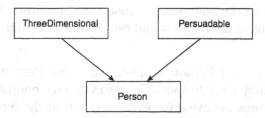

**Figure 8.2** Person's hierarchy seen in graphical terms.

Persuadable's manipulate() and ThreeDimensional's manipulate()conflict. AspectJ lets the programmer decide which method Person will support by giving you a compilation error. This behavior stays consistent with how AspectJ treats all conflicts. Recall that Caching and Tracing could not both declare a compute() method unless the declarations were private (see Listing 8.7). To solve the problem you could rename one of the methods (rotate() instead of manipulate()).

The conflict sharpens when you add a common supertype to Person's two parents. You can do this by creating a Manipulable interface:

```
interface Manipulable{}

public interface Persuadable extends Manipulable{}

public interface ThreeDimensional extends Manipulable{}

/* in the aspect: */
public void Manipulable.manipulate(){
    System.out.println("Manipulating something.");
}
```

Now the inheritance relationship resembles a diamond—hence *diamond problem* (see Figure 8.3).

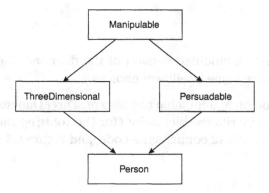

**Figure 8.3** Now Person's parents share an ancestor.

You don't want to rename one of the methods, because each one overrides the method on Manipulable. Changing the name would remove the overriding relationship.

Java avoids this headache by forcing Person to choose. Because Person takes responsibility for implementing all interfaces, it resolves any conflicts by default. The Person class defines behavior for every method of the interface regardless of whether it conflicts with a method from another interface.

AspectJ's uses the same solution—with a difference. If you implement manipulate() on Person, you resolve the conflict: Person's method overrides both interface methods. See Listing 8.11 for the details.

```
public class Person implements ThreeDimensional, Persuadable{
    /*
     * This method solves the conflict.
     */
    public void manipulate(){
        System.out.println("I'm convinced.");
    }
}
public static void main(String[] args){
        Person p = new Person();
        p.manipulate();
}
/* Output */
I'm convinced.
```

**Listing 8.11**  Person steps up to resolve the conflict.

The difference with AspectJ's solution to the diamond problem is that programmers must only resolve conflicts—you don't have to implement non-conflicting behavior.

### The Triangle Problem

The triangle problem manifests a modified version of the diamond dilemma. This time the compiler can make some intelligent choices.

If you define a toString method on Manipulable and also on ThreeDimensional, but *not* on Persuadable, the inheritance hierarchy (for the toString method) looks a bit like a triangle. (Listing 8.12 contains the code, and Figure 8.4 shows the inheritance diagram.)

```
/* these declarations appear in an aspect */
public String Manipulable.toString(){
    return "I'm Manipulable.";
}


public String ThreeDimensional.toString(){
    return "I'm 3D!";
}
```

**Listing 8.12** The situation becomes more complicated.

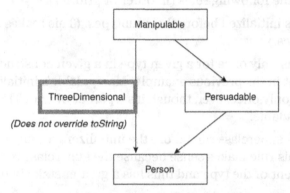

**Figure 8.4** Person inherits toString by two paths, one longer than the other.

Here the compiler has a little more information to go on. Because ThreeDimensional *already* overrides Manipulable's toString, it represents the most specialized version of the method. Person thus uses ThreeDimensional's version (as you can see from the following main method and output):

```
public static void main(String[] args){
    Person p = new Person();
    System.out.println(p.toString());
}
/* Output */
I'm 3D!
```

You could argue that there's still a conflict and the compiler should flag it. In fact, the issue *was* argued on the AspectJ mailing list. The consensus was that the current behavior best represents user intent in most cases.

### Final Thoughts on Conflicts

As you can see, deep multiple inheritance hierarchies can lead to confusing situations. Although it's too early to tell exactly what the structures of mainstream aspect-oriented programs will look like, we feel they will posses simpler hierarchies with more type-based behavior defined in terms of shallow, crosscutting interfaces. Deep inheritance chains with specialized branches should become a thing of the past. If we're right, you won't have to think about these sorts of conflicts very often.

### Order of Initialization

Because field declarations in interfaces can contain initialization code, multiple supertype initializations can run for the same type. AspectJ resolves the order of the initialization with the following rules (in order of priority):

1. Supertypes are always initialized before their subtypes. (This makes sense and follows Java's rules.)

2. Initialization code runs only once for a given type in a given construction chain. This means that in the previous example, Manipulable's initialization code (if any) will run only once, even though it's a parent of both ThreeDimensional and Persuadable.

3. Initializers for a type's superclass run before the initializers for any implemented interfaces. This rule makes sense because the superclass represents the primary parent of the type and thus has a greater stake in object construction.

For the previous example, these rules mean that when you construct a Person, initializers run in the following order:

   Object, Manipulable, ThreeDimensional, Persuadable, Person

(ThreeDimensional and Persuadable may swap places, depending on the whim of the compiler.) Most of the time, you won't have to think about the order of initialization. If you are trying to pin it down, it's easiest to add tracing advice that will tell you what's going on.

## Possibilities of Interfaces with Concrete Members

The next two sections explore uses for interfaces that have concrete members and point out some interesting possibilities.

### Role Definition

As you saw with the Persistence example, interfaces can help you reuse aspect-oriented code. Because aspects can crosscut classes that know nothing about them, you can use aspects in all sorts of systems, even those written without aspects in mind. The dynamic weaving capabilities of AspectJ 1.1 dramatically expand this possibility. Of course, in order to operate on components, aspects must know something about *them*. This poses a problem—if the aspects are supposed to be generic and reusable, they cannot be tied to their targets.

Component-oriented software also faces this problem. Unfortunately, the solution exhibits undesirable properties. Anyone familiar with Java servlets or EJBs knows about this territory. In these spaces, a *container* (similar for the purposes of discussion to a set of aspects) hosts and provides services to components that run within it. For example, servlet filters provide a form of around advice applicable to servlet requests. EJB containers provide transactional wrappers around method invocations. In order to participate in this relationship, components implement marker interfaces. For instance, all servlets (by definition) implement javax.servlet.Servlet. Doing so allows containers to interact with components they know little or nothing about.

Similar to containers, reusable aspects can define their interactions with target components in terms of interfaces. However, aspects allow more control over how much knowledge the components have about the relationship. In a component-container relationship, affected components must declare their role (MyServlet implements Servlet). Aspect-oriented systems have this option too (SomeNewClass implements PersistentObject). However, with inter-type declarations, targets can participate in a role without their knowledge. Adapter aspects can make declarations such as the following:

```
declare parents : com.mycompany.entities..* implements PersistentObject;
```

With this sort of adapter, a set of off-the-shelf components can have their role in complex crosscutting behavior defined for them.

This technique opens a wide range of possibilities. In contrast, the component-container model suffers from effort impedance. In other words, only the most common and widespread concerns are worth the effort of standardizing an interface, creating containers, and modifying components to operate within them. The EJB component-container model promoted by Sun illustrates this situation. Early versions of the EJB specification met the needs of large-scale enterprise systems and often ignored or marginalized concerns applicable to smaller market segments. As more organizations adopted the EJB model, EJB containers began to handle a wider range of concerns.

Assuming a basic familiarity with the principles of AOP, aspects require less effort to integrate and develop than defining a container and promoting it as a standard. As a result, smaller-scale concerns can be captured and sold without a marketing campaign (or grass-roots support) to back them. Design patterns such as Observer or Flyweight can be captured in a reusable aspect library and incorporated into any system the way collections libraries are today.

Chapter 13, "Aspect-Oriented Examples: Patterns and Reuse" explores this territory further.

## Mixin Style Inheritance

Often a set of classes needs to access services provided by their environment. These services could range from sophisticated application-specific behavior to something as simple as logging. Often these services are implemented as statically accessible methods (System.out.println) or as objects available through a globally accessible source (such as JNDI). Each solution has problems—static methods cannot be overridden, leading to less customizable behavior. Globally accessible objects suffer from complexity—first you must access the object, and then you invoke the service.

It would be great if you could build a service into affected objects so you could call, say, logging, like this

```
int i = frob(param);
log("result of frob " + i);
```

instead of

```
System.out.println("result of frob " + i);
```

As you might have guessed, AspectJ interfaces allow this sort of behavior. Classes can declare that they implement an interface and thereby gain access to any concrete behavior that has been defined on the interface. This situation resembles mixin inheritance in languages such as C++. Let's look at an example based around logging.

## An Idiom for Interface Bodies

Although AspectJ allows inter-type declarations to add behavior to interfaces, it does not permit you to directly add members the way you would to a class. For that reason, to create a standalone interface with concrete behavior, you must combine an aspect and an interface. Listing 8.13 shows this technique.

```
public interface LogService {

    /* 1 */
    static aspect BODY{
        private static boolean getDebug(){
            return "true".equals(
                System.getProperty("debug"));
```

**Listing 8.13** The LogService interface uses a static inner aspect to define concrete methods. (continues)

```
        }

    public void LogService.log(String s){
        System.out.println(s);
    }

    public void LogService.warn(String s){
        System.err.println("WARNING: " + s);
    }

    public void LogService.debug(String s){
        if(getDebug()){
            System.out.println("DEBUG: " + s);
        }
    }
    }
    }
}
```

**Listing 8.13** The LogService interface uses a static inner aspect to define concrete methods. (continued)

The LogService interface provides a set of simple logging methods that any class can use. The static inner aspect named BODY (location 1) defines the interface and implementation for all of LogService's methods. Using this idiom, the interface and implementation remain together while respecting AspectJ's limitation on directly implementing interface members.

Listing 8.14 shows a sample class that implements and uses the LogService interface.

```
public class ShoppingCart implements LogService{
    private double itemTotal;

    public ShoppingCart(double itemTotal) {
        this.itemTotal = itemTotal;
    }

    public void checkOut() {
        double grandTotal = calculateTotal(itemTotal);
        log("Customer's total: " + grandTotal);
        sendOrderToFulfillment(grandTotal);
    }

    private void sendOrderToFulfillment(double grandTotal) {
```

**Listing 8.14** The ShoppingCart uses LogService to communicate. (continues)

```
        warn("Fulfillment server down!");
    }

    public double calculateTotal(double itemTotal){
        double grandTotal = itemTotal;
        grandTotal = calculateShipping(grandTotal);
        grandTotal = calculateTax(grandTotal);
        return grandTotal;
    }

    private double calculateTax(double grandTotal) {
        double taxTotal = grandTotal + grandTotal * .05;
        debug("Tax total: " + taxTotal);
        return taxTotal;
    }

    private double calculateShipping(double grandTotal) {
        double shipTotal = grandTotal + grandTotal * .10;
        debug("Ship total: " + shipTotal);
        return shipTotal;
    }


    public static void main(String[] args) {
        new ShoppingCart(100).checkOut();
        System.setProperty("debug", "true");
        new ShoppingCart(200).checkOut();
    }
}
/* Output */
Customer's total: 115.5
Fulfillment server down!
DEBUG: Ship total: 220.0
DEBUG: Tax total: 231.0
Customer's total: 231.0
Fulfillment server down!
```

**Listing 8.14** The ShoppingCart uses LogService to communicate. (continued)

ShoppingCart uses the methods of LogService just as if it had inherited them from an abstract class. As you can see from the output, they operate that way, too.

### Thoughts on Mixins

Services implemented through mixin-style interfaces are flexible. Because interfaces follow well-defined inheritance rules, other aspects (or even the classes involved) can override portions of the behavior. Suppose you've decided that warnings from the shopping cart demand urgent attention. Listing 8.15 shows how easy it is to add this functionality using inheritance.

```
public interface CriticalLogging extends LogService{
    static aspect BODY{
        public void CriticalLogging.warn(String s){
            System.out.println(s +
                "-Paging systems administrator.");

        }
    }
}
aspect ApplyCriticalLogging{
    declare parents :
        ShoppingCart implements CriticalLogging;
}
/* New output */
Customer's total: 115.5
Fulfillment server down!-Paging systems administrator.
DEBUG: Ship total: 220.0
DEBUG: Tax total: 231.0
Customer's total: 231.0
Fulfillment server down!-Paging systems administrator.
```

**Listing 8.15** Inheritance allows easy customization of logging behavior.

The CriticalLogging interface at overrides the warn method defined on LogService. The new method pages an administrator in the event of a warning. The ApplyCriticalLogging aspect uses declare parents to apply the new interface to the classes that need it. Now, when ShoppingCart calls warn(), CriticalLogging's implementation executes, and the sysadmin receives a page.

### Template Methods

You can also use interfaces to implement the template method pattern in AspectJ. For example, if the logic for calculating totals appeared in several classes you could define a generic implementation of calculateTotal() and defer the details to implementing classes. Listing 8.16 contains a template interface.

```
public interface TotalAlgorithm {

    static aspect BODY{
        public double TotalAlgorithm.
                        calculateTotal(double itemTotal){
```

**Listing 8.16** TotalAlgorithm defines a template method that ShoppingCart fills out. (continues)

```
            double grandTotal = itemTotal;
            grandTotal = calculateShipping(grandTotal);
            grandTotal = calculateTax(grandTotal);
            return grandTotal;
        }

        /* first hook method*/
        public abstract double TotalAlgorithm.
                        calculateShipping(double total);

        /* second hook method*/
        public abstract double TotalAlgorithm.
                        calculateTax(double total);
    }
}

/* Modified shopping cart */
    public class ShoppingCart implements LogService, TotalAlgorithm{
    //...same definition except calculateTotal() not declared
}

/* Output */
//...identical
```

**Listing 8.16** TotalAlgorithm defines a template method that ShoppingCart fills out. (continued)

In standard Java, TotalAlgorithm would be an abstract class (the only choice for combining a mix of abstract and concrete behavior). In AspectJ, you can use an interface similar to LogService. The interface declares two abstract hook methods (calculateShipping and calculateTax). By doing so, it requires subclasses to complete the algorithm by filling in the implementations.

The exciting thing about this example is that ShoppingCart now extends two modules of concrete behavior: CriticalLogging and TotalAlgorithm. Without AspectJ, ShoppingCart would have to choose one or the other (or unite them into an artificial TotalAlgorithmAndCriticalLogging base class).

## Declaring Precedence

Chapter 7 covered advice precedence. Specifically, it dealt with the different effects of precedence and explained how each type of advice reacts to precedence. That chapter also contained several situations in which you had to alter precedence to make advice execute according to your intent. However, we postponed a full consideration of how to declare inter-aspect precedence until this chapter.

## An Example of Precedence

As an example, imagine a join point that several aspects are interested in. These aspects declare before advice on the doSomething() method of SomeObject. You'll give them descriptive names, but for the moment you'll just have them print a message to the console about what they're doing:

```
public aspect Notification {

    before() : call(void doSomething()){
        System.out.println("Notification:" +
            " Sending update somewhere.");
    }
}
```

To specify which aspect has precedence over which, you can include a precedence declaration, either in one of the relevant aspects or in another aspect. For this example, you can use a coordinator aspect:

```
public aspect Coordinator {

    declare precedence : Notification, Tracing, *;
}
```

If you run some code that calls doSomething(), you'll see the following:

```
Notification: Sending update somewhere. //from Notification
Tracing: logging call. //from Tracing
Finally doing something. //the join point
```

Notification prints its message to the console first—indicating that its before advice took precedence over Tracing's before advice. (Precedence doesn't always mean *executes first*; different types of advice react to precedence differently—see Chapter 7 for details.)

## Declare Precedence: The Mechanics

The syntax for a precedence declaration is as follows:

```
PrecedenceDeclaration ::= declare precedence ":" TypePatternList ";"
```

Type patterns that show up in a precedence declaration list conform to some special rules. First, the same aspect cannot be selected by more than one type pattern in the list. The following violates this rule:

```
declare precedence : Notification, Tracing, Not*;
```

Second, the special * pattern means "any aspect not selected by a pattern in the same list." The * pattern allows the declaration to place any non-listed aspects before, between, or in front of listed aspects. For instance, this declaration places any other aspects between Notification and Tracing in terms of precedence:

```
declare precedence : Notification, *, Tracing;
```

Because * essentially means "all other aspects," it cannot appear more than once in the same precedence list.

Multiple aspects can make precedence declarations, and multiple declarations can appear in a single aspect. AspectJ will define a total precedence order for each join point that draws on information from all the precedence declarations in the system. However, it cannot resolve circularity (see the section "Circularity").

## More About Type Patterns

If you add a type pattern to a precedence list that does not match any concrete aspects, AspectJ ignores it. As an example, let's add Exception to the type pattern list:

```
declare precedence : Exception, Notification, Tracing, *;
```

The addition of Exception does not change the precedence of the aspects. Notification will come first, Tracing second, and others third. AspectJ treats Exception as a type pattern without any valid matches.

Because abstract aspects are (by definition) not concrete, adding them to the type pattern list will have no effect. At the time of this writing, the AspectJ compiler does not flag this situation with a -Xlint warning. However, in the future, it will probably do so. Although you cannot add abstract aspects to the list directly, the + type pattern will grant precedence to all aspects that extend a given type. Let's look at two concrete aspects—MoreSecurity and CustomSecurity—that extend a common abstract aspect named Security. Listing 8.17 contains the code.

```
public abstract aspect Security {

    before() : call(void doSomething()){
        System.out.println("Security: checking policy.");
    }
}
public aspect MoreSecurity extends Security {

    before() : call(void doSomething()){
        System.out.println("More security: checking policy.");
    }
}
public aspect CustomSecurity extends Security {

    before() : call(void doSomething()){
```

**Listing 8.17**  Security+ grants precedence to its subaspects. (continues)

```
         System.out.println("CustomSecurity: checking policy.");
    }
}
public aspect Coordinator {

    declare precedence : Security+, Notification, Tracing;
}

/* Output: */
More security: checking policy.
CustomSecurity: checking policy.
Security: checking policy.
Security: checking policy.
Notification: Sending update somewhere.
Tracing: logging call.
Finally doing something.
```

**Listing 8.17**  Security+ grants precedence to its subaspects. (continued)

The Coordinator aspect uses Security+ to match all concrete aspects that extend the Security type. As you can see from the output, MoreSecurity and CustomSecurity now take precedence over Notification and Tracing.

### Subaspects Precede Superaspects

As you may remember from Chapter 7, advice in subaspects takes precedence over advice defined in its parent(s). This explains why the advice from Security appears *after* the advice from either subaspect in Listing 8.17. Unfortunately, there's no way to reverse this order in AspectJ 1.1 (it was possible in AspectJ 1.0).

### The Effects of Multiple Concrete Aspects

If you examine the output in Listing 8.17, you'll see that the advice for Security (the abstract superaspect) executes twice on the same join point. It does so because each concrete aspect instantiates and operates independently of other concrete aspects. Two aspects of type Security crosscut the system—one extended by MoreSecurity, and the other by CustomSecurity. Just as with two totally unrelated aspects (say, Notification and Tracing), each gets a chance to execute its advice at a given join point.

### Marker Interfaces

As with other areas (such as inter-type member declarations), marker interfaces can appear in precedence lists. This ability allows flexibility in applying precedence policies. As an example, the following Coordinator aspect accomplishes the same effect as the previous version:

```
public aspect Coordinator {
    public static interface HighestPriority{};

    declare parents : *Security implements HighestPriority;
    declare precedence : HighestPriority+, Notification,
                         Tracing;
}
```

First the aspect declares a marker interface, HighestPriority. Then it uses declare parents to mark all aspects whose names end with *Security* with the HighestPriority interface. Finally, it uses declare precedence with a + type pattern to state that any concrete aspects that implement HighestPriority receive precedence over all other aspects. (Remember, if HighestPriority appeared without the plus, it would have no effect.)

## Circularity

Two types of precedence circularity are possible: those caused by the same declaration and those caused by multiple declarations. As the mechanics section stated, the same aspect cannot appear more than once in the same precedence list. The following two declarations result in clear circularity—Notification cannot precede itself:

```
declare precedence : Notification, Tracing, Notification;
declare precedence : Notification, Tracing, Not*;
```

You can think of this error as a convenience to the programmer. With only a quick look, you might miss that Not* matches Notification.

Despite this convenience, AspectJ will forgive the following two declarations (even if they appear in the same aspect):

```
declare precedence : Notification, Tracing;
declare precedence : Tracing, Notification;
```

To be more precise, it will forgive them on one condition: *that Tracing and Notification do not declare advice that affects the same join point.* (The example you've been working with up until now would violate the rule.)

Why should AspectJ treat these two conditions (which seem to amount to the same circularity) differently? AspectJ's implementers may have decided on this behavior to allow more precedence declarations to coexist in the same system. Recall from Chapter 7 that AspectJ determines precedence on a per-join-point basis. If advice from two aspects never shares a join point, AspectJ need never determine the exact precedence. Although the declarations cause circularity *in theory*, they might not in practice. Thus two aspects (possibly from different libraries) can make circular precedence declarations without causing unnecessary errors.

## Effects of Precedence

Aspect precedence primarily affects advice. Chapter 7 detailed the effects on each type of advice. However, advice is not the only thing affected by precedence. Recall from earlier in the chapter ("Conflicts and Precedence") that inter-type members from aspects with higher precedence supplant conflicting members from aspects with lower precedence.

## Other Static Crosscutting

You've already seen the big guns in AspectJ's static crosscutting arsenal. The next two subsections cover some of the less expansive—but still very useful—features in the set. Softened exceptions provide a way around Java's sometimes restrictive exception policy. Custom compilation messages allow you to enforce constraints such as coding standards and architectural rules. Both features depend on a certain subtype of pointcut: those whose scope can be determined entirely at compile time. The next subsection discusses these pointcuts.

### Statically Determinable Pointcuts

Pointcuts that operate only on compile-time information are called *statically determinable*. The primitive pointcuts that fit this description are call(), execution(), adviceexecution(), get(), set(), handler(), intialization(), staticinitialization(), within(), and withincode(). User-defined pointcuts that consist entirely of these pointcuts are also considered statically determinable.

Non-statically determinable pointcuts include all pointcuts that expose context (because context is necessarily a runtime concept). The full list of disallowed pointcuts follows:

- **cflow() and cflowbelow()**—Because the control flow of even a moderately complex program cannot be determined at compile time, these pointcuts necessarily operate on runtime information. Some of the functionality of these pointcuts can be replicated with within() and withincode().

- **if()**—If() operates specifically on runtime information, allowing more dynamic crosscutting expressions. As such, it can't be used at compile time.

- **this(), target(), and args()**—These pointcuts are designed to expose runtime context. They can also act as discriminators. If you need to replicate some of their discriminating functionality, you can use the signatures of other pointcuts. For example, call(* foo(..)) && args(int) is close to call(* foo(int)). within() can mimic the function of this() for some purposes.

# Custom Compilation Messages

One of the most interesting features of AspectJ is its ability to specify custom compilation errors and warnings. There are coding practices that should be discouraged and others that should be outright disallowed. Some of these coding practices are matters of style, and tools have been available for years that enforce such concerns as naming conventions. Other concerns are architecture specific. For example, once you have defined a reusable LogService interface (see the section on mixin-style interfaces), you may wish to disallow calls to System.out.println in any class that implements it. AspectJ allows aspects to warn or error on the occurrence of any join point that can be picked out by a statically determinable pointcut.

## *Enforced Thread Safety*

Certain types of components are designed to execute in a multithreaded environment. Java servlets, for instance, often handle concurrent HTTP requests. Such components need to be built so that they do not they do not store thread-specific state in instance variables. If they did, the data from one thread could overwrite data from another. The next example shows how to use a marker interface called ThreadSafe to specify that a component needs to abide by these design rules. An aspect enforces that no state can be set in instance variables (except during initialization). See Listing 8.18 for the full code.

```
public interface ThreadSafe {
    public void init(Object context);

    public static aspect ThreadSafety{

        /* 1
         * Selects any field assignments in
         * a ThreadSafe class that do not
         * occur within init code.
         */
        pointcut notWithinInit() :
            set(!static * *)
```

**Listing 8.18**  The ThreadSafe interface uses an aspect to require that implementers adhere to design rules. (continues)

```
                && within(ThreadSafe+)
                && ! initCode();

        /* 2
         * Picks out init code.
         */
        pointcut initCode() :
            withincode(void init(Object))
            || withincode(new(..));

        /* 3
         * Declares an error on any join
         * point selected by the first
         * pointcut.
         */
        declare error : notWithinInit():
            "Instance variables of a ThreadSafe class cannot be
set outside of the init method or constructor.";
    }

}
public class Demo implements ThreadSafe{
    private int foo;

    public Demo(){
        foo = 0;//ok
    }

    public void init(Object o){
        foo = Integer.parseInt((String)o);//ok
    }

    public void doWork(){
        foo++;//not ok
    }
}
/* Compiler output */
ThreadSafe.java: Instance variables of a ThreadSafe class cannot
be set outside of the init method or constructor [...line
information...]
```

**Listing 8.18**  The ThreadSafe interface uses an aspect to require that implementers adhere to design rules. (continued)

The ThreadSafe interface defines a single method—init(Object)—that mimics the initialization methods found on such components as servlets. It also defines a static aspect with a single declare error form. The notWithinInit pointcut at location 1 picks out any field assignment join points (set(* *)) that occur within any type that implements ThreadSafe (within(ThreadSafe+)) and do not happen in initialization code (! initCode()).

The user-defined pointcut initCode() selects any join points that fall within either the constructor (withincode(new(..))) or the init method (withincode(void init(Object))). Because the first pointcut already narrows affected types to ThreadSafe+, there's no need to specify this information again.

The error declaration operates on the notWithinInit pointcut. It will print an error at each join point matched by the pointcut (the error will stop the compilation). Because the join point foo++ assigns a value to an instance field outside of initialization code, it matches the pointcut. When you compile the example, you get an error stating that the field assignment in doWork is illegal.

## NOTE

This example deliberately simplifies the issue of when field sets should be allowed for complete thread safety. For example, inner types aren't addressed.

### Utility of Custom Compilation Messages

Because of the expressiveness of AspectJ's join point model, declare error and warning allow for sophisticated error conditions. In the ThreadSafe example, you saw how interfaces can allow declarative participation in design enforcement. You can also enforce the design of all classes (omit any type information from the pointcuts), classes with certain names (within(*JDBC)), or classes in a certain package (com.mycompany.model..*).

Using AspectJ in this manner allows you to familiarize yourself with AspectJ's join point model and other AOP concepts without forcing production code to depend on AspectJ. Development and QA builds can use the AspectJ compiler/weaver while the production system uses standard Java tools. This scenario can be attractive to technical managers seeking to build familiarity with a new technology while minimizing risks.

## *Declare Error/Warning: The Mechanics*

There's not a lot to the mechanics of declare error and declare warning. The official syntaxes are as follows:

```
MessageDeclaration ::=
    declare [ error | warning ] ":"
    StaticallyDeterminablePointcut ":"
```

```
      Message ";"
StaticallyDeterminablePointcut ::= ;(a statically determinable
pointcut as described in the previous section)
Message ::= ;(a Java string literal)
```

The pointcut selects all join points that should generate messages if the compiler encounters them. Message constitutes the String the compiler will print if it encounters a match for the pointcut. The only difference between error and warning is that errors will stop the compilation.

### The PatternTesting Project

If you're intrigued by the possibilities of declare error and warning, you're not alone. The PatternTesting project on SourceForge (founded by noted Open Source/testing figure Vincent Massol) exists to provide reusable pattern tests. These pattern tests use both runtime tests and declare error/warning to enforce frequently encountered design rules. At the time of this writing, the project is in its early stages, but it's growing quickly. If you're interested in learning more about AspectJ's capabilities in this area or want to suggest one of your own favorite design guidelines, head to http://patterntesting.sourceforge.net.

## Softening Exceptions

AspectJ allows users to bypass Java's exception checking system by *softening* exceptions. As experienced Java developers are aware, Java ensures that all subclasses of Exception (except those that subclass RuntimeException) are either declared in signatures or caught and handled. Sometimes this feature reminds programmers to handle exceptional conditions. Often, however, exceptional conditions indicate flaws in program design or infrequently encountered combinations of state and input. Intermediary callers may not have any better idea of how to deal with the condition than did the original thrower. As such, a lot of error handling that we've seen in practice amounts to logging the exception or rethrowing an unchecked exception in the place of the original checked exception.

In recognition of this state of affairs, AspectJ's designers incorporated the ability to selectively silence exceptions and rethrow them as unchecked exceptions using the declare soft form.

### Softening IOExceptions

Let's say you want to create a helper class that writes data to a temporary file-based cache. Listing 8.19 contains such a class.

```
public class CacheManager {
    File tempDir = determineTempDir();

    private File determineTempDir(){
        File t =
            File.createTempFile("tmp",null);//1 IOException
        File tempDir  = t.getParentFile();
        t.delete();
        return tempDir;
    }

    public void write(int id, byte[] cacheData){
        File cache  = new File(tempDir, ""+ id);
        cache.createNewFile();//2 IOException
        cache.deleteOnExit();
        OutputStream out = //3 FileNotFoundException
            new FileOutputStream(cache);
        out.write(cacheData);//4 IOException
    }


    static aspect SuppressIOE{
        /* 5 */
        declare soft : IOException : within(CacheManager);
    }

    public static void main(String[] args){
        CacheManager manager = new CacheManager();
        manager.write(0, new byte[]{1,2,3});
    }
}
```

**Listing 8.19** The CacheManager calls several methods that throw IOExceptions.

We've included an end-of-line comment at each method call where an exception might be thrown. Let's look at the potential exceptional conditions. The first occurs at location 1. An IOException while creating a temporary file seems unlikely—perhaps something is wrong with the temporary directory. In any case, it seems like something that should halt the application rather than something which CacheManager's caller could react to. Assuming the IDs passed to write() are unique, the exception at location 2 is also unlikely. At 3, you see the potential for a FileNotFoundException. This seems implausible, because you created the file two lines ago. Finally, at 4 you face another IOException when writing data to the file. In all cases, the exceptions don't seem like normal program conditions. Callers of the CacheManager aren't likely to have a meaningful response either.

To silence the exceptions without inserting identical handler blocks, you can use the declare soft form shown at location 5. The declaration tells AspectJ to soften any IOException thrown from a join point within CacheManager. *To soften* in this context means that AspectJ will catch the exception and rethrow it wrapped in an org.aspectj.lang.SoftException.

### Further Developing the Example

Let's say you add another method to the cache manager that reads data from the cache, and you adjust the main method to exercise it:

```
public InputStream read(int id){
    File cache = new File(tempDir, ""+ id);
    return new FileInputStream(cache);
}
public static void main(String[] args){
    CacheManager manager = new CacheManager();
    manager.write(0, new byte[]{1,2,3});
    manager.read(0);
    manager.read(1);//uh oh
}
```

If you run this code, the output will be something like this:

```
Exception in thread "main"
    org.aspectj.lang.SoftException
at introduction.CacheManager.new$constructor_call0
    (CacheManager.java:41)
at introduction.CacheManager.read
    (CacheManager.java:28)
at introduction.CacheManager.read$method_call0
    (CacheManager.java:48)
at introduction.CacheManager.main
    (CacheManager.java:48)
```

The first stack line takes you to line 41—the aspect where the declare soft conversion takes place. The second line (28) takes you to the read method where the underlying exception was thrown. This outcome brings up two questions: How informative is the soft exception? And, should you have included the read method in the softening?

## NOTE

This stack trace was generated from an earlier version of AspectJ—the exact stack frames are likely to change over time. The basic point (that the stack trace does not reflect that of the original exception) is likely to remain true as the language evolves.

### How Informative Is the SoftException?

The stack trace of the SoftException more accurately reflects the implementation details of the softening mechanism than the chain of events that led to the error. To see this, let's change the declare soft to affect only method execution join points defined in the CacheManager class:

```
declare soft : IOException :
    execution(* *(..))
    && within(CacheManager);
```

Now your stack trace is as follows:

```
Exception in thread "main" org.aspectj.lang.SoftException
at introduction.CacheManager.read
    (CacheManager.java:41)
at introduction.CacheManager.main
    (CacheManager.java:48)
```

Note that you can no longer see line 28 where the exception was thrown. (The exception is softened at a different join point—the method execution rather than the constructor call that caused the problem.) In addition to being unable to track the exception back to the source, you also have no idea what type of exception caused the problem—all you can see is SoftException.

To regain this information, you can access the root cause of a SoftException by calling getWrappedThrowable(). However, most top-level exception handlers will not automatically unwrap and display the root cause for you. As such, unless you operate with care, the SoftException may hinder your bug hunting.

### Use Your Own Soft Exception

You can help matters by using your own wrapper exception instead of the one that ships with AspectJ. A future version of the language will probably support doing this declaratively. In the meantime, you can do it with a bit of advice. Listing 8.20 contains the revised aspect.

```
static aspect SuppressIOE{
    pointcut IOThrowers() :
        execution(* *(..))
        && within(CacheManager);

    after() throwing (IOException e) : IOThrowers(){
        e.printStackTrace();
        /* provide your own wrapper below */
        throw new RuntimeException("" + e);
        //JDK 1.4 allows throw new RuntimeException(e);
```

**Listing 8.20**   New after advice allows a custom wrapper. (continues)

```
    }

    declare soft : IOException : IOThrowers();

}
```

**Listing 8.20**  New after advice allows a custom wrapper. (continued)

The aspect now defines a pointcut—IOThrowers()—that selects all executions of methods defined in the CacheManager class. The aspect reuses the pointcut in both the declare soft form and in after throwing advice. The advice logs the original exception and throws a runtime exception. It could easily use a custom wrapper exception or the exception chaining mechanism standardized in Java 1.4. The advantage of using a different wrapper exception is that the exception itself can automatically display the stack trace of the root cause. (JDK 1.4's chained exceptions do this.) Even without a chained exception, you can examine the logs to see your stack trace:

```
java.io.FileNotFoundException:
    /tmp/1 (No such file or directory)
at java.io.FileInputStream.open(Native Method)
at java.io.FileInputStream.<init>(FileInputStream.java:59)
at java.io.FileInputStream.<init>(FileInputStream.java:90)
at introduction.CacheManager.read(CacheManager.java:28)
at introduction.CacheManager.main(CacheManager.java:60)
```

Now you know what went wrong.

This seems like a lot of trouble to save a few try blocks! Of course, we've deliberately limited the scope to a single class. Your soft declaration could be applied to whole packages if you wished. Having a consistent, cross-system exception handling policy in one place, where it can be easily customized, saves significant code complexity.

### Selective Softening

Now that you have the failure information, let's turn to the second question: Should you soften all the exceptions? The answer belongs to the application authors. If callers of CacheManager can respond to a read problem intelligently (perhaps by generating the non-cached data), then it makes sense to declare the FileNotFoundException in the signature of read(). Because declare soft operates on pointcuts, you can easily adjust which join points' exceptions are softened. For example, you could redefine IOThrowers to read as follows:

```
pointcut IOThrowers() :
    execution(!static * *(..))
    && !execution(* read(..))
    && within(CacheManager);
```

The first line selects non-static method executions (excluding main). The second line excludes the read method by name. The third-line (again) restricts the set of join points to those appearing within CacheManager. Defining the pointcut this way allows the unlikely exceptions to be ignored and the informative exceptions to be propagated normally.

### Softening Exceptions: The Mechanics

Exception handling is inherently tricky. As you've seen in this section, AspectJ allows very different handler effects with a few lines of code. That being said, the syntax of declare soft is not complicated:

```
SoftenDeclaration ::=
    declare soft ":" Type ":"
    StaticallyDeterminablePointcut ";"
```

Type selects the type of exception to soften. As of this writing, it's illegal for Type to refer to a non-Throwable. Keep in mind that many types subclass Exception. The following declaration is *very* broad:

```
declare soft : Exception : somePointcut();
```

In particular, this declaration affects RuntimeException (because it subclasses Exception). Furthermore, AspectJ's SoftException subclasses RuntimeException. Because RuntimeExceptions are already soft, you run the risk of softening the same exception multiple times, making the resultant stack trace difficult to wade through.

## What's Next

This chapter covered AspectJ's inter-type declarations and other static crosscutting forms. We explored the mechanics and motivation behind inter-type members, discovered how and why aspects can alter inheritance hierarchies, and looked closely at AspectJ's treatment of interfaces. We ended the chapter with precedence, exception softening, and custom compilation messages. Each of these features contributes to AspectJ's crosscutting power, although none does so as visibly as the join point and advice combination.

Inter-type declarations open up Java's type system, making it a more suitable ground for complex and powerful aspect behavior. Chapter 13, "Aspect-Oriented Examples: Patterns and Reuse," continues to explore this territory by showing how AspectJ's features can work together to provide reusable crosscutting.

The next chapter will explore aspects, the basic unit of crosscutting modularity in AspectJ.

# CHAPTER 9

# Aspects

If you've worked through the examples in the previous chapters, you'll remember that all the pointcuts, join points, and advice were encapsulated using the *aspect* keyword. AspectJ uses the aspect keyword to denote a structure designed to encapsulate all the code necessary to implement a crosscutting concern, in much the same fashion as the Java keyword class. Without the aspect, the code for implementing a crosscutting concern would simply contribute to the code-tangling problem we are attempting to solve. In this chapter, we will look at:

- Aspect structure
- Aspect extensions
- Instantiation and associations
- Domination
- Giving aspects class privilege
- Example aspects

## Aspect Structure

An aspect looks and acts just like a Java class by providing a convenient container for the encapsulation of join points, pointcuts, and advice code. The aspect can contain its own attributes and methods to further support object-orientation within the concerns the aspect represents. The format of an aspect is as follows:

```
aspect ::= <access> [privilege] [static] aspect <identifier>
<class identifier><instantiation>
<access> ::= public | private [abstract]
<identifier> ::= letter { letter | digit }
<class identifier> ::= [dominates] [extends]
<instantiation> ::= [issingleton | perthis | pertarget | percflow
| perflowbelow]
  //pointcuts
  //advice
  //methods/attributes
}
```

The most common access for an aspect is public, but sometimes an aspect is declared abstract or private (as you will see later in this chapter). The access specified for an aspect follows the rules set up for Java classes. If you don't specify an access type, the aspect will default to package access.

## Writing Aspects

There are several ways to write an aspect and associate it with the primary application code; these approaches relate directly to the concern being implemented through the aspect. An aspect can be located in its own file much as a high-level Java class has its own file. On the other hand, if the aspect affects only a single class in the primary code, you can write it in the same file as the Java class.

The types of concerns that need to be implemented through AspectJ can be grouped according to the level of primary application source they will affect. If a concern indicates that all writes to the file system need to be logged based on their source call, then the concern probably will crosscut a large portion of the code, because the concern requires that the source call for the write be logged. This type of system-level concern generally warrants its own implementation file.

In contrast, the concern may require that all writes to the file system be logged, but only with low-level information about the write. If the primary application has been written appropriately, a database or file system class or two probably is designed to handle all such writes. The aspect can be written in one of the class files to maintain a level of encapsulation.

Finally, a concern may be identified where the functionality is close to the requirements of a system object, but agreement cannot be reached to include the functionality in the Java class. In this case, you can include the aspect as a member of the Java class. In this design, the concern can be implemented as either part of the Java class code or an aspect. By using an aspect, you make an implied statement that the functionality doesn't belong in the primary class definition—the aspect allows it to be pulled out, but you maintain a deep association. In addition, if the AspectJ constructs are the easiest way to implement the functionality, you should use an aspect.

All these situations lead to three possible placements for aspect code as it relates to the primary Java code. The sections that follow cover these placements:

- Separate aspect file
- Aspect combined with a source file
- Aspect embedded in a source class

Listing 9.1 shows the primary Java code used to describe how to add an aspect.

```
public class Simple {
  private String name;

  public String getName() {
    return name;
  }
  public static void main(String args[]) {
    Simple simple = new Simple();
    System.out.println(simple.getName());
  }
}
```

**Listing 9.1**   Simple Java class.

## Separate Aspect File

When a concern crosscuts a large percentage of your primary Java code—or, sometimes, more than a few classes—typical object-oriented design rules dictate that the aspect be created in its own file and not directly associated with any other aspect or class. Using the example Java code in Listing 9.1, you would expect to find a file on the system called Simple.java. Using the same format, you can create an aspect with its own source file by giving the file the same name as the aspect. Consider this aspect definition:

```
public aspect SimpleAspect {
  pointcut namePC() : call(public String Simple.getName());
  before() : namePC() {
  }
}
```

Although this code is short, it creates a new aspect called SimpleAspect that matches all calls to the public String getName() method of the Simple class. The code is contained in a file called SimpleAspect.java. Using the command-line compiler shown in Chapter 3, "Obtaining and Installing AspectJ," the Simple.java and SimpleAspect.java files are compiled with this statement:

```
ajc -classpath ".\;c:\aspectj1.0\lib\aspectjrt.jar" Simple*.java
```

The result is two class files: Simple.class and SimpleAspect.class. Subsequently, the Simple class's main() method can be executed with the following command:

```
java Simple
```

The main() method executes, and appropriate actions are taken when the call is made to the getName() method.

### Combining an Aspect and a Source File

When an aspect affects only a single class or several embedded classes, it is proper to locate it in the same class file as the primary code. Consider the code in Listing 9.2, which is pulled from a source file called SimpleCombined.java. In this source file, a primary code Java class called SimpleCombined is based on the Simple class defined earlier. After the class is the definition of an aspect that has a join point defined specifically on the SimpleCombined class.

```java
public class SimpleCombined {
  private String name;

  public String getName() {
    return name;
  }
  public static void main(String args[]) {
    SimpleCombined simple = new SimpleCombined();
    System.out.println(simple.getName());
  }
}


public aspect SimpleCombinedAspect {
  pointcut namePC() :
    call(public String SimpleCombined.getName());
  before() : namePC() {
  }
}
```

**Listing 9.2**   Aspect and primary code in one file.

As you know, the Java compiler does not like two public classes in the same file, and the compiler will definitely have a problem with both a class and an aspect. To find out what the AspectJ compiler does with code that appears in a single file and contains both a class and an aspect, you need to compile the program using the -preprocess option. The compiler places intermediate java files in the ./ajcworkingdir directory. Even though there is only a single source file, two files are found in the directory: SimpleCombined.java and SimpleCombinedAspect.java. As you might expect, the AspectJ compiler pulled out the aspect in the combined source code and created a new source file for the resulting class. If you are using the latest AspectJ System (1.1 or greater), the -preprocess option isn't available, so you will not see the intermediate steps.

### Embedding an Aspect in a Source Class

If you have a concern that only crosscuts a single class, such as a database connection class, you can embed a concern directly in the class as a class member. The code in Listing 9.3 shows an example of putting a private aspect into a Java class.

```
public class SimpleEmbedded {
  private String name;

  public String getName() {
    return name;
  }
  public static void main(String args[]) {
    SimpleEmbedded simple = new SimpleEmbedded();
    System.out.println(simple.getName());
  }

  private static aspect SimpleCombinedAspect {
    pointcut namePC() : call(public String getName());
    before() : namePC() {
      System.out.println("getName() method found");
    }
  }
}
```

**Listing 9.3**   Embedded aspect and class.

You should notice two things about the internally defined aspect. First, the aspect is declared static; this is a requirement for all such aspects. Second, the access type is declared private. By using a private access type, you fully encapsulate the aspect in the defined class, and no other classes have access to it. However, depending on the application design, the aspect could be public.

# Aspect Extensions

The previous discussion provided some insight into how aspects are created and their conversion from aspects into classes. To further support the development of code to implement concerns, the AspectJ language lets you extend abstract aspects in a number of ways. You can extend an aspect by first building an abstract aspect and using it as a foundation for other aspects. In addition, you can extend aspects by inheriting from other classes and interfaces. However, the AspectJ language does not allow a class to either extend or implement an aspect.

## Building Abstract Aspects

To determine where it would be most beneficial to extend aspects, let's consider an example concern that requires all calls to a sorting algorithm to be timed. The primary application is made up of three classes:

- VectorSort implements the shell, bubble sorts on a Java Vector class, and uses the VecObj as the stored object (Listing 9.4).
- VecObj holds and compares integers (Listing 9.5).
- Work makes appropriate calls to the VecObj and VectorSort classes. Within the Work class, a main() method builds a VectorSort structure, populates the structure, and sorts it (Listing 9.6).

The shell and bubbleSort algorithms are demonstrated in the main() method with repeated calls to populate the vector and sort it.

```
public class VectorSort extends java.util.Vector{
    public VectorSort() {
      super();
    }

    public void shellSort() {
        int i, j, h = 1, n = size(), v;
        VecObj o;

        do {
            h = (3 * h) + 1;
        } while (h <= n);

        do {
            h /= 3;
            for (i = h + 1; i <= n; i++) {
                o = (VecObj) elementAt(i - 1);
                j = i;
                while (o.compare((VecObj) elementAt((j - h) - 1))
< 0) {
                    setElementAt(elementAt((j - h) - 1), j - 1);
                    j = j - h;
```

**Listing 9.4**   VectorSort class source code. (continues)

```
                        if (j <= h) {
                            break;
                        }
                    }
                    setElementAt(o, j - 1);
                }
            } while (h > 1);
        }

        public void bubbleSort() {
            int i, j;

            for (i = 0; i < size(); i++) {
                for (j = i + 1; j < size(); j++) {
                    VecObj o1, o2;

                    o1 = (VecObj) elementAt(i);
                    o2 = (VecObj) elementAt(j);
                    if (o1.compare(o2) > 0) {
                        setElementAt(o2, i);
                        setElementAt(o1, j);
                    }
                }
            }
        }
    }
```

**Listing 9.4**  VectorSort class source code. (continued)

```
public class VecObj {
  private int value;

  public VecObj(int inValue) {
    value = inValue;
  }

  public int getValue() {
    return value;
  }

  public int compare(VecObj o) {
    if (o.getValue() < value)
      return 1;
    else if (o.getValue() == value)
      return 0;
```

**Listing 9.5**  VecObj class source code. (continues)

```
    else
      return -1;
  }
}
```

**Listing 9.5**   VecObj class source code. (continued)

```java
import java.util.Random;

public class Work {
  private VectorSort vs;
  private Random random;

  public Work() {
    vs = new VectorSort();
    random = new Random();
  }

  public void fillVector(int size) {
    vs.clear();

    for (int i=0;i<15;++i) {
      VecObj a = new VecObj(random.nextInt(50));
      vs.add(a);
    }
  }

  public void bubbleSort() {
    vs.bubbleSort();
  }

  public void shellSort() {
    vs.shellSort();
  }

  public void printVector() {

    for (int i=0;i<vs.size();++i) {
      System.out.print(((VecObj)vs.elementAt(i)).getValue() + ",
");
    }
    System.out.println("");
  }

  public static void main (String args[]) {
```

**Listing 9.6**   Work class source code. (continues)

```
    Work work = new Work();

    work.fillVector(10000);
    work.bubbleSort();

    work.fillVector(10000);
    work.shellSort();
  }
}
```

**Listing 9.6**  Work class source code. (continued)

To implement a concern to time all sort calls, you must add code to both the shellSort() and bubbleSort() methods. This seems easy, because you're dealing with only two methods; but in a larger system, the concern could be extended to a large number of operations that need to be timed. Some luckless developer would be given the task of looking through all the code and adding the appropriating timing routines. Later, when a better timing mechanism was developed or the output format needed to be changed, the developer would have to go back and locate every place the original timing information was added. Both tasks are very time consuming, but they can be solved with AspectJ in a matter of minutes. Consider the aspect found in Listing 9.7.

```
import java.util.Date;
import java.text.DateFormat;

public aspect VectorSortAspect {

  pointcut methods() : execution(public void VectorSort.shellSort()) ||
                       execution(public void VectorSort.bubbleSort());

  before() : methods() {
    System.out.println("-->" + thisJoinPoint.getSignature() + ":"
+ (new Date()).getTime());
  }

  after() : methods() {
    System.out.println("<--" + thisJoinPoint.getSignature() + ":"
+ (new Date()).getTime());
  }
}
```

**Listing 9.7**  VectorSortAspect aspect source code.

In this aspect, a pointcut is created to match specific join points in the Vector-Sort class. The *methods* pointcut groups all the methods that need to be timed.

The goal is to use before and after advice based on the execution of the join points to display the start time and end time information. When the aspect is matched against the Work class, the following output is obtained:

```
-->void VectorSort.bubbleSort():1026085802000
<--void VectorSort.bubbleSort():1026085802010
-->void VectorSort.shellSort():1026085802010
<--void VectorSort.shellSort():1026085802010
```

The bubbleSort() method took a total of 10 milliseconds to execute, and the shellSort() method took less than a millisecond to perform the requested sort.

The aspect works for the example code, but let's change it a bit to be more general. In some cases, timings need to be at the nanosecond level; in other cases, milliseconds are fine. The abstract aspect can even be implemented to store timing results in a database. You can provide full flexibility, yet ensure consistency throughout the application. AspectJ allows you to generalize an aspect by declaring it abstract, giving you more flexibility when implementing the timing routines. Listing 9.8 contains an example of the timing aspect in abstract form.

```
abstract aspect AbstractTiming {

  abstract pointcut methods();
  public abstract String getTime();

  before() : methods() {
    System.out.println("-->" + thisJoinPoint.getSignature() + ":"
+ getTime());
  }

  after() : methods() {
    System.out.println("<--" + thisJoinPoint.getSignature() + ":"
+ getTime());
  }
}
```

**Listing 9.8**  Abstract timing aspect.

An aspect must be declared abstract if any of the pointcuts or methods in the aspect are abstract. You create *methods*—a single, abstract pointcut—by prepending the keyword *abstract* to the pointcut and ending the pointcut definition with a semicolon instead of putting a body on the pointcut. The methods pointcut is designed to be defined within a concrete class indicating the join points in a specific application that need to be timed. Further, the getTime() method is abstract so you can provide the specific time precision. Once you've created the abstract aspect, you must create a specific one. Listing 9.9 shows a concrete aspect that extends the abstract aspect.

```
import java.util.Date;
import java.text.DateFormat;

public aspect VectorTiming extends AbstractTiming {

  pointcut methods() :
    execution(public void VectorSort.shellSort()) ||
    execution(public void VectorSort.bubbleSort());

  public String getTime() {
    return new String((new Date()).getTime());
  }
}
```

**Listing 9.9**  Concrete timing aspect.

For the concrete aspect, the use of the *extends* keyword in the VectorTiming definition tells the AspectJ compiler that the concrete aspect needs to define each abstract method and pointcut in the abstract aspect.

You might be required to write another concrete aspect for database access. Using the same abstract timing aspect, the new concrete aspect is easy to write:

```
public aspect DatabaseTiming extends AbstractTiming {

  pointcut methods() :
    execution(public void DatabaseAccess.runQuery()) ||
    execution(public void DatabaseAccess.getMetadata());

  public String getTime() {
    return new String((new Date()).getTime());
  }
}
```

AspectJ only allows inheritance from abstract aspects; the compiler will not allow inheritance from a concrete aspect. In addition, if your derived aspect attempts to override a concrete pointcut in the inherited aspect, a compile-time error will occur.

## Inheriting from Classes and Interfaces

In the previous example, you saw how an aspect can extend an abstract aspect. In addition, an aspect can extend traditional Java classes and interfaces. The VectorTiming aspect in Listing 9.9 handles all the time functionality itself. You can also create a timing interface, called Timings (see Listing 9.10).

```
public interface Timings {
  int PRECISION = 10;

  public String getTime();
  public long getTimeLong();
}
```

**Listing 9.10**　Timings interface.

Listing 9.11 shows how the VectorTiming2 aspect can not only extend the AbstractTiming aspect but also implement the Timings interface. In order to implement the Timings interface, the VectorTiming2 aspect must define both the getTime() and getTimeLong() methods. By using an interface, separate developers can implement specific functionality while maintaining consistency.

```
import java.util.Date;
import java.text.DateFormat;

public aspect VectorTiming2 extends AbstractTiming implements
Timings {

  pointcut methods() :
    execution(public void VectorSort.shellSort()) ||
    execution(public void VectorSort.bubbleSort());

  public String getTime() {
    return new String((new Date()).getTime()+"");
  }

  public long getTimeLong() {
    return (new Date()).getTime();
  }
}
```

**Listing 9.11**　Aspect using an interface and abstract aspect.

# Aspect Instantiation and Associations

As we discussed earlier in this chapter, the AspectJ compiler converts aspects into traditional Java classes for compilation by the Java compiler. During conversion and before any of the system code executes, the new class is given a static attribute that is assigned an object of the aspect class type. This type of object creation is the default for all aspects and is considered a singleton approach. One object of the aspect class type is instantiated for use in all primary class and aspect code. Aspect instantiation is performed by static code in the class definition because, by design, no public constructor is available.

The AspectJ language provides several types of instantiation methods for aspects in a system:

- Singleton
- Per-object
- Per-control-flow

The different types can be assigned directly or inherited from a parent aspect. If an aspect doesn't have a parent, the default singleton type is used.

## Singleton Aspects

Singleton is the default type assigned to all aspects that do not have parent aspects or declare a specific instantiation type. The singleton type can be assigned to an aspect to ensure that only one object of the aspect class type is created for the entire primary application. One concrete use of this instantiation type is to change the instantiation type inherited from a parent and force only one object to be created. The format to create a singleton aspect is as follows:

```
aspect ID issingleton {
}
```

## Per-Object Aspects

If you need an aspect object created for each object associated with a this or target designator, then you can use the perthis(pointcut) and pertarget(pointcut) aspect instantiation keywords. In most cases, these keywords cause a unique aspect class object to be created for each object encountered with this or target. When the join point associated with an aspect using these keywords is matched, the appropriate aspect class object is used for execution of the aspect advice. This differs from the singleton approach, where only a single object is available to the entire Java application. The format for using the perthis and pertarget keywords is as follows:

```
aspect ID perthis(pointcut) {
}
aspect ID pertarget(pointcut) {
}
```

The example code in Listing 9.12 and the aspect in Listing 9.13 show how perthis instantiation works.

```
import java.util.Random;
import java.util.Date;

public class Work implements Runnable {
  private VectorSort vs;
  private Random random;
  private int count;

  public int getCount() {
    return count;
  }

  public void setCount(int i) {
    count = i;
  }

  public Work() {
    vs = new VectorSort();
    random = new Random(new Date().getTime());
  }

  public void fillVector(int size) {
    vs.clear();

    for (int i=0;i<count;++i) {
      VecObj a = new VecObj(random.nextInt(50));
      vs.add(a);
    }
  }

  public void bubbleSort() {
    vs.bubbleSort();
  }

  public void run() {
    setCount(random.nextInt(5000));
    fillVector(count);
    bubbleSort();
  }

  public static void main (String[] args) {
    for(int i=0;i<5;i++) {
      try {
        Work work = new Work();
        Thread thread = new Thread(work);
        thread.sleep(5);
```

**Listing 9.12**   perthis keyword example. (continues)

```
        thread.start();
      } catch(Exception e) { }
    }
  }
}
```

**Listing 9.12**  perthis keyword example. (continued)

```
import java.util.Date;
import java.text.DateFormat;

public aspect VectorTiming extends AbstractTiming perthis(this(Work)) {

  String startTime;

  pointcut methods(Work obj) :
    execution(public void Work.bubbleSort()) &&
    this(obj);

  before(Work obj) : methods(obj) {
    startTime = getTime();
  }

  after(Work obj) : methods(obj) {
    System.out.println("Count: " + obj.getCount() + " Start Time
= " + startTime);
    System.out.println("Count: " + obj.getCount() + " End   Time
= " + getTime());
  }

  public String getTime() {
    return new String((new Date()).getTime()+"");
  }
}
```

**Listing 9.13**  perthis keyword aspect.

In Listing 9.12, five different Work objects are created. Each object generates a random number of values in a Vector object and then sorts the vector using the bubble sort algorithm. The aspect in Listing 9.13 builds a new aspect object for each new Work object, as indicated by the this(Work) designator in the perthis keyword. Each aspect object attempts a match on the bubbleSort call in the Work object. When a match occurs, the before advice gets the current time and stores it in a private attribute. The after() advice for the same match outputs both the value of the private attribute and the ending time. Here's the output when the example code is executed with the perthis aspect:

```
Count: 6 Start Time = 1030497141697
Count: 6 End    Time = 1030497141797
Count: 1534 Start Time = 1030497141747
Count: 1534 End    Time = 1030497142067
Count: 1534 Start Time = 1030497141697
Count: 1534 End    Time = 1030497142107
Count: 3887 Start Time = 1030497141487
Count: 3887 End    Time = 1030497143399
Count: 4116 Start Time = 1030497141927
Count: 4116 End    Time = 1030497143650
```

Notice that all the start times are different, as you would expect if you had five different aspect objects. Here's the result if the same example code is executed but the aspect doesn't use perthis:

```
Count: 184 Start Time = 1030497196966
Count: 184 End    Time = 1030497196986
Count: 184 Start Time = 1030497196966
Count: 184 End    Time = 1030497197157
Count: 2814 Start Time = 1030497196966
Count: 2814 End    Time = 1030497198228
Count: 2814 Start Time = 1030497196966
Count: 2814 End    Time = 1030497198438
Count: 3427 Start Time = 1030497196966
Count: 3427 End    Time = 1030497198629
```

In this case, all the start times are the same. The first thread that executes the bubbleSort() method sets the private attribute, and all other matches write over it when they execute. The last thread to set the attribute dictates its value for all the matches. This starting value is printed by all the threads in the after advice.

## Per-Control-Flow Aspects

When you use the cflow and cflowbelow designators in an aspect, a flow of execution is matched based on the associated join points for the designators. You can use the percflow(pointcut) and percflowbelow(pointcut) keywords with an aspect to force the instantiation of an aspect class object each time the flow of execution is entered. The format of the keywords is as follows:

```
aspect ID percflow(pointcut) {
}
aspect ID percflowbelow(pointcut) {
}
```

To explore how these designators can be used, consider Listing 9.13. If you replace perthis(Work) with percflow(execution(public void Work. bubbleSort())), you will significantly narrow the scope of where the aspect objects are created and destroyed. Once the scope is narrowed, you can use different join points within the execution flow to time specific elements of the code. A new aspect is shown in Listing 9.14, where only the timings associated with calls to the compare() method are matched.

```
import java.util.Date;
import java.text.DateFormat;

public aspect VectorTiming extends AbstractTiming percflow(execution(public
void VectorSort.bubbleSort())) {

  String startTime;

  pointcut methods() :
    call(public int VecObj.compare(..));

  before() : methods() {
    startTime = getTime();
  }

  after() : methods() {
    System.out.println(" Start Time = " + startTime);
    System.out.println(" End   Time = " + getTime());
  }

  public String getTime() {
    return new String((new Date()).getTime()+"");
  }
}
```

**Listing 9.14**  Percflow used in aspects.

The output from the aspect is similar to that for perthis, except the timings are very small because the calls to the compare() method are quick.

# Aspect Domination and Precedence

In addition to hierarchies, there is another way to allow aspects to dominate or wrap each other. *Aspect domination* occurs when pointcuts are defined in two separate aspects, and those pointcuts consist of common join points. Consider the aspect in Listing 9.13, where a join point is defined on the execution of the bubbleSort() method. Everything works well until another aspect is defined on the same join point, but for a different crosscutting concern (such as logging):

```
aspect LogBubble {
  pointcut method() :
    call(public void Work.bubbleSort());
  before() : method() {
    //do logging
  }
}
```

You now have two different aspects based on the same join point. A number of factors dictate which advice code associated with a matched pointcut will evaluate first. If the advice and pointcuts are defined in different aspects, then the order of execution is undefined—either pointcut and advice could execute first. If one aspect is a subaspect of another, the subaspect pointcut/advice will execute first.

In the previous example, the timing advice might execute before the logging advice. This could be a problem, because you are timing your logging as well as the bubble sort algorithm. You can prevent this behavior by using the *dominates* keyword. Using the aspect in Listing 9.13, change the first lines as follows:

```
public aspect VectorTiming
   extends AbstractTiming
   dominates LogBubble
   perthis(this(Work) {
```

When the bubbleSort() method is matched, the timing aspect will execute instead of the LogBubble aspect, because it dominates the aspect. (See the end of Chapter 7, "Advice," for more information about aspect precedence.)

## Accessing Aspect Objects

During the execution of the application, the object(s) created for a specific aspect in a system are made available to other aspects using the aspectOf() method. When the aspectOf() method is executed within another aspect, the system attempts to return the object currently associated with the specific aspect. Consider the code in Listing 9.15.

```
public aspect VectorLogging dominates VectorTiming {

  pointcut methods() :
    call(public void Work.bubbleSort());

  before() : methods() {
    System.out.println("Start time = " + VectorTiming.aspectOf(thisJoin-
Point.getThis()).getTime());
  }

  after() : methods() {
    System.out.println("End time = " +
VectorTiming.aspectOf(thisJoinPoint.getThis()).getTime());
  }
}
```

**Listing 9.15** Aspect using the AspectOf() method.

The new aspect called VectorLogging dominates VectorTiming (defined in Listing 9.15). When the application in Listing 9.14 executes, the VectorLogging aspect dominates the VectorTiming aspect when the bubbleSort() method is matched. In this case, you still want some timing information, so both the before and after advice code blocks execute the aspectOf() method against the VectorTiming aspect. The aspectOf() method tries to find an aspect object associated with the current join point based on the specific aspect (VectorTiming, in this case). If the object is found, the code calls the object's getTime() method.

The aspectOf() method has two different signatures, which relate to the instantiation method for the aspect:

- **aspectOf( )**—Used with singleton and percflow/percflowbelow
- **aspectOf( object)**—Used with perthis and pertarget

The VectorTiming aspect uses perthis, so your VectorLogging aspect must pass the current object using the getThis() method call.

# Aspect Privilege

As you begin to write aspects, sometimes you will want to access a private attribute of a class being crosscut. Generally, you can use a simple accessor method to obtain the attribute's value. Consider the primary code in Listing 9.16.

```
public class PrivateAttribute {
  private int cannotSeeMe;
  private int accessorAvailable;

  public PrivateAttribute(int a, int b) {
    cannotSeeMe = a;
    accessorAvailable = b;
  }

  public int getAccessorAvailable() {
    return accessorAvailable;
  }

  public static void main (String args[]) {
    PrivateAttribute pa = new PrivateAttribute(5, 10);
  }
}
```

**Listing 9.16** Primary code with private attributes and accessor methods.

The PrivateAttribute class has two private attributes that are available to the code in the class. There is a single accessor method for the accessorAvailable attribute, but not for the cannotSeeMe attribute. External objects cannot access the cannotSeeMe attribute. If you were to write an aspect that tried to access the cannotSeeMe attribute, an error would result. Consider the aspect in Listing 9.17.

```
public aspect PrivateAttributeAspect {
  pointcut startIt(PrivateAttribute obj) :
    initialization(PrivateAttribute.new(..)) &&
    target(obj);

  after(PrivateAttribute obj) : startIt(obj) {
    System.out.println(obj.getAccessorAvailable());
    System.out.println(obj.cannotSeeMe);
  }
}
```

**Listing 9.17** Aspect with private attribute attempt.

When the aspect and the primary code in Listing 9.18 are compiled, the following error results:

```
.\PrivateAttributeAspect.java:8:28:
    PrivateAttribute.cannotSeeMe has private access
    System.out.println(obj.cannotSeeMe);
                       ^

1 errors
```

The compiler does not allow the aspect to access any of the protected or private attributes in the target/this returned object by default. This behavior clearly is a good thing, because the Java compiler is maintaining the access types defined for the aspects and classes. However, what if you really need to access the private/protected attribute, and there is no accessor method? The answer is to define the aspect as privileged. Consider the aspect in Listing 9.18.

```
privileged aspect PrivateAttributeAspect {
  pointcut startIt(PrivateAttribute obj) :
    initialization(PrivateAttribute.new(..)) &&
    target(obj);

  after(PrivateAttribute obj) : startIt(obj) {
    System.out.println(obj.getAccessorAvailable());
    System.out.println(obj.cannotSeeMe);
  }
}
```

**Listing 9.18** Privileged aspect.

The privileged keyword added to the aspect in Listing 9.20 allows the aspect to have internal access to the private cannotSeeMe attribute. Clearly this is a violation of encapsulation and security for the primary code class. Just as the friend functionality in C++ was a hot topic of discussion concerning its breakage of encapsulation in a class, the privileged keyword is also troublesome. There could be times when it is absolutely necessary to access a private attribute of a class—say, when there is no accessor method—but you should take extreme care when doing so.

## NOTE

The astute reader will notice from the formal definition at the beginning of the chapter that the protected access type is missing. The AspectJ language does not allow you to assign the protected access type to an aspect. Attempting to use protected will result in a compile-time error.

## What's Next

In this chapter, we have taken a comprehensive look at the aspect and the various ways aspects can be written to fully implement a concern. The AspectJ language combines all the major concepts like join points and pointcuts and brings them into the aspect, allowing designers and developers to maintain class encapsulation.

The next section of the book covers *using* AspectJ: examples, common problems, tools, and finally two case studies that apply aspect-oriented techniques to real applications. In Chapter 10, we begin our look at the practical uses of AspectJ.

# CHAPTER 10

# Development Uses of AspectJ

A s our attention turns away from the specifics of the AspectJ language and toward using the system to solve real problems, we focus on introducing AspectJ to your development team members so that they understand its benefits and endorse using the language. This chapter examines these topics:

- Adopting AspectJ
- Testing uses
- Addressing crosscutting concerns
- Understanding the production aspects
- Tuning performance

## Adopting AspectJ

Suppose we're sitting in a conference room with our development team, listening as team leaders express the goals of our project. The business leaders talk about the domain of the user, how we have to develop a complete product that fits the needs of the user, how we don't have enough time, and how extremely tight the budget is. The quality assurance (QA) team leader explains how the code must be bulletproof, how the concepts of Extreme Programming will be used to develop tests up front, and how we need to keep the code modular so we can incorporate testing with ease. Finally, the development leader gets up, looks at the business leader, looks at the QA leader, and then goes down the road of writing quality software. The team must reuse code, build fully encapsulated classes, and document all appropriate functionality. The code must fulfill the needs of the user as well as internal organizations, and above all, the requirements must be met.

At the end of the leadership speeches, the team is clapping and ready to dive into analyzing and designing the solution to the problem. All the while you may be quietly sitting in your seat wondering where the reuse will come from, the 2.1 release of the software or the 3.0 version (and the code wasn't written all that well in those versions). You are also thinking about the concept of building fully encapsulated classes. Is this even possible? You remember that in your last project, all calls to the database had to be logged and the result of the actual database transaction was also saved for logging purposes. These requirements absolutely violated the concept of encapsulation. It's like the use of the C++ friend keyword became a requirement in itself instead of a forbidden keyword.

After reading about AspectJ and how it can help with the process of building new software (as well as retrofitting code that is also in production), you may want AspectJ to be part of the process for your next project. But first, you have to convince team members and management that AspectJ will make for better code and better coders. In the interim, you can use AspectJ for your own testing, logging, QA activities, and other functions.

## Why Adopt AspectJ?

Throughout this book, we have discussed why individual developers and organizations should adopt the use of AspectJ, but a few points are worth repeating. AspectJ allows you to separate the concerns that comprise your system. By separating concerns, you are able to build classes that represent the primary requirement of a system without having to add more support code to them. If all of the calls to a database transaction class need to be logged and timed, the additional code for this task doesn't have to be part of the database class itself. The class doesn't care about being logged and timed—it just wants to perform a transaction against the database. The support or ancillary logging and timing code doesn't belong in the class.

This is a simple example to get your team thinking. All it takes is a whiteboard and a few minutes to draw out a simple database class and show how adding extraneous support code breaks all the object-oriented rules the language itself is trying to enforce. After a few strokes of the marker, you will have a number of the team members agreeing that forcing all this additional information into the primary classes isn't a good idea. In addition to addressing the development side of things, you can provide examples for the testing group.

In a simple manner, full-parameter verification can be provided for key methods of a class or all methods. Verification can be switched on for testing to ensure the code catches all conditions and then switched off in production for efficient code execution. Finally, you can pull in the business leadership because AspectJ is still Java, it doesn't cost anything, and the analysis of the problem will still produce the same information—but now instead of forcing requirements into unrelated classes, independent ones will be created. Management will also be able to see the benefits AspectJ brings in the area of refactoring, adding new requirements, and less time searching for bugs.

## How to Put AspectJ into the Process

During your discussions, someone will ask where AspectJ and crosscutting fit into the software development process. Before answering this question, let's quickly review the development process. When a new project is starting, or an existing application requires increased functionality, someone is responsible for gathering user requirements. These requirements are typically written or typed long-hand, and then converted to a more formal product like use cases or functional specs. This conversion is called the *specification*; it provides both the user and the design team with information about what the system must do. In most cases, the use cases are more verbose and provide a level of application flow, but both contain the necessary information about the end system.

Once the specification document has been created, a design team begins the process of developing the packages, classes, and relationships between all of them. The goal of the design is to create a system of classes that is able to work together to handle all the requirements of the system. Where does AspectJ come into play? There are a couple places where you can use the concepts behind AspectJ.

The first is when the specification document is created. While the analysis team is building the document, those requirements that stand out as being core or primary to the developer and use of the system should be marked as such. Determining whether or not a requirement crosscuts the system is sometimes challenging, but they can be identified by looking for requirements that touch many parts of the system. Also, many broadly defined requirements will crosscut that system as they try to gather information. At design time if the analysis team has separated the requirements, the primary requirements are written using Java and the secondary or crosscutting ones are written using AspectJ. If the analysis team has not separated the requirements, the design team should build the classes for the system with an eye to those requirements that involve placing attributes and methods in more than a few classes. These requirements are secondary and crosscut the primary functionality of the code. When the design is finished, another pass of the classes should be performed in order to identify any other requirements that crosscut the system classes. In some cases, such as logging, the crosscutting will entail a large number of classes, but a memory pool requirement might affect only a small percentage of classes. In both these cases, however, pulling the requirement and writing it in AspectJ will create a more modular and encapsulated design.

## Previous Development Work

If your team is in the middle of development or you are currently doing maintenance work on a legacy Java application, AspectJ can still be of use. During the refactoring of a class or even while you're making a relatively minor change, you can analyze the class structure to determine if any of the methods or attributes appear to crosscut the class. You can pull these out of the code and put them into the AspectJ language without affecting too much of the code. The aspect could even be included in the class as a member to avoid having to add a file to the system.

## Backing It Out

During software development, AspectJ can be easily backed out because you have the code in the form of an advice and the location to place the code based on the join points. You'd just need to add the advice code to all places in the system when the join point is found. Of course, this could be a huge issue if requirements crosscut many of the system classes, and would add greatly to the complexity of the system. Even more important is the fact that you'd be tangling the application code on purpose! Avoiding spaghetti code is one of the reasons we want to use AspectJ in the first place.

## Development Uses

There are many places in the development of a system where temporary code is needed to handle such tasks as tracing and condition checking on method parameters. Just imagine the excitement from the QA group when you show them how a use case flows through the system. You can show arguments going into all methods and validating their contents.

## Tracing

When you're developing a system, it can be helpful to follow the flow of information and methods calls made during execution. This is especially true when you're modeling a use case with the code. Since most developers rely on the class's API and related documentation, possibly written by a fellow developer, they won't know what occurs within the other object. By using tracing, all the method calls can be mapped from the moment the execution enters the method until it exits.

Before we discuss how AspectJ enables detailed tracing, let's consider how we would write tracing into our own code. One of the most common methods for tracing an application is using the step function available in many IDEs. The debugger provides the ability to execute the code and follow the statement line by line. Within JBuilder, for example, you can set a breakpoint in the code and execute each statement with the press of a button. You can watch the code as it moves from object to object executing methods along the way. This works well for small traces, but it you have even 20 or 30 objects, or the code relies on some level of timing, the IDE isn't a good solution. If you have a very large application that relies on specific timings, the debugger probably cannot be used—it might rely on a specific Java Virtual Machine, for instance. Of course, if your application is executing in a production environment and the execution isn't directly reproducible in a development environment, you need another option.

A better way is to put console or file output statements in each of the methods of all classes. The code might be as simple as this:

```
System.out.println("--> enter move method");
System.out.println("<-- exit move method");
```

As the code above is activated, enter and exit text will be displayed based on the exact execution path. It is a fairly easy task to insert these two statements in 30 different classes, each of which has 10–15 methods. But don't forget that QA doesn't want to see these statements when the code is submitted for testing, so you might need to wrap the code with a condition to keep the code from executing when a release build is created. In that case, every method would need a minimum of four additional lines of code for tracing purposes.

A much better solution is to use an aspect. For example:

```
public aspect trace {
pointcut method() : execution(* *.*(..));
before() : method() {
System.out.println("--> enter "+ thisJoinPoint.getSignature() + "
method");
  }
after() : method() {
System.out.println("<-- exit " + thisJoinPoint.getSignature() + "
method");
  }
}
```

In this aspect, the pointcut catches all methods in all classes. The before advice prints the enter text, and the after advice prints the exit text. In a matter of

10 minutes, all the code in your application can be traced without affecting the individual methods of the classes.

## Condition Checks

For the most part, as developers we are responsible for handling any and all data that is passed to a method from any source, whether from the local object or another object. We use many lines of code to determine if an argument value falls within acceptable ranges or even has a value at all. During development, we anticipate the values passed to the method and code appropriately. Wouldn't it be great to have something within the methods that recorded the values coming to the method through the parameter and possibly analyze them for us so we know what additional checks to put in the production code?

Using Java to add this type of functionality to class's methods would require several lines of code to perform the recording of the value, but there really isn't any way to capture the incoming value and change it into either an appropriate value or an inappropriate one for testing purposes. However, AspectJ does provide this ability:

```
public aspect paramTest {
pointcut method(String s) :
call(public void myClass.func1(String)) &&
args(s);
void around(String s) : method(s) {
If (s == null || s == "")
proceed("empty")
else If (s.length > 64) {
proceed("string too long")
else
proceed(s);
  }
}
```

In this example, we are catching all calls to the func1() method of the myClass class. When the join point is matched, a quick check is made of the incoming string parameter. If the value is ever null or an empty string, a new string is passed with the value of "empty"; otherwise, the length of the string is checked and if the value is greater than 64, a smaller string is passed to the method. If neither of these cases is true, the method is passed the original string. This check is important because the output display might have a 64-character limitation and strings longer than 64 become unreadable. The code could be further enhanced by putting the incoming string value into a file for later checking.

The QA group as well as the developer can take advantage of the values being passed to the method during integration of the class into the full system as well as during the unit test phase. The output shows if adequate values are being tested and if additional code needs to be incorporated to handle obscure values. In many systems, a failure occurs when a value is passed to a method that we just didn't think could be passed. During the testing of an application with the preceding aspect, the QA team, as well as the development team, could have a task in their methodology for analyzing the values to the method. This analysis would provide information on the largest, smallest, most frequent, and other values passed. The code could be optimized for specific values or other changes as needed.

These types of aspects would be most beneficial in the development and testing of the application. When the application is put into production, the aspects could either be removed or made nonfunctional. However, if an issue occurs in production, we could easily add the aspects back to the application, and additional information would be made available to a production support team.

# Production Aspects

As you can tell from the previous discussion, a large amount of data can be produced from the aspects. This isn't something that you would want to occur during production. It would even be too dangerous to output large amounts of data to a file because the file system could become full without maintenance. There are some requirements in the development of a system that also crosscut the primary functionality and must be available during production. In this section, we look at two such requirements:

- Logging and timings
- Authorization

## Loggings and Timings

During the implementation of a trace aspect, we as developers gain a better understanding of the execution of our application. As you might already know, if you provide your users with a GUI filled with buttons and edit lines, they will click the buttons and put all kinds of data in the edit lines. You don't have too much control over what they will put in the edit lines, nor do you control the order in which the user clicks the buttons.

When users report an error with your software, they won't always know what they did to receive the error. This type of situation suggests the need for some level of logging within production code. In addition, key areas of the system also benefit from the use of timings to determine if they are holding up under the stress of live production use.

In a traditional development environment, logging of the application would be accomplished by creating a log class such as this:

```
public class log {
public log() {
//open log file or connect to db
  }
public void store(String msg) {
// place msg in db or file
  }
}
```

When the application starts, a log object is instantiated to be used globally by the application or instantiated locally for each of the major objects. Each time an error, warning, or simple log message needs to be placed in the file or the database, a call is made to the store() method passing in the necessary text. We place the method in the primary code to be called during execution. We can create the same type of class for the timing concern with start() and end() methods that make appropriate calls to either the log class or internal methods for storing the timing information in a file or database.

It is up to us to place the log and timing methods in the right places and methods. Any changes to the method calls or text that should be saved will require a search for all possible calls.

The use of an aspect makes our job much easier. Using either a common join point or a combination of numerous specific join points, we can accomplish the logging using a comprehensive aspect. For example:

```
public aspect log {
pointcut CPMethods() : execution(* CFClass.*(..));
pointcut EPMethods() : execution(* EPClass.*(..));
pointcut DBMethods() : execution(* DBClass.*(..));
pointcut EPDBMethods() : EPMethods() || DBMethods();
before() : CPMethods() {
  }

after() : CPMethods() {
  }

before() : EPDBMethods() {
  }

after() : EPDBMethods() {
  }
}
```

In this aspect, we've used three separate pointcuts to obtain the join points of methods specific to three classes of the application. When any of the methods of the CPClass, EPClass, and DBClass are matched, before advice is executed. It is expected that this advice will put some type of text into a database or file indicating that the beginning of a method has started. The after advice is used to indicate successful execution of the method. In discussing the log class versus the log aspect, it can be argued that there is finer control available with the log class because the log.store("here") call can be put anywhere in a method, not just at the beginning or end of a method, as is the case with an aspect.

Although true, a good system design states there should be a small number of statements, 10 or so, in a typical method. If this is the case, there isn't much difference between putting the advice at the beginning and end of the methods as opposed to including several statements in a method. Of course, if there is another method call within the current one, it will be matched by an appropriate join point.

In the next aspect example, we consider a timings aspect that will place specific start and end clock values into the database or appropriate log file:

```
public aspect timings dominates log{
pointcut DBMethods(String s) :
execution(public void DBMethods.*(String)) &&
args(s)
before(String s) : DBMethods(s) {
    }
after(String s) : DBMethods(s) {
    }
}
```

One of the first things you notice is the use of the dominates keyword in the timings aspect. The timings aspect is said to dominate the log aspect previously defined: all methods with a join point matching public void DBMethods.*(String) will trigger the timings DBMethods() pointcut instead of the DBMethods() pointcut also defined more generally in the log aspect. Basically, we want all methods in the DBMethods class to be logged, but for those methods that have a single String argument, we want timing information provided in their record. These methods might be used to send SQL statements to the database; the amount of time used by the methods has a direct effect on performance, so it should be recorded and reviewed.

In both the timings and log aspects, we are able to provide basically the same level of performance and functionality of the log/timing classes but in a much better encapsulation of the code.

## Authorization

Many Web applications now require a username and password. In most cases, the authorization of a person has to be passed from one page to another or maintained in some sort of database state. In many traditional applications, the issue of authorization is also a consideration, so access to particular parts of a system needs to be restricted to specific individuals. When a user attempts to select a particular option, control will more than likely be transferred to a specific method for the requested functionality. The first line of the method generally determines if the user has rights to access that particular part of the application. Many applications have differing levels of authorization from the module to the screen and even down to a specific field. All of these different levels relate to an object instantiated in the system. For example:

```
public class Profile {
private String name;
private String address;

public void setName(Caller c, String s) {
if (Caller.credentials("nameprofile") == 'y') {
name = s;
    }
  }
public void setAddress(Caller c, String s) {
if (Caller.credentials("addressprofile") == 'y') {
address = s;
    }
  }
}
```

In this simple class, there exists a private variable called *name* that represents the username of a person in our medical application. The name associated with the object is sensitive data and shouldn't be changed by just anyone. In order to accomplish this goal, the setName() method requests the credentials of the current user of the system specifically referencing the nameprofile field. If the user has the appropriate credentials, the user is allowed to make the name change.

Now take a look at the setAddress() method. Our application allows a user to change the address but not the name of a medical client. If the code attempts to call the setAddress() method, the code checks the addressprofile credentials of the user to determine if the user should be allowed to change the address. Just imagine all of the code necessary to check city, state, zip, and many other fields. Instead, an aspect can handle the authorization automatically. Consider the following:

```
public aspect authorization {
pointcut name(Caller c, String s) :
(setName(Caller, String) ||
setTelephone(Caller, String)) &&
args(c, s);

pointcut address(Caller c, String s) :
```

```
(setAddress(Caller, String) ||
setCity(Caller, String) ||
setState(Caller, String)) &&
args(c, s);
around(Caller c, String s) : name(c, s) {
if (Caller.credentials("nameprofile") == "y") {
proceed(c, s);
    }
  }
around(Caller c, String s) : address(c, s) {
if (Caller.credentials("addressprofile") == "y") {
proceed(c, s);
    }
  }
}
```

In this aspect, all the join points related to the changing of sensitive data for the client are grouped in the name() pointcut and all address-related methods in the address() pointcut. When a join point is matched, the appropriate pointcut will be matched and the selected around advice executed. The code checks the credentials of the user of the code and determines if the original code should proceed or be bypassed. Any necessary changes to the way authorization is done within the application can be easily determined by looking at the aspect code itself.

# What's Next

In this chapter, we provided important information for those of you who want to adopt AspectJ and the AOP methodology but have to convince managers and team members. By understanding how AOP can be used in both development and production phases, you can realize the full power of AOP. In the next chapter, we present a handful of examples to show practical uses of AOP.

# Using AspectJ Tools

The AspectJ system is designed to be more than just an extension to Java and a compiler for converting the extension keywords into Java-compliant code. In the quest to build a comprehensive solution for aspect-oriented programming (AOP), the AspectJ team has included the following tools in the package:

- The AspectJ compiler
- The AspectJ structure browser
- IDE extensions
- Ant support
- The AspectJ debugger (ajdb)
- The AspectJ documentation creator (ajdoc)

In this chapter, we cover each of these and provide examples along the way.

## AspectJ Compiler Options

For most of the examples in this book, we've used the AspectJ compiler without having to use command-line options other than –classpath and –preprocess. In this section, we detail all of the command-line flags available with the AspectJ compiler:

**–argfile** *path*—Specifies the location of a line-delimited file containing possible command-line options. You place the options in the command line of the compiler.

**–aspectpath**—Specifies the path to aspects found in JAR or CLASS files.

**–bootclasspath** *path*—Specifies the location of the default boot CLASS files.

**–classpath** *path*—Specifies the location of any support files needed for the compiler.

**–d** *directory*—Specifies where the compiler should place the final CLASS files it produces. The default directory is the current directory.

**–emacssym**—Produces symbols from the compiled code for use with Emacs.

**–encoding** *Encoding*—Specifies the encoding used in the source files to be compiled.

**–extdirs** *path*—Specifies the location of the extension files.

**–incremental**—Instructs the compiler to use incremental compiling.

**–injars** *path*—Specifies JARs used in the weaving process. You separate multiple JARs with a colon (:) or a semicolon (;).

**–noweave**—Causes Java code to be compiled but not woven.

**–O**—Optimizes the code produced by the AspectJ compiler.

**–outjars**—Specifies the path and name of the JAR in which the compiler should place the compiled code.

**–source 1.4**—Causes the compiler to treat assert as a true language keyword as defined in version 1.4 of the Java language.

**–usejavac**—Forces the system to use the Javac compiler when producing final CLASS files.

**–verbose**—Produces output messages from the compiler about its various activities.

**–version**—Displays the current version of the compiler. For example: ajc version 1.0.5 (built Jun 27, 2002 4:59 PM PST) running on java 1.4.0_01.

**–workingdir** *directorypath*—Specifies the location of intermediate files produced when the AspectJ compiler compiles aspects and weaves them into the primary Java code. All of the files in this directory are removed unless you use the –preprocess flag.

## Filenames

The AspectJ compiler recognizes all files with an extension of .java and produces files with the .java extension as well. However, the compiler also supports files with the .aj extension. The designers of AspectJ recommend you use the .aj extension if the files contain any type of AspectJ code. This includes files containing just aspects and those containing both classes and aspects. The AspectJ team does not recommend using any other type of mechanism to differentiate the AspectJ code from the Java application code.

**NOTE**

As is often the case when we're building large projects, the number of source files can become large and adding aspects only increases the file count. Trying to list all the files on a command line for either the Java or AspectJ compiler isn't very practical. Both compilers will accept a simple build file listing all the files to be used during the compilation phase. The file can have any filename but typically ends with the extension .lst. All the files to be built by the compiler are listed in the build file using either absolute or relative file paths. Here's an example of a build file:

```
C:\aop\software\chapter08\Product.java
\aop\software\chapter08\ProductAspect.java
..\..\aop\software\chapter08\DVD.java
..\GUI\*.java
```

## The Structure Browser for Aspects

One of the early access tools made available by the AspectJ developers is the structure browser. This application is designed to provide a graphical view of Java and aspect source files located within a build file. In addition, you can use the structure browser to launch the AspectJ compiler and edit files from the build list. All of these features suggest that the structure browser is a simple programming IDE; however, the features are limited and a development environment like Eclipse is recommended.

The browser is located in the \bin directory of the default installation directory. You can execute the application by typing *ajbrowser* in a command prompt or terminal window. You can follow the command with the name of a build file:

```
ajbrowser
ajbrowser product.lst
```

Figure 11.1 shows the main screen of the browser after we've loaded a build file. We'll refer to the numbers on the image to highlight some of the core features of the browser. If you don't use a build file in the command line, the error dialog box shown in Figure 11.2 will appear. In this case, a build file will have to be opened through the browser itself.

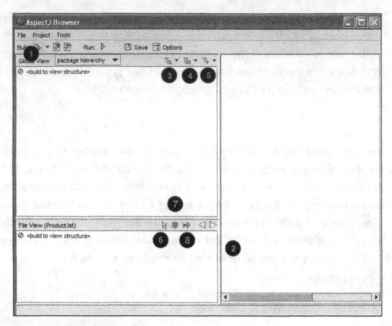

**Figure 11.1**   The AspectJ structure browser.

**Figure 11.2**   The Build File message from the AspectJ structure.

In order for you to see the source file information made available in the build file, the project must be built by the browser. To do the build, select Build from the Project menu or click the Build button (#1 in Figure 11.1). The browser launches the AspectJ compiler and builds all of the files in the project. During the build, any error messages from the compiler are displayed in a window (#2 in Figure 11.1). Once a successful build is completed, the files associated with the build are made available in the browser, as shown in Figure 11.3. You can expand each of the product files by simply clicking on the filename. The contents of the file appear in the far-right window of the browser. The expanded file shows all imports as well as inherited classes. You can see a fully expanded view of the file in the lower-left window of the browser. The attributes of the class associated with the selected file are shown with a small box icon. Class methods have a gear icon assigned to them. If an entry in the view has a toggle switch next to it, this means additional information or elements are associated with the entry. Click the entry to toggle the display of the additional information.

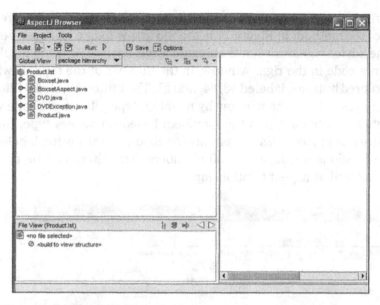

**Figure 11.3**   Build files available in the browser.

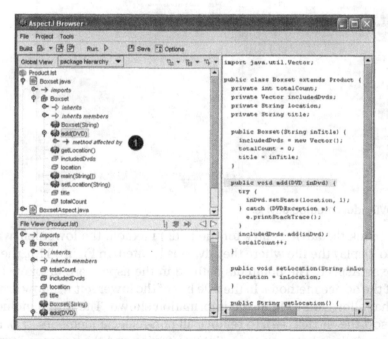

**Figure 11.4**   The DVD add() method.

In Figure 11.4, the add() method has been toggled. Notice that the source code in the right window automatically displays the method in question. Underneath the add() method in the left window is a red arrow with the description "method affected by." This means aspect advice exists that could affect the execution of the method. In Figure 11.5, the red arrow toggle has been selected to reveal the advice signature and the signature has been selected to display the advice source code in the right window. In the title bar of the top-left window are three colored buttons, labeled #3, #4, and #5. The button labeled 3 filters the information presented in the window by member, type, file, or package visibility. The button labeled 4 filters the members based on access type, member type, and possible keywords, such as static or abstract. The button labeled 5 filters the associations displayed for all members. The filters can be based on inheritance as well as aspect relationship.

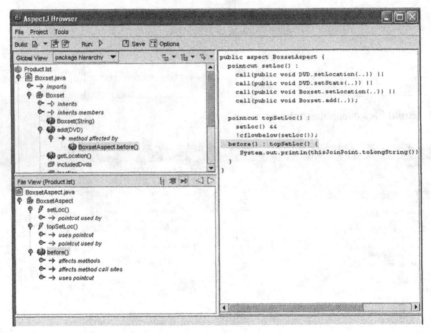

**Figure 11.5** The DVD add() method advice.

When you click the advice entry for the add() method, the lower-left window changes to display the file where the advice is located. In Figure 11.5, the file is called BoxsetAspect. The pointcuts defined in the aspect are displayed along with all of the advice methods. In the title bar of the lower-left window are small buttons that allow you to limit the information shown. The filters include the ability to sort the entries (#6), to remove all non-AspectJ members (#7), and to hide all associations between the pointcuts/advice and the primary Java code (#8).

The browser allows you to execute classes as well as build them. In order to execute the code, you have to specify the fully qualified name for the main class. You specify the class by selecting the Options option under Tools on the main menu. The resulting Settings dialog box has three tabs on it for setting various browser options. The middle tab, called AJBrowser Options, has a text area in which you can enter the name of the class where the system can find and execute the appropriate main() method. For our example, we entered the class Boxset. Once you've entered the class, click the green run arrow on the main browser window to run the code.

In addition to allowing you to specify the class you want to use for running the application, the Settings dialog box includes a host of other options for setting directory paths and controlling strictness of the compiler, as well as a couple of compiler options.

# Using AspectJ IDE Extensions

One of the goals of the AspectJ development group is widespread acceptance of the language. We can help with this goal by developing extensions to some of the major programming environment tools such as JBuilder and Forte. The extensions allow the direct integration of aspects into the Java language typically using a visual presentation versus a simple editor. The current IDE extensions available are

- JBuilder
- Forte
- Emacs
- Eclipse

As the AspectJ FAQ states, the criteria for choosing IDEs included the extensibility of the IDE, the size of the community involved in using and extending the IDE, and the time available to the AspectJ team. In this section, we examine each of the extensions for the given IDEs.

## JBuilder

JBuilder from Borland is one of the premier development environments available to the Java community. The IDE is available in three different flavors: personal, professional, and enterprise. The personal version is available free of charge as long as you run it for personal use only. The enterprise edition is available in a trial format. Both versions are available at www.borland.com/products/downloads/download_jbuilder.html. Borland requires that you create a login for its downloads, but this isn't an extensive process. Version 6 of the product became available earlier this year and is very stable. The Java SDK provided with version 6 is 1.3.1, but you can also use 1.4.0. Version 7 became available at the end of June/early July 2002. Figure 11.6 shows an example of the IDE with a Java project loaded into the environment.

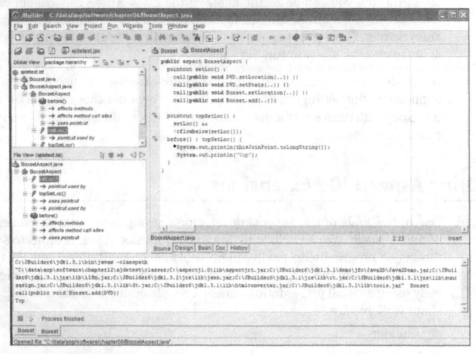

**Figure 11.6** A JBuilder project example.

To obtain the information we provide in the next section, we used version 6 of the Personal Edition, and we also tested version 7 and found no problems. Out of the box, JBuilder doesn't provide any type of AspectJ support. In order to extend JBuilder, a quick trip to the AspectJ Web site is in order. On the page http://aspectj.org/servlets/AJSite?channel=download&subChannel=compilerAndTools, you'll find a download file toward the bottom of the page called ajde-jbuilderOpenTool-1.0.5.jar. Download this file to the local machine where JBuilder is installed.

### The AJDE for JBuilder Installation

To begin, type the following at a command prompt or terminal window:

```
java –jar ajde-jbuilderOpenTool-1.0.5.jar
```

This command launches the installation program contained within the specified file. You'll see the splash screen shown in Figure 11.7.

The splash screen provides information about the version of the extension as well as the type and location of the license. Once you've read the information, click the Next button to display the screen shown in Figure 11.8.

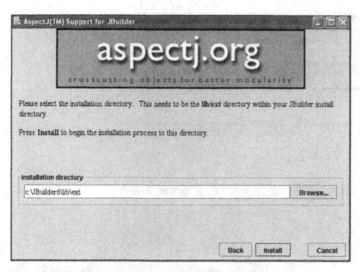

**Figure 11.7** The JBuilder AspectJ Extension splash screen.

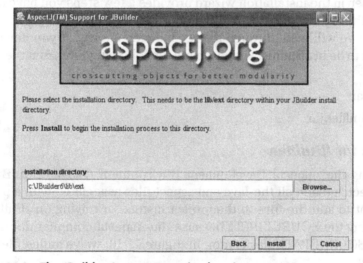

**Figure 11.8** The JBuilder AspectJ Extension location screen.

The location screen provides an edit line for you to enter the location of the lib\ext directory created during your installation of the JBuilder product. The default location will be c:\jbuilder6\lib\ext. After entering the location or leaving the default one, click the Install button to begin the short process of copying the necessary files to the ext directory. When the system is finished, you will see the screen shown in Figure 11.9. Click the Next button to bring up a release notes screen.

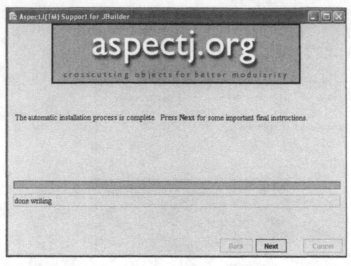

**Figure 11.9** This screen tells you the install was successful.

The final screen in the installation wizard provides a few steps you have to take before using the extension. First, if JBuilder is currently executing, you have to shut it down. We will walk through the second step shortly. If you don't want the extension to be in JBuilder, simply delete the following files from the lib/ext directory:

- aspectjrt.jar
- ajdeForJBuilder.jar

### Using AJDE for JBuilder

To begin using the AspectJ Development Environment (AJDE) for JBuilder, create a project and add all the Java and aspect files associated with a project. It is important to add the files to the project instead of relying on JBuilder to find them using the SOURCEPATH because the AspectJ compiler doesn't use the JBuilder SOURCEPATH designator. In Figure 11.10, we've added files for a simple project.

If you attempt to use JBuilder's build functionality, errors will occur because JBuilder uses the standard Java compiler. To activate AJDE for JBuilder, click the red/blue AJ button located on the toolbar of JBuilder (#1 in Figure 11.10). Or, you can click Tools, choose AspectJ, and then select Start AJDE. When AJDE is started, not much occurs in the JBuilder IDE right away except for a couple additional windows and an expanded AspectJ toolbar. The additional icons are

- AspectJ Browser—#2
- AspectJ Options—#3
- Compile Using AspectJ Compiler—#4

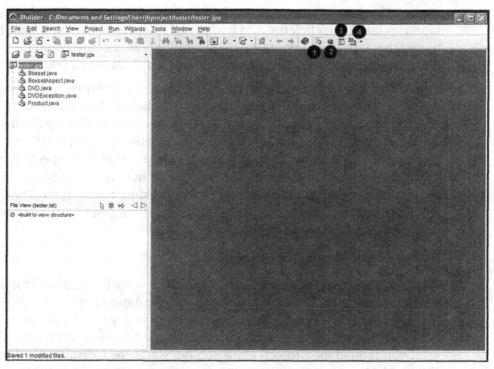

**Figure 11.10**  Our JBuilder project and files.

With all the files added to the project and AJDE activated, you can now compile the project by clicking on the button called Compile Using ajc or by pressing Ctrl+F11. The ajc compiler will compile all the files loaded in the current project as well as all packages and subpackages. If the build is successful, text will appear at the bottom of the JBuilder windows telling you that the "Build succeeded in $X$ seconds." If there is an error, an additional window appears displaying the appropriate error message. Simply double-click the error message to open the file with the error and then edit the file. To run the project, click the Run Project icon (the green arrow) or press Ctrl+F12. The system will execute the Java Runtime Environment against the compiled code. You might see a dialog box that prompts you for the class where the main() method can be found. Add the class to the appropriate edit line and click OK.

At this point, the runtime will continue to run the project; however, you might see an error message containing the text *java.lang.NoClassDefFoundError: org/aspectj/lang/Signature*. This means the system is unable to find the AspectJ runtime. If you look at the command line that the system was attempting to use to execute the project, you'll note that the path associated with the AspectJ runtime begins with the text *c:\apps...* This path is probably not available on your system. To edit the path for the correct location of the AspectJ runtime on your system, click the Project menu item in JBuilder. Select the Default

Project Properties option and in the resulting dialog box, click the Required Libraries tab. Then click the Add button and select AspectJ Runtime. Click OK to add the AspectJ library as a default required library. You could do this only for the current project if you don't want it as a default for all your projects.

In the Required Library combo box of the Project Properties dialog box, you'll see an entry called AspectJ Runtime. Double-click on that entry to bring up a dialog box called Configure Library. In a text area labeled Library Settings you'll see a path associated with the runtime library. Select the path and then click the Edit button. Change the path to the correct location of the AspectJ runtime— probably *c:\aspectj1.0\lib\aspectjrt.jar*. Keep clicking OK until you exit the Project Properties box, and then try to execute the project again. This attempt should be successful, and you'll see the output displayed in a JBuilder window or through an application GUI if one is available.

## Using AspectJ Browser in JBuilder

As part of the AJDE for JBuilder, the AspectJ browser is embedded for easy traversal of the Java primary code as well as the AspectJ code. To activate the browser, click the AspectJ Browser button (#3 in Figure 11.10). Although this activates the browser, the information about the classes might not be available until you rebuild the project. Once you do, you'll see a display like the one in Figure 11.11.

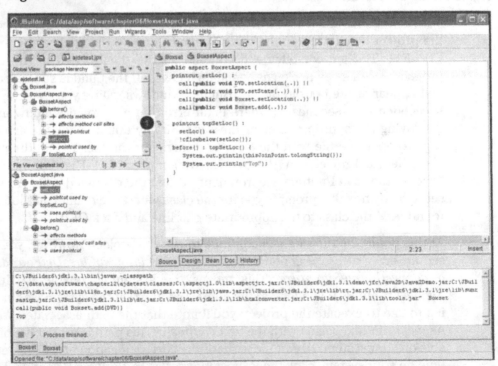

**Figure 11.11** The AspectJ browser in JBuilder.

You'll find all of the browser functionality we described earlier; in fact, there is an additional piece of functionality, as shown in Figure 11.11 (#1). By right-clicking the arrow, you display a menu that contains links to source code associated with that item. This includes, for example, inherited methods, join points, and pointcuts. Figure 11.12 shows an example of one such menu and its links.

**Figure 11.12**   Link points in code.

Note that all of the same filters are available in the JBuilder browser just as they were in the stand-alone browser.

## Using Build Files

You can also create projects in JBuilder to handle .lst build files. Create a normal JBuilder project and add a .lst build file to the project. Double-click the project's .lst entry (#1 in Figure 11.13) to reveal a number of tabs in the rightmost window. Click the tab labeled lst Designer (#2). You can edit the .lst file using the Designer tab or through the Source tab manually.

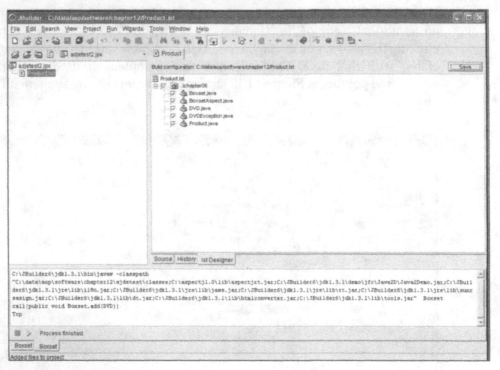

**Figure 11.13** The lst Designer in JBuilder.

## Forte and NetBeans

The Forte and NetBeans IDEs are alternatives to the JBuilder product. They are available at http://forte.sun.com and http://netbeans.org, respectively. Both of the IDEs provide the same level of development support and can also be used for AspectJ development with an extension. The extension, called AJDE for Forte, is available at http://aspectj4netbean.sourceforge.net/. Before installing the extension, you must install either Forte or NetBeans. Once you do, launch the extension installation file in a command prompt or terminal window by issuing the command:

```
java –jar ajde-forteModule-1.0.5.jar
```

The installation program begins with a splash screen that displays the version of the extension and license information. Follow these steps:

1. Click the Next button to display a dialog box requesting information about the installation location for the code. The default is c:\forte4j\modules. If you have installed the software on another drive, then enter the correct installation path. Do not change the modules subdirectory path because this is where the IDE expects to find extensions.

2. Click Install to start the process of copying the files from the installation JAR to the modules subdirectory.

3. Click Next when the installation wizard indicates that all of the files have been copied.

4. Read the final wizard dialog box and note the availability of a readme HTML file. Click Finish.

### Uninstalling AJDE for Forte

Uninstalling AJDE for Forte is simple. Just remove the file ajdeForForte.jar from the *<installation drive>*\Forte4J\modules directory and the file aspectjrt.jar from the *<installation drive>*\Forte4J\lib\ext directory. After you shut down Forte and then launch it again, the extension will not be in the IDE.

### An AJDE for Forte Example

Let's look at the steps for using AJDE for Forte with some of the example code from Chapter 6 (all the code in this book is available at www.wiley.com/comp-books/gradecki). You can generally follow these steps with any project.

1. Start Forte.

2. Create a new project using the Project Manager under the Project menu. Mount the chapter12 directory because this directory contains a build list that will be used to pull in the necessary files for the example. You should also mount the chapter06 directory since the source files are located in this directory.

3. Start AJDE for Forte by navigating to the Tools menu, selecting AspectJ, and then choosing Start AJDE. Or you can click the AJ button on the Forte IDE toolbar. Either of these actions results in the addition of several buttons on the IDE, as shown in Figure 11.14. Also, note that a new tab, called AspectJ, is added to the Explorer window. The new additions are

   #1—The Start/Stop AJDE button

   #2—The Rebuild button

   #3—The Build Selection button

   #4—The Options button

   #5—The AspectJ Explorer tab

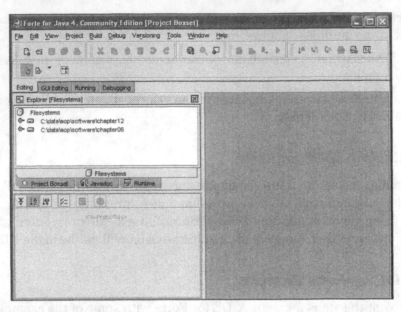

**Figure 11.14** The Forte AJDE extension.

4. When you mounted the chapter12 directory in step 2, all of the build files in the directory were assigned to the Build Selection button. At this point, click the button to see the builds. For this example, we selected the build called Product.lst, and the AspectJ Explorer tab displays the appropriate files in the build list.

5. Click the Build button to build the files in the project. You can navigate the various attributes and methods of the classes within the AspectJ tab of the IDE. The navigation works and looks the same as in the stand-alone AspectJ browser. Source files will appear in the rightmost window when you double-click an attribute or method on the class hierarchy.

6. When the code is ready to be executed, select the FileSystems tab in the GUI Explorer window. Double-click on the entry where the actual code file can be found for the class to be executed. In our case, double-click on the entry for chapter06 and select the Boxset class. Right-click the entry and select Execute. The GUI launches a virtual machine and executes the main() method in the Boxset class. When the results have been displayed, click the Editing tab to return to the original Explorer tabs.

## Emacs

Outside of vi, Emacs is the longest-running editor in the UNIX community. Emacs provides exceptional support for developers who need to write code on a continual basis. Some developers wouldn't dream of using anything other than Emacs for their source code development. With this type of backing, the AspectJ team created an extension to the application that provides support for the new language within the editor.

The Emacs extension is called AspectJ-mode, and it works with GNU-emacs and XEmacs. For GNU-emacs, install version 20.3.1 or higher from www.gnu.org/software/emacs/. For XEmacs on Linux/UNIX, install version 21.1.14 or higher and Windows 21.4 or higher from www.xemacs.org. The steps for installing the Emacs extension (based on XEmacs for Windows) are as follows:

1. Download the extension from http://aspectj4emacs.sourceforge.net/.

2. Extract the files from the aspectj-emacsMode-1.0.5.tgz file into the installation directory for Xmacs/XEmacs/xemacs-packages.

3. The AspectJ extension comes with a sample .emacs file in the directory created during step 2. Copy this file to your home directory.

## NOTE

On a UNIX box, finding a home directory is easy; on Windows it is not. For Windows NT/2000, a home directory is provided based on the path c:\Documents And Settings\<*your login*>\My Documents. On XP, it will be c:\Documents And Settings\<*your login*>. For Windows 9*x* or if XEmacs cannot find your home directory, create an environment variable called HOME and set it equal to a path on your system to a default directory.

4. Using a command prompt, change to your home directory and execute the command:

```
Mkdir .xemacs
```

5. Change into the .xemacs directory and execute the command

```
edit init.el
```

6. Copy the following into the directory:

```
(setq load-path (cons "c:/program files/XEmacs/xemacs-
packages/aspectj-emacsMode-1.0.5" load-path))

(require 'aspectj-mode)

(when (eq system-type 'windows-nt)
  (setq shell-file-name "c://windows//system32//cmd.exe")
    (setq explicit-shell-file-name shell-file-name)
      (setenv "SHELL" shell-file-name))

(when (not (string-match "XEmacs" emacs-version))
  (global-font-lock-mode t))
```

7. Change into the xemacs-packages\lisp directory of your XEmacs installation and either remove the jde directory or move it to your temp directory in order to keep the normal Java mode from executing when Java files are loaded into the editor.

8. Launch XEmacs.

## AspectJ-Mode Features

In order to see the features available in AspectJ-mode, use XEmacs to open a Java file with the AspectJ keywords. The system might ask if you want to merge your .emacs with the system .emacs. Answer yes and allow the merge to occur. Once the Java file is loaded into the editor, you'll see that the AspectJ keywords have been highlighted as valid keywords, as shown in Figure 11.15. Notice the addition of the AspectJ menu in the toolbar.

**Figure 11.15**   Using XEmacs to edit AspectJ code.

The AspectJ menu includes an option for compiling code using the AspectJ compiler. From the AspectJ menu choose the Compile option. At the bottom of the resulting window enter the compile files you want to use in the compilation or enter a build file. Once the code has been built, you'll discover another feature of AspectJ-mode. In Figure 11.16, the Boxset.java file is visible in the editor window. Notice the annotations to the right of the methods where join points have been defined. The annotations, controlled by the AspectJ menu item, let you know which file contains an aspect relating to the method.

**Figure 11.16**    The Boxset class annotations.

Click the BoxsetAspect.java tab in the editor window to reveal annotations associated with the advice defined for the aspect, as shown in Figure 11.17.

The AspectJ-mode package also features the concept of a jump menu. Click the Boxset.java file and select the method name where you've defined advice code. Then, select Jump from the AspectJ menu to open a jump menu at the bottom of the XEmacs window. Click the X or SPC button, and the editor "jumps" to the advice code and displays it in the center window. Figure 11.18 shows an example of this functionality.

# Eclipse

One of the most exciting achievements in the development tools community has been IBM's release of Eclipse. This extensible IDE isn't specific to one language, but it provides an API in which we can achieve support for many languages with moderate effort. Probably the most important aspect of the new IDE is the fact that it has been released open source with an extensive community already behind it.

**Figure 11.17** The BoxsetAspect annotations.

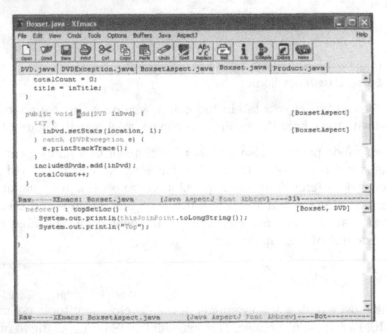

**Figure 11.18** Using the jump menu.

Before you can install the extension, you must install Eclipse. You can find the application at www.eclipse.org. The application is simple to install, and the Web site includes comprehensive instructions. For our example, we installed the Eclipse application in the c:\eclipse-SDK-2.0-win32 directory.

You can find the AspectJ plug-in for Eclipse on the eclipse.org Web site at www.eclipse.org/ajdt. You need two files for the plug-in:

```
AJDT Plug-in
AJDE Tools Plug-in
```

The two files are available for various versions of AspectJ. You should unzip those files in the Eclipse installation's plugins directory. Once you've installed the two files, you must complete a few more steps to verify that the installation was successful and that the Eclipse IDE is properly configured to use the AJDE.

### The Eclipse AJDE Installation Check

To check the installation of AJDE, launch the Eclipse application by double-clicking the Eclipse icon in the installation directory. Once the application launches, click the Help menu and select About. At the bottom left of the result-ing dialog box, click the Plug-in Details button to display the dialog box shown in Figure 11.19. At the top you should see a plug-in named org.aspectj.ajde. The version of the plug-in should be 1.0.5. This verifies that the primary AJDE has been installed successfully. Next, scroll to the bottom of the plug-in details grid to find a plug-in named org.eclipse.ajdt.ui, version 0.5.0. This verifies the instal-lation of the other necessary plug-in, as shown in Figure 11.20.

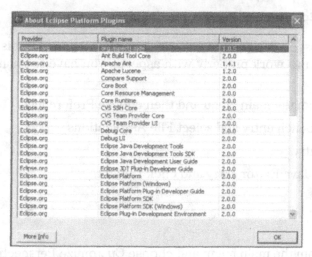

**Figure 11.19** The Plug-in Details screen.

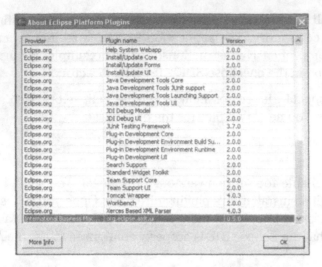

**Figure 11.20** The Plug-in Details screen for org.eclipse.ajdt.ui.

## The Eclipse Configuration Setup

In order for the AspectJ Development Tools (AJDT) plug-in to work properly, you must set several configuration options in the Eclipse IDE. These changes are documented in the AJDT release notes found in the directory \plugins\org.eclipse.ajdt.ui_0.5.0\releaseNotes\readme.html (complete with screenshots). The following is a summary of those steps (without the screenshots). You must follow these steps in order for the AJDT plug-in to work correctly.

### The Eclipse Default Editor

Out of the box, Eclipse is designed to use the Java Development Tools (JDT) editor. For the plug-in to work properly with aspects, you have to change the default editor:

1. Select Window from the main menu and then choose Preferences.
2. Expand the Workbench entry and select File Associations
3. Click the *.java entry.
4. Click the AspectJ/Java Editor entry and click Default.
5. Click OK.

### A Wizard Shortcut

1. Select Window from the main menu and choose Customize Perspective.
2. Expand the File New entry.

3. Click the Aspect and/or AspectJ Project button if you want them on the New menu list.

### Disable Early Indication

The Disable Early Indication option highlights errors while you type but it isn't AspectJ aware. The option doesn't cause any problems, but it can be annoying. To disable the option:

1. Select Window from the main menu, and then choose Preferences.

2. Expand the Java node.

3. Click Editor.

4. Select the Problem Indication tab.

5. Deselect the option Show Problems Before Compiling.

6. Click OK.

## Things You Should Know

The release notes document provides information about the functionality of Eclipse in cooperation with the AJDT plug-in. To summarize:

1. Changes to the code will not automatically change the view; only a rebuild changes the view.

2. There is no incremental building in the IDE since AspectJ doesn't support this option in 1.0.6 or earlier; however, it is supported in 1.1.

3. The AJDT plug-in supports multiple builds. Select a different build using the down arrow drop-down next to the Build button.

## Eclipse Example

Let's look at a simple example to see how we can use the AJDT plug-in with the Eclipse IDE. We use example files and a build file from the chapter06 and chapter12 directories of the example code. You can use the following steps for the development of projects using AspectJ and Java:

1. Launch Eclipse.

2. Select File, then New, and then Project to bring up the New Project wizard.

3. In the first screen of the wizard, select AspectJ in the left window and select AspectJ Project in the right window, as shown in Figure 11.21. Click the Next button to continue.

4. Give the project a name and select the location where you want to place the project directory. The default is in the workspace, as shown in Figure 11.22. Click Next to continue.

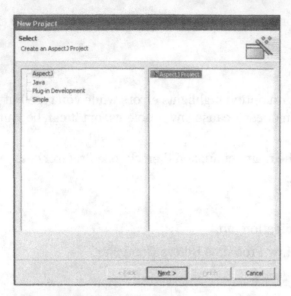

**Figure 11.21** The Eclipse AspectJ project dialog box.

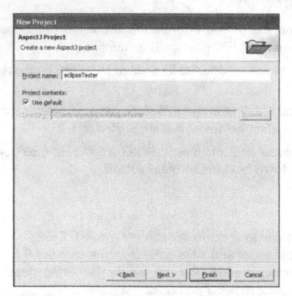

**Figure 11.22** Naming the project and selecting a location.

5. In the Java Settings window, you must add the AspectJ runtime JAR to the project. Click the Libraries tab and then click the Add External Jars button.

6. In the resulting dialog box, find the aspectjrt.jar file in the plugins/org.aspectj.ajde.1.0.5 directory of the default Eclipse installation. Click the file and then click OK.

7. You should now see a screen like the one shown in Figure 11.23. Click Finish to continue building the new AspectJ project.

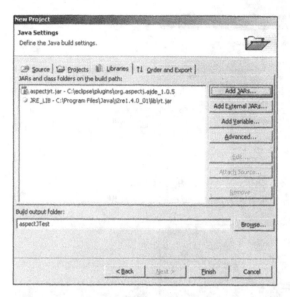

**Figure 11.23**   The Eclipse AspectJ project Java Settings dialog box.

8. The new project is loaded into the Eclipse IDE. To add source files to the project that have already been created, click File, then Import. To add new classes, packages, or interfaces to the project, click File, then New. For this example, let's use files from the chapter06 directory.

9. In the Import dialog box, double-click on the Filesystems entry to gain access to the example files. In the Directory edit line, enter the path to the chapter06 directory (or use the Browse button to locate the directory). The files from the directory will be visible in the right window of the dialog box. At this point, select the files that you wish to add to the current project.

10. In the Destination Folder edit line, add the name of the project where you want to put the imported files (or use the Browse button and select the current project). Figure 11.24 shows the dialog box at this point.

11. Click the Finish button. The files are added to the current project; you can display them by clicking the + expander button next to the project name, as shown in Figure 11.25.

12. To build the project, click the Build button or select Rebuild Project from the Project menu. The IDE launches the compiler and builds the entire project.

13. To execute the built code, click the Run button (or select Run from the Project menu). The IDE displays a Launch Configurations wizard that lets you determine the class and method you want to use when launching the project.

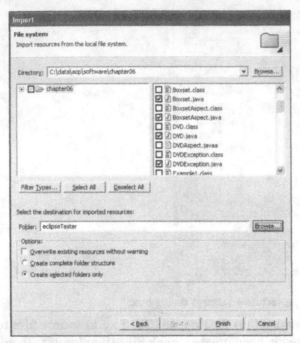

**Figure 11.24** The Import dialog box.

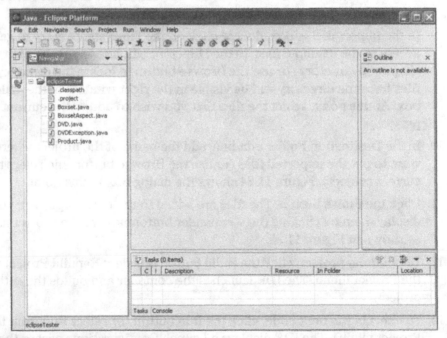

**Figure 11.25** The Eclipse IDE with a project.

14. Click the Java Application entry in the Launch Configurations combo box and expand the entry to automatically create a new launch configuration. Give the configuration entry a name in the right part of the dialog box. The

project entry should be automatically filled; its value is based on the current project. In the Main Class edit box, enter the class name *Boxset* since it contains the main() method. Figure 11.26 shows the dialog box at this point.

The results of the project are displayed in the IDE, as shown in Figure 11.27.

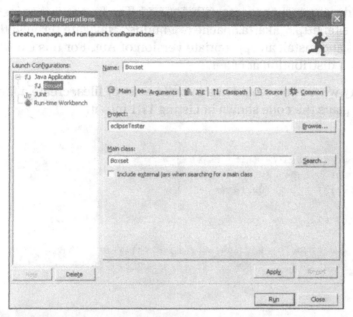

**Figure 11.26** The Launch Configurations dialog box.

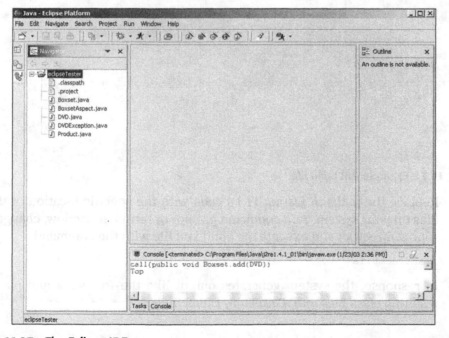

**Figure 11.27** The Eclipse IDE.

# Ant

Ant is a build tool designed to allow you to compile code across platforms and without the problems associated with the various make tools. It is possible to use Ant in the development process with AspectJ. The first step is to install Ant from this Web site: http://jakarta.apache.org/builds/. Navigate through the various directories and install an appropriate version of Ant. For this example, we installed the Ant distribution at c:\ant.

In the directory where you would like to build a set of files, create a file called build.xml and place the code shown in Listing 11.1 into it.

```
<project name="Product" default="init" basedir=".">
  <property name="src" value="."/>
  <property name="build" value="build"/>

  <taskdef name="ajc" classname="org.aspectj.tools.ant.taskdefs.Ajc" >
    <classpath>
      <pathelement location="c:/ant/lib/aspectj-ant.jar"/>
      <pathelement location="c:/aspectj1.0/lib/aspectjtools.jar"/>
    </classpath>
  </taskdef>

  <target name="init">
    <mkdir dir="${build}"/>
  </target>

  <target name="compile" depends="init">
    <ajc  srcdir="${src}" destdir="${build}" >
    <classpath>
      <pathelement location="c:/aspectj1.0/lib/aspectjrt.jar"/>
    </classpath>
    </ajc>
  </target>
</project>
```

**Listing 11.1**  Example Ant build file.

Replace the paths in Listing 11.1's code with the specific location of the JAR files on your system. At a command prompt or terminal window, change to the source directory and execute the build.xml file with the command

```
ant compile
```

In response, the system generates output like the following and places the resulting class files into a directory called build:

```
C:\data\aop\software\chapter12\ant>ant compile
Buildfile: build.xml

init:

compile:
     [ajc] Compiling 5 source and 0 arg files to
C:\data\aop\software\chapter12\ant\build

BUILD SUCCESSFUL

Total time: 3 seconds
C:\data\aop\software\chapter12\ant>
```

# Debugging with AspectJ

Debugging is an activity required in all software development methodologies and something all developers will be faced with at some point. It is important to be able to walk through the source code when you're faced with a tricky bug. AspectJ supports source-level debugging according to FSR-45, which is also written into Java 1.4's debugger. If you are writing against 1.4, there is a good chance that you can use any of the current development environments to walk through the source code.

If your development environment doesn't support AspectJ code debugging, don't despair. As long as you are using version 1.0.6 of AspectJ or earlier, the language support tools include a debugger that you can use to walk through the code. Version 1.1 isn't supported by the AspectJ debugger tool (ajdb). The ajdb application is currently able to debug AspectJ code in both a command-line and GUI environment. The debugger is available only for AspectJ version 1.0 because it is expected that better FSR-45 support will be available in the common IDEs. The commands supported by ajdb are the same as those for Java's debugging tool, jdb, and can be found in the jdb documentation. We provide a short tutorial here to get you started. Start the debugger by issuing the command jdb in the command-line version and jdb –gui in the GUI version. The full command summary for the debugger is

```
ajdb <command-line options><class><arguments>
```

For command-line options you can use one or more of the command-line flags listed here. The class option represents the class that you want to receive control once the debugger starts and arguments are passed to the starting class.

The command-line flags are

**–classpath** *path*—Specifies the path the executing code should use to find CLASS files

**–Dname=***value*—Defines the property name with the starting value of *value*.

**–help**—Displays the ajdb help summary.

**–read** *file*—Specifies a file to be read by the debugger with line-delimited initialization commands.

**–sourcepath** *path*—Specifies the path the executing code should use to find source files.

**–gui**—Launches the debugger into GUI mode.

**–v | verbose [:class|:gc|:jni]**—Provides additional information about class, garbage collection, or dynamic library loading. The default is class loading.

**–workingdir** *directory*—Sets the working directory for ajdb.

**–Xoption**—Specifies Java Runtime Environment commands passed by the debugger to the JRE.

## An ajdb Command-line Tutorial

The ajdb tool works in a manner identical to jdb; therefore, this tutorial will be a short introduction to the tool. This tutorial begins with the execution of the ajdb tool.

Compile the project that you wish to debug with the AspectJ compiler using the –preprocess command-line option. For this tutorial, we are compiling the Boxset class in the chapter06 code. The compiler command used within the c:\data\aop\software\chapter06 directory is

```
ajc –preprocess Product.java DVD.java DVDException.java Boxset.java
```

Start the command-line debugger by typing *ajdb* in a command prompt or terminal window. The tool first displays the default working directory it will be using. Let's assume that you started the compiler and debugger in the same directory and did not specify a working directory for the –preprocess command-line option. (If you did specify a working directory, you must provide the same working directory to the debugger by using the –workingdir option.)

In this example, let's debug the add() method associated with the Boxset class. The first thing we need to do is tell the debugger where it can find the source files for the project. The use command handles this job:

```
use c:\data\aop\software\chapter06 directory
```

One difference between ajdb and jdb is the ajdb's ability to list the contents of a file within the debugger before starting to debug it. For example, we want to debug the add() method of the Boxset class. Let's use the following list command:

```
list Boxset.java
```

The options available for the list command are

**no option**—Lists the source code containing the point the debugger is currently stopped at; this requires a running virtual machine.

*class*—Lists the specified class.

*class linenumber*—Displays line number *linenumber* of the class *class*.

*class start end*—Displays lines *start* through *end* of the class *class*.

Figure 11.28 shows what the output from the debugger looks like up to this point.

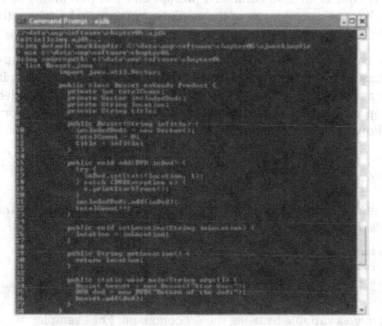

**Figure 11.28**   ajdb example output.

Next, let's set a breakpoint on the main() method of the Boxset class with the *stop* command:

```
stop on Boxset.main
```

The command is accepted by the debugger; the resulting output looks like this:

```
> stop on Boxset.main
Set breakpoint Boxset.main
Deferring breakpoint Boxset.main
It will be set after the class is loaded.
>
```

Although this resembles an error message, it isn't, because the debugger hasn't loaded the Boxset class yet and cannot set the breakpoint until it does. The message just informs us that the breakpoint will be set when the class is loaded.

Once the breakpoint is set, we can instruct the debugger to execute the code using the command *run*:

```
run Boxset
```

When the debugger comes to the breakpoint, it will interrupt execution, display breakpoint information, and wait for you to enter a command. For example:

```
Breakpoint hit: thread="main", Boxset.main(), line=34, bci=0
34              Boxset boxset = new Boxset("Star Wars");
main[1]
```

The main[1] code is an ajdb command prompt and will poll until you enter a command. You can access a list of the available commands by typing the *help* command.

One of the commands, *step*, will execute the command at the current cursor position. Based on the code in line 8, the debugger sits on line 34 waiting to instantiate a new Boxset object. When the statement is executed, the debugger outputs step information as well as the next line in the application. For example, the following output is generated when the *step* command is executed:

```
Step completed: thread="main", Boxset.<init>(), line=9, bci=0
9               public Boxset(String inTitle) {
main[1]
```

If you are interested in seeing the values of current local variables, use the command *locals*. For example:

```
main[1] locals
Method arguments:
  inTitle = "Star Wars"Local variables:
main[1]
```

You can change a variable by using the *set* command. For example:

```
main[1] set inTitle = "Star Wars set"
Changed 'inTitle' from '"Star Wars"' to '"Star Wars set"'
main[1]
```

When you finished debugging the application, enter the *exit* command at the main[1] command prompt.

It is possible to set a breakpoint on the aspect code using the information contained in the BoxsetAspect.java class source file. The method that will be called when a join point is found is called before0$ajc. Using the *stop* command, you can set a breakpoint on the method. For example, the command

```
Stop on BoxsetAspect.before0$ajc
```

produces output like this:

```
Breakpoint hit: thread="main", BoxsetAspect.<advice #>(), line=12, bci=0
12              System.out.println(thisJoinPoint.toLongString());
main[1]
```

It is also possible to use the *stop* command to set a breakpoint based on a line number. For example:

```
Stop on BoxsetAspect.java:13
```

This aspect will cause a breakpoint to be added to the add() method.

## An ajdb GUI Tutorial

The ajdb tool also has a GUI component that makes using the debugger easier for those without ajdb experience. The GUI is designed to provide the most basic jdb commands in a button/menu format but still allows the developer to enter individual commands manually. Let's see how to use the graphical debugger.

Begin by executing the debugger with the following command to produce the application shown in Figure 11.29:

```
ajdb -gui
```

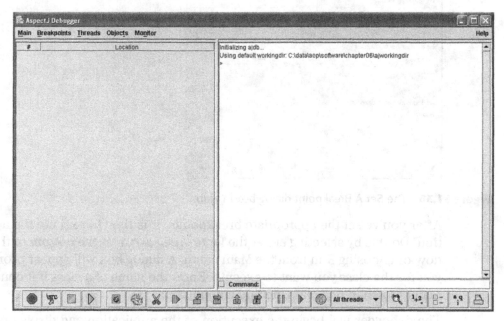

**Figure 11.29** The ajdb GUI starting screen.

Once the debugger starts, you can access most of the common jdb commands from the menu or by clicking the buttons at the bottom of the window. To start using the debugger, you must specify the source location of the files you want to debug by using the *use* command. There three ways to accomplish this task: Click the SRC button at the bottom of the window, select Use from the main menu, or type the command in the Command text box. The button and menu will bring up a dialog box where you can enter the path to the source. Use one of these methods to specify the source code location for the files you want to debug. Our example uses c:\data\aop\software\chapter06. Regardless of how you accomplish this task, the debugger will display the outcome in the right-most window of the application.

Now set a breakpoint for the main() method of the Boxset class by typing the command, by clicking the button that looks like a green arrow on a red button, or by selecting Breakpoint from the main menu. The menu and button display a dialog box, as shown in Figure 11.30. You have the option of setting a method breakpoint on a class method, a line number based on a class, or a line number based on a source file. In Figure 11.30, we have specified a method breakpoint.

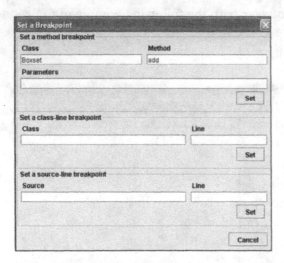

**Figure 11.30** The Set A Breakpoint dialog box in ajdb.

After you've set the appropriate breakpoints, it is time to execute the application. Do this by selecting either the large green arrow at the bottom of the window or choosing Run from the Main menu. A dialog box will appear prompting you for the class you want to execute. Enter the name of a class if it contains a main() method or a class.method combination.

The debugger will begin the execution of the application and display console messages in the right window.

### Breakpoint Lines

In both the command-line and GUI versions of the debugger, you can set breakpoints based on lines numbers; however, the debugger must be in the middle of execution in order for the breakpoints to be set. Once a single breakpoint has been triggered, you can use the *stop* on command to set the line number breakpoints. An example of a line breakpoint is

```
stop on Boxset:54
```

This breakpoint is triggered when the debugger hits line 54 of the Boxset class once the application starts to execute again.

# Using ajdoc

The AspectJ documentation creator tool (ajdoc) lets you output AspectJ projects in the same format that Javadoc handles traditional Java projects. The new tool takes all Java or .aj files provided to it and relates all the methods, join points, and advice. The classes in the project will be fully documented between the primary Java and AspectJ code. The format for using ajdoc is

```
ajdoc <options> <packagenames> <sourcefiles> <classnames> <@files>
```

The command line for the tool includes various option flags, package names you can include in the documentation, source files you can use as input, class names you want to include, and possible @ files.

The options available to the ajdoc tool are

**–argfile** *file*—Specifies a line-delimited file consisting of files to be used in the command line. For example: ajdoc –argfile tobeincluded.txt.

**–bootclasspath** *path*—Specifies a path to the files needed by the bootstrap classloader. Using this option overrides the default location path.

**–classpath** *path*—Specifies the location(s) for CLASS files needed for execution of the primary Java code.

**–encoding** *encoding*—Specifies the encoding used in the source files.

**–extdirs** *path*—Specifies the path to the installed extensions. Using this option overrides the default location path.

**–help**—Displays the help information compiled into the command.

**–locale name**—Specifies the locale you want to use with the command.

**–log**—Tells the tool to log each pass necessary for document creation.

**–overview file**—Specifies an HTML file you want to use as overview documentation in the final output.

**–public**—Specifies that the tool should only show public classes and members.

**–protected**—Specifies the tool should only show public and protected classes and members.

**–package**—Specifies the tool should only show package/protected/public classes and members.

**–private**—Specifies the tool should show all classes and members.

**–sourcepath path**—Specifies the path to where source files can be found.

**–standard**—Specifies that the com.sun.tools.doclets.standard.Standard doclet should be used.

**–verbose**—Specifies the tool should show display messages about its execution.

## An ajdoc Example

Producing documents for your Java code and aspects is quite easy with the ajdoc application. While all the kinks aren't worked out of the applications yet, in general you will find the application works as you'd expect. Consider some of the code from Chapter 6. The Boxset class inherits from Product and also has an associated aspect in BoxAspect. We can produce documentation for these three classes/aspects with the following command:

```
ajdoc -d doc -standard -private Boxset.java BoxsetAspect.java
Product.java
```

After we enter this command in a terminal window or command prompt, the application sends the following output to the console:

```
Starting compile...
Loading source file C:\data\aop\software\chapter06\Boxset.java...
Loading source file C:\data\aop\software\chapter06\BoxsetAspect.java...
Loading source file C:\data\aop\software\chapter06\Product.java...
Creating root...
Generating documentation...
Standard Doclet version 1.4.0

Generating doc\constant-values.html...
Building tree for all the packages and classes...
Building index for all the packages and classes...
Generating doc\overview-tree.html...
Generating doc\index-all.html...
Generating doc\deprecated-list.html...
Building index for all classes...
Generating doc\allclasses-frame.html...
Generating doc\allclasses-noframe.html...
```

```
Generating doc\index.html...
Generating doc\packages.html...
Generating doc\Boxset.html...
Generating doc\BoxsetAspect.html...
Generating doc\Product.html...
Generating doc\package-list...
Generating doc\help-doc.html...
Generating doc\stylesheet.css...
```

The HTML for the documentation of the selected classes and all their members is written to the doc directory. As you can see by checking the information displayed on the console, all the standard Javadoc files are written. Figure 11.31 shows the class hierarchy of the classes provided to the application. Notice the BoxsetAspect aspect is shown as a class instead of an aspect in order to maintain consistency with Javadoc.

**Figure 11.31** The Boxset hierarchy from ajdoc.

# What's Next

In this chapter, we devoted considerable attention to the numerous support application provided in the AspectJ system. Debuggers and IDE extensions allow for comprehensive solutions necessary for the complete adoption of aspect-oriented programming and especially AspectJ. In the next chapter, we analyze the errors that you might encounter in both the compile and execution phases of AspectJ.

# Error Handling and Common Problems

Throughout the development cycle with aspect-oriented programming and AspectJ, you will develop code and attempt compilations that produce errors. You will also want to do things with AspectJ that aren't possible based on the current implementation of the language. This chapter brings together many of the errors and limitations the authors have experienced, as well as some from the AspectJ mailing list. We hope this information will help you through the difficult times when you're using the language.

## Compilation Errors

A compilation error can occur when the Java or AspectJ compiler is executed against a single file or a group of files. This section introduces errors commonly encountered during the compile phase.

### Wrong Compiler

Consider the following class snippet:

```
public class CompileTest {
  public CompileTest() {
    //do nothing default constructor
  }

  private aspect CompileTestAspect {
    pointcut grabConstructor() : execution(CompileTest.new());
```

```
      before() : grabConstructor() {
         System.out.println("I'm in the constructor");
      }
   }
}
```

Suppose you try to compile this code with the following command:

```
java -classpath "c:\aspectj1.0\lib\aspectjrt.jar"
CompileTest.java
```

Most of us are familiar with using the Java compiler, and won't anticipate any error with this compile attempt. However, the compiler will immediately flag the keyword *aspect* as a syntax error. Here is the error produced:

```
CompileTest.java:6: ';' expected
   private aspect CompileTestAspect {
                                    ^
CompileTest.java:6: cannot resolve symbol
symbol  : class aspect
location: class CompileTest
   private aspect CompileTestAspect {
           ^
2 errors
```

You can't use the standard Java compiler to compile a class file that contains AspectJ code. You must first use the AspectJ compiler, ajc; it will in turn execute the Java compiler if the -preprocess command-line flag isn't used. If you use the -preprocess flag in the execution of the AspectJ compiler, you can use the Java compiler to compile the previously weaved code contained in the working directory where ajc places the files.

## Unable to Find Aspectjtools.jar

Using the same source code provided for the previous example, you can see another error when you use the AspectJ compiler to compile the class. Consider this command for executing the compiler.

```
C:\data\aop\software\chapter12>ajc -classpath
  "c:\aspectj1.0\lib]aspectjrt.jar" CompileTest.java
```

This command will not work correctly, and a rather extensive error will be generated:

```
Can't find org.aspectj.lang.JoinPoint on your classpath anywhere.
You need to include aspectjrt.jar on your classpath when
 compiling or
running applications with ajc.
See README-TOOLS.html in the top directory of
the distribution for more details on how to configure this
correctly.
```

```
I looked in:
    c:\j2sdk1.4.0_01\jre\lib\rt.jar
    c:\j2sdk1.4.0_01\jre\lib\i18n.jar<not found>
    c:\j2sdk1.4.0_01\jre\lib\sunrsasign.jar
    c:\j2sdk1.4.0_01\jre\lib\jsse.jar
    c:\j2sdk1.4.0_01\jre\lib\jce.jar
    c:\j2sdk1.4.0_01\jre\lib\charsets.jar
    c:\j2sdk1.4.0_01\jre\classes
    c:\j2sdk1.4.0_01\jre\lib\ext\dnsns.jar
    c:\j2sdk1.4.0_01\jre\lib\ext\ldapsec.jar
    c:\j2sdk1.4.0_01\jre\lib\ext\localedata.jar
    c:\j2sdk1.4.0_01\jre\lib\ext\sunjce_provider.jar
    c:\aspectj1.0\lib]aspectjrt.jar<not found>
```

This error results when the AspectJ compiler is unable to find the aspectrt.jar file in your classpath. Although it appears that you included the file in your classpath, further analysis of the command reveals a ] character in the path to the JAR file instead of a \ character. The system doesn't flag the wrong character, but instead returns an error saying the JAR file cannot be found. The same error will be produced no matter why the system can't find the file. To find the root cause, note that the AspectJ compiler command, ajc, is ultimately a script file for executing a Java virtual machine (JVM) and providing it with a class to execute that handles the code necessary to compile the aspect code. The code for the execution of the AspectJ compiler is as follows:

```
"%JAVA_HOME%\bin\java" -classpath "%ASPECTJ_HOME
%\lib\aspectjtools.jar;%JAVA_HOME%\lib\tools.jar;%CLASSPATH%"
-Xmx64M org.aspectj.tools.ajc.Main %1 %2 %3 %4 %5%6 %7 %8 %9
```

Notice the execution of the Java Runtime using a classpath and a number of options. One of those options is the class to execute: org.aspectj.tools.ajc.Main. Without the aspectjrt.jar file, the compiler cannot execute.

## Out of Memory Error

Sometimes the JVM associated with the compiler runs out of memory during the compilation of a project. Such projects are large, with numerous classes and aspects. When this occurs, you need to open the ajc compiler script or batch file and change the JVM memory option from its initial flag of -Xmx64M to a larger value such as -Xmx128M or -Xmx256M.

## Wrong JSDK

When you install the AspectJ compiler and support JAR files on the local system through the installation wizard, the wizard asks for the location of the Java Software Development Kit (JSDK). This path is put into the compiler startup scripts, which are located in the /bin directory of the AspectJ installation. The Windows batch file contains the following information:

```
@echo off
REM This file generated by AspectJ installer
REM Created on Sat Jul 13 07:24:01 MDT 2002 by User

if "%JAVA_HOME%" == "" set JAVA_HOME=C:\Program
Files\Java\j2re1.4.0_01
if "%ASPECTJ_HOME%" == "" set ASPECTJ_HOME=c:\aspectj1.0

if exist "%JAVA_HOME%\bin\java.exe" goto haveJava
if exist "%JAVA_HOME%\bin\java.bat" goto haveJava
if exist "%JAVA_HOME%\bin\java" goto haveJava
echo java does not exist as %JAVA_HOME%\bin\java
echo please fix the JAVA_HOME environment variable
:haveJava
"%JAVA_HOME%\bin\java" -classpath
"%ASPECTJ_HOME%\lib\aspectjtools.jar;%JAVA_HOME%\lib\tools.jar;
%CLASSPATH%" -Xmx128M org.aspectj.tools.ajc.Main %1 %2 %3 %4 %5
%6 %7 %8 %9
```

If you change JSDK versions, you don't want to go through the hassle of reinstalling AspectJ—and you don't need to. Just open the shell script or bat file in the /bin directory (depending on your operating system) and edit the line that sets *JAVA_HOME* to a specific version. Note that if the environment already has a variable named *JAVA_HOME* and that variable is set to a value, the set command for *JAVA_HOME* will be skipped. So, if you previously set *JAVA_HOME* in your .cshrc file or through the Environment Variables button under Windows, you don't need to change the startup scripts for the compiler.

## No Java Compiler

The AspectJ compiler requires the use of several JAR files in the system. The first is the aspectjrt.jar file located in the /lib directory of the AspectJ installation. The second is the tools.jar file located in the Java installation. However, if the system is unable to find the tools.jar file located in the /lib directory of the Java SDK installation, an error will be produced.

An error can also result if the *JAVA_HOME* path isn't valid, because the first thing the AspectJ compiler script does is try to execute the java command. Such an error might look like this:

```
java does not exist as c:\j2sdk1.4.0_011\bin\java
please fix the JAVA_HOME environment variable
The system cannot find the path specified.
```

In such cases, you need to verify the *JAVA_HOME* environment variable or the value placed in the compiler script.

# Extended Runtime Error Handling

Runtime errors can occur during the execution of a primary application that has been enhanced with AspectJ code. Other times, the code may not work as you expect. In this section, we'll cover the most common situations in which these problems take place.

## Stack Overflow

If you aren't careful, an overflow condition can occur. Consider the following Java code:

```java
public class Recursive {
  public print() {
    System.out.println("Test");
  }
  public static void main(String args[]) {
    Recursive recursive = new Recursive();
    recursive.print();
  }
}
```

Now let's build a simple aspect that matches any println() statements in the Java primary code:

```java
public aspect RecursiveAspect {
  pointcut print() : call(* System.out.println(..));
  before() : print() {
    System.out.println(thisJoinPoint.getSignature());
  }
}
```

This aspect matches on the println() method call and displays the signature where the match was found. If you compile and execute this code, you will receive a stack overflow. In addition, the output will not be what you expect—you expect a single signature to be displayed, but lines of output will begin to scroll off your screen.

The problem with the code is the System.out.println() method call in the advice of the aspect. This output call will also be matched, thus calling the advice, which calls println()—and thus a recursive situation is formed. It is a good idea to use either this() or target() designators to limit the scope of the match. You can also use the negation operator, !, to exclude classes/aspects.

## Join Point Not Matching

One of the most frustrating parts of using AspectJ happens when you execute the primary and aspect code—and code you expect to execute, doesn't. The problem is most likely in the join point definition of an aspect. In this section, we'll consider some of the different errors that can occur when you're writing join point definitions.

## Misspelled Name

The join points for an aspect are based on method signatures and object class names. When the AspectJ compiler compiles the aspect code and weaves it into the primary Java code, all attempts will be made to match the join points in the aspect against the methods or possibly the classes in the primary code. If a match can be made, appropriate changes are made to the primary code based on the pointcut's advice. If a match cannot be made against a join point and methods/classes in the primary code, then the join point's advice code is not added to the primary code. Consider the following code:

```
public class CompileTest {
  public CompileTest() {
  }

  public int returnOne() {
    return 1;
  }

  public static void main(String args[]) {
    CompileTest compileTest = new CompileTest();
    compileTest.returnOne();
  }

  private static aspect CompileTestAspect {
    pointcut grabOne() : call(* *.return1());
    before() : grabOne() {
      System.out.println("I've got One");
    }
  }
}
```

In the primary code, the returnOne() method returns the value 1 to the caller. An aspect associated with the code has a pointcut called grabOne(). The designator used in the pointcut is a call that attempts to match a join point called return1(), which is associated with any object in the primary code. When the code is executed, the before() advice for the grabOne() pointcut does not fire, because the AspectJ compiler is unable to make a match between the return1() join point and any of the methods in the primary code class.

The concept of correct join point matching can extend to the join point's parameters. If the join point specifies that there are no parameters but the methods of the class all have parameters, no match will be made.

## No Package Declaration

When you're using join points that are part of a package, you must be careful how the join point is written in a pointcut designator. Consider the following example primary code:

```
package com.gradecki;

public class CompileTest2 {
  public CompileTest2() {
  }

  public int returnOne() {
    return 1;
  }

  public static void main(String args[]) {
    CompileTest2 compileTest = new CompileTest2();
    compileTest.returnOne();
  }
}
```

The CompileTest2 class is contained in a package declaration starting with com.gradecki. Now consider the following aspect:

```
public aspect CompileTest2Aspect {
  pointcut grabOne() : call(* CompileTest2.returnOne());
  before() : grabOne() {
    System.out.println("I've got One");
  }
}
```

This aspect contains a join point definition designed to match against the returnOne() method of the CompileTest2 class. When the AspectJ compiler begins the weaving process, it tries to find the appropriate class/method based on the code in its intermediate directory. Unfortunately, there is no CompilerTest2 class in the intermediate directory, because the class is in a path of com.gradecki. In order to match a join point associated with a class/method in a package, you must use either the package or wildcards. The following two aspects show the possibilities:

```
public aspect CompileTest2Aspect {
  pointcut grabOne() : call(* com.gradecki.CompileTest2.returnOne());
  before() : grabOne() {
    System.out.println("I've got One");
  }
}
public aspect CompileTest2Aspect {
  pointcut grabOne() : call(* *.returnOne());
  before() : grabOne() {
```

```
                System.out.println("I've got One");
        }
    }
```

## More Subtype Matching

Let's look at another common problem when you're writing aspects that you want to match all calls to methods declared in a class or its derived classes. The designator is written as follows, assuming a class name of Foo:

```
call(* Foo+.*(..))
```

This call designator says to match all methods of Foo or its derived classes, regardless of return type, method name, or the type/number of method parameters. However, this will not match methods like toString(), hashCode(), and so on.

To absolutely match all methods, you can use the following designator:

```
call(* *(..)) && target(Foo)
```

Here, the call designator matches all methods called on any method in the system—something you will probably never do except when combined with the target designator as in the example. The call() designator is combined with target(Foo) to narrow the matched calls to those where the target object is Foo. The new designator will match toString(), and so forth.

## Type/Type+ Commonality

As you read the mailing lists and other materials for AspectJ, you will note that in some places a type name like Foo is used, and in other places the name is Foo+. As we mentioned in Chapter 5, "Join Points," Foo matches only against the Foo class, whereas Foo+ matches on Foo and any derived classes. As you write aspects you must pay attention to this distinction, because in many cases, you will want to write Foo+ instead of Foo in order to handle extensions to your code.

## Matching All Types

If you are interested in matching all types in a package or subpackage, the type pattern must be in the following format:

```
call(com.gradecki..*);
```

Notice the two periods (..) between the text and *. This double period is a wild-card indicator just like that used in parameters:

```
call(void int myFoo(..));
```

## Improper Use of args()

Another possible problem when you're defining join points and pointcuts is the use of logical operators and the args() designator. Consider the following primary code method:

```
public void showTwo(int a, float b) {
}
```

Suppose you want to build a pointcut to match the showTwo signature, and the pointcut should have two parameters of type int and float. You use the call() and args() designators for this purpose, combined with a logical AND operator. Here's one possibility for the definition of the pointcut:

```
pointcut matchShowTwo() : call(public void showTwo(..)) &&
                                    args(int) &&
                                    args(float);
```

At first glance, it appears the pointcut has been created to match a call to the showTwo() method that has zero or more parameters and also two arguments (a and b) passed back to the pointcut advice. However, args(int) && args(float) really says to match on the method showTwo() that has one argument where the first parameter is both of type int and float. Obviously this cannot happen, so the pointcut will never be triggered.

The problem comes down to the args() designator, which is supposed to use comma separators between the parameters. For example:

```
pointcut matchShowTwo() : call(public void showTwo(..)) &&
                                    args(int, float);
```

This new pointcut tells the system to match the showTwo() method where the arguments to the method are defined as int followed by float.

## Using call() && execution()

A very common error occurs during the development of aspects when you attempt to match a call and execution of a method. For example:

```
call(* Foo.getFoo(..));
This designator will match all calls to the Foo.getFoo()
methods. Now consider
execution(* Foo.getFoo(..));
```

This designator matches the execution of the method Foo.getFoo(). What does the following join point match?

```
call(* Foo.getFoo(..)) && execution(* Foo.getFoo(..));
```

Nothing! There can never be a point in the execution of code where both the call and execution occur at the same time.

## Using the IDE to Determine Join Point Access

Chapter 11, "Using Aspect J Tools," discusses the use of IDEs for AspectJ development. Note that if you aren't able to get an aspect to match on a join point successfully, turning to one of the IDEs may be the right decision—most provide indicators in the code where a match will be made.

# Exception Throwing and Catching

A recent mailing list thread discussed join points for catching exceptions—either thrown and caught or thrown and not caught. Ultimately, the system will catch an exception if no other catch() is capable. Consider the following primary and aspect code:

```java
public class CompileTest3 {
   public CompileTest3() {
   }

   public int returnOne() {
      try {
         int i[] = new int[1];
         i[4] = 1;
      } catch(ArrayIndexOutOfBoundsException e) {
         System.out.println("In catch");
         return 0;
      }
      return 1;
   }

   public int returnTwo() {
      int i[] = new int[1];
      i[4] = 1;
      return 2;
   }

   public static void main(String [] args) {
      CompileTest3 compileTest = new CompileTest3();
      System.out.println(compileTest.returnOne());
      System.out.println(compileTest.returnTwo());
   }

   private static aspect CompileTestAspect {
      pointcut grabHandler() : handler(ArrayIndexOutOfBoundsException);
      pointcut grabMain() : execution (void main(..));

      after() : grabHandler() {
         System.out.println("In Handler");
      }

      before() throwing(ArrayIndexOutOfBoundsException e) :
grabMain() {
```

```
        System.out.println("In main");
    }
  }
}
```

This CompileTest3 class has two methods called returnOne() and returnTwo(). Both methods make the mistake of allocating memory in a small integer array but use a cell outside of the currently allocated bounds. In returnOne(), the code for allocating and using the array is wrapped by a try-catch block. In returnTwo(), there is no try-catch block. You are interested in catching both exceptions when they are thrown, due to the i[4]=1; statement.

Two pointcuts are defined In the aspect. The first one, grabhandler(), uses the handler designator to specify that the pointcut should be triggered when a catch handler is activated to handle an ArrayIndexOutOfBoundsException. The advice is to be executed before the actual handler code. The second pointcut, grabMain(), has an execution designator with a join point defined to be the main() method. Obviously, this pointcut alone won't catch any exceptions.

Moving to the advice, you see the grabHandler pointcut assigned to before advice. This advice will execute when any catch code is executed. The grabMain pointcut is used with an after() throwing advice designator. So, if an ArrayIndexOutOfBoundsException is thrown and not handled, this advice code will execute.

The result of running the previous code is as follows:

```
In Handler
In catch
0
In main
Exception in thread "main" java.lang.ArrayIndexOutOfBoundsException
        at CompileTest3.returnTwo(CompileTest3.java:18)
        at CompileTest3.main(CompileTest3.java:25)
```

The code begins displaying output when the array exception is thrown and execution transfers to the before() advice. Once the code in the advice finishes, the code in the catch() block executes, returning 0 to the main method. Next, the returnTwo() method executes, and another exception is thrown but not caught. After the exception is thrown, the after() advice code executes; then the Java system outputs the error to the console, because no catch() blocks are defined to catch the second exception.

# Using TraceJoinPoints.java

Some time ago, a discussion on the AspectJ mailing list talked about tracing join points in a piece of code. The result of the discussion was a piece of

AspectJ code designed to trace all the join points in an application and output those join points in XML format. Listing 12.1 shows the TraceJoinPoints.java aspect.

```
//---------------------- TraceJoinPoints.java

/*
Copyright (c) Xerox Corporation 2001, 2002. All rights reserved.

Use and copying of this software and preparation of derivative
works based upon this software are permitted. Any distribution
of this software or derivative works must comply with all
applicable United States export control laws.

This software is made available AS IS, and Xerox Corporation
makes no warranty about the software, its performance or its
conformity to any specification.
*/

package aj;

import org.aspectj.lang.*;
import org.aspectj.lang.reflect.*;
import java.io.*;

public abstract aspect TraceJoinPoints dominates * {
    protected abstract pointcut entry();
    protected pointcut exit(): call(* java..*.*(..));

    final pointcut start(): entry() && !cflowbelow(entry());

    final pointcut trace():
        cflow(entry()) && !cflowbelow(exit()) && !within(TraceJoinPoints+);

    before(): start() { makeLogStream(); }

    before(): trace() { logEnter(thisJoinPointStaticPart); }
    after(): trace() { logExit(thisJoinPointStaticPart); }

    after(): start() { closeLogStream(); }

    //------------ added
    /**
     * Emit a message in the log, e.g.,
     * <pre>TraceJoinPoints tjp = TraceJoinPoints.aspectOf();
     * if (null != tjp) tjp.message("Hello, World!");</pre>
     */
```

**Listing 12.1** The TraceJoinPoints.java aspect. (continues)

```java
    public void message(String s) {
        out.println("<message>" + prepareMessage(s) + "</message>");
    }
    public void message(String sink, String s) {
        if (null == sink) {
            message(s);
        } else {
            out.println("<message sink=" + quoteXml(sink)
                        + " >" + prepareMessage(s) + "</message>");
        }
    }
    protected String prepareMessage(String s) { return s; } //
XXX implement

    //--------- end of added

    PrintStream out;
    int logs = 0;
    protected void makeLogStream() {
        try {
            out = new PrintStream(new FileOutputStream("log" +
logs++ + ".xml"));
        } catch (IOException ioe) {
            out = System.err;
        }
    }

    protected void closeLogStream() {
        out.close();
    }


    int depth = 0;
    boolean terminal = false;
    protected void logEnter(JoinPoint.StaticPart jp) {
        if (terminal) out.println(">");
        indent(depth);
        out.print("<" + jp.getKind());
        writeSig(jp);
        writePos(jp);

        depth += 1;
        terminal = true;
    }

    void writeSig(JoinPoint.StaticPart jp) {
        out.print(" sig=");
```

**Listing 12.1**   The TraceJoinPoints.java aspect. (continues)

```
        out.print(quoteXml(jp.getSignature().toShortString()));
    }

    void writePos(JoinPoint.StaticPart jp) {
        SourceLocation loc = jp.getSourceLocation();
        if (loc == null) return;

        out.print(" pos=");
        out.print(quoteXml(loc.getFileName() +
                        ":" + loc.getLine() +
                        ":" + loc.getColumn()));
    }

    String quoteXml(String s) {
        return "\"" + s.replace('<', '_').replace('>', '_') +
"\"";
    }

    protected void logExit(JoinPoint.StaticPart jp) {
        depth -= 1;
        if (terminal) {
            out.println("/>");
        } else {
            indent(depth);
            out.println("</" + jp.getKind() + ">");
        }
        terminal = false;
    }

    void indent(int i) {
        while (i-- > 0) out.print("  ");
    }
}
```

**Listing 12.1**   The TraceJoinPoints.java aspect. (continued)

The TraceJoinPoints aspect is abstract and must be derived from in order to operate correctly. Listing 12.2 shows an example of using the aspect.

```
import aj.TraceJoinPoints;

public class CompileTest4 {
  private int [] i;

  public CompileTest4() {
```

**Listing 12.2**   Using the TraceJoinPoints.java aspect. (continues)

```
  }

  public int returnOne() {
    try {
      i = new int[1];
      i[4] = 1;
    } catch(ArrayIndexOutOfBoundsException e) {
      System.out.println("In catch");
      return 0;
    }
    return 1;
  }

  public int returnTwo() {
    i = new int[1];
    i[4] = 1;
    return 2;
  }

  public static void main(String [] args) {
    CompileTest4 compileTest = new CompileTest4();
    System.out.println(compileTest.returnOne());
    System.out.println(compileTest.returnTwo());
  }

  private static aspect CompileTestAspect {
    pointcut grabHandler() : handler(ArrayIndexOutOfBoundsException);
    pointcut grabMain() : execution (void main(..));

    before(): grabHandler() {
      System.out.println("In Handler");
    }

    after() throwing(ArrayIndexOutOfBoundsException e) :
grabMain() {
      System.out.println("In main");
    }
  }
}

public aspect CompilerTestAspect extends TraceJoinPoints {
    protected pointcut entry() :
        execution(static void CompileTest4.main(String[]));

    public static void main (String[] args) {
        CompileTest4.main(args);
    }
}
```

**Listing 12.2**   Using the TraceJoinPoints.java aspect. (continued)

The aspect CompilerTestAspect extends the TraceJoinPoints aspect and overrides the entry and main methods of the aspect. The entry point for most applications is a main() method, but it can be any other valid method of a class. The rest of the code executes and performs various common Java activities like constructor calls, method calls, attribute access, and exceptions. The result of the TraceJoinPoints aspect on the primary Java code is as follows:

```
- <method-execution sig="CompileTest4.main(..)"

   pos="CompileTest4.java:26:3">
- <constructor-call sig="CompileTest4()"
   pos="CompileTest4.java:27:32">
- <initialization sig="CompileTest4()"
   pos="CompileTest4.java:3:27">
  <instanceinitializer-execution sig="CompileTest4._init_"
   pos="CompileTest4.java:3:1" />
  <constructor-execution sig="CompileTest4()"
   pos="CompileTest4.java:6:3" />
  </initialization>
  </constructor-call>
  <field-get sig="System.out" pos="CompileTest4.java:28:12" />
- <method-call sig="CompileTest4.returnOne()"
   pos="CompileTest4.java:28:24">
- <method-execution sig="CompileTest4.returnOne()"
   pos="CompileTest4.java:9:3">
  <field-set sig="CompileTest4.i" pos="CompileTest4.java:11:7"
/>
  <field-get sig="CompileTest4.i" pos="CompileTest4.java:12:7"
/>
- <initialization sig="CompileTest4.CompileTestAspect()"
   pos="CompileTest4.java:32:43">
  <instanceinitializer-execution
   sig="CompileTest4.CompileTestAspect._init_"
   pos="CompileTest4.java:32:3" />
  <constructor-execution sig="CompileTest4.CompileTestAspect()"
   pos="CompileTest4.java:32:3" />
  </initialization>
  <staticinitialization
   sig="CompileTest4.CompileTestAspect._clinit_"
   pos="CompileTest4.java:32:3" />
- <advice-execution sig="ADVICE:
   CompileTest4.CompileTestAspect.before()"
   pos="CompileTest4.java:36:5">
  <field-get sig="System.out" pos="CompileTest4.java:37:15" />
  <method-call sig="PrintStream.println(..)"
   pos="CompileTest4.java:37:8" />
  </advice-execution>
- <exception-handler
   sig="catch(ArrayIndexOutOfBoundsException)"
   pos="CompileTest4.java:13:7">
```

```
<field-get sig="System.out" pos="CompileTest4.java:14:14" />
<method-call sig="PrintStream.println(..)"
  pos="CompileTest4.java:14:7" />
</exception-handler>
</method-execution>
</method-call>
<method-call sig="PrintStream.println(..)"
  pos="CompileTest4.java:28:5" />
<field-get sig="System.out" pos="CompileTest4.java:29:12" />
<method-call sig="CompileTest4.returnTwo()"
  pos="CompileTest4.java:29:24">
<method-execution sig="CompileTest4.returnTwo()"
  pos="CompileTest4.java:20:3">
<field-set sig="CompileTest4.i" pos="CompileTest4.java:21:5"
/>
  <field-get sig="CompileTest4.i" pos="CompileTest4.java:22:5"
/>
</method-execution>
</method-call>
</method-execution>
```

The output from the aspect clearly shows the join points available in the primary code as well as an encapsulation of where they will be when executed. All this information is helpful when you're creating join points and limiting them with cflow and cflowbelow.

# Differentiating Between Call and Execution Designators

A common discussion point on the mailing lists centers around a call() designator versus execution() and how those designators interact with the within/withincode and other issues. Briefly, you know that call() is matched when a caller makes a method call against a callee object. The call() will always be matched before the called method executes. However, the scope of the call() designator doesn't end until the method returns or throws an exception. In the case of the execution() designator, it is matched when the method begins to execute and continues until after the last statement. The execution() designator is always within the scope of a call() designator if one is matched.

## Using this() and target()

In this section, we'll to consider situations where the call() and execution() designators are combined with this() and target(). There are four combinations and possible results, as Table 12.1 shows.

**Table 12.1** Possible combinations of call/execution with this/target

| && | THIS() | TARGET() |
|---|---|---|
| call() | A type in the this() designator, this(DVD), means the call join point must be made from a DVD object. | A type in target(), target(DVD), means the call join point will match when the join point is associated with a DVD object. |
| | A variable in this(), this(obj), will pass the object making the call to the advice. | A variable in target(), target(obj), will pass the object that is the recipient of the join point. |
| execution() | A type in the this() designator, this(DVD), means the executing join point must be within a DVD object. | A type in target(), target(DVD), means the call join point will match when the execution is occurring in the specified type. |
| | A variable in this(), this(obj), will pass the object executing the join point to the advice. | A variable in target(), target(obj), will pass the object executing the join point. |

## Effects of within/withincode

Dealing with the within()/withincode() designators can be tricky when you're using call() and execution(). A call() designator combined with within() or withincode() will be matched only when the join point method associated with call() is found within the execution of the code matched by within()/withincode().

Consider a method called A(). within()/withincode() is used to match the execution of A(). In addition, there is a call() designator for method B(). The pointcut might look like this:

```
pointcut wacky() : within(execution(* *.B(..))) &&
                              call(* *.A(..));
```

The wacky pointcut is valid only when a call to method A() occurs within the execution scope of method B().

## What's Next

In this chapter, we have looked at some of the common errors that can occur when you use AspectJ, its compiler, and weaved code. In Chapters 13 and 14, we'll pull together everything we've discussed and use AspectJ in two real-world situations: adding functionality to an existing application and building an application from the ground up.

# CHAPTER 13

# Aspect-Oriented Examples: Patterns and Reuse

If you're like us, you learn by example. With something as revolutionary as AspectJ, examples can be critical to understanding both the potential of a new technology as well as successful techniques for using it. Accordingly, we've tried to put examples into every chapter to help you understand language issues and the types of concerns that AspectJ can modularize. This chapter and the next take a step backward to consider larger issues. In this chapter, we delve into patterns and reuse, and explore how to turn a unit of crosscutting behavior into something that you can reapply to different situations. Chapter 14 looks at AspectJ in context, weaving crosscutting concerns into complete applications. By the time you've finished reading these two chapters, you should have a better sense of how to apply aspects to your own applications.

The examples in this chapter draw from the skeleton of an Employee management system introduced in Chapter 7, "Advice," and the beginnings of a persistence solution presented in Chapter 8, "Inter-type Declarations." You might consider glancing back at those examples to refresh your memory before you proceed.

We begin this chapter by refactoring the persistence example from Chapter 8. This chapter turns the solution into a fully reusable aspect that we can apply to any object in our system. After the refactoring, we explain some of the general features of reusable aspects. Once we've developed a familiarity with aspect reuse we apply the concept to design patterns. It turns out that AspectJ can represent design patterns as aspects. We test the idea of aspect reuse by using a third-party implementation of the Observer pattern to help us with cache invalidation.

Throughout the chapter, we attempt to present design considerations and highlight areas where aspect-oriented programming (AOP) can improve the modularity and understandability of your software systems.

# Reusable Persistence

We've already been through two iterations of persisting the objects in our Employee management system (you can see the latest iteration of the design in Chapter 8, Listing 8.9). However, we're a long way off from a total solution.

Here's a little bit about what we've developed so far:

- Each persistable class implements a marker interface (PersistentObject) that allows it to interact with a persistence container. (We're thinking of bean-managed persistence entity beans in an EJB container, but the example does not tie directly to EJBs.)

- The PersistentObject interface defines a store() method that takes responsibility for writing a persistent representation of the object to a database. (A complementary read() method would be required in a real system, but we'll focus on store() for now).

- The container (outside of our control) decides when to call the store() method.

- Since database updates are expensive, we only want to execute them if the object's state has changed since it was last stored. The persistence aspect implements this behavior by storing a "dirty" flag that we set to true if we determine that the object's state has changed.

- We can apply the role of "PersistentObject" to any class in the system without modifying the class. The persistence aspect allows this by adding concrete members to the PersistentObject interface. (Chapter 8 applies the interface to the Employee and Department classes.)

- In order to make the persistence solution fully reusable, we need to customize the persistent behavior of each affected object. Each persistent class needs its own store() method, and each class should similarly decide which operations change its state.

The pointcuts that we used to describe state changes in Chapter 8 were the same for both affected objects. For this reason, our previous example missed some important methods that would "dirty" the Department object. Specifically, we could add and remove Employees from a Department without triggering a "state change." Furthermore, we did not customize the store() method for each class.

# The PersistenceProtocol Aspect

To provide aspect-oriented behavior that can be customized, you use an abstract aspect. As you may recall from Chapter 9, "Aspects," aspects can extend other aspects. Just as with extending a class in Java, extending an aspect allows the subtype to inherit generic behavior from its supertype. The subtype overrides or adds members to tailor the generic behavior to its specific requirements. Creating an abstract persistence aspect allows us to create sub-aspects that customize persistence behavior for each class we wish to persist.

Listing 13.1 contains the code for the abstract aspect. It defines a number of pieces of advice, as well as some abstract methods and pointcuts. Subaspects take responsibility for filling in the abstract behavior.

```
/**
 * Marks that a class fills the role of a persistable
 * entity. The example makes the interface public
 * because it posists that a container will use the role.
 * Otherwise the interface might be made package access
 * to keep other code from depending on it.
 */
public interface PersistentObject{
    public void store();
}


public abstract aspect PersistenceProtocol {

    /** 1
     * Declares a private member variable on
     * the PersistentObject interface.
     */
    private boolean PersistentObject.dirty = false;

    /** 2
     * Fulfills the contract required by the third
     * party container, overridden to only call
     * store(Connection) when the object is dirty.
     */
    public final void PersistentObject.store() {
        if(dirty){
            store(getConnection());
        }else{
```

**Listing 13.1**  PersistenceProtocol defines the general persistence behavior of PersistentObjects.
(continues)

```
                    System.out.println("This PersistentObject " +
                "does not need to be stored.");
        }
      dirty=false;
}


/** 3
 * Takes the place of the no-arg store() method.
 * Each PersistentObject must implement this
 * method to customize its storage.
 */
public abstract void
    PersistentObject.store(Connection c);



/** 4
 * Each subaspect must define this pointcut
 * to identify those operations which change
 * a PersistentObject's state.
 */
abstract pointcut stateChange(PersistentObject po);

/** 5
 * Sets the dirty flag on the object after each
 * state change.
 */
after(PersistentObject po) returning : stateChange(po){
    po.dirty = true;
}

/** 6
 * Each subaspect has the chance to override
 * this method on their persistent objects if they need
 * to get a connection from a different source.
 */
Connection PersistentObject.getConnection(){
    Connection conn = null;
    //get connection from some source
    return conn;
}

}
```

**Listing 13.1** PersistenceProtocol defines the general persistence behavior of PersistentObjects. (continued)

Let's take a look at the features of the aspect. If you remember the earlier incarnations of this example, the dirty flag declared onto the PersistentObject interface (location 1) should come as no surprise. The exact mechanics differ, but the intent of the flag remains the same. It serves to mark the object as requiring storage at the next opportunity.

The store() method at location 2 meets the (supposed) contract of the third-party persistence container.. As in previous examples, store() uses the dirty flag to determine whether the object should store itself. If storage is necessary, the method calls the abstract store(Connection) method. Subaspects implement store(Connection) to write the object to the database. (Notice that PersistenceProtocol declares the inter-type store() method final so that subaspects will override store(Connection) instead.) Once the store operation completes, the aspect marks the PersistentObject as "clean."

PersistenceProtocol supplies the connection to store(Connection). This allows it to take responsibility for obtaining the connection. Using this technique, the aspect provides important context to the storage operation. In a real application, the aspect could even open the connection before passing it to store(Connection) and close it afterward. In this manner, common behavior (obtaining a connection, opening it, and so on) remains in a common location rather than appearing in each persistent object. Also, notice that the getConnection() method can be overridden by subaspects if necessary. That way, if Employee needs a different connection than Department, the change will be easy to make.

The stateChange pointcut and associated advice at locations 4 and 5 implement the dirtying behavior. The advice simply sets the dirty flag after any join points selected by stateChange. PersistenceProtocol delegates the exact definition of stateChange to its subaspects. This way, the abstract aspect (PersistenceProtocol) defines common behavior (dirtying the object) while the subaspects determine under what circumstances the behavior takes effect.

To review, PersistenceProtocol defines an interface for persistent objects. It interacts with these objects through the interface. It stores persistent objects only when dirty and dirties them at join points defined by its concrete subaspects.

## Applying PersistenceProtocol with Subaspects

At this point you've seen the general behavior. The picture remains incomplete without applying PersistenceProtocol to target classes. To successfully apply PersistenceProtocol, we need to write a subaspect that does three things:

1. Declares that a class (or set of classes) implements PersistentObject. Currently AspectJ supports no way to enforce that a subaspect does this, but the subaspect will make little sense without it.

2. Defines a pointcut (stateChange) that captures any operations which alter the state of the persistent object.

3. Defines a store(Connection) method for the classes affected by the aspect. This method writes the state of the persistent object to the database.

Let's demonstrate two concrete implementations of PersistenceProtocol: EmployeePersistence and DepartmentPersistence.

### A Simple Subaspect: EmployeePersistence

EmployeePersistence is the simpler of the two cases. You can peruse the full source of the aspect in Listing 13.2.

```
public aspect EmployeePersistence extends
                              PersistenceProtocol{

    /* 1 */
    declare parents : Employee implements PersistentObject;

    /** 2
     * Defines state changes as assignments to
     * any instance variables of Employee.
     */
    pointcut stateChange(PersistentObject emp) :
        set(!static !transient * *)
        && target(emp) && target(Employee);

    /* 3 */
    public void Employee.store(Connection conn){
        System.out.println("About to store " + this);
        //omitting actual details of SQL statements
    }
}
```

**Listing 13.2** EmployeePersistence customizes the persistence policy applied to Employees.

As you can see, customizing the persistence policy is a matter of a few lines. At location 1, the aspect declares that Employee will participate in the persistence protocol. At location 2, it overrides the stateChange pointcut. This pointcut resembles those found in Chapter 8. Specifically it defines a state change as an assignment to a nontransient instance variable. Notice that stateChange includes *two* target() pointcuts. The first exposes the PersistentObject as join point context. The second (target(Employee)) limits the scope of the pointcut to field assignments on Employees. The reason we need two targets is that the signature of an overriding pointcut must match the signature of the overridden pointcut exactly. Thus, the exposed context must be typed to PersistentObject. However, the pointcut does not want to target all PersistentObjects—it's only concerned with Employees. Therefore, we add the second target() designator.

Finally the store(Connection) method at location 3 writes data to the database. We've omitted the gory details and simply added a println() to indicate that the method executes.

## A More Complex Subaspect: DepartmentPersistence

Sections 1 and 3 of DepartmentPersistence resemble EmployeePersistence. The store() method has an added println() to signify the update to the Department's list of Employees. The real difference lies in the stateChange pointcut. Namely, it incorporates add() and remove() methods. Because the addEmployee() and removeEmployee() methods of Department clearly alter the state of the object but do not set any instance variables, the pointcut cannot rely solely on set(! static !transient * *). Take a look at Listing 13.3.

```
public aspect DepartmentPersistence extends
                                PersistenceProtocol{
   /* 1 */
   declare parents : Department implements PersistentObject;

   /* 2 */
   pointcut stateChange(PersistentObject po) :
      (
         set(! static !transient * *) ||
         addsAndRemoves ()
      )
      && target(po) && target(Department);

   /* 3 */
   pointcut addsAndRemoves():
      call(* add*(..)) || call(* remove*(..));



   /* 4 */
   public void Department.store(Connection conn){
      System.out.println("About to store " + this);
      System.out.println(" Updating employee list: " +
         getEmployees());
      //omitting actual details of SQL statements
   }
}
```

**Listing 13.3** The DepartmentPersistence aspect sports a different stateChange pointcut.

In addition to looking at instance variables, the stateChange pointcut in DepartmentPersistence looks at method calls. The addsAndRemoves pointcut (location 3) uses || to select calls any method whose name begins with "add" or "remove". stateChange combines this new pointcut with a set() pointcut similar to the one in EmployeePersistence.

## The Persistence Aspects in Action

The Main class in Listing 13.4 demonstrates the behavior of the Persistence-Protocol and its subaspects. An employee and a department are constructed and modified several times. The main() method calls the store() method on each object at various points in its lifecycle. We use println()s to specify our expectations about whether the object should write to the database at each call to store(). Just after the demo class appears a short aspect that decorates println() methods from the Main class. Although we won't consider it in detail, it illustrates AspectJ's power to quickly implement a small crosscutting concern (the aspect surrounds each println() from Main with "[]:").

```
public class Main {

    public static void main(String[] args) {
        Employee janet = new Programmer("J. Smythe", 99000);
        System.out.println("New employee, should store");
        janet.store();
        System.out.println("No changes, shouldn't");
        janet.store();
        janet.raiseSalary(2300);
        System.out.println("Should store");
        janet.store();

        System.out.print("-------------");
        System.out.println("Now trying a department");
        System.out.println();

        Department hr = new Department("Human Resources",
                                        250000);
        System.out.println("New dept., should store");
        hr.store();
        System.out.println("No changes, shouldn't");
        hr.store();
        hr.addEmployee(janet);
        hr.addEmployee(new Employee("Bill Buxley", 29000));
        System.out.println("Employees added, should store");
        hr.store();
        System.out.println("Shouldn't");
        hr.store();
        hr.removeEmployee(janet);
        System.out.println("Employee removed," +
```

**Listing 13.4** This Main class demonstrates the effects of the persistence aspects. (continues)

```
                        " should store");
        hr.store();
    }
}

aspect DecoratePrintlns{

    /* Selects printlns in the Main class. */
    pointcut printlnsInMain(String s):
        call(void println(String)) && args(s)
        && within(Main);

    /* Calls proceed() with a new argument,
     * effectively decorating the fucntion.
     */
    void around(String s) : printlnsInMain(s){
        proceed("["+s +"]:");
    }
}

/* Output */
[New employee, should store]:
About to store Programmer J. Smythe:$99,000.00
[No changes, shouldn't]:
This PersistentObject does not need to be stored.
[Should store]:
About to store Programmer J. Smythe:$101,300.00
-------------[Now trying a department]:

[New dept., should store]:
About to store Department Human Resources budget: 250000
  Updating employee list: []
[No changes, shouldn't]:
This PersistentObject does not need to be stored.
[Employees added, should store]:
About to store Department Human Resources budget: 250000
  Updating employee list: [Programmer J. Smythe:$101,300.00,
  Employee Bill Buxley:$29,000.00]
[Shouldn't]:
This PersistentObject does not need to be stored.
[Employee removed, should store]:
About to store Department Human Resources budget: 250000
  Updating employee list: [Employee Bill Buxley:$29,000.00]
```

**Listing 13.4**  This Main class demonstrates the effects of the persistence aspects. (continued)

There's nothing unexpected in the output. When either an Employee or a Department is created, or its state modified, the persistence aspects conspire to ensure that the object will store its state at the next call to store().

## Thoughts on Reusable Aspects

Aside from demonstrating how AspectJ can capture persistence behavior, this example illustrates several aspect-oriented design principles. Most of these revolve around coupling. As we've mentioned before, the use of inter-type declarations allows component code to be entirely unaware of aspects. Let's look a little more closely at what that means.

### Patterns and Roles

The PersistenceProtocol aspect defines a pattern. Since *pattern* has come to be a widely used (and sometimes misused) software term, let's narrow its meaning. PersistenceProtocol defines a behavior pattern for code that interacts with it. Objects that implement the PersistentObject interface play a role within a set of actions and interactions defined by the aspect. For now, we'll use the term *behavior pattern* to differentiate this meaning from the many other meanings that "pattern" brings to mind.

Object-oriented programming (OOP) and AOP systems realize behavior patterns differently. In traditional Java, behavior patterns range from informally organized sets of interactions scattered through related classes to well-defined containers that provide services to installed components. In aspect-oriented programs, behavior patterns can be constructed as aspects. With or without aspects, behavior patterns must define roles that that participants play. Java and AspectJ treat the matter of role definition very differently.

### Who Knows What about Whom

In our example, the PersistenceProtocol aspect knows only about the role that components play within it. It does not know about Employees or Departments and interacts with those classes only through a narrowly defined interface. The same can also be said of many established object-oriented behavior patterns. A container usually interacts with components through a similar type of interface.

Things begin to differ when we consider what the component knows. In our example, all Employee knows about is its *central abstraction*. In other words, it models a real-world employee. After countless examples and wild new behaviors, the Employee class has scarcely changed since we first looked at it. To implement a persistence pattern in traditional Java, the Employee would need to know about its role. Perhaps it would implement an interface like PersistentObject directly. The result would be a sort of persistent-Employee that blended the central abstraction with an external role. The definition of Employee would depend on the definition of PersistentObject. Such a class would serve as a classic example of close coupling.

**NOTE**

Some frameworks get around the issue component to container coupling by using such techniques as reflection and metadata descriptor files. We would argue that these systems also exhibit AOP properties (to a limited extent).

The disadvantages of close coupling are well known. If, for instance, the interface for PersistentObject needed to change, that change would ripple to all affected classes. Furthermore, the persistent-Employee couldn't be reused in a system with a different notion of persistence.

Blending persistence directly into Employee also reduces Employee's cohesion. With only a single role, the effect is minimal. However, as it supported more and more roles, the Employee would represent its primary abstraction less and less well. A persistent-Employee is one thing. A remote-persistent-notifying-Employee is another.

Instead of blending roles into affected classes, AspectJ offers "bridge" aspects. In our example, the bridge aspects were EmployeePersistence and DepartmentPersistence. These aspects concretized the PersistenceProtocol and adapted it to suit Employee and Department. These bridge aspects *are* very closely coupled—they have intimate knowledge of both the behavior pattern and the component classes. If something were to change on either side, you can bet that we would need to revisit these aspects in short order. However, this sort of close coupling is different. The next section explores why.

### Encapsulated Coupling

Despite their coupling, bridge aspects offer a compelling advantage—they encapsulate the coupling. In other words, they act as adapters between the components and the pattern. Neither the role-players nor the role-definers need to know about each other. The end result is more independent modules. With a new set of bridge aspects, PersistenceProtocol could be applied to a new system. Similarly, the Employee class can play multiple roles without increasing in complexity or blurring its central abstraction. With AspectJ we're closer to an off-the-shelf component model than ever before.

# Method Caching

The next section steps away from design considerations to look at another example of how AspectJ can capture a crosscutting concern. But before we've finished with the example we'll be back to considering patterns and reuse.

As we've seen several times throughout the book, around advice can be used to dynamically replace join points. Aspects can use this power to neatly replace method calls, among other things. For example, around advice can replace a method call with a less expensive method call. This section considers how you can use around advice to transparently cache the results of a method call, thereby improving performance.

# Caching XML Representations

In Chapter 8 we added methods to classes from our Employee management system that rendered the objects as XML. Creating XML representations can be time-consuming. Therefore, these toXML() methods seem like good candidates for our caching strategy. This example focuses on the caching the results of toXML()on Department.

## Department's XML Representation

Listing 13.5 contains the code for rendering a department as XML. There's not a lot of aspectual behavior to consider beyond the inter-type declaration of the toXML() method onto Department (location 1). Since a Department contains a list of Employees, the XML representations of all of the Employees are included in the output.

```
public aspect DepartmentXML {

    /* 1 */
    public void Department.toXML(PrintStream out){
        out.println("<department>");
        printContents(this, out);
        out.println("</department>");
    }

    private static void printContents(Department d,
                                      PrintStream out){
        out.println("<title>");
        out.println("  " + d.getTitle());
        out.println("</title>");
        out.println("<budget>");
        out.println("  " + d.getBudget());
        out.println("</budget>");
        out.println("<employees>");
        printEmployees(d, out);
        out.println("</employees>");
```

**Listing 13.5** Department's XML representation depends on the XML representation of its Employees. (continues)

```
        }

        private static void printEmployees(Department d,
                                           PrintStream out){
            Iterator it = d.getEmployees().iterator();
            while(it.hasNext()){
                ((Employee)it.next()).toXML(out);
            }
        }

        public static void main(String[] args){
            Department it =
                new Department("IT", 200000);
            Employee joe = new Programmer("Joe", 85000);
            Employee nick = new Programmer("Nick", 85000);
            it.addEmployee(joe);
            it.addEmployee(nick);
            it.toXML(System.out);
        }
}
/* Output */
<department>
<title>
  IT
</title>
<budget>
  200000
</budget>
<employees>
<programmer>
  <name>
    Joe
  </name>
  <salary>
    85000
  </salary>
  <language>
    null
  </language>
</programmer>
<programmer>
  <name>
    Nick
  </name>
  <salary>
    85000
```

**Listing 13.5**  Department's XML representation depends on the XML representation of its Employees. (continues)

```
   </salary>
   <language>
     null
   </language>
 </programmer>
 </employees>
 </department>
```

**Listing 13.5**  Department's XML representation depends on the XML representation of its
Employees. (continued)

The output of the main method shows a department as (very untidy) XML.

## Caching the toXML() Method

Assume we've decided that Department's toXML() method is too slow. To
improve performance, we'd like to execute it only if the Department has
changed since the last time it was called. Otherwise, we can safely reuse the
results of the last call. To keep things simple, this example applies caching only
to Department. If we wanted to, we could easily make the caching aspect
abstract and apply it to several different classes (just as we did with PersistenceProtocol). Listing 13.6 contains the CacheToXML aspect.

```
public aspect CacheToXML {

    /** 1
     * Identifies calls to the toXML method.
     */
    pointcut cacheableCalls (PrintStream out, Department d) :
        call(void toXML(PrintStream))
        && target(d) && args(out);

    /** 2
     * Declares a cache field on the Department itself.
     */
    private String Department.xmlCache;

    /** 3
     * Executes instead of calls to toXML.
     *
     * Calls proceed and stores result if no
     * cache exists. Otherwise uses cached
```

**Listing 13.6**  CacheToXML stores and reuses the results of Department's toXML() method.
(continues)

```
    * data.
    */
   void around(PrintStream out, Department d):
       cacheableCalls (out, d){

       if(d.xmlCache == null){
           System.out.println("(generating fresh)");
           ByteArrayOutputStream data =
               new ByteArrayOutputStream();

           proceed(new PrintStream(data), d);

           d.xmlCache = data.toString();
       }
       else{
           System.out.println("(using cached data...)");
       }
       out.print(d.xmlCache);
   }

   /** 4
    * Dirtying behavior similar to Persistence
    * example. (See advice at 5).
    */
   pointcut stateChange(Department d) :
       (
           set(! static !transient * *) ||
           call(* add*(..)) || call(* remove*(..))
       )
       && target(d);


   /** 5
    * Clears the cache if dept. changes.
    */
   after(Department d) :
       stateChange(d) &&
       !within(CacheToXML){

       d.xmlCache = null;
   }
}
/* Test class */
public class Main {

   public static void main(String[] args){
```

**Listing 13.6**  CacheToXML stores and reuses the results of Department's toXML() method.
(continues)

```
        Department it =
            new Department("IT", 200000);

        Programmer joe = new Programmer("Joe", 85000);
        it.addEmployee(joe);

        System.out.println("new dept. should use fresh");
        it.toXML(System.out);

        System.out.println("no changes should use cache");
        it.toXML(System.out);

        Programmer nick = new Programmer("Nick", 85000);
        it.addEmployee(nick);

        System.out.println("new employee");
        it.toXML(System.out);
        nick.setLanguage("AspectJ");
        joe.setLanguage("AspectJ");

        System.out.println(
            "languages changed-should use fresh");
        it.toXML(System.out);
    }
}
/* Output */
[new dept. should use fresh]:
(generating fresh)
<department>
... <!-- nothing unexpected -->
</department>
[no changes should use cache]:
(using cached data...)
<department>
...
</department>
[new employee]:
(generating fresh)
<department>
... <!-- added nick -->
<programmer>
  <name>
    Nick
  </name>
  <salary>
    85000
```

**Listing 13.6** CacheToXML stores and reuses the results of Department's toXML() method. (continues)

```
    </salary>
    <language>
      null
    </language>
  </programmer>
  </employees>
</department>
[should use fresh-languages changed]:
(using cached data...) ...<!-- problem! -->
<department>
  <programmer>
    <name>
      Joe
    </name>
    <salary>
      85000
    </salary>
    <language>
      null <!--should be AspectJ! -->
    </language>
  </programmer>
  <programmer>
    <name>
      Nick
    </name>
    <salary>
      85000
    </salary>
    <language>
      null <!--should be AspectJ! -->
    </language>
  </programmer>
  </employees>
</department>
```

**Listing 13.6** CacheToXML stores and reuses the results of Department's toXML() method. (continued)

The pointcut and around advice at locations 1 and 3 do the majority of the interesting work in this aspect. The cacheableCalls pointcut selects calls to Department's toXML() method and exposes the Department as well as the PrintStream argument as context. The around advice at location 3 makes use of the context. If the Department's cache lies empty, the advice will call proceed and cache the results. If the cache contains data, or the advice is done caching, it writes the contents of the cache to the original PrintStream. The pointcut and advice at locations 4 and 5 serve to empty the cache if the Department changes state. For an in-depth discussion on the stateChange pointcut, see the persistence example earlier in the chapter.

There's a problem, however. If we look at the last XML rendering of the department, we can see it prints Nick and Joe's skills as "null" rather than "AspectJ." If we look at the stateChange pointcut, we can see why. There's no provision to select state changes on Employees in the Department! The next subsection seeks to remedy this.

# Design Patterns as Aspects

To invalidate the Department's cache, we must notify the Department every time one of its employees changes state. If there's one thing we know by now, it's that AspectJ is good at notifications. However, this problem may prove thorny.

## Adding Invalidation to the Aspect's API

In order to pave the way for additional invalidation conditions, we need to refactor our invalidation mechanism somewhat. We don't want to expose other code to the implementation details of the cache. Accordingly, we add a public invalidate() method to the aspect so that other code can invalidate a Department's cache without manually clearing the cache field. Listing 13.7 shows the new API.

```
/** 5
* Clears the cache if dept. changes.
*/
after(Department d) : stateChange(d){
    invalidate(d);
}

/** 6
* Allows other callers to programmatically
* clear the cache.
*/
public void invalidate(Department d){
    d.xmlCache = null;
}

/* Sample use*/
CacheToXML.aspectOf().invalidate(someDept);
```

**Listing 13.7** The invalidate() method hides the implementation details of the aspect.

Using the aspect's method to clear a Department's cache clarifies the client's dependency on the aspect. It also allows the aspect to change its caching implementation without disturbing clients who use it. This idiom (going *through* an aspect to access behavior added *by* the aspect) appears often in the AspectJ documentation.

### Detecting State Changes on Employee

Ordinarily we might just set up another pointcut and advice to call the new invalidate() method. However, we have a small problem: we can't notify a department after a change to Employee unless we know which department to notify. We can check if an Employee belongs to a department easily enough:

```
d.getEmployees().contains(emp)
```

We could even use that expression in advice: *if(d.getEmployees().contains(employee)){...}*. However, the association is unidirectional. That is, there's no way to ask an Employee for his or her Department. We could add a bidirectional association using inter-type declarations and automatically update it using advice. However, we plan to go a step beyond that.

# The Observer Pattern

Those of you familiar with design patterns, especially those popularized in *Design Patterns* by Gamma, et. al (Addison-Wesley, 1995) can probably see what's coming. The Observer pattern suits this sort of need perfectly. Let's review the pattern briefly.

### Observer in a Nutshell

The Observer pattern's intent, according to the Portland Pattern Repository Wiki (http://c2.com/cgi/wiki?ObserverPattern) is to:

"Define a one-to-many dependency between objects so that when one object changes state, all its dependents are notified and updated automatically."

This looks like exactly what we want. We want to maintain a dependence between Employees and Departments so that when an Employee changes state, its department is notified and updated (its cache cleared).

#### Implementing Observer in Java

In ordinary Java, a Subject class keeps track of any objects that need to know about changes in its state (they're usually stored in a list on the Subject). When the Subject's state changes, it iterates through the list and notifies each Observer of the change.

Observer, like many patterns, suffers from scattering. The Subject implements some parts, and the Observer others. Unless you're familiar with the pattern, you might not understand that these pieces cooperate. Furthermore, you can't simply pull the Observer pattern out of a third-party pattern library and drop it into your code. You need to make changes to both of the involved classes and then hook them together at the right time. In our case, we'd have to modify the Department so that it began observing each Employee as soon as it was added and stopped observing once the Employee left. This approach is worthwhile perhaps, but somewhat invasive. Will the code really be better off with all this added complexity? Do we really need this performance improvement?

# Reusing Observer in AspectJ

Think back to the persistence example. We used the PersistenceProtocol aspect to define interactions between code and to specify roles for participants. We then customized the behavior pattern to suit two different classes. Surely we can apply the same principles to this situation. We could create an abstract aspect and then customize it to the Employee/Department caching situation. At the end of the day we'll have built a pattern we can actually reuse instead of reimplementing it when we need it again.

Building a reusable pattern would be great. But our lives would be even easier if we could use an already tested and debugged pattern from a library. After all, who wants to reinvent the wheel? It turns out that Jan Hannemann and Gregor Kiczales have created a reusable library of AspectJ pattern implementations as part of a project for the Software Practices Lab at the University of British Columbia (UBC). Sure enough, the library contains an implementation of Observer.

This example looks like a perfect situation in which to test AspectJ's claims of enhanced modularity and reuse. Let's attempt to solve our caching problem by extending the ObserverProtocol aspect that ships with the library. If we can successfully add the Observer pattern to our code without complicating our core classes, we'll know we have a new tool in our design chests.

## The ObserverProtocol Aspect

Since we're big fans of open source software and the practice of reading code, we reprint the full source for the ObserverProtocol aspect in Listing 13.8. As you can see, the source is thoroughly commented. We'll add a few points of our own at the end.

```
package ca.ubc.cs.spl.pattern.library;
/* -*- Mode: Java; tab-width: 4; indent-tabs-mode: nil;
 * c-basic-offset: 4 -*-
 *
 * This file is part of the design patterns project at UBC
 *
 *The contents of this file are subject to the Mozilla Public
 * License Version 1.1 (the "License"); you may not use this
 * file except in compliance with the License. You may
 * obtain a copy of the License at either
 * http://www.mozilla.org/MPL/ or http://aspectj.org/MPL/.
 *
 * Software distributed under the License is distributed on
 * an "AS IS" basis, WITHOUT WARRANTY OF ANY KIND, either
 * express or implied. See the License for the specific
 * language governing rights and limitations under the
 * License.
 *
 * The Original Code is ca.ubc.cs.spl.patterns.
 *
 * Contributor(s):
 */

import java.util.WeakHashMap;
import java.util.List;
import java.util.LinkedList;
import java.util.Iterator;

/**
 * Defines the general behavior of the observer design
 * pattern.
 *
 * Each concrete sub-aspect of ObserverProtocol defines one
 * kind of observing relationship.  Within that kind of
 * relationship, there can be any number
 * of subjects, each with any number of observers.
 *
 * The sub-aspect defines three things: <ol>
 *
 *    <li> what types can be subjects or observers <br>
 *          this is done using +implements
 *
 *    <li> what operations on the subject require updating the
```

**Listing 13.8**    A reusable implementation of the Observer design pattern from UBC's Aspect-Oriented Pattern Implementation project. (continues)

```
 *         observers <br> this is done by concretizing the
 *         changes(Subject) pointcut
 *
 *   <li> how to update the observers <br>
 *         this is done by defining a method on
 *         updateObserver(Subject, Observer)
 * </ol>
 *
 * Note that in this implementation, the work of updating is a
 * method on the sub-aspect, not a method introduced on the
 * observer. This allows one class of object to be the
 * observer in different kinds of observing relationships,
 * each of which
 * has a different updating behavior. For observers that just
 * have a single generic update behavior, the method on
 * updateObserver will just be a simple call that generic
 * updater.
 *
 * @author  Gregor Kiczales
 * @author  Jan Hannemann
 * @version 1.0, 05/13/02
 *
 */

public abstract aspect ObserverProtocol {


    /**
     * This interface is used by extending aspects to say
     * what types can be subjects. It models the subject
     * role.
     */

    protected interface Subject  { }


    /**
     * This interface is used by extending aspects to
     * say what types can be observers. It models the
     * observer role.
     */

    protected interface Observer { }


    /**
```

**Listing 13.8** A reusable implementation of the Observer design pattern from UBC's Aspect-Oriented Pattern Implementation project. (continues)

```
 * Stores the mapping between <code>Subject</code>s
 * and <code>Observer</code>s. For each subject, a
 * <code>LinkedList</code> is of its observers is stored.
 */

private WeakHashMap perSubjectObservers;


/**
 * Returns a <code>Collection</code> of the observers of
 * a particular subject. Used internally.
 *
 * @param s the subject for which to return the observers
 * @return a <code>Collection</code> of s's observers
 */

protected List getObservers(Subject s) {
    if (perSubjectObservers == null) {
        perSubjectObservers = new WeakHashMap();
    }
    List observers = (List)perSubjectObservers.get(s);
    if ( observers == null ) {
        observers = new LinkedList();
        perSubjectObservers.put(s, observers);
    }
    return observers;
}


/**
 * Adds an observer to a subject. This is the equivalent
 * of <i>attach()</i>, but is a method on the pattern
 * aspect, not the subject.
 *
 * @param s the subject to attach a new observer to
 * @param o the new observer to attach
 */

public void    addObserver(Subject s, Observer o) {
    getObservers(s).add(o);
}

/**
 * Removes an observer from a subject. This is the
 * equivalent of <i>detach()</i>, but is a method on the
 * pattern aspect, not the subject.
```

**Listing 13.8**    A reusable implementation of the Observer design pattern from UBC's Aspect-Oriented Pattern Implementation project. (continues)

```
 *
 * @param s the subject to remove the observer from
 * @param o the observer to remove
 */

public void removeObserver(Subject s, Observer o) {
    getObservers(s).remove(o);
}

/**
 * The join points after which to do the update.
 * It replaces the normally scattered calls to
 * <i>notify()</i>. To be
 * concretized by sub-aspects.
 */

protected abstract pointcut subjectChange(Subject s);

/**
 * Call updateObserver after a change of interest to
 * update each observer.
 *
 * @param s the subject on which the change occured
 */

after(Subject s): subjectChange(s) {
    Iterator iter = getObservers(s).iterator();
    while ( iter.hasNext() ) {
        updateObserver(s, ((Observer)iter.next()));
    }
}

/**
 *Defines how each <code>Observer</code> is to be updated
 * when a change to a <code>Subject</code> occurs. To be
 * concretized by sub-aspects.
 *
 * @param s the subject on which a change of interest
 *          occured
 * @param o the observer to be notifed of the change
 */

protected abstract void updateObserver(Subject s,
                                       Observer o);
}
```

**Listing 13.8** A reusable implementation of the Observer design pattern from UBC's Aspect-Oriented Pattern Implementation project. (continued)

What does the aspect actually *do*? Well, first it defines two roles, Subject and Observer. When we extend the aspect, we'll use our subaspect to apply these roles to Employee and Department, respectively. Second, it maintains a set of mappings between Subjects and Observers. Each Subject can have a number of Observers. (The aspect maintains this with a WeakHashMap with Subjects as keys and LinkedLists of Observers as values.) Client code or subaspects can use the addObserver() and removeObserver() methods to alter these mappings.

It's important to realize that the relationship between Subjects and Observers varies dynamically. The two classes enter the pattern only when they're passed as arguments to addObserver(). This means that a given component could be added to any number of Subject-Observer relationships—possibly playing different roles in each. It also means that, to apply the pattern, another entity must take responsibility for pairing Subjects and Observers by calling addObserver() and removeObserver(). This entity could be anything from component code to another aspect to a front end that accepts input from the user. (We plan to use our subaspect to handle this responsibility).

The aspect defines after advice relative to the abstract subjectChange pointcut. Subaspects implement subjectChange to select join points that signal a state change for the subject. The advice on subjectChange then calls the abstract method updateObserver() for each Observer that's watching the changed Subject.

As you can see, the number of implemented lines of code is low—the real usefulness of the aspect comes from the order it imposes on the pattern. All of the relationships and interactions are captured in code or delegated to subaspects to fill in.

### Extending ObserverProtocol

So far, so good. The real test comes when we apply the aspect to our situation. Let's review the questions our subaspect must answer in order to successfully implement the pattern:

1. Who are the Subjects and who are the Observers?
2. What constitutes a change in the Subject?
3. What constitutes an update to the Observer?
4. When does the Observer begin watching the Subject, and when does it stop?

The ObserverProtocol aspect does not require subaspects to answer question 4 in the same manner it requires them to answer 1 through 3. However, the pattern will only activate when we call addObserver() to pair the Employee and

Department. In our case, we know exactly when we want to activate the pattern: after the addEmployee() method executes. Accordingly, we can use advice to automate the call to addObserver().

Listing 13.9 showcases our use of ObserverProtocol. We've commented the aspect to indicate which segments of code answer each question.

```
public aspect EmployeeObserver extends ObserverProtocol {

    /**
     * Question 1.
     * Who are the Subjects and who are the Observers?
     */
    declare parents : Employee implements Subject;
    declare parents : Department implements Observer;

    /**
     * Question 2.
     * What  constitutes a change in the Subject?
     */
    protected pointcut subjectChange(Subject emp) :
        set(!static !transient * *)
        && target(emp) && target(Employee);

    /**
     * Question 3.
     * What constitutes an update to the Observer?
     *
     * A: Updating the observer consists of invalidating
     * its cache.
     */
    protected void updateObserver(Subject emp,
                                  Observer dept){

        CacheToXML.aspectOf().invalidate((Department)dept);
    }

    /**
     * Question 4.
     * When does the Observer begin watching the Subject,
     * and when does it stop?
     */

    /**
     * Identifies addEmployee and exposes the players.
     */
```

**Listing 13.9** EmployeeObserver fills in the details of the Observer pattern. (continues)

```
private pointcut additions(Employee emp,
                           Department dept):
    call(public void addEmployee(Employee))
    && target(dept) && args(emp);

/**
 * Does the same for removeEmployee.
 */
private pointcut removals(Employee emp, Department dept):
    call(public void removeEmployee(Employee))
    && target(dept) && args(emp);

/**
 * After additions, create the relationship.
 */
after(Employee emp, Department dept) returning :
    additions(emp, dept){

    addObserver(emp, dept);
}

/**
 * After removals, remove the relationship.
 */
after(Employee emp, Department dept) returning :
    removals(emp, dept){

    removeObserver(emp, dept);
}

public static void main(String[] args){
    Department dept =
        new Department("IT", 200000);
    Programmer joe = new Programmer("Joe", 85000);
    dept.addEmployee(joe);
    Programmer nick = new Programmer("Nick", 85000);
    dept.addEmployee(nick);
    System.out.println("new dept, fresh");
    dept.toXML(System.out);

    System.out.println("no change, cache");
    dept.toXML(System.out);

    nick.setLanguage("AspectJ");
    joe.setLanguage("AspectJ");
    System.out.println("changes to Nick and Joe, fresh");
    dept.toXML(System.out);
```

**Listing 13.9**  EmployeeObserver fills in the details of the Observer pattern. (continues)

```
        dept.removeEmployee(joe);
        System.out.println("joe removed, fresh");
        dept.toXML(System.out);

        joe.raiseSalary(3000);
        System.out.println("Changes to Joe, but Department");
        System.out.println("no longer observing him, cache");
        dept.toXML(System.out);
    }

}

/* Output */
[new dept, fresh]:
(generating fresh)
...
[no change, cache]:
(using cached data...)
...
[changes to Nick and Joe, fresh]:
(generating fresh)
<department>
...
<employees>
<programmer>
  <name>
    Joe
  </name>
  <salary>
    85000
  </salary>
  <language>
    AspectJ <!-- correct! -->
  </language>
</programmer>
<programmer>
  <name>
    Nick
  </name>
  <salary>
    85000
  </salary>
  <language>
    AspectJ <!-- correct! -->
  </language>
</programmer>
```

**Listing 13.9**  EmployeeObserver fills in the details of the Observer pattern. (continues)

```
</employees>
</department>
[joe removed, fresh]:
(generating fresh)
...
[Changes to Joe, but Department]:
[no longer observing him, cache]:
(using cached data...)
...
```

**Listing 13.9**   EmployeeObserver fills in the details of the Observer pattern. (continued)

The aspect answers question 1 early. It uses declare parents to mark an Employee as a Subject and a Department as an Observer. It answers question 2 by defining (a now familiar-looking) subjectChange pointcut, thereby overriding the abstract version from ObserverProtocol. EmployeeObserver also overrides the abstract updateObserver() method. The overridden version calls CacheToXML's invalidate() method on the Department. (In this manner, it answers question 3.)

Question 4 (when does the relationship between Employees and Departments start and end) deserves a little more attention. First the aspect defines two pointcuts: additions and removals. These pointcuts identify the start and end of the relationship. Essentially, every time an Employee enters a Department it simultaneously enters into the Subject-Observer relationship with that Department. When it exits the Department it also exits the relationship. Two pieces of after returning advice implement this behavior by calling addObserver() and removeObserver(), respectively.

Notice that the EmployeeObserver aspect could easily serve several departments and that Employees could work for multiple Departments. Each Department would receive notifications for all its Employees, regardless of how many other departments that Employee belonged to.

### More Patterns in AOP?

AspectJ's claims for enhanced modularity and reuse have proven themselves—at least with regards to patterns. In this example, we took an off-the-shelf design pattern and customized it to our application with a single subaspect. Now the Department's cache will invalidate whenever a dependent Employee changes.

With a little thought, you may see other uses for the ObserverProtocol aspect. Observer made it into the GoF patterns because it was a widespread best practice for dealing with dynamic notification. Because AspectJ makes it easy to reuse already-implemented patterns, we wouldn't be surprised if the number of patterns in the average application increased with the adoption of AOP.

# Aspect-Oriented Design

This chapter has focused on design and reuse by showing:

- An example of how to turn a special-purpose aspect into a generic solution to a problem (PersistenceProtocol)
- An example of how to add crosscutting behavior to your code by extending a third party pattern aspect (ObserverProtocol)

So, now that we've looked at these topics, what can we say about the emerging shape of aspect-oriented design?

AspectJ clearly shows an aptitude for encapsulating what we called behavior patterns. In this area AspectJ shows the programmer more forest and fewer trees. It does this by capturing and organizing interactions between classes. In object-oriented systems these interactions remain scattered through the participants in the behavior pattern. In aspect-oriented systems they are localized by the language's crosscutting constructs (pointcuts, advice, marker interfaces, and so on). The this organization gives programmers the ability to reason about more concerns (and more complicated concerns) simultaneously. Futhermore, behavior patterns can be tested and perfected in isolation, free from contextual distractions. This leads to higher potential for the reuse of generic code, meaning that teams can spend less time reinventing the wheel and more time adding unique value.

The emergence of byte-code weaving in AspectJ 1.1 intensifies the situation. In theory it will be possible to buy components from one vendor, behavior patterns from another, and weave them together into a coherent system with a few adapter aspects. Component-based reuse has been the pie-in-the-sky dream of software engineers and managers for years, if not decades. Will AspectJ really make it happen?

The answer is...yes and no. AspectJ cannot modularize everything, nor does it provide convenient idioms for every operation that a programmer can express in thought or words. Third-party software may prove resistant to modification unless it's designed for simplicity. Toolkits and frameworks that "do everything" may hamper clean aspect compositions.

However, the results of applying the "off-the-shelf" Observer pattern are encouraging. Previous attempts at truly component-oriented software missed two important capabilities that AspectJ provides. First, they lacked the ability to significantly alter a module's behavior without modifying its source code.

Java 2 Platform Enterprise Edition (J2EE ), for instance, offers XML descriptors that can customize a component—but only in limited ways. AspectJ allows modifications that the component designers may never have dreamed of. Second, previous solutions forced components to adhere to specialized interfaces, meaning that components for one set of behavior patterns couldn't be reused with another set.

In a sense, AspectJ offers only a foretaste of the possibilities of aspect-oriented design. As the language evolves, it will continue to offer more elegant and precise encapsulations of a wider variety of concerns. Already the prospects of generic typing loom on the horizon. Beyond even aspect-oriented software lies intentional software—software that makes the source code resemble the design. For the moment, however, we're excited by AspectJ, and even a little overwhelmed. As deep as we've gotten, we've only scratched the surface.

# What's Next

The final chapter in the book continues our examination of the larger issues involved in using AspectJ. The chapter applies aspects to two complete applications. In the first example, we use AspectJ to add new features to an application. In the second, we refactor the application with AspectJ—moving crosscutting concerns from components into aspects. The chapter considers issues such as UML notation for aspects, designing with aspects in mind, and interfacing with existing code.

If after Chapter 14 you still hanker for examples of AspectJ in action, you might want to check out these likely sources:

**The AspectJ documentation:**
(http://dev.eclipse.org/viewcvs/indextech.cgi/~checkout~/aspectj-home/documentation.html). The examples include a very nice sample application (Spacewar) that implements some heavy-duty concerns (aspect-oriented thread synchronization is a sight to behold). The docs also ship a few smaller scale examples.

**The Aspect-Oriented Design Pattern Implementation Project:**
(www.cs.ubc.ca/labs/spl/projects/aodps.html). Aside from the Observer pattern, Jan Hanneman and Gregor Kiczales implemented the other 22 "Gang of Four" (GoF) design patterns in AspectJ and Java simultaneously. If you're familiar with the GoF patterns, you may find their implementation in AspectJ to be a good tool for understanding aspects in general. This project is also a great place to see reusable aspects in action. Hanneman and Kiczales's paper, *Design Pattern Implementations in Java and AspectJ*, does an excellent job of discussing patterns and aspects and influenced the shape of this chapter a great deal.

# CHAPTER 14

# Using AspectJ in the Real World

To show how aspect-oriented programming can affect a complete project, this chapter walks you through the software development cycle when using aspects. We'll consider two scenarios: adding a new application feature and refactoring a previous project.

The first example centers around the addition of logging and thread pooling to a piece of software found on an open-source Java Web site. This is a good example of how you can add a new feature to source code you haven't developed (or even seen before). The software shows a graphical representation of a projectile being shot from a cannon. The projectile has a given mass, and the cannon has an angular position relative to the ground. The velocity is also controllable through a slide control on the application's GUI. The software looks nice graphically, but it doesn't keep a record of changes made to the controls or final outcome values. Some of the software's fictitious users are interested in knowing when any control is changed, even if the Fire button isn't clicked. In addition, you'll make all intermediate plotted values and the final distance available in a log.

The second example focuses on refactoring an application to remove logging and timing values from the original code. Your primary intent will be to bring the modularity of some of the classes back to a more acceptable state instead of allowing extraneous code to work its way into otherwise encapsulated classes.

# Adding Features

In most cases where a developer can get the attention of the chief architect (or happens to be the chief architect), AOP isn't given the red-carpet treatment. Like most new technologies, it requires a trying-out period during which things like usability, performance, and maturity can be proven. This try-out period is typically associated with either a very small project or a new feature being added to a project.

## Initial Application

Many developers will be familiar with this situation: You go to work knowing all the tasks you need to accomplish, only to be informed of a change in direction. The boss lets you know that an important customer has raised a high-priority issue and you need to add a new feature or two to production code already in the field. You've never used the software, and there is very little documentation. Fortunately, the customer wants the job done right, so you have an unrealistic due date instead of an impossible one.

In this example, the current application is called Projectile Motion; you can find the source code at www.phys.virginia.edu/classes/109N/more_stuff/Applets/ ProjectileMotion/applet.html. This software, which is covered by the GNU GPL license, provides scientists around the world with a graphical representation of the flight path of a projectile that has a specific mass and is fired from a cannon at a specified angle and velocity.

## Features to Be Added

The customer has indicated that the Projectile Motion application does its required job well, but they would like a few problems addressed:

- The application cannot provide output in a form other than the graphical format. The customer would like results from the calculations to be output to a file. For each run, the starting values entered by the user, all intermediary values, and the final distance should be put into a text file for later processing.

- The customer wants a tracking feature that records all values set for mass, velocity, and angle. This information should be noted when the user starts the projectile in motion. In addition, every time the user selects a value for one of these three variables, all three values should be recorded.

- The customer wants to affect time in the calculation of the projectile, by letting the user move time ahead or behind. The code should display an input box asking the user if time should be changed from the present value. You might even tell the application not to bother asking for a change until a certain time is reached. Ultimately, you will be able to give the software the ability to replay data based on a new system time and also to determine the system's response to bad data.

## Current Design

Figure 14.1 shows the sample output after you download the source code for the application, compile it, and execute it to determine what it does. Now you can set out to understand the design structure of the code; this exercise leads to the UML class diagram shown in Figure 14.2.

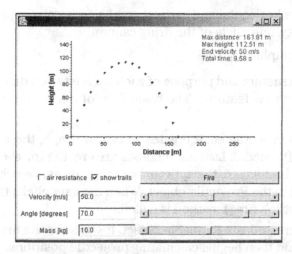

**Figure 14.1** Application sample output.

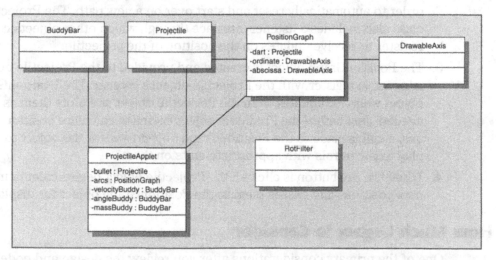

**Figure 14.2** Projectile Motion UML class diagram.

From the UML diagram, you can see that the application includes six classes. Two of those classes, ProjectileApplet and PositionGraph, do the most work. From the comments in the source code, you can determine the purpose of each class:

**ProjectileApplet**—Contains the logic for handling setup, getting input from the user, and firing a projectile

**Projectile**—Calculates where a projectile is located, based on mass, velocity, and the angle of the firing cannon

**PositionGraph**—Draws the projectile on a graph

**BuddyBar**—Displays input sliders to the user

**DrawableAxis**—Draws horizontal and vertical graphs with units appropriate for the mass, velocity, and angle of the firing cannon

**RotFilter**—Rotates a graphical image

Understanding the class structure and purpose of each class lets you determine where to add code for the new features. The basic flow of execution follows these steps:

1. A ProjectileApplet object is created. It creates a PositionGraph, three BuddyBar controls, and a Projectile. Listener methods are created for each control. When a slider is changed, the appropriate value, mass, velocity, and angle are changed in the Projectile object. When the user clicks the Fire button, the Projectile's fire() method is called.

2. The Projectile object created is a Runnable object. It waits for the fire() method to be called, and then begins calculating projectile positions. [awk.]The code interrupts the current processing of a projectile path in order to automatically reset and start over on a new path. The Projectile class also includes a listener interface through which other objects can register to receive updates on the position of the projectile.

3. The PositionGraph object is created and provided to the Projectile object in order to register with the Projectile object's listener. The PositionGraph object waits for updates from the Projectile object and plots them as needed. Just before the Projectile object begins to calculate position values, a call is made to the PositionGraph object to allow the object to display axis controls with appropriate units on them.

4. When the fire button is clicked, the Projectile object begins calculating new positions and passes them to the PositionGraph object for display.

## How Much Legacy to Consider

One of the primary considerations after you review the design and code of the current application is the mix of new code versus AspectJ code to use to implement the new tasks. In other words, you must decide whether to write code in AspectJ because it's available and you want to use it, or whether to spend time considering the design of the application and use all available features to implement the new concern.

The answer is simple: If the new concern that needs to be added to the application will crosscut the legacy application, then you should write an aspect. If you can write the concern as a stand-alone class and plug it into the current code without upsetting the previously written classes, then you should use the primary language.

## Writing Aspects and Primary Code

Your goal is to add the new concerns to the current application without resorting to tangled code in the classes already defined. As you look at the first concern—which deals with handling logging of starting, intermediate, and ending values—it should occur to you that the Projectile object already provides the ability to obtain this information. Recall that the PositionGraph object registers itself with the Projectile object to receive updates when a position changes. Upon inspection of the two classes, you find that the Projectile's listener class is actually an interface, defined in Listing 14.1.

```
public interface ProjectileListener {
 public void setPosition(double x,double y,
   double vx,double vy,double time,boolean mark);
 // Initial velocity and angle.
 public void beginFiring(double velocity, double angle,
   double[] endStats);
 // shotStats[0] endDistance [1] end velocity [2]
 // maxHeight [3] endTime
 // endStats[0] kappa [1] gamma
 // endStats[2] vx0 [3] vy0 [4] t0 -- all three scalings.
 public void endFiring(double[] shotStats);
}
```

**Listing 14.1** The ProjectileListener class.

The interface has three primary methods: beginFiring(), setPosition(), and endFiring(). All three methods fit perfectly with the information you need to log based on the first new concern. You don't need to create an aspect for this concern, because you can build a new class that implements these three methods and registers itself with the Projectile object. When the beginFiring() method is called, the new class opens a log file and inserts the initial values from the application. The setPosition() method adds intermediate position information to the file, and the endFiring() method records final information and closes the file. After all that, you don't even need an aspect.

A simple version of the new class is shown in Listing 14.2.

```java
import java.io.*;
public class PathLogging implements Projectile.ProjectileListener
{
 Logger logObj;

 public PathLogging (Projectile bullet) {
  bullet.addListener(this);
  logObj = Logger.instance();
 }

 public void setPosition(double x,double y, double vx,double
vy,double time,boolean mark) {
   logObj.write("x= " + x + " time= " + time);
 }

 public void beginFiring(double velocity, double angle, double[]
endStats) {
   logObj.write("Begin Firing");
 }

 public void endFiring(double[] shotStats) {
   logObj.write("End Firing\n");
 }
}
```

**Listing 14.2**   The PathLogging class.

## Logger Helper Class

A helper class called Logger, shown in Listing 14.3, handles opening the log file, closing the file, and appending a string to the current file contents. This helper class logs the projectile path information as well as the information to be recorded as indicated in the second concern (discussed next).

```java
import java.io.*;
public class Logger{

 FileWriter fw;
 static private Logger _instance = null;
```

**Listing 14.3**   The Logger class. (continues)

```
static public Logger instance() {
  if(_instance == null) {
    _instance = new Logger();
  }
  return _instance;
}


protected Logger() {
 try {
  fw = new FileWriter("log.txt");
 } catch(IOException e){}
}


public void close() {
 try {
  fw.close();
 } catch(IOException e){}
}


public void write(String s) {
 try {
  fw.write(s + "\n");
 } catch(IOException e){}
 }
}
```

**Listing 14.3** The Logger class. (continued)

One of Java's more painful characteristics is the need to either declare an exception thrown or add try/catch blocks to all code that might throw an exception. Such is the case for the FileWriter code defined in Listing 14.3. However, AspectJ lets you remove the try/catch blocks or signature definitions by setting up a software exception in an aspect. Consider the following aspect, which handles the exceptions in constructor, write, and close methods:

```
public aspect LoggerAspect {
  declare soft : IOException : within(Logger);

  pointcut writerCall(Logger obj) :
   call(* Logger.*(..)) &&
   this(obj);

  after (Logger obj) throwing (Exception e) : writerCall(obj) {
   obj.close();
  }
}
```

In this aspect, a soft exception is declared based in the Logger class. This means any method with the class could potentially throw an IOException. Next, the constructor and write methods are selected as join points using a call designator. When either of these join points is matched and the method is throwing an exception, the after advice will execute. The after advice calls the close() method of the FileWriter object to make sure the object is cleaned up when an error has occurred.

With this base aspect in place, any new methods added to the Logger class don't need to include try/catch blocks or declare they are throwing IOException. Although this might seem like a small win, it makes a big difference when the class has a large number of methods.

## Adding PathLogging

The PathLogging class must be incorporated into the application so it can be instantiated and registered with the Projectile object. The most logical approach is to make the new class an attribute in the ProjectileFrame class in the same manner as PositionGraph. The code is as follows:

```
PathLogging pl = new PathLogging(bullet);
```

Once the application is executed, the movement of a projectile is recorded to a file. Here's a small piece of the output in the file:

```
Begin Firing
x= 0.0 time= 0.0
x= 0.0 time= 0.07663140638417193
x= 1.310474229738103 time= 0.15326281276834386
x= 2.620948459476206 time= 0.2298942191525158
x= 3.9314226892143087 time= 0.3065256255366877
```

Moving to the second concern, which specifies that all changes to the mass, velocity, and angle controls should be logged, you have to look in the ProjectileApplet code to see how the control changes are handled. The code that does the work is as follows:

```
public void buddyValueChanged(BuddyBar changer, double dVal){
    if (changer==velocityBuddy) {
      bullet.setVelocity(dVal);
    } else if (changer == angleBuddy) {
      bullet.setAngle(dVal*Math.PI/180);
    } else if (changer == massBuddy) {
      bullet.setMass(dVal);
    }
}
```

The code sets the new velocity, mass, or angle value on the Projectile object and returns. All you need to do is add code to open a log file when the ProjectileApplect code starts; you can add writes to the log file in this method. Of course, doing so violates the objective of avoiding tangled code. Therefore, the second concern is a perfect opportunity to use an aspect. This aspect is based on the call to the method and requires you to access the variables passed to the code (see Listing 14.4).

```
public aspect LogIntermediate {
  Logger logObj = Logger.instance();

  private void writeInfo(double mass, double velocity, double
angle) {
    logObj.write("Mass="+mass+" Velocity="+velocity+"
Angle="+angle);
  }

  pointcut valueChange(Projectile bullet) :
    (execution(public void Projectile.setVelocity(double)) ||
    execution(public void Projectile.setAngle(double)) ||
    execution(public void Projectile.setMass(double))) &&
    this(bullet);

  after(Projectile bullet) : valueChange(bullet) {
    writeInfo(bullet.getMass(), bullet.getVelocity(),
bullet.getAngle());
System.out.println(bullet.getVelocity());
  }
}
```

**Listing 14.4** The LogIntermediate aspect.

The aspect intercepts the call to each of the ProjectileApplet object's set methods. *After* advice is executed when the method has completed its work, and a write is made to the log file associated with the application. This aspect catches all changes to the slider controls for each of the variables *mass*, *velocity*, and *angle*. The output from changing the three variables is saved in the log file. Here is an example of the output:

```
Mass=10.0 Velocity=56.935 Angle=0.7068583470577035
Mass=10.0 Velocity=57.43 Angle=0.7068583470577035
Mass=10.0 Velocity=57.925 Angle=0.7068583470577035
Mass=10.0 Velocity=58.42 Angle=0.7068583470577035
Mass=10.0 Velocity=58.915 Angle=0.7068583470577035
Mass=10.0 Velocity=59.41 Angle=0.7068583470577035
Mass=10.0 Velocity=59.905 Angle=0.7068583470577035
Mass=10.0 Velocity=59.905 Angle=0.7068583470577035
Mass=10.0 Velocity=59.905 Angle=1.2252211349000193
Mass=10.0 Velocity=59.905 Angle=1.233075116533994
```

The third concern is a little more involved and causes a change to occur in the execution of the application that isn't meant to occur in the original design. Comments in the source code discuss the possibility of changing the parameters of the project in mid-flight. You don't alter the characteristics of the projectile, but instead change the current time. Doing so can be handy for replaying a projectile's flight or stepping through its flight.

The Projectile object is the primary place for the flight calculations. The method calcPosition(double) takes a double value representing the time and updates the internal attributes of the object. Time starts at zero and is incremented by a value of .008 units during each iteration within an internal loop. The aspect you add intercepts the call to calcPosition(double) and gives the user an opportunity to provide an input time other than that used by the application. The aspect uses a small input dialog, shown in Figure 14.3, to obtain the value from the user.

Listing 14.5 shows the aspect.

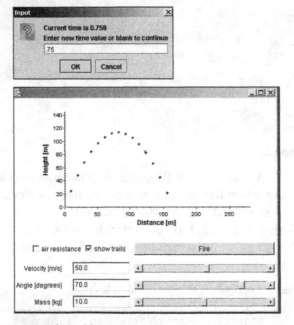

**Figure 14.3** CalcPosition input box.

```
import java.awt.Graphics;
import javax.swing.*;
```

**Listing 14.5** The TimeAspect aspect. (continues)

```
public aspect TimeAspect {
 pointcut interceptTime(double time, Projectile bullet) :
  execution(private void calcPosition(double)) &&
  args(time) &&
  this(bullet);

 void around(double time, Projectile bullet) :
interceptTime(time, bullet) {
  String input = JOptionPane.showInputDialog("Current time is "
+ time + "\n" +
                          "Enter new time
value or blank to continue\n");

  if (!input.equals("")) {
   double newTime = Double.parseDouble(input);
   bullet.t = newTime;
   proceed(newTime, bullet);
  } else {
   proceed(time, bullet);
  }
 }
}
```

**Listing 14.5**  The TimeAspect aspect. (continued)

The aspect begins with a definition of a pointcut using an execution designator against the join point private void calcPosition(double). Because you must access the incoming time parameter, the args designator is specified as well. The source code for the Projectile class shows that the time value passed to the method is based on a class attribute called t. If you want the calculations to change based on a new time value, the t attribute must also be set to the new time value. For this reason, the object where the join point is matched is passed to the code as well, through the *this* designator. The interceptTime pointcut is associated with around advice, so you can affect the outcome of the matched method. The parameter to the calcPosition() method and the affected object are both passed to the advice.

The advice code begins by creating and displaying a dialog box, shown in Figure 14.3. The dialog displays the current value passed into the method as a reference value for the user. The user has the option of clicking OK to use the original value or entering their own value for use in the calcPosition() method. In either case, the advice code checks the string returned from the dialog box. If the string is empty, then the user wants the current time value to be used. If the string isn't empty, then the user has changed the time, and the code extracts a double value from the string. Once the time value has been determined to be either the old or a new value, the proceed keyword is used to pass both the new time value and the Projectile object back to the system so the original code can continue processing.

Figure 14.4 shows an example of advancing the projectile in time. The projectile has an arc graph just after it was fired; the graph continues its downward fall when the time advances forward.

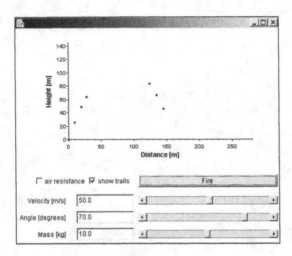

**Figure 14.4**   Interrupted flight path.

## Testing

One of the benefits of incorporating the concerns for this example is the testing group's unprecedented access to a large number of variables in the application while the application is running. In addition, the group can change the time value to determine how the code reacts to bad data and so on.

## Documentation

When you make any changes to an existing application, it's important to keep the documentation consistent. In this case, no initial design information existed outside the code itself. A UML-based class diagram was created to help you understand the application's architecture. Because the diagram has already been created, it will be useful to keep it up to date.

A number of articles have been written about expanding UML to handle AOP concepts. Figure 14.5 shows why there is so much discussion about adding AOP to UML diagrams.

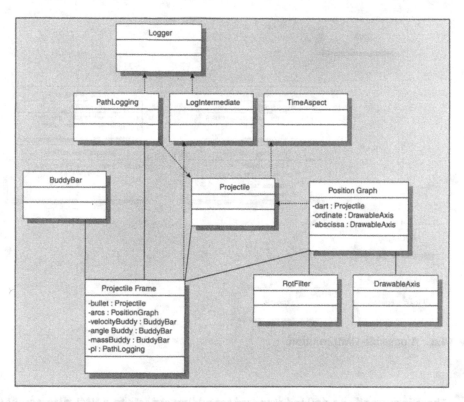

**Figure 14.5**  Initial concern placement in UML.

The UML class diagram in Figure 14.5 shows how the PathLogging class, which addresses the first concern, was added to the application. The class is a normal Java class and doesn't lead to problems with the UML diagram. The second concern was addressed with an AspectJ aspect called LogIntermediate. From the diagram, it appears that the aspect is just another class in the application; there is no indication that the aspect crosscuts the application, nor are any constructs, such as pointcuts, shown. The third concern was also addressed with an aspect—but again, it looks like a class. You could add a number of notes to the UML diagram; however, it's better to represent the aspects and their related concepts in a form that brings out the fact that the aspects are ancillary to the application, and that in many cases they could be removed with affecting the application.

Figure 14.6 shows another UML diagram in which the LogIntermediate and TimeChange aspects are defined in terms more appropriate for aspects. These aspects are shown to be dependent on the Projectile class, and the LogIntermediate aspect <has-a> Logger object associated with it. Each of the aspects is drawn into the diagram using a dotted box to represent the fact that these aspects are easy removed from the application without upsetting the primary functionality.

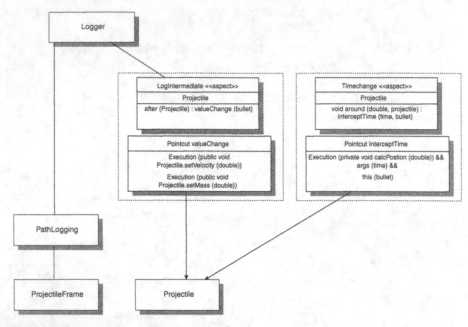

**Figure 14.6** A possible UML solution.

NOTE

There is currently no defined standard for adding aspects to a UML diagram. At the following Web site, you can find a number of articles that show how aspects should be added to class diagrams, collaboration diagrams, and others: http://lglwww.epfl.ch/workshops/aosd-uml/papers.html.

Each aspect figure is designed to provide as much information as necessary about its structure so a designer can accurately convey the purpose and relationship of the aspect to the rest of the primary code. At the top of each aspect is its name, followed by the classes it will potentially match. This portion of the aspect may be quite large if the aspect can match a large number of methods spread across many classes. After the list of affected classes, the advices found in the aspect are listed, along with their associated pointcuts.

The pointcuts defined in the aspect are listed in boxes under the aspect's labeled box. The first part of the pointcut is its name, followed by the designators specifying the join points the pointcut will use to match primary code. If the aspect includes more than one pointcut, you'll create additional boxes within the aspect.

As you look at this example and read the articles at the link in the preceding Note, you will come to understand the need for a standard way to represent aspects in UML—and there are as many ideas for how to do this as there are designers.

# Conclusion

A popular question about AspectJ is whether you should use it instead of incorporating the feature directly into the primary application through a refactoring exercise or a hack job. This question can be answered intelligently, but the answer depends on the application and the state of the source code.

First, hacking the feature into the code isn't a good option; although quick, this approach will lead to problems down the road. Adding a feature during the refactoring process isn't necessarily a good idea either, because the focus of the exercise will vacillate between the refactor and adding the feature. If you have source code and accurately encapsulated classes, adding the feature may be best in the primary language, unless it will crosscut the classes and components.

In this section's example, adding the ability to log and control the play time of the projectile crossed many classes. This fact alone makes AspectJ a good choice for the implementation.

# Refactoring Web Spider

In all projects, there comes a time when the code is used in a production setting, features are being added, and the original developers have moved on to different projects. Eventually, the code begins to get messy and performance may start to suffer. One solution is to refactor the code. This process can entail the entire system, a complex method of one class, or a single feature.

During the refactoring process, a primary goal should be better encapsulation of the classes and components. Even in the best of circumstances, you'll need to place some code in multiple classes, where it breaks the classes' encapsulation. In these circumstances, the solution is to use AOP, and AspectJ specifically.

When the project was written in Java, you can use AspectJ to write better code. To show how you can refactor an application using AspectJ, this section takes the open-source Web spider called WebLech (available at http://weblech.sourceforge.net), removes some of the crosscutting concerns, and replaces the concerns with aspects. The section is roughly broken into subsections based on the concern to be removed from the primary code.

As we move through the sections, we'll show most of the aspect code but only a small portion of the primary code, for space reasons. We recommend that you download the code for this example from the book's Web site (www.wiley.com/compbooks/gradecki) so you'll have a full picture of the changes. It may also be helpful to have the original source code available, as found at the weblech.sourceforge.net site.

# Logging

When you review the code for the Web spider, it will become clear that logging is one of the first crosscutting concerns that needs to be removed from the code. Within the code, all the logging is handled using the Log4J package. The Log4J package is encapsulated within a Logger class, where a static attribute called _logClass holds a logging instance based on a WebLech category.

Any class in the code that wants to log information needs to import either the Log4J or Logger class and pull the log instance. Once this has been accomplished, information can be logged using the instance's info(), error(), and debug() methods. In the spider's source code, there are anywhere from 2 to 10 calls to the logger in any given method. This is quite a bit of crosscutting, and it must be evaluated. The evaluation is multifaceted:

1. Do all the different logging events need to occur? In other words, do you need to use info(), error(), and debug() without any criteria, or would simple logging statements suffice? Answer: For this application, there's no reason to use multiple levels of logging criteria.

2. What impact does the logging crosscutting concern have on the readability and maintainability of the code? Answer: The logging is dispersed throughout the code and detracts from its readability.

3. Will pulling logging into an aspect help with encapsulation and modularization? Answer: Yes.

The result of the evaluation determines whether logging should be an aspect (yes) and how much functionality and complexity should be contained in the aspect. The last part addresses question 1: If you need the logging granularity, it can be obtained through a level of logic in the aspect code and how the join points are handled.

To refactor the logging concern to an aspect, you will start with the logger's output mode.

## *Logger Output*

As we mentioned, the logging used in WebLech is Log4J, and it has been used extensively throughout all the code. You don't have to abandon the use of Log4J if it provides a capability necessary for analysis.

The following code implements a logger aspect using Log4J. The code is based on Listing 14.3, except the aspect is defined to be abstract. To promote modularization, each class in the system has an associated logging aspect. When a class is changed, it will be easy to find the aspect to update:

```
package weblech.util;
import org.apache.log4j.Category;
import weblech.util.Log4j;

abstract aspect LoggerAspect {
 protected static final Category _logClass =
Category.getInstance("LoggerAspect");

 static {
  Log4j.init();
 }
}
```

At this moment, all the aspect does is obtain a Log4J instance and make sure it is initialized. The next few sections walk through the application code, showing how it is refactored to use a logging aspect. Note that all the code could easily be logged with a single aspect matching all methods in the code. Remember the evaluation questions? The granularity of logging captured by the logging aspects is directly proportional to the complexity of the join points, advice, and aspects. For this example, assume that a higher level of complexity is necessary in order to provide intelligent logging.

For the most part, the aspects you add to the project will not use introduction. However, in a few places, accessor methods are supplied for class attributes needed to provide accurate logging.

### Refactoring DumbAuthenticator.java

The DumbAuthenticator.java file implements a class to handle passing a username and password to Web sites that need authentication. The class includes two methods with a total statement count of five; two of those statements are dedicated to logging. The class's code includes five additional lines of code for logging. About half of this class deals with logging, and although the logging is necessary, the class is a prime example of how a simple concern can crosscut and even dominate a class. Listing 14.6 shows the original object code.

```
package weblech.spider;
import org.apache.log4j.Category;
import java.net.Authenticator;
import java.net.PasswordAuthentication;

import weblech.util.Log4j;
public class DumbAuthenticator extends Authenticator
{
```

**Listing 14.6** The DumbAuthenticator class. (continues)

```
  private final static Category _logClass = Category.getInstance(DumbAuthen-
ticator.class);

  static
  {
    Log4j.init();
  }

  private final String user;
  private final String password;

  public DumbAuthenticator(String user, String password)
  {
    _logClass.debug("DumbAuthenticator(" + user + ", ***)");
    this.user = user;
    this.password = password;
  }

  public PasswordAuthentication getPasswordAuthentication()
  {
    _logClass.debug("getPasswordAuthentication()");
    return new PasswordAuthentication(user, password.toCharArray());
  }
}
```

**Listing 14.6**   The DumbAuthenticator class. (continued)

The first method in the class is the constructor, which logs the username passed to the constructor. The second method returns the object's authentication information and logs just the method name. In both cases, the logging is accomplished with a call to the debug() method. It's quite simple to create an aspect for this class. Listing 14.7 shows the resulting LoggingAspectDumbAuthenticator aspect.

```
package weblech.spider;
public aspect LoggerAspectDumbAuthenticator extends LoggerAspect
{
 pointcut logConstructor(String username, String password) :
  initialization(public DumbAuthenticator.new(..)) &&
  args(username, password);

 pointcut logGet() :
  call(* getPasswordAuthentication());
```

**Listing 14.7**   The LoggerAspectDumbAuthenticator aspect. (continues)

```
before(String username, String password) :
    logConstructor(username, password) {
 _logClass.debug("DumbAuthenticator(" + username + ", ***)");
 _logClass.info("DumbAuthenticator(" + username + ", ***)");
}


before() : logGet() {
 _logClass.debug(thisJoinPoint.getSignature());
 _logClass.info(thisJoinPoint.getSignature());
 }
}
```

**Listing 14.7** The LoggerAspectDumbAuthenticator aspect. (continued)

This aspect extends the abstract LoggingAspect aspect. The extension allows automatic instantiation of the Log4j object and lets the code log to both the screen and a log file without further programmer action. Within the aspect are two pointcuts: logConstructor and logGet. The logConstructor pointcut uses the initialization designator to match a join point on the method constructor. The logGet pointcut uses a call designator to match the getPasswordAuthentication() method. You use two different pointcuts because the logging output for each join points is different. For both pointcuts, before advice is defined in which information is presented to the console as well as a log file.

To test the DumbAuthenticator and its aspect, you can use the following test application:

```
package weblech.test;
import weblech.spider.DumbAuthenticator;
import java.net.Authenticator;
import java.net.PasswordAuthentication;

public class TestDumbAuthenticator {
 public static void main(String [] args) {

   DumbAuthenticator da = new DumbAuthenticator("Gradecki", "password");

   PasswordAuthentication pa = da.getPasswordAuthentication();
 }
}
```

This tester allocates a DumbAuthenticator object, thus triggering a match on the LogConstructor pointcut. The code makes a call to the getPasswordAuthentication() method to trigger the logGet pointcut. You can compile and execute the code with this command:

```
java -classpath "C:\aspectj1.0\lib\aspectjrt.jar;.\classes;
  .\lib\log4j-1.1.3.jar" weblech.test.TestDumbAuthenticator
```

The following output appears on the screen and in a log file called weblech.log:

```
Log4j configured to use weblech.log -- view full logging here
2002-08-01 00:06:00,710 [main] INFO
   LoggerAspectDumbAuthenticator.java;weblech/
spider/LoggerAspect.java[1k]:14 - DumbAuthenticator(Gradecki,
***)
2002-08-01 00:06:00,730 [main] INFO
LoggerAspectDumbAuthenticator.java;weblech/
spider/LoggerAspect.java[1k]:19 - PasswordAuthentication
weblech.spider.DumbAuth
enticator.getPasswordAuthentication()
```

With the addition of the aspect, the original DumbAuthenicator class code becomes dramatically smaller, as shown in Listing 14.8.

```
package weblech.spider;
import java.net.Authenticator;
import java.net.PasswordAuthentication;

public class DumbAuthenticator extends Authenticator {
  private final String user;
  private final String password;

  public DumbAuthenticator(String user, String password)
  {
    this.user = user;
    this.password = password;
  }

  public PasswordAuthentication getPasswordAuthentication()
  {
    return new PasswordAuthentication(user,
password.toCharArray());
  }
}
```

**Listing 14.8**  The final DumbAuthenticator class.

### Refactoring URLGetter.java

URLGetter.java is the next class to be refactored away from using the logging classes directly. The class takes a URL to a Web site, creates a connection object, connects to the site, downloads the provided HTML, and returns a URLObject with the site HTML enclosed. The majority of the information logged is for basic tracing of the connection process, with a few logs when an exception occurs. Because of the length of the source file, we won't reproduce it here; you can find it in the download file mentioned earlier in the chapter. The aspect is as shown in Listing 14.9.

```
package weblech.spider;
import java.net.URL;
import java.io.*;

public aspect LoggerAspectURLGetter extends LoggerAspect {
 pointcut logConstructor() :
  initialization(public URLGetter.new(..));

 pointcut logGetURL(URLToDownload url) :
  execution(URLObject getURL(URLToDownload)) &&
  args(url);

 pointcut logGetURLNoArgs() :
  execution(URLObject getURL(..));

 pointcut catchSleep() :
  call(* Thread.sleep(..));

 pointcut logFailureRate(URLGetter ug) :
  this(ug) &&
  cflow(catchSleep());

 pointcut logOpenConnection(URLToDownload url) :
  call (public java.net.URLConnection java.net.URL.openConnection()) &&
  cflow(logGetURL(url));

 pointcut logConnect() :
  call (public void java.net.HttpURLConnection.connect()) &&
  cflow(logGetURLNoArgs());

 pointcut logResponse() :
  call (public String java.net.HttpURLConnection.getResponseMessage()) &&
  cflow(logGetURLNoArgs());

 pointcut logHeaderField(String key) :
  call (public String java.net.HttpURLConnection.getHeaderField(String)) &&
  cflow(logGetURLNoArgs()) &&
  args(key);

 pointcut logStream() :
  call(java.io.BufferedInputStream.new(..));

 pointcut logStats(URLGetter url) :
  call(* java.net.HttpURLConnection.getContentLength()) &&
```

**Listing 14.9** The LoggerAspectURLGetter aspect. (continues)

```
   cflow(logGetURLNoArgs()) &&
   this(url);

 pointcut logFileNotFound(FileNotFoundException e) :
  handler(FileNotFoundException) &&
  args(e);

 pointcut logIOException(IOException e) :
  handler(IOException) &&
  args(e);

/************************/
 before() : logConstructor() {
  _logClass.debug("URLGetter()");
  _logClass.info("URLGetter()");
 }

 before(URLToDownload url) : logGetURL(url) {
  String text = new String(thisJoinPoint.getSignature().toString());

  _logClass.debug(text + url);
  _logClass.info(text + url);
 }

 after(URLGetter ug) : logFailureRate(ug) {
  _logClass.warn("Lots of failures recently, waiting 5 seconds
before attempting download");
 }

 before(URLToDownload url) : logOpenConnection(url) {
  URL requestedURL = url.getURL();
  _logClass.debug("Creating HTTP connection to " +
requestedURL);
 }

 after(URLToDownload url) : logOpenConnection(url) {
  URL referer = url.getReferer();
  if (referer != null)
   _logClass.debug("Setting Referer header to " + referer);
 }

 before() : logConnect() {
  _logClass.debug("Opening URL");
 }

 after() returning (String resp) : logResponse() {
  _logClass.debug("Remote server response: " + resp);
```

**Listing 14.9** The LoggerAspectURLGetter aspect. (continues)

```
}

after(String key) returning (String value) : logHeaderField(key) {
  _logClass.debug("Received header " + key + ": " + value);
}

before() : logStream() {
  _logClass.debug("Getting buffered input stream from
    remote connection");
}

after(URLGetter url) returning (int length): logStats(url) {
 _logClass.info("Downloaded " + url.content.length + " bytes,
" + url.bytesPerSec + " bytes/sec");
 if (url.content.length < length)
 _logClass.warn("Didn't download full content for URL: " +
url);
 }

before(FileNotFoundException e) : logFileNotFound(e) {
 _logClass.warn("File not found: " + e.getMessage());
}

before(IOException e) : logFileNotFound(e) {
 _logClass.warn("File not found: " + e.getMessage());
 }
}
```

**Listing 14.9**  The LoggerAspectURLGetter aspect. (continued)

We'll discuss each of the pointcuts and related advice. Some of the pointcuts
are built creatively to handle the original logging commands. At one point, a
variable local to a method had to move to the class level in order for the logging
command to provide necessary information. This change will be noted in the
particular pointcut.

This pointcut produces a log entry when the constructor for the URLGetter
class is used:

```
pointcut logConstructor() :
  initialization(public URLGetter.new(..));
```

This pointcut produces a log entry when the getURL() method begins to execute. The advice for this pointcut needs to output the URL passed to the
method; thus the args designator is used to access the parameter:

```
pointcut logGetURL(URLToDownload url) :
  execution(URLObject getURL(URLToDownload)) &&
  args(url);
```

Some of the pointcuts described later are scoped directly to the getURL()
method. The cflow designator must be used to be sure the join points are only
matched within the specific method:

```
pointcut logGetURLNoArgs() :
  execution(URLObject getURL(..));
```

The first part of the getURL() method contains code that logs a message when
more than 10 attempts are made to download a specific URL. The code appears
as follows:

```
pointcut logFailureRate(URLGetter ug) :
  this(ug) &&
  call(* Thread.sleep(..));
```

As you can see, there isn't anything in the conditional to use as a join point,
because AspectJ doesn't yet support join points on conditional statements. Fortunately, the sleep() method only occurs within the conditional, and you can
use it as a join point to indicate that more than 10 failures have occurred:

```
  if(failureCount > 10) {
    _logClass.warn("Lots of failures recently, waiting 5
seconds before attempting download");
    try { Thread.sleep(5 * 1000); } catch(InterruptedException e) { };
    failureCount = 0;
  }
```

The next join point is based on the opening of a connection to a specific URL.
The point is defined based on the openConnection() method call and its location in the getURL() method. The URL object passed to the getURL() method is
obtained so the log can indicate which URL is being opened:

```
pointcut logOpenConnection(URLToDownload url) :
  call (public java.net.URLConnection java.net.URL.openConnection()) &&
  cflow(logGetURL(url));
```

When the code tries to connect to the Web site based on the URL specified to the
getURL() method, a call is made to the connect() method. The logConnect()
pointcut is triggered when a call is made to the connect() method; the call is
made within the getURL() method:

```
pointcut logConnect() :
  call (public void java.net.HttpURLConnection.connect()) &&
  cflow(logGetURLNoArgs());
```

After a connection to a Web server is attempted, the response from the server
is captured through the getResponseMessage() method and output to the log.
Because you only want to match on the join point when it occurs within
getURL(), you use the cflow designator:

```
pointcut logResponse() :
  call (public String java.net.HttpURLConnection.getResponseMessage())
```

```
&&
  cflow(logGetURLNoArgs());
```

Before the text of the HTML page associated with the URL is downloaded, you obtain and log HTTP headers. The getHeaderField() method is called a number of times with a specific parameter. The logHeaderField pointcut includes the args designator to pull the value passed with the method:

```
pointcut logHeaderField(String key) :
  call (public String java.net.HttpURLConnection.getHeaderField(String))
&&
  cflow(logGetURLNoArgs()) &&
  args(key);
```

However, it's also important to show the value returned by the getHeader-Field() method. You can obtain the return value in the advice used with this pointcut:

```
after(String key) returning (String value) : logHeaderField(key) {
  _logClass.debug("Received header " + key + ": " + value);
}
```

Notice the use of the *returning* keyword so you get access to the value from the method after it executes.

The headers are followed by the code needing a stream to keep track of the text from the URL:

```
pointcut logStream() :
  call(java.io.BufferedInputStream.new(..));
```

Because the stream is created as an object using new(), you can use the same initialization as a join point to indicate the stream object has been created:

```
pointcut logStats(URLGetter url) :
  call(* java.net.HttpURLConnection.getContentLength()) &&
  cflow(logGetURLNoArgs()) &&
  this(url);
```

The logStats pointcut is a problem, because the code must be able to output values from two local variables. These local variables aren't accessible using AspectJ. For this reason, their definition appears in the attribute section of the class. To access the variables, you pass to the advice code the URL object where the getContentLength() method is called.

The last pointcuts in the aspect are associated with exceptions that can occur in the code. In both pointcuts, information about the exception is put in the log as well:

```
pointcut logFileNotFound(FileNotFoundException e) :
  handler(FileNotFoundException) &&
  args(e);
```

```
pointcut logIOException(IOException e) :
 handler(IOException) &&
 args(e);
```

### Refactoring HTMLParser.java

The last refactored class we will look at in detail is HTMLParser. This class parses the HTML text returned from the Web site, with the goal of determining whether there are additional links to follow or files to download. The resulting aspect from this class is shown in Listing 14.10.

```
package weblech.spider;
import java.io.IOException;
import java.net.URL;
import java.util.List;

public aspect LoggerAspectHTMLParser extends LoggerAspect {
 pointcut logParse(URL sourceURL, String textContent) :
  execution(* HTMLParser.parseAsHTML(URL, String)) &&
  args(sourceURL, textContent);

 pointcut logSize(URL sourceURL, String textContent) :
  call(int java.util.ArrayList.size()) &&
  cflow(logParse(sourceURL, textContent));

 pointcut logExtract(String tag, String attr) :
  call(private void HTMLParser.extractAttributesFromTags(
    String, String, ..)) &&
  args(tag, attr, ..);

 pointcut logMail() :
  execution(private void logMailURL(String));

 pointcut logMailException(IOException e) :
  handler(IOException) &&
  cflow(logMail()) &&
  args(e);

//****************************************************
 before(URL sourceURL, String textContent) : logParse(sourceURL,
textContent) {
  _logClass.info("parseAsHTML()");
 }

 after(URL sourceURL, String textContent) returning (int size) :
logSize(sourceURL, textContent) {
```

**Listing 14.10**  The LoggerAspectHTMLParser aspect. (continues)

```
   if(size == 0) {
     _logClass.debug("Got 0 new URLs from HTML parse, check
HTML\n" + textContent);
   }
   _logClass.info("Returning " + size + " urls extracted from
page");
   }

  before(String tag, String attr) : logExtract(tag, attr) {
   _logClass.info("extractAttributesFromTags(" + tag + ", " +
attr + ", ...)");
   }

  before() : logMail() {
   _logClass.info("logMailURL()");
   }

  before(IOException e) : logMailException(e) {
   _logClass.warn("Caught IO exception writing mailto URL:" +
e.getMessage());
   }
 }
```

**Listing 14.10**  The LoggerAspectHTMLParser aspect. (continued)

This aspect includes three pointcuts of particular importance. The first, log-
Parse(), is defined as follows:

```
pointcut logParse(URL sourceURL, String textContent) :
   execution(* HTMLParser.parseAsHTML(URL, String)) &&
   args(sourceURL, textContent);
```

The primary method in the HTMLParser class is parseAsHTML(), which
accepts both a URL and the text obtained from the URL. The logParse pointcut
is triggered on the parseAsHTML() method and provides access to the two
parameters for logging purposes:

Once the logParse() method has done its work, the number of URLs obtained
from the HTML text is checked to see if any additional ones were found. You
want to log the situation when no additional links are found. The logParse
pointcut is used within a cflow designator. The pointcut is pulled out for
examination here because of the binding of the parameters to the logParse
pointcut. Because you want to have access to the parameters in the new pointcut, you must provide the types and names in the pointcut definition as well:

```
pointcut logSize(URL sourceURL, String textContent) :
   call(int java.util.ArrayList.size()) &&
   cflow(logParse(sourceURL, textContent));
```

The final pointcut of note is logExtract, which matches on a join point based on the extractAttributesFromTags() method:

```
pointcut logExtract(String tag, String attr) :
  call(private void HTMLParser.extractAttributesFromTags(
    String, String, ..)) &&
  args(tag, attr, ..);
```

This method accepts six parameters, but four of them are not important to logging activity—you are only interested in the first two. As you can see in the pointcut definition, the first two parameters are defined, and the remaining ones are defined using the .. parameter. Using .. in the definition matches any calls to extactAttributesFromTags() where the first two parameters are Strings and the last four parameters are anything else. When you want to access these parameters, they must be defined in the args designator as well. This isn't enough, though, because in order to accurately bind the first two parameters, you must use the .. parameter in the args designator as well.

### Refactoring Spider.java

For completeness, Listing 14.11 shows the aspect used for the Spider class.

```
package weblech.spider;
import java.io.IOException;
import weblech.spider.URLToDownload;

public aspect LoggerAspectSpider extends LoggerAspect {
 boolean html, xml, image;

 pointcut logStart() :
  execution(public void Spider.start());

 pointcut logThread() :
  initialization(Thread.new(..)) &&
  cflow(logStart());

 pointcut logWriteCheckPoint() :
  execution(private void writeCheckpoint());

 pointcut logReadCheckPoint() :
  execution(public void readCheckpoint());

 pointcut logWriteCheckPointException(IOException e) :
  handler(IOException) &&
  cflow(logWriteCheckPoint()) &&
```

**Listing 14.11** The LoggerAspectSpider aspect. (continues)

```
  args(e);

  pointcut logReadCheckPointException(IOException e) :
    handler(IOException) &&
    cflow(logReadCheckPoint()) &&
    args(e);

  pointcut logThreadStop() :
    execution(public void Spider.run());

  pointcut logDownloadURL(URLToDownload url) :
    execution(private List downloadURL(URLToDownload, ..)) &&
    args(url, ..);

  pointcut logDownloadURLNoArgs() :
    execution(private List downloadURL(..));

  pointcut logQueue(URLToDownload url) :
    cflow(logDownloadURL(url)) &&
    execution(* *.existsOnDisk());

  pointcut logIsHTML() :
    cflow(logDownloadURLNoArgs()) &&
    call(* URLObject.isHTML());

  pointcut logIsXML() :
    cflow(logDownloadURLNoArgs()) &&
    call(* URLObject.isXML());

  pointcut logIsImage(URLToDownload url) :
    cflow(logDownloadURL(url)) &&
    call(* URLObject.isImage());

//****************************************************

  before() : logThread() {
    _logClass.info("Starting Spider thread");
  }

  before() : logWriteCheckPoint() {
    _logClass.debug("writeCheckpoint()");
  }

  before(IOException e) : logWriteCheckPointException(e) {
    _logClass.warn("IO Exception attempting checkpoint: " +
e.getMessage(), e);
  }
```

**Listing 14.11**   The LoggerAspectSpider aspect. (continues)

```
before(IOException e) : logReadCheckPointException(e) {
  _logClass.warn("IO Exception attempting checkpoint: " +
e.getMessage(), e);
}

after() : logThreadStop() {
 _logClass.info("Spider thread stopping");
}

before(URLToDownload url) : logDownloadURL(url) {
 _logClass.debug("downloadURL(" + url + ")");
}

after(URLToDownload url) : logQueue(url) {
 _logClass.info("Q: " + url);
}

after() returning (boolean value) : logIsHTML() {
 html = value;
}

after() returning (boolean value) : logIsXML() {
 html = value;
}

after(URLToDownload url) returning (boolean value) :
logIsImage(url) {
  if (!value && !html && !xml)
   _logClass.warn("Unsupported content type received: ");
   _logClass.info("URL was " + url);
}
}
```

**Listing 14.11**   The LoggerAspectSpider aspect. (continued)

### *Refactoring URLObject.java*

The URLObject aspect is shown in Listing 14.12.

```
package weblech.spider;
import java.io.*;
import weblech.spider.SpiderConfig;
import java.net.URL;
```

**Listing 14.12**   The LoggerAspectURLObject aspect. (continues)

```
public aspect LoggerAspectURLObject extends LoggerAspect {
 pointcut LogURLObject(URL sourceURL) :
  initialization(public URLObject.new(URL, SpiderConfig)) &&
  args(sourceURL, ..);

 pointcut LogIOExceptionInConstructor(IOException e, URL
sourceURL) :
  handler(IOException) &&
  args(e) &&
  cflow(LogURLObject(sourceURL));

 pointcut LogWrite(String filename) :
  execution(public void writeToFile(String)) &&
  args(filename);

 pointcut LogIOExceptionInWrite(IOException e, String filename)
:
  handler(IOException) &&
  args(e) &&
  cflow(LogWrite(filename));


//*****************************************************

 before(IOException e, URL sourceURL) :
   LogIOExceptionInConstructor(e, sourceURL) {
 _logClass.warn("IO Exception reading disk version of URL " +
sourceURL);
 }

 before(String filename) : LogWrite(filename) {
 _logClass.debug("writeToFile(" + filename + ")");
 }

 before(IOException e, String filename) :
  LogIOExceptionInWrite(e, filename) {
 _logClass.warn("IO Exception writing to " + filename);
 }

}
```

**Listing 14.12**   The LoggerAspectURLObject aspect. (continued)

## Timings

The URLGetter class includes code for timing how long it takes to pull HTML
text from a provided URL. The time is used in a calculation to show the system's

file-download speed in bytes per second. You could make the case that this timing and byte calculation should be part of the URLGetter object; but if you look at the code, you will see that the calculation isn't a major component of the class. By pulling the timing code into an aspect, it can be potentially utilized in other parts of the code.

Within the getURL() method, the timing of the URL download begins when the connect() method is called. At this point, a call is made to the System.current-TimeMillis() method to obtain the start time. Once the HTML text has been pulled, another call is made to currentTimeMillis(), and the difference is calculated. The resulting aspect is shown in Listing 14.13.

```
package weblech.spider;
public aspect TimingAspectURLGetter extends LoggerAspect{
 long startTime;

 pointcut logGetURLNoArgs() :
  execution(URLObject getURL(..));

 pointcut logStartTime() :
  call (public void java.net.HttpURLConnection.connect()) &&
  cflow(logGetURLNoArgs());

 pointcut logEndTime(URLGetter url) :
  call(* java.net.HttpURLConnection.getContentLength()) &&
  cflow(logGetURLNoArgs()) &&
  this(url);

 before() : logStartTime() {
  startTime = System.currentTimeMillis();
 }

 before(URLGetter url): logEndTime(url) {
  long timeTaken = System.currentTimeMillis() - startTime;
  if(timeTaken < 100) timeTaken = 500;

  int bytesPerSec = (int) ((double) url.content.length /
((double)timeTaken / 1000.0));
  _logClass.info("Downloaded " + url.content.length + " bytes,
 " + bytesPerSec + " bytes/sec");
 }
}
```

**Listing 14.13**  The TimingAspectURLGetter aspect.

Because the timing aspect is really just a specialization of a logging aspect, it inherits the LoggerAspect; thus it has the ability to log the timing information. The aspect includes only three pointcuts:

- **logGetURLNoArgs** allows the getURL() method to be matched, but you ignore all the arguments to the method because they aren't needed.

- **logStartTime** uses a join point based on the method call to connect(), but only in the execution of getURL(). When the pointcut triggers, the advice records the current system time in milliseconds to an attribute of the aspect for later use.

- **logEndTime** uses a join point based on the method call to getContentLength(). Before this method call, the advice calculates the ending system time, determines the total time of the download, and displays the results in the log.

# Checkpointing

The Web spider can checkpoint the URLs in its download queue as well as read from the checkpoint into the current queue. The code for checkpointing is found in the Spider class. The aspect created to handle checkpointing is shown in Listing 14.14.

```
package weblech.spider;
import weblech.spider.Spider;
import java.io.FileOutputStream;
import java.io.ObjectOutputStream;
import java.io.IOException;

public aspect CheckpointAspect {
 private void checkpointIfNeeded(Spider spider) {

  SpiderConfig config = spider.getConfig();
  long checkpointInterval = config.getCheckpointInterval();

  if(checkpointInterval == 0) {
   return;
  }

  if(System.currentTimeMillis() - spider.getLastCheckpoint() >
checkpointInterval) {
   synchronized(spider.getQueue()) {
    if(System.currentTimeMillis() - spider.getLastCheckpoint() >
     checkpointInterval) {
     writeCheckpoint(spider);
spider.setLastCheckpoint(System.currentTimeMillis());
   }
  }
 }
```

**Listing 14.14** The CheckpointAspect aspect. (continues)

```
  }

private void writeCheckpoint(Spider spider) {
  try {
    FileOutputStream fos =
      new FileOutputStream("spider.checkpoint", false);
    ObjectOutputStream oos = new ObjectOutputStream(fos);
    oos.writeObject(spider.getQueue());
    oos.writeObject(spider.getURLsDownloading());
    oos.close();
  } catch(IOException ioe) {}
}

pointcut spiderRun() :
 execution(public void Spider.run());

pointcut checkPoint(Spider spider) :
 call(* *.queueSize()) &&
 cflow(spiderRun()) &&
 this(spider);

after(Spider spider) : checkPoint(spider) {
 checkpointIfNeeded(spider);
 }
}
```

**Listing 14.14** The CheckpointAspect aspect. (continued)

The original spider code included two methods called checkpointIfNeeded()
and writeCheckpoint(). The checkpointIfNeeded() method was called within a
while loop during each iteration. Unfortunately, no method call surrounded
the call to checkpointIfNeeded(). Upon analysis of the code, we found that
three calls were made to the downloadQueue's queueSize() method. By changing the code a little, you can create a temporary variable to capture the size:

```
size = queue.queueSize();
```

Using this small code change, you can create a join point for the checkpointing.
When the call is made to queueSize(), the checkPoint join point is triggered.
The join point advice calls the checkpointIfNeeded() method, and subsequently
calls writeCheckpoint() if necessary.

This process seems simple, but you will probably encounter problems when
refactoring your own code. First, the checkpoint routines need access to attributes of the main Spider object. No accessor methods were originally written for
the attribute, so they were added. You will know private attributes are a problem if the AspectJ compiler indicates it cannot bind a variable you are using
within an advice or a method within an aspect. If you are comfortable with the

notion, you can set up your aspects to have privilege access and thus allow them direct access to the private attributes. After you get beyond the private attributes, you'll have created a complete encapsulated and modular checkpoint aspect.

## What's Next

That's it! We have spent the past 397 pages introducing you to a new coding paradigm. We hope you will take your new knowledge and begin writing cleaner, much less tangled code. The team at AspectJ.org is dedicated to bringing the community the best in aspect programming and constantly works to expand the tools usable with aspects.

# AspectJ API

This appendix provides an overview of the major classes and interfaces used in the development of AspectJ. Because AspectJ is a new language, this information is more volatile and likely to change as the language matures.

## Interface Hierarchy

```
interface org.aspectj.lang.JoinPoint
interface org.aspectj.lang.JoinPoint.StaticPart
interface org.aspectj.lang.Signature
interface org.aspectj.lang.reflect.CatchClauseSignature
interface org.aspectj.lang.reflect.MemberSignature
        interface org.aspectj.lang.reflect.CodeSignature
        interface org.aspectj.lang.reflect.AdviceSignature
        interface org.aspectj.lang.reflect.ConstructorSignature
        interface org.aspectj.lang.reflect.InitializerSignature
        interface org.aspectj.lang.reflect.MethodSignature
interface org.aspectj.lang.reflect.FieldSignature
interface org.aspectj.lang.reflect.SourceLocation
```

## Class Hierarchy

```
class java.lang.Object
class java.lang.Throwable (implements java.io.Serializable)
        class java.lang.Exception
```

```
class java.lang.RuntimeException
class org.aspectj.lang.NoAspectBoundException
class org.aspectj.lang.SoftException
```

# AspectJ API Descriptions

The following descriptions apply to AspectJ 1.06 through 1.x. We've created appropriate examples where needed to help you better understand the code.

## Interface: JoinPoint

**Definition:** org.aspectj.lang.JoinPoint

**Description:** The JoinPoint interface provides reflective access and static information to a matched join point.

**Attributes:** None

### Methods

**Method Signature:** java.lang.Object[] getArgs()

**Description:** This method returns an array of Objects representing the arguments of the matched join point.

**Example:**

```
pointcut test() :
  execution(public int test(int, String));

before() : test() {
  Object[] args = thisJoinPoint.getArgs();

  for (int i = 0;i<args.length;++i)
    System.out.println(args[i].toString());
}
```

**Output:**

```
4
test
```

**Method Signature:** java.lang.String getKind()

**Description:** This method returns a String representing the kind of join point matched.

**Example:**

```
pointcut test() :
  execution(public int test(int, String));

before() : test() {
  System.out.println(thisJoinPoint.getKind());
}
```

**Output:**

```
method-execution
```

**Method Signature:**   Signature getSignature()

**Description:**   This method returns a Signature object representing the signature where a join point has matched.

**Example:**

```
pointcut test() :
  execution(public int test(int, String));

before() : test() {
  Signature sig = thisJoinPoint.getSignature();
  System.out.println(sig.getName());
}
```

**Output:**

```
test
```

**Method Signature:**   SourceLocation getSourceLocation()

**Description:**   This method returns a SourceLocation object of the matched join point.

**Example:**

```
pointcut test() :
  execution(public int test(int, String));

before() : test() {
  SourceLocation src = thisJoinPoint.getSourceLocation();
  System.out.println(src.getColumn());
}
```

**Method Signature:**   org.aspectj.lang.JoinPoint.StaticPart getStaticPart()

**Description:**   This method returns a StaticPart object representing the static parts of the matched join point.

**Example:**

```
pointcut test() :
  execution(public int test(int, String));

before() : test() {
  StaticPart src = thisJoinPoint.getStaticPart();
}
```

**Method Signature:** java.lang.Object getTarget()

**Description:** This method returns the Target object of the matched join point. This method is typically associated with the call designator.

**Example:**

```
pointcut test() :
  execution(public int test(int, String));

before() : test() {
  Object this = thisJoinPoint.getTarget();
}
```

**Method Signature:** java.lang.Object getThis()

**Description:** This method returns the object where the currently matched join point is executing.

**Example:**

```
pointcut test() :
  execution(public int test(int, String));

before() : test() {
  Object this = thisJoinPoint.getThis();
}
```

**Method Signature:** java.lang.Object toLongString()

**Description:** This method returns a String representation of the matched join point in a long format with extended information.

**Example:**

```
pointcut test() :
  execution(public int test(int, String));

before() : test() {
  System.out.println(thisJoinPoint.toLongString());
}
```

**Output:**

```
execution(public int example.test(int, java.lang.String))
```

**Method Signature:** java.lang.String toShortString()

**Description:** This method returns a String representation of the matched join point in a short format.

**Example:**

```
pointcut test() :
  execution(public int test(int, String));

before() : test() {
  System.out.println(thisJoinPoint.toShortString());
}
```

**Output:**

```
execution(example.test(..)
```

**Method Signature:** java.lang.String toString()

**Description:** This method returns a String representation of the matched join point.

**Example:**

```
pointcut test() :
  execution(public int test(int, String));

before() : test() {
  System.out.println(thisJoinPoint.toString());
}
```

**Output:**

```
execution(int example.test(int, String))
```

# Interface:   JoinPoint.StaticPart

**Definition:**   org.aspectj.lang.JoinPoint.StaticPart

**Description:**   The JoinPoint.StaticPart interface contains methods that return information about the static part of the matched join point. Using this interface through the JoinPoint.getStaticPart() method is a performance-enhanced operation as opposed to using the full JoinPoint interface.

**Attributes:**   None

### Methods

The methods available in the JoinPoint.StaticPart interface have the same signature and functionality as in the JoinPoint interface.

## Interface:   Signature

**Definition:**   org.aspectj.lang.Signature

**Description:**   The Signature interface is used to obtain signature information about a matched join point. A Signature object is obtained using the getSignature() method found in both the JoinPoint and JoinPoint.StaticPart interfaces.

**Attributes:**   None

### Methods

**Method Signature:**   java.lang.Class getDeclaringType()

**Description:**   This method returns a Class object based on the class, interface, or aspect that originally declared the member.

**Example:**

```
pointcut test() :
  execution(public int test(int, String));

before() : test() {
  Signature sig = thisJoinPoint.getSignature();
  System.out.println(sig.getDeclaringType());
}
```

**Output:**

```
class example
```

**Method Signature:**   int getModifiers()

**Description:**   This method returns all of the modifiers associated with this signature as an integer.

**Example:**

```
pointcut test() :
  execution(public int test(int, String));

before() : test() {
  Signature sig = thisJoinPoint.getSignature();
  System.out.println(sig.getModifiers());
}
```

**Method Signature:**   java.lang.String getName()

**Description:**   This method returns the identifiers part of the signature.

**Example:**

```
pointcut test() :
  execution(public int test(int, String));

before() : test() {
  Signature sig = thisJoinPoint.getSignature();
  System.out.println(sig.getName());
}
```

**Output:**

```
test
```

**Method Signature:**   java.lang.String toLongString()

**Description:**   This method returns a string representation of the signature in a long format.

**Example:**

```
pointcut test() :
  execution(public int test(int, String));

before() : test() {
  Signature sig = thisJoinPoint.getSignature();
  System.out.println(sig.toLongString());
}
```

**Output:**

```
public int example.test(int, java.lang.String)
```

**Method Signature:**   java.lang.String toShortString()

**Description:**   This method returns a string representation of the signature in a short format.

**Example:**

```
pointcut test() :
  execution(public int test(int, String));

before() : test() {
  Signature sig = thisJoinPoint.getSignature();
  System.out.println(sig.toShortString());
}
```

**Output:**

```
example.test(..)
```

**Method Signature:** java.lang.String toString()

**Description:** This method returns a string representation of the signature.

**Example:**

```
pointcut test() :
  execution(public int test(int, String));

before() : test() {
  Signature sig = thisJoinPoint.getSignature();
  System.out.println(sig.toString());
}
```

**Output:**

```
int example.test(int, String)
```

# Interface: CatchClauseSignature

**Definition:** org.aspectj.lang.reflect.CatchClauseSignature, derived from org.aspectj.lang.Signature

**Description:** This interface is derived from Signature and is used when the signature of a matched join point is a catch statement.

**Attributes:** None

### Methods

**Method Signature:** java.lang.String getParameterName()

**Description:** This method returns the name of the parameter associated with the matched catch join point.

**Method Signature:** java.lang.String getParameterType()

**Description:** This method returns the type of the parameter associated with the matched catch join point.

# Interface: MemberSignature

**Definition:** org.aspectj.lang.reflect.MemberSignature, derived from org.aspectj.lang.Signature

**Description:** This interface is derived from Signature and is used when the signature of a matched join point is a member method of a class or interface.

**Attributes:** None

### Methods

None

# Interface: CodeSignature

**Definition:** org.aspectj.lang.reflect.CodeSignature, derived from org.aspectj.lang.reflect.MemberSignature

**Description:** This interface is used when a join point is code-based.

**Attributes:** None

### Methods

**Method Signature:** java.lang.Class[] getExceptionTypes()

**Description:** This method returns an array of the exception types found in the code associated with the matched join point.

**Method Signature:** java.lang.String[] getParameterNames()

**Description:** This method returns an array of the parameter names found in the code associated with the matched join point.

**Method Signature:** java.lang.String[] getParameterTypes()

**Description:** This method returns an array of the parameter types found in the code associated with the matched join point.

# Interface: AdviceSignature

**Definition:** org.aspectj.lang.reflect.AdviceSignature, derived from org.aspectj.lang.reflect.CodeSignature

**Description:** This interface is used to return information associated with advice code.

**Attributes:** None

### Method

**Method Signature:** java.lang.Class getReturnType();

**Description:** This method returns the class associated with the advice code.

# Interface:   ConstructorSignature

**Definition:**   org.aspectj.lang.reflect.ConstructorSignature, derived from org.aspectj.lang.reflect.CodeSignature

**Description:**   This interface is used when a matched join point is associated with a Constructor.

**Attributes:**   None

### *Methods*

None

# Interface:   InitializerSignature

**Definition:**   org.aspectj.lang.reflect.InitializerSignature, derived from org.aspectj.lang.reflect.CodeSignature

**Description:**   This interface is used when a matched join point is associated with an Initializer.

**Attributes:**   None

### *Methods*

None

# Interface:   MethodSignature

**Definition:**   org.aspectj.lang.reflect.MethodSignature, derived from org.aspectj.lang.reflect.CodeSignature

**Description:**   This interface is used when a matched join point is associated with a method.

**Attributes:**   None

### *Method*

**Method Signature:**   java.lang.Class getReturnType();

**Description:**   This method returns the class associated with the method code.

# Interface: FieldSignature

**Definition:** org.aspectj.lang.reflect.FieldSignature, derived from org.aspectj.lang.reflect.MemberSignature

**Description:** This interface is used when a matched join point is associated with an attribute of a class or interface.

**Attributes:** None

## *Method*

**Method Signature:** java.lang.Class getFieldType()

**Description:** This method returns the class associated with a field.

# Interface: SourceLocation

**Definition:** org.aspectj.lang.reflect.SourceLocation

**Description:** This interface provides information about the class and location within the source file of the matched join point.

**Attributes:** None

## *Methods*

**Method Signature:** int getColumn()

**Description:** This method returns the column where the join point is matched.

**Example:**

```
pointcut test() :
   execution(public int test(int, String));

before() : test() {
  SourceLocation src = thisJoinPoint.getSourceLocation();
  System.out.println(src.getColumn());
}
```

**Output:**

```
3
```

**Method Signature:** java.lang.String getFileName()

**Description:** This method returns the filename where the join point is matched.

**Example:**

```
pointcut test() :
  execution(public int test(int, String));

before() : test() {
  SourceLocation src = thisJoinPoint.getSourceLocation();
  System.out.println(src.getFileName());
}
```

**Output:**

```
example.java
```

**Method Signature:** int getLine()

**Description:** This method returns the line number where the join point is matched.

**Example:**

```
pointcut test() :
  execution(public int test(int, String));

before() : test() {
  SourceLocation src = thisJoinPoint.getSourceLocation();
  System.out.println(src.getLine());
}
```

**Output:**

```
3
```

**Method Signature:** java.lang.Class getWithinType()

**Description:** This method returns the class or interface where the join point is matched within.

**Example:**

```
pointcut test() :
  execution(public int test(int, String));

before() : test() {
  SourceLocation src = thisJoinPoint.getSourceLocation();
  System.out.println(src.getWithinType().toString());
}
```

**Output:**

```
class example
```

# Class:   SoftException

**Definition:**   org.aspectj.lang.SoftException

**Description:**   This class is used to wrap Java exceptions declared as soft in AspectJ.

**Attributes:**   None

## Methods

**Method Signature:**   SoftException(java.lang.Throwable)

**Description:**   This method is a Constructor for a SoftException object.

**Method Signature:**   java.lang.Throwable getWrappedThrowable()

**Description:**   This method returns the Throwable object associated with the SoftException.

# Class:   NoAspectBoundException

**Definition:**   org.aspectj.lang.NoAspectBoundException

**Description:**   This exception can be thrown when a call is made to the aspectOf() method and no aspect is currently bound.

**Attributes:**   None

## Method

**Method Signature:**   NoAspectBoundException()

**Description:**   This method is a Constructor for the class.

# Useful Web Sites

In this appendix, we've listed some of the major Web sites covering AspectJ and Aspect-Oriented Programming.

## Overview Sites

**AspectJ Project home site** (www.eclipse.org/aspectj)

***Mastering AspectJ: Aspect-Oriented Programming in Java* book Web site** (www.wiley.com/compbooks/gradecki)

**Aspect-Oriented Software Development** (www.aosd.net)

**Research on Aspect-Oriented Programming** (www.emn.fr/sudholt/research/aop.html)

**University of Washington—Gregor Kiczales Presentation** (http://murl.microsoft.com/LectureDetails.asp?185)

## People

**Gregor Kiczales, ApectJ team lead** (www2.parc.com/csl/members/gregor/)

**Concurrent Programming Research Group** (www.iit.edu/~concur/)

# Tutorial in Nature

**Improve Modularity with Aspect-Oriented Programming** (www-106.ibm.com/developerworks/java/library/j-aspectj/)

**I Want My AOP! Part 1** (www.javaworld.com/javaworld/jw-01-2002/jw-0118-aspect.html)

**I Want My AOP! Part 2** (www.javaworld.com/javaworld/jw-03-2002/jw-0301-aspect2.html)

**I Want My AOP! Part 3** (www.javaworld.com/javaworld/jw-04-2002/jw-0412-aspect3.html)

**PowerPoint Presentation on Aspect-Oriented and Adaptive Programming** (www.ccs.neu.edu/research/demeter/talks/erfurt-keynote/erfurt-talk.ppt)

**Aspect-Oriented Programming in Java** (www.voelter.de/data/articles/aop/aop.html)

**Aspect-Oriented Decomposition and Composition** (www.prakinf.tu-ilmenau.de/~czarn/aop/)

**Three Examples of Aspect-Oriented Programming** (www.cse.ogi.edu/~black/3AspectExamples/)

**Aspect-Oriented Programming with AspectJ** (www.sauria.com/presentations/Seajug-12-2001.pdf)

**Aspect-Oriented Programming with C# and .NET** (www.dcl.hpi.uni-potsdam.de/folien/Net-Days/AOP-with-NET_files/frame.htm)

**Aspect-Oriented Programming with AspectJ: A Short Introduction** (http://rzserv2.fhnon.de/~lg002556/basics/AspectOrientedProgramming.pdf)

**Untangle Your Code with Aspect-Oriented Programming** (www.trcinc.com/knowledge/presentations/Untangle_Your_Code_with_Aspect-Oriented_Programming_TRCInc.ppt)

**Aspect-Oriented Programming** (www.cs.tut.fi/~bitti/generat-seminaari/aop.pdf)

# Papers

**Aspect-Oriented Programming** (www2.parc.com/csl/groups/sda/publications/papers/Kiczales-ECOOP97/)

**Untangling Code** (www.technologyreview.com/articles/tr10_kiczales0101.asp)

**Emerging Technologies That Will Change the World** (www.technologyreview.com/articles/tr10_toc0101.asp)

**Aspect-Oriented Programming Enables Better Code Encapsulation and Reuse** (http://msdn.microsoft.com/msdnmag/issues/02/03/AOP/AOP.asp)

**Separation of Concerns** (ftp://www.ccs.neu.edu/pub/people/crista/papers/separation.ps)

**Thoughts on Aspect-Oriented Programming** (http://openmap.bbn.com/~kanderso/aop/AOP-thoughts.html)

**Gregor Kiczales' Publications** (www2.parc.com/csl/groups/sda/publications.shtml)

**Semantics of Aspect-Oriented Programming** (www.cwi.nl/~ralf/saop/)

**AOP Publications** (www.emn.fr/sudholt/research/by_name.html)

**An Initial Assessment of Aspect-Oriented Programming** (www.cs.ubc.ca/labs/se/papers/1999/icse99-aop.pdf)

**Applying Aspect-Oriented Programming to Security** (www.viega.org/papers/aop-cutter.pdf)

**The Impact of Aspect-Oriented Programming on Future Design** (www.inf.ethz.ch/vs/edu/WS0001/UI/slides/ui_08AspectOP.pdf)

**Aspect-Oriented Programming with Reflection and Dynamism** (www.ai.mit.edu/~gregs/dyn-aop.html)

**Can Aspect-Oriented Programming Lead to More Reliable Software?** (www.computer.org/software/so2000/s6019abs.htm)

**Aspect-Oriented Programming with Model Checking** (www.graco.c.u-tokyo.ac.jp/~tamai/pub/aosd2002.pdf)

**Treecc: An Aspect-Oriented Approach to Writing Compilers** (www.southern-storm.com.au/treecc_essay.html)

## Other Paradigms

**Multi-Dimensional Separation of Concerns: Software Engineering using Hyperspaces (IBM)** (www.research.ibm.com/hyperspace/)

**IBM's Subject-Oriented Programming** (www.research.ibm.com/sop/)

## Software Development and Systems

**Demeter: Aspect-Oriented Software Development** (www.ccs.neu.edu/research/demeter/)

**Java Aspect Components** (http://jac.aopsys.com/)

**TransWarp and Python** (www.zope.org/Members/pje/Wikis/TransWarp/HomePage)

**Aspect-Oriented Programming and the CLR** (www.iunknown.com/Weblog/fog0000000093.html)

**Aspect-Oriented Modeling with UML** (http://lglwww.epfl.ch/workshops/aosd-uml/papers.html)

## Events

**Tutorial and Workshop on Aspect-Oriented Programming and Separation of Concerns** (www.comp.lancs.ac.uk/computing/users/marash/aopws2001/)

**Third International Conference on Metalevel Architectures and Separation of Crosscutting Concerns (Reflection 2001)** (www.openjit.org/reflection2001/)

**OOPSLA 2001 Workshop on Advanced Separation of Concerns in Object-Oriented Systems** (www.cs.ubc.ca/%7ekdvolder/Workshops/ OOPSLA2001/ASoC.html)

**ETAPS 2002 Software Composition Workshop** (http://www.easycomp.org/sc2002/index.hei?&card=heises.8f16020fdfb773a08 7b31726d96698b0)

**First International Conference on Aspect-Oriented Software Development** (http://trese.cs.utwente.nl/aosd2002.htm)

**Aspect-Oriented Software Development Conference 2003 in Boston**
(http://aosd.net/conference)

**Aspect-Oriented Programming Conference 1997**
(http://trese.cs.utwente.nl/aop-ecoop99/aop97.html)

**Aspect-Oriented Programming Conference 1998**
(http://trese.cs.utwente.nl/aop-ecoop99/aop98.html)

**Aspect-Oriented Programming Conference 1999**
(http://trese.cs.utwente.nl/aop-ecoop99/)

**Foundations of Aspect-Oriented Programming**
(www.cs.wustl.edu/~cytron/FOAL/)

## Universities

**Aspect-Oriented Software Development** (www.comp.lancs.ac.uk/computing/aop/)

**MIT Technology Review and Aspect-Oriented and Adaptive Programming** (www.ccs.neu.edu/research/demeter/aop/publicity/mit-tech-review.html)

**AOP at Northeastern University**
(www.ccs.neu.edu/home/lorenz/center/aop.html)

# Other AOP Language Bindings

A lthough this book specifically references the AspectJ language and its implementation of aspect-oriented programming (AOP) principles, bindings are available that allow you to directly use AOP in other programming languages. This appendix provides a short introduction to the current bindings. You can find a comprehensive collection for AOP bindings at www.aosd.net. Consult this Web site from time to time if your favorite language isn't listed in this appendix.

## AspectR

AspectR is a binding for AOP against the Ruby language. The primary location for AspectR information is http://aspectr.sourceforge.net.

### Description

AspectR handles the addition of advice code to the primary Ruby source by wrapping the advice around specific methods. The wrap code is passed a number of arguments, including the arguments to the wrapped method, the name of the wrapped method, the object receiving the method call, and the return value. A subset of the functionality found in AspectJ is available in AspectR, but the features continue to grow with each new release.

## Requirements

AspectR requires version 2.0 of Ruby and can execute on any platform where Ruby is available.

## Example Code

```
require 'aspectr'
include AspectR

class Verify < Aspect
  def log_enter(method, object, exitstatus, *args)
    $stderr.puts "#{self.class}##{method}: args = #{args.inspect}"
  end

  def log_exit(method, object, exitstatus, *args)
    $stderr.print "#{self.class}##{method}: exited "
  end
end

class HelloWorldClass
  def sayHelloWorld
    puts "Hello World"
  end
end

Verify.new.wrap(HelloWorldClass, :verify_enter, :verify_exit,
/say/)
HelloWorldClass.new.sayHelloWorld
end
```

# AspectS

AspectS is a binding for AOP against Squeak/Smalltalk. The primary location for AspectS information is www.prakinf.tu-ilmenau.de/~hirsch/Projects/ Squeak/AspectS/.

## Description

Squeak is an open and portable version of Smalltalk available at www.squeak.org. Squeak is based on a virtual machine and is available for many platforms. AspectS, an implementation of AOP for Squeak, combines the extensions used for AspectJ and the concept of a wrapper for adding the secondary concerns to the compiled Squeak code.

## Requirements

AspectS is designed to be used with Squeak.

# Apostle

Apostle is a Master's thesis project for incorporating AOP into Smalltalk. The primary Web site for Apostle is www.cs.ubc.ca/labs/spl/projects/apostle/.

## Description

Apostle is an implementation of AOP for Smalltalk designed as a project under the supervision of Gregor Kiczales and is currently a port of AspectJ 0.8. At this time, it appears to be behind the development put into AspectS.

## Requirements

Apostle is designed to be used with IBM's VisualAge for Smalltalk 4.5, which is available for most major operating systems at www-3.ibm.com/software/ad/smalltalk/?c=0035016165&n=befree_affiliate&t=aff.

# AspectC

AspectC is an attempt to bring AOP to the C programming language. You can find information on the extension at www.cs.ubc.ca/labs/spl/projects/aspectc.html.

## Description

Some of the original designers of AOP and AspectJ have been involved in the development of AspectC. As of this writing, the AspectC system is being used in-house by the developers and hasn't been released for public use. Based on the information available, it appears that AspectC works in the same prepro-cessing method as AspectJ, where the primary and aspect code is parsed and weaved into a final set of code.

## Requirements

Not known.

## Example Code

Although we don't have the language available, you can obtain information about AspectC from a document found at www.cs.ubc.ca/labs/spl/papers/2001/coady-psc.pdf. Based on the code in the paper, an aspect associated with a Hello World program written in C might look like the following:

```
aspect MainTest {
  pointcut hello() : calls(void sayHello());
  before() : hello() {
    printf(-Before sayHello() call");
  }
}

#include <stdio.h>

void sayHello() {
  printf("Hello World!");
  }

void main() {
  sayHello();
}
```

# AspectC++

AspectC++ brings AOP concepts to the C++ programming language. The Web site for the language binding is http://www.aspectc.org.

## Description

AspectC++ works in the same way as AspectJ in that it performs a preprocessing of the source code and weaves the aspect code to form a final C++ source. The source is compiled using an appropriate C++ compiler. The current system supports Microsoft Windows, Linux, and Solaris.

## Requirements

The current implementation of AspectC++ executes on Windows, Solaris, and Linux. Under Windows, Borland C++ 5.5 (a free compiler is available from www.borland.com) is supported. For Solaris and Linux, the gcc compiler is used as the traditional compiler. The AspectC++ precompiler, called ac++, is compiled with gcc 2.95.3 and statically linked in order to produce a stand-alone compiler.

## Example Code

The following is an example of code (primary C++) for a Hello World program and an aspect to catch calls to the sayHello() method of the HelloWorld class:

```
#include <iostream.h>

pointcut hello() =
    call ("void HelloWorld::sayHello()");

aspect HelloWorldAspect {
 public:
    advice hello() : void after () {
      cout << ("Saying Hello");
    }
};

class HelloWorld {
  public:
    void sayHello() {
      cout << "Hello";
    }
};

int main () {
  HelloWorld hello = new HelloWorld();
  hello.sayHello();
}
```

This code would be precompiled with the AspectC++ compiler ac++. A C++ file would then be generated combining the primary and aspect code for final compilation by a traditional C++ compiler. If you become familiar with AspectJ, moving to AspectC++ for those situations where C++ is required won't be a huge stretch.

# Pythius

Pythius allows the Python language to use AOP. The Web site for Pythius is http://sourceforge.net/projects/pythius/.

## Description

Pythius is designed to add AOP concepts to Python. The distribution contains lengthy documentation written into the code, complete with example code to get you started.

## Requirements

Pythius requires Python 2.2.1 or higher and must be built when first installed. Refer to the Install document of the download.

## Example Code

The following is a simple example of using Pythius to add AOP functionality to Python:

```
import aop
class Check(aop.Aspect):
  def __init__(self):
    aop.Aspect.__init__(self)   # don't forget this!
    self.after('getattr', 'area', self.log)

  def log(self, cxt):
    value    = cxt['value']
    name     = cxt['name']
    print 'Attribute %s (value of %s)' % (name, value)

class DoubleIt:
  def __init__(self, x):
    self.x = x*x
    self.quad = x*x*x*x

  check = Check()
  DoubleIt = check.affect(DoubleIt)

  doubleit = DoubleIt(4)
  print 'Double Value = %d' % doubleit.x

  print 'Quad Value = %d' % doubleit.quad
```

# Index

## Symbols

&& (and) operator, 86
\* (asterisk) character, 62
! (not) operator, 86
|| (or) operator, 62, 86

## A

abstract aspects, building,
    246–251
abstract methods, 201
access control, inter-type
    declarations, 203–205
accessing aspects, 258–259
access types, aspects, 242, 261
advice, 16
    before advice, 35, 147–150
        unwanted join points,
            150–154
    after advice, 35, 147
    after returning advice, 147,
        162–165
    after throwing advice, 147,
        157–162
        adding new error
            conditions, 160–161
        detecting errors, 161–162
        FailedRaisePolicy
            example, 158–159
        passing thrown
            exceptions, 159–160
    around advice, 35, 147, 165
        altering context with,
            172–179
        getProperty() call
            example, 165–170
        proceed(), 169–170,
            178–179
        replacing join points,
            167–168

return values, 168–169,
    170–171
defining, 132–137
    AddSourceInfo aspect
        listing, 135–136
    advice body, 134–135
    advice type, 133
    formal syntax, 136–137
    parameters, 133
    pointcuts, 134
    printIn() example,
        132–133
exception restrictions,
    145–146
Hello World example, 35–36
inter-type declarations and,
    196–199
passing context to
    Employee class example,
        137–139
    formal parameters,
        139–144
    reflective access, 144
precedence, 179
    circular relationships, 182
    importance of, 179
    inter-aspect precedence,
        180
    intra-aspect precedence,
        181–182
    pseudo precedence, 184
    runtime execution,
        182–184
unqualified advice, 147
unqualified after advice,
    154–157
adviceexecution designators,
    86, 123
AdviceSignature interface, 407
after advice, 35, 147, 182

after returning advice, 147,
    162–165
after throwing advice, 147,
    157–162
    adding new error conditions,
        160–161
    detecting errors, 161–162
    FailedRaisePolicy example,
        158–159
    passing thrown exceptions,
        159–160
ajdb (debugger), 303–304
    command-line options,
        303–304
    command-line tutorial,
        304–307
    GUI tutorial, 307–309
AJDE for JBuilder, 282–288
ajdoc (documentation tool),
    309–311
and (&&) operator, 86
anonymous classes,
    within/withincode
    designators, 121–122
anonymous pointcuts, 125
Ant, 302–303
AOP (aspect-oriented
    programming), 1, 9
    bindings
        Apostle, 421
        AspectC, 421–422
        AspectC++, 422–423
        AspectR, 419–420
        AspectS, 420–421
        Pythius, 423–424
    design, 360–361
    development process, 10–12,
        13
    goals, 9–10